FOOLS AND HEROES

The Changing Role of
Communist Intellectuals in Czechoslovakia

FOOLS AND HEROES

The Changing Role of
Communist Intellectuals in Czechoslovakia

BY

PETER HRUBY
Western Australian Institute of Technology

PERGAMON PRESS

OXFORD · NEW YORK · TORONTO · SYDNEY · PARIS · FRANKFURT

U.K.	Pergamon Press Ltd., Headington Hill Hall, Oxford OX3 0BW, England
U.S.A.	Pergamon Press Inc., Maxwell House, Fairview Park, Elmsford, New York 10523, U.S.A.
CANADA	Pergamon of Canada, Suite 104, 150 Consumers Road, Willowdale, Ontario M2J 1P9, Canada
AUSTRALIA	Pergamon Press (Aust.) Pty. Ltd., P.O. Box 544, Potts Point N.S.W. 2011, Australia
FRANCE	Pergamon Press SARL, 24 rue des Ecoles, 75240 Paris, Cedex 05, France
FEDERAL REPUBLIC OF GERMANY	Pergamon Press GmbH, 6242 Kronberg-Taunus, Pferdstrasse 1, Federal Republic of Germany

First edition 1980

British Library Cataloguing in Publication Data

Hruby, Peter
Fools and heroes.
1. Czechoslovakia — History — 1945-
I. Title
943.7′04   DB2216   79-40768
ISBN 0 08 024276-6

Printed and bound in Great Britain by
William Clowes (Beccles) Limited, Beccles and London

TO SHIRLEY

Contents

PART III SEARCHING FOR TRUTH AND REALITY

Abbreviations

CC	Central Committee
C.I.A.	Central Intelligence Agency
CPC	Communist Party of Czechoslovakia
CPI	Communist Party of Italy
CPS	Communist Party of Slovakia
ČS.	Československý (Czechoslovak)
ČSAV	Československá akademie věd (Czechoslovak Academy of Sciences)
ČSM	Československý svaz mládeže (Czechoslovak Youth Association)
ČSR	Československá Republika (Czechoslovak Republic)
ČSSR	Československá Socialistická Republika (Czechoslovak Socialist Republic)
Cz.	Czechoslovak
KSČ	Komunistická strana Československa (Czechoslovak Communist Party)
KSS	Komunistická strana Slovenska (Slovak Communist Party)
OKN	Okresní národní výbor (District National Committee)
RFER	Radio Free Europe Research
ROH	Revoluční odborové hnutí (Revolutionary Trade Union)
TV	Television
U.S.	United States
U.S.S.R.	Union of Soviet Socialist Republics
ÚV	Ústřední výbor (Central Committee)
VLP	Vydavateľstvo politickej literatúry (Publishers of Political Literature)
VSAV	Vydavateľstvo slovenskej akadémie vied (Publishers of the Slovak Academy of Sciences)

Acknowledgements

FIRST of all, I would like to express my thanks to my wife who shared with me all the inevitable agonies engendered by the preparation and writing of a work of this scope. Her help was substantial.

To the sponsor of my Ph. D. thesis (on which this book is based)[1], Professor Jacques Freymond, then Director of the Graduate Institute of International Studies in Geneva, I am grateful for his unlimited endurance with which he followed and regularly helped my research and writing which proceeded slowly and mostly at a distance. To him as well as to my second reader, Professor Rudolf Bystrický, are due my thanks for the largesse of spirit manifested in their allowance of a free development of my research and ideas. Their suggestions were always beneficial and welcome. I would like to add that my repeated stays at the Institute were always enjoyable and that I am thankful to all the other professors I had the pleasure of meeting and working with.

When I was looking for sources on the earlier years of my study period, I was lucky to receive an invitation from Dr. Johann W. Bruegel to come and explore the treasures of his personal archives in his London house where I was offered generous hospitality. I am also grateful to Dr. Rudolf Urban who invited me to use the resources of the archives and library of the J. G. Herder Institute in Marburg an der Lahn.

I would like to acknowledge my grateful indebtedness to Radio Free Europe in Munich for the opportunity of using their archives as well as for the excellent monitoring and press photocopying service.

I am much obliged to Mrs. Milena Hoenig for her long lasting help in sending me copies of important articles and clippings from publications to which I did not have access.

In Perth (W. A.) on 27 December 1978   P. H.

---

[1] "Czechoslovakia between East and West. The Changing Role of Communist Intellectuals, 1948-1968," University of Geneva, Switzerland, 1978. The text was here abbreviated and the references to sources shortened.

Introduction
Aims of the work, its methods, and contribution

Interest

TWENTIETH-century European history is an unfinished story of wars, upheavals, revolutions, and destruction as well as creation of empires. The carefully kept balance of power of the nineteenth century definitely disappeared. The crucial age not only of the masses and of efficient methods of communication but, alas, also of manipulation brought into existence modern totalitarian and imperialist states, industrially developed, heavily armed, and buttressed by aggressive ideologies. Small or middle-sized countries had lost their security and repeatedly also their independence. Internal and external peace has been permanently threatened and often shattered.

In all of the upsetting history of modern times, Czechoslovakia was deeply involved. Its statesmen's creative efforts to master the unsettled European affairs have been, in the long run, mostly discouraging. A few times they served as decisive warnings of dangers present. During the last sixty years, this small state in the heart of Europe, at least four times, played a pivotal role — in 1918, 1938, 1948, and 1968. It was worth watching as a sensitive barometer of hopes, tensions, and dangers on the European continent.

Of these dates only 1918 was ever celebrated in Czechoslovakia by the majority of the population with joy, and for some time appeared to have beneficial influence on world developments. An attempt was made then to transplant the peaceful condition of the Republic of Geneva to the center of Europe by creating there a new state, which on several occasions during the war was discussed and prepared on the lovely shores of Lake Léman. The effort continued throughout two decades at the League of Nations, but in 1938 the principle of collective security, after repeated disasters, failed also for this new Republic. The fairy-tale of a philosopher-king on the Hradčany Castle, who would have liked to reproduce Switzerland in Central Europe, and of his capable foreign minister, who was distinguishing himself in disarmament and other talks in the Palais des Nations, could not survive unscathed the Nazi and Fascist drive to power, when France and England did not feel obliged to keep their arrangements of Versailles.

The first of the three terms by which Czechoslovakia enriched the contemporary political vocabulary was then coined — the *Munich appeasement*. A useless sacrifice of a small but well-armed state, which until then was the only one in Central and East Europe which managed to keep and develop liberal rights and a democratic system of government, became a warning against attempts to satisfy expansionist powers by concessions made at the expense of small allies.

Unfortunately, in the 1940s it took too many years before that lesson would be heeded in international politics by the Truman Doctrine, the Marshall Plan, and by the establishment of NATO. Again, what helped was the next alarming signal coming from Prague in the form of a bloodless *coup d'état* carefully prepared in advance and executed by the Communist party against divided, dispirited democrats and with a manifest lack of interest on the part of Western powers. The second future cliché of international politics of Czechoslovak provenience was born — the *coup of Prague*. Watching recent developments in Portugal and in Italy, foreign observers were often mentioning the 1948 experience and pondering its tactics and dangerous implications.

Finally, when someone thought about calling the speeding up liberalizing and democratizing evolution in Czechoslovakia of 1968 the *Prague Spring*, the term quickly caught the imagination of both domestic participants and foreign sympathizers. Another terminological short-cut for complicated historical events entered the realm of international politics.

All three trite expressions of Czechoslovak origin — Munich appeasement, *coup* of Prague, and Prague Spring — concern questions of independence, human rights, and democracy threatened or trampled on by an expansionist great power. Only the last one was positive and inspiring. Its promise had to be crushed by invading tank divisions, making it in its consequences another symbol of a tragic lack of decent prospects for a country squeezed in Eastern Europe between great powers. In all three instances the small state was left abandoned, without any help from Western democracies, as a prey to the appetite of international bullies, always just serving as a strong warning.

Although all three historical dates involved a sharp clash between opposing sets of values (democracy versus dictatorship), especially the last one had created a stir in intellectual circles, since thanks to the creative energy of the Czechoslovak intelligentsia a totalitarian system was almost dismantled and a new variation of communism, "socialism with a human face", was replacing the often brutal and stupid neo-Stalinist order. It helped to focus attention on questions of humanism or the lack of it in Marxism and in movements claiming its heritage. Czech lands, which once before in European history initiated a reform movement on a large scale (fifteenth-century religious reformation), might have again encouraged a process of reformation of a twentieth-century political faith. The fashionable discussions of Eurocommunism would have been impossible without the impetus of Prague.

Thus, it is not a limited local history of a small Central European state which is the topic of this work. Even the problem of Czechoslovakia's international relations, basically a result of its geographic position between the West and the East, is not peculiar to this country. On the contrary, it is now the foremost actual problem of the world. In addition, from the beginning of the Khrushchevian coexistence policy, whose name was in the Brezhnev era changed into détente, the Kremlin ideologues have been stressing that the main battles between the two camps are, and will be, taking place on the ideological front. Therefore, it should be instructive to follow their development and results. In this ideological warfare the intellectuals either become tools in the hands of political manipulators, spreading their slogans, or create an atmosphere in which change for the better can take place.

Aims

This book will concentrate mainly on the two crucial years of 1948 and 1968 since they marked the climax of contradictory developments; namely, the acceptance and repudiation of Soviet ideology and statecraft. As the title suggests, the Czechoslovak dilemma between the East and the West will be seen through the eyes of the communist intelligentsia, whose role in the historically short time of two decades changed radically.

The revolution of 1968 in Czechoslovakia was prepared and led by communist intellectuals — historians, writers, economists, sociologists, philosophers, and other educated people. Yet, twenty years before, in February of 1948, many of them worked for the *coup d'état* by which the Communist Party of Czechoslovakia took over complete control of the country; later, they actively helped in applying at home the Soviet model of dictatorial socialism. In 1968, often the same men wanted to radically reform the system and replace it with a new model in which domestic and Western democratic traditions played a major role. In 1948 both the leading and the budding communist intellectuals were under the spell of Soviet ideology and power; in 1968, however, they tried to liberate their country from this overwhelming Soviet impact.

I would like to explore reasons for such a radical change of *optique*, of perspective, and orientation. Why and how in a country, placed at the crossroads of Europe, was the Eastern attraction of the 1940s and 1950s replaced by Western attractiveness in the 1960s? What kind of an ideological mutation took place in the mind of many influential communist men of culture and science?

Czechoslovakia could be viewed as a laboratory testing Soviet ideology and methods in an industrially and educationally developed European environment, whose cultural and political past markedly differed from Russia.

The activist intellectuals of 1948 were violating national traditions but resurrecting them in 1968. Soviet tool in 1948, anti-Soviet in 1968, they turned against the inhuman — by implication — face of Soviet socialism. In a way, since they embraced many ideals of the Czechoslovak year of 1918, their revolution of 1968 was an answer not only to the 1948 *coup d'état* in Prague, but also to the Petrograd *coup d'état* of 1917, commonly called the Bolshevik Revolution. In 1948 the communist intellectuals tried to repudiate and replace much of the Czech and Slovak heritage by Soviet examples. But their cultural inheritance influenced them during the twenty years of sustained implementation of the Soviet model and finally led them against its import.

In 1948 the Communist Party of Czechoslovakia was a willing instrument for Stalin's intention to bring the country under direct domination by the Soviet Union. The CPC was used in order to satellize Czechoslovakia, Russify it culturally, turn it into an industrial colony, impose fully the Soviet system of command socialism, and cut it away from the West culturally, politically, and economically. Twenty years later, the same party, led by its profoundly changed communist intellectuals, attempted to relax at least some of the existing bonds, to renew contacts with the West, and to apply Western democratic socialism, which was discarded with contempt in 1948. Two decades of experiences with a totalitarian dictatorship in culture, justice, government, and economics radically changed the value attributed to sets of ideas and policies. We could observe a process from the satellization of a country to an attempt at its desatellization by the same party, by more or less the same political and cultural élite. The problem of liberalization of Stalinism remains acute, and a study of the Czechoslovak attempt is useful. In the protracted conflict between programs of individual freedoms and collectivist social order, intellectual fanaticism continues to be a problem.

Of particular interest is the "workshop of the intellectuals" who first helped to introduce a totalitarian system of power and then experienced, analyzed, refused, undermined, and finally replaced it through a bloodless revolution, first of its kind. The famous "treason of the clerks" (Julian Benda), observable in Czechoslovakia, especially between 1945 and 1955, was followed by a systematic effort of the intellectuals (writers, historians, scientists, theatre and movie directors, journalists, Radio and TV commentators, etc.) to restore their nations' mental health, refute the system of official lies and false pretenses, overcome their own and their compatriots' fears, and encourage resistance. An important part of this renaissance of the arts and sciences was the rediscovery of a national heritage and its reassertion: gradual removal of many artificial taboos and renewal of contacts with Western sciences, literature, theatre, and fine arts. It also involved the rethinking of problems of socialism and democracy, often under the influence of Western scientific literature and under the impact of successful integration of Western Europe. Of importance in solving some of our contemporary problems is a study of contradictory ideas and policies as they were contemplated and resolved by Czechoslovak communists: crucial problems of violence in social movements; democracy versus dictatorship; evolution or revolution; spontaneity or dirigism; single party or pluralism; "class struggle" and technological development.

Between 1945 and 1948 some communist scholars tried to persuade their students of Lenin's supremacy over T. G. Masaryk, although the Party still officially venerated the first President. In the 1950s a violent campaign was conducted against "Masarykism". But Czechoslovak history from 1948 till 1968 clearly led many Communist writers and scholars to refute Lenin and confirm Masaryk's negative analysis of the Soviet version of socialism.

After they helped to destroy a democratic system, the same men faced the much harder problem of liberalizing and democratizing a totalitarian system of their own making.

Throughout its history Czechoslovakia has been at the crossroads of Western and Eastern socialism, Western and Eastern conceptions of democracy. What general deductions can be made on the basis of these two confrontations (1948 and 1968) about the impact of Soviet ideas and methods on a country that was attracted to both socialism and democracy? Is there anything general and objective that could be determined from observations of the fateful meeting of communism and democracy on this Prague bridge between the West and the East? What about the ideas of the Italian "historical compromise", of the "unity of the Left", or of Eurocommunism? How do the slogans of the co-existence, détente, or convergence appear under the light of Czechoslovak experience? Recent Czechoslovak history should be studied and described as a fascinating and highly instructive chapter in the cultural and political history of modern Europe.

Methods

Summing up: my book is a study of a cultural élite and its Soviet influenced perspective at the beginning and at the end of twenty years of testing an ideology in practice and considering the results obtained through social engineering. The questions I will be asking are, for instance: what led many intellectuals to the Soviet type of communism and what led them later away from it? What opinions, hopes, and certainties turned out to be illusions or mistakes? Why people like Karel Bartošek, Eduard Goldstücker, Milan Hübl, Karel Kaplan, Pavel Kohout, Karel Kosík, Eugen Loebl, Artur London, Pavel Machonin, Zdeněk Mlynř, Ota Šik, Ivan Sviták, and others, who felt enthusiastic about "February1948", prepared and welcomed "January 1968?" Why persuaded anti-democrats in time became more democratic? Why were they *for* a foreign system in 1948 and why were they *against* it and for something quite different in 1968? I would like to explore personal reasons for both attitudes as expressed in ideas, plans, and activities of representative individuals who played prominent or supporting roles both in 1948 and 1968.

"It is a question of great psychological and political significance to understand the real motivations of people in the service of a dictatorial regime," wrote Erich Fromm.[1] We do not know enough about it. And we should know more about ways in which dangerous fanatics, led by their misleading millenial hopes to destruction and crimes, could be persuaded in time that other ways might be more constructive and fruitful.

I do not intend to write a history of twenty years of Soviet–Czechoslovak relations but a comparative study of two models of socialism, as seen — mainly in 1948 and 1968 (but also before, in between, and after these years) — through the minds of communist intellectuals in Czechoslovakia, placed between the East and the West. It is a comparative study of two sorts of thought patterns, since the change in outlook, in mentality, in basic beliefs and attitudes between the 1940s and the 1960s has been substantial and is fascinating. In Czechoslovakia "the shifting temper of the times"[2] showed fast and in a very revealing way.   How much chance is there that a militant communist would ever become a democrat? I propose to study this and similar questions (for instance, the relationship between intellectuals and workers) in a series of *case studies* of some thirty members of the communist intelligentsia — writers, journalists, economists, sociologists, political scientists, historians, philosophers, and political activists. I am interested in the way they imagined present and historical reality, how they saw their role in the world, according to this image, and how and why their aims, theories, and activities developed throughout twenty to thirty years of experience with their own social engineering, molding of the future, and manipulation of the masses. By reading their articles, poems, essays, and speeches, beginning in the second half of the 1940s and continuing until our days, I would like to confront their views in the process of formation as well as later transformation.

The emphasis on personal motivation and experience in historical events is

[1] See his introduction to John M. Steiner, *Power Politics and Social Change in National Socialist Germany* (The Hague: Mouton, 1975).
[2] Maurice Ashley, *England in the Seventeenth Century* (London: Penguin Books, 1968), p. 180.

intentional for several reasons. First, the institutional and political developments have been studied and described exhaustively in many books and articles, but until now almost no attention has been paid to individual histories and motives of people who helped to generate the developments between 1948 and 1968. It should be interesting to a historian, since their outlook showed, in the relatively short span of time, some remarkable evolution. Usually, it is believed that people form their basic ideas about the world and their part in it quite early, and that in their early twenties their views have been already formed and would remain preserved until the end of their days. The Czechoslovak history of the communist intelligentsia after 1945 proves that it is not always true.

Second, it is becoming clear that personal views and motivations of actors in the political arena can easily lead to crimes perpetrated on a mass scale. If humanity wants to survive at all, it would have to understand the motivations of crime and develop preventive measures before fanatics and lunatics had a chance of enslaving millions of people and of liquidating thousands or millions of them under any ideological pretext. This is of prime importance not only in the microcosm of individual or small group terrorism, but especially in the macrocosm of highly organized criminal societies, led by mass exterminators of the human race. Megalomaniacs, such as Stalin or Hitler, should be discovered in time and kept in a safe place. The same is true about their henchmen and helpers, even propagandists. We must comprehend false values and crises which lead otherwise, if not normal, at least harmless people into murderous activities. Politics is now the area of the highest incidence of criminality.

There is another reason for this study of historical problems from personal experiences of the participants. Images that lead people into actions and their perception of events might be approximately right or completely false; they might make much or no sense at all. What matters is that for them, in that moment, they were real. (How much art was inspired by superstition and nonsense?) Intellectuals do not necessarily see better than ordinary people — often they see much worse — but they verbalize their thoughts and leave records of them. Therefore, it is easier to study their reflections of "reality" than that of uneducated people. Many books have been written on the Czechoslovak tragedy but in most of them, in spite (or because?) of their sometimes meticulous recollection of all major and minor events, the moving drama disappeared and what is left looks like faded flowers in a herbarium. It is my intention, for the purpose of this study and for its vividness, to resurrect this drama from the inside, from the individual points of view, from the personal participation of the actors, without much interference, without theoretical encumbrances, allowing them as much time as possible to present their cases. Instead of the usual transcription of original sources in a factual prose which could distort the meaning and which often kills the life, I have tried to preserve the style and moods of my sad heroes in order not to lose the local flavor and the feel of changing times. Paradoxically but truthfully, a collectivist movement will be presented from the points of view and perceptions of the individuals — since only they are real — in a kind of a mosaic. The organizing pattern, although it should be true, is mine but the little stones and colours should be theirs. I hope that with their unwilling help the work will remain scholarly but will also be readable by mediating the living reality of recent historical happenings.

Selection

A few words of explanation are due about my choice of persons for the case studies. I have tried to introduce communist intellectuals on whose unfolding activities it would be possible to show at best a variety of approaches and fields as well as different developments. I wanted to have represented not only Czechs but also Slovaks, Jews, and Germans. A reader can easily rearrange for himself parts of the work and, if he so wishes, to study the Slovak, German, or Jewish question, the economic reform, problems of internationalism, open Marxism, workers' corruption and resistance, intellectuals' collaboration or stimulation of reforms, etc., by looking them up in the index. Not everything, naturally, was covered, but the main areas were. My prevailing interest was, however, in a comparative study of motivations in two or three decades of an international conflict of political culture.

Some actors suggested themselves because of their prominent parts in the drama or because they published more than others (both Kohout and Mňačko, for instance, were the most printed authors of the 1950s), and did not hesitate to reveal things of interest. Major heroes of the media from the year 1968 had to be chosen. The availability of resources, however, sometimes decided for one and eliminated the other; for example, some authors used to sign their articles in the 1950s (editors of *Tvorba*, Karel Kosík and Jan Štern), some did not. Also I wanted to study various types of intellectuals from different generations, avoiding documents too much analyzed.

In order to take into account the neo-Stalinist regime's preferences for hate and condemnation of the main "counter-revolutionaries" I have consulted several of their black lists.[3] Since this selection had to take place many years ago, when I had a chance of doing research in a few archives, I was pleased to realize, in due course, that many of my chosen authors proved to be the most active dissenters who have been attracting attention until our days. I regret some omissions, but limitations of time and place seriously curtailed my possibilities. Since the thesis kept bursting out of the originally intended size and scope, at the end I had to put aside quite a few of my targets for case studies, although I had a lot of material in files. Still, I hope that my selection is both interesting and representative, in order to fulfill the intentions of this study.

All of my surveyed heroes played important, although sometimes only supporting roles. All of them belonged to the "school of communist intellectuals" that had prepared and influenced the Prague Spring or what followed it (with the exception of Margolius who did not live long enough but whose wife later wrote one of the best and the most humanly moving testimony of the whole period). Some left the country soon after the tanks came to pay a visit to Czechoslovak cities, some later, but some stayed to face the music and to remind the rulers, from time to time, that there was still fire in the ashes and that no winter can last forever.

This might be an appropriate place to remind the reader that this work is concerned almost exclusively with communist intellectuals and that often the best

---

[3] For example, the one officially announced to Communist party members in a letter emanating from the CPC CC and published in *Rudé právo*, 3 Feb. 1970, mentioned in *Le Monde*, 4 Feb., and quoted by it *in extenso* on Feb. 1970.

writers, philosophers, journalists, and others as non-communists had to leave the scene in 1948 or soon after. Many of them disappeared for decades in prisons and concentration camps. All of them were silenced. So we are dealing only with a slice of Czechoslovak life and not with the whole Czechoslovak culture, which, at best, had to go abroad or underground. The future heroes of 1968, in most cases, helped the Party policemen to suppress and oppress the liberal, democratic, social democratic, Christian (or Buddhist, for that matter), and any other men of culture and education. For some time, at least till 1956, the communists had the stage free for themselves and therefore fast careers could be made on very narrow intellectual bases and so much junk could be published in many thousand copies. Only in 1956 two of the most decent and courageous poets, František Hrubín and Jaroslav Seifert, began to claim publicly that their colleagues should be released from unmerited punishment in dungeons. And only in the 1960s some of them who managed to survive their ordeals obtained limited possibilities of publication. The famous Czech school of film from the 1960s was mostly non- and anti-communist, although often in the West mistakenly celebrated by superficial pro-communist dreamers as "socialist art." Even around 1968 some of the best works came from non-communists. So this is a story of communist culture — or sometimes rather the lack of it, and not of Czechoslovak culture as a whole.

Part I
The class struggle and moral problems

Chapter 1

Moral and national hara-kiri

SINCE Alexander Solzhenitsyn's arrival in the West, the impression has grown that contemplation of world problems from a moral point of view is something peculiarly Russian. F. M. Dostoyevsky's analysis of growing nihilism and revolutionary attitudes in nineteenth-century Russia and his warnings against atheist and anti-Christian trends, especially in his novels *Crime and Punishment* and *The Possessed*, were taken over by Solzhenitsyn. He has the advantage over Dostoyevsky in that the old prophesy now seems to have been overwhelmingly proved by experience with the communist rule in the Soviet Union. Such a moral and markedly Christian view of the world is accepted in the West with interest but skeptically as something odd and old-fashioned. Although trust in law and democratic institutions has recently been shaken, civic and rational thinking is still preferred to moral and prophetic attitudes.

In Russia there has never been a steady development of democratic institutions or of enlightened and rational thought. In many ways, Lenin and other Russian Bolsheviks only continued the ingrained tradition of their orthodox or even liberal predecessors who did not like the Western preference for law, civic freedoms, and tolerant if not critical relationship to Christianity. Therefore, when Russian dissidents are looking for a philosophy of life, a *Weltanschauung*, that would help them to find a way out of their troubles, they often fall back on their strong tradition of religious and moral postulates.

Religion and morality have been separated in the West more successfully than in the East or, at least, there are other secular positions and institutions available making it possible to base moral values on liberal and civic virtues rather than on strictly religious grounds. Since religious preaching and moral admonitions often become the specialty of hypocritical, conservative, or even reactionary circles, they are not held in high esteem.

It came as a surprise when the Czechoslovak revolution of 1968, to a large degree led by members of the atheist Communist Party, put great stress on moral values and succeeded in keeping the revolutionary processes unusually clean, without blood-letting and without any violence. Compared with the Hungarian revolution of 1956 the difference was striking. (Naturally, the Czechs had the advantage of acting later, with Hungarian experiences present in their mind.)

In order to get an insight into one of the crucial problems of our age, let us explore one of the ethical issues involved; namely, the question of class struggle and moral problems.

Czechoslovakia between 1948 and 1968 could serve as an unusually ideal laboratory for social scientists' testing of Marxist-Leninist hypotheses. Many lessons can be learned and the subject is complex. In this part I will concentrate on one aspect only — are moral values simply class concepts and prejudices?

According to almost all varieties of Marxism, including Leninism and Stalinism, violence forms a necessary part of class struggle, both before and after the revolutionary seizure of power. "Denigration of rational thought and worship of action has led, historically, to worship of violence and the concept of violence as a therapeutic force."[1] In the mutation that Marxism went through on its way from Marx to Lenin and Stalin, revolutionary violence meant, more and more, not only physical replacement in power of one class by another but also unhindered use of all forms of violence against the "enemies" — lies, torture, physical liquidation, and terror. All was acceptable that supposedly helped the sacred cause. Followers of Stalin wholeheartedly believed in the new Machiavellian Prince and practiced his teachings. They claimed that their historical mission absolved them from any personal responsibility and feelings of guilt since the "bourgeois" morality of truth, human rights, and justice was just a prejudice based on class interests and had to be discarded as such. In this hopeful belief that a collective myth (be it tribal, religious, national, racial, or class) would absolve them from any personal responsibility, they followed other fanatical movements, such as Christianity, Islam, Nazism. The modern myth of communism was founded on a peculiar understanding of the latest two new man-made gods — history and science.

A Polish philosopher who went through similar experiences as his Czechoslovak, Hungarian, and other comrades, expressed this fateful fallacy in the subtitle in one of his books *On Historical Understanding and Individual Responsibility*. He wrote:

> The morality of everyday life cannot be deduced from our knowledge of alleged historical necessities. . . . Rules of moral behavior cannot be derived from any theory of historical progress, and . . . no such theory can justifiably be used for the violation of certain rules of whose validity we are otherwise convinced.[2]

Most of the Czech and Slovak communist intellectuals would have probably agreed with that statement in 1968 but not in 1948. Then they believed in and practiced a class approach to all problems and felt contempt for a so-called bourgeois morality which would not be allowed to stop them on their march to the glorious future of classless communism. Not the individual, but society must be changed. "The true basis of morality is not individual conduct, but social organization," as explained by Eugene Kamenka in his exploration of Marxism and its ethics.[3] When the communist intellectuals in Czechoslovakia thought about these problems around the decisive year of 1948, they were persuaded that it was up to them to get rid of all "bourgeois prejudices" and especially of moral scruples. Against the "class enemy" only a merciless fight to the end would do and every fighter for communism had to harden himself or herself to the point where no pity would be felt, no conscience, no hesitation, just the resolve to win and destroy all that would oppose the final victory.

Between 1943 and 1948, I was a lucky (and unhappy) witness to this process,

---

[1] Martin Oppenheimer, "The Limits of Revolution," in *On Revolution*, ed. by William Lutz and Harry Brent (Cambridge, Mass.: Winthrop Publishers, 1971), p. 86.

[2] Leszek Kolakowski, *Marxism and Beyond* (London: Paladin, 1971), pp. 159 and 172.

[3] *The Ethical Foundations of Marxism* (New York: St. Martin's Press, 1962 and 1969), p. 38.

especially watching as a friend, the best Czech recitor of poetry, was strenuously fighting all her humanist education and orientation as mere class prejudices and was trying to achieve complete victory over her 'bourgeois" past, till she became a steeled representative of the Bolshevik cause. Countless Czech intellectuals were then involved in a similar process of moral and mental mutilation. Too many of them accepted the Stalinist thesis that fascism was the last stage of capitalism. They expected all bourgeois democracies to develop into fascist systems and at the same time they imagined that the Soviet Union was a paradise of political as well as economic democracy.

Naturally, not only then and not only Czechs attempted their own moral hara-kiri in order to qualify for service to the Marxian myth as believed by aspirants to participation in the final solution of the "bourgeois class." For the Yugoslavs, Milovan Djilas wrote in prison: "For dogmatic — and not only dogmatic — reasons, we communists proclaimed that the normal human concepts and ethical values are petty bourgeois. In this way we are creating two mutually irreconcilable worlds."[4]

How much self-doubt and self-hate on the part of mainly bourgeois people was here involved has not yet been fully analyzed, in spite of the bourgeois origin, education, and outlook of almost all Bolshevik leaders, beginning with Lenin. Surely Marx and Engels cannot be considered typical proletarians. Certainly the drama of the Czechoslovak Communist intellectuals almost always involved in its first act this type of pathological "purification," masochistic purging, and self-mutilation of the soul.

In his film *Innocence Protected* the Yugoslav film director Dušan Makavejev portrayed this typical communist self-indoctrination, self-stylization as folkheroes, supposedly chosen to lead the masses to a victory of the proletarian Saint George over the dragon of capitalism devouring people. The whole mystification of struggle, liberation, and victory, all the expected heroic deeds had as a condition a self-molesting attempt at a purification. All that was not supposed to be there, had to be cut out: bourgeois habits and morality, attachment to individualism, anarchism, symbolism, surrealism, cubism, and on and on. The agents and victims of this crippling destruction of personality did not realize how close they came to the Nazi effort of reviving the old German myths; for example, of Siegfried's purifying blood-bath, and eagerly helped to create out of themselves willing depersonalized robots of a totalitarian dictatorship. Makavejev showed well how such masochism of systematic strengthening of their "class consciousness," socialist progressivity, and revolutionary violence liberated their sense of cruelty and sadistic impulses. To non-believers all this seemed to be a ridiculous and dangerous myth. The phony warriors looked funny in their borrowed armor. The feeling of unreality, self-stylization, and pretense of life was prevailing, but the tragic consequences were sadly real.

Such a drastic self-censorship and suppression of any doubts continued after 1948. A non-communist Czech writer, an observer of similar processes in

---

[4] *Parts of a Lifetime*, ed. by M. and D. Milenkovich (New York: Harcourt Brace Jovanovich, 1975); reprinted as "Jail Diary," *Dissent*, summer 1975, p. 269.

Czechoslovakia for a longer period of time than I was able to do, by some twenty years, expressed a part of it in one of his books in the following way:

> When a conditioned artist arrived at a dilemma between the official truth as it was proclaimed by the Cultural Secretariat, and the concrete truth as he experienced it in everyday life, he began to doubt not the proclaimed truth but his own progressiveness. "Do I have enough of class-consciousness?" he would ask himself according to the account of one of the film critics, Jaroslav Bocek. "Are not my doubts just the remnants of intellectualization, or some other individualistic anachronism, which I must negate?"[5]

The awakening from such a mass psychosis had to be, and was, shocking and full of consequences.

Many Czech and Slovak intellectuals who enthusiastically worked for the Communist Party around the crucial year of 1948, when it seized absolute power in a *coup d'état*, believed in and practiced revolutionary violence in the name of the historically necessary class struggle — first, against their "bourgeois" enemies and, later, against their own comrades who were denounced as lackeys of capitalism and Titoist or Slovak or other nationalists. A whole set of implacable principles was established and used in order to legitimize terror against all "class enemies." Everything was allowed as long as it served "historical necessities."

When some of them became victims of these theories, in prison and in concentration camps, the comrades attempted to rethink the problems of socialist justice and of all sorts of violence. New experiences with their co-prisoners — many of them their past victims, some of whom sometimes saved their lives from lynching in prison by other inmates — often led to a reassertion of general moral principles not based at all on class origin. Even those who did not get into gaols themselves could observe numerous consequences of Party policies on the whole society and gradually changed their outlook.

Considerations of non-class morality and justice, rediscovered and adopted by many leading communist intellectuals, played a major role in the preparation and execution of the revolution in 1968. It was one of the main reasons for its decency and lack of blood-letting.

A comparison of the years 1948 and 1968 allows us a comparative study of principles and attitudes concerning moral issues in the relatively short span of twenty years, as often manifested by the same individuals in two different revolutions. Quotations from their articles, studies, and novels will document one of the important problems of our times.

It is hard to imagine the atmosphere of February 1948 in Prague. The democrats found themselves defeated without much if any resistance. Many of them did not even know what was going on until it was too late.

---

[5] Josef Škvorecký, *All the Bright Young Men and Women: A Personal History of the Czech Cinema* (Toronto: Peter Martin Associates Ltd., 1971), p. 62.

From my personal experience I can add a few typical details to facts already well known from memoirs of participants or historical books.[6]

For a while I watched on the Old Town Square the phony atmosphere of a *coup d'état* that was being staged as a pretended people's revolution. In a slight snowfall, in order to come even closer to the image of the Bolshevik seizure of power in 1917, Premier Klement Gottwald, acting more in his capacity of chairman of the Communist Party, wore a Russian hat and addressed the crowds of workers and Party activists who were brought to the plaza in trucks not only from Prague factories but also from towns miles away from the capital; for instance, the "Red" Kladno. It became clear to me that the Communist Party was seizing total power, that it was the expected *putsch*, and I went to Professor František Kovárna who did not live far away and who was one of the leading intellectuals of the Czech Socialist Party as well as one of the most courageous critics of Bolshevik trends in Czechoslovakia. He used to warn the communist intellectuals that the fight for democracy was also for their benefit. I hoped to find him in the middle of preparations for countering the *coup* and wanted to offer help. He was in his apartment and had just finished listening to Gottwald's harangue. When I told him about my observations and their conclusion, he said that our nation would not follow such a demagogue as Gottwald, that President Beneš was holding everything in his hands, and that surprisingly I, who always seemed to be so calm, was exaggerating, becoming hysterical for no good reason, should go home, and calm down, that nothing would happen, and that there was no need to take any action.

I met him again a few days later, at a meeting of the Cultural Union, which associated some of the leading creative and performing artists, writers, and journalists of the country. (I was present only as a representative of its Youth Club which I had founded for young artists and writers and of which I was the general secretary. The older gentlemen wanted to know what "the youth" was thinking about the events). He already knew what it was all about, acknowledged his slow comprehension: "Such things shouldn't be done in a democracy!", and together with Ferdinand Peroutka reproached the communists for their antidemocratic

---

[6] A *personal note* concerning my position between 1945 and 1948 as well as later might be in order. Since the reopening of the universities in Czechoslovakia, after a six-year hiatus, I had studied philosophy and literature at the Charles University in Prague. I was not affiliated with any political party but my views could be described as closest to the Social Democratic Party program. But I did not like the Fierlinger's wing of the party and its preference for Stalinism when in conflict with democracy. Some of my friends were either non-party people or belonged to the young, liberal and democratic trends, mainly — since I was an infidel — in the Social Democratic or Czech Socialist Party. Several Slovaks were among them. My girl-friend was a member of the Communist Party as were quite a few of my other acquaintances. A continuous and sharp exchange of views on democracy and socialism was then going on among students. I was worried about the partial dehumanization and about the threatening Bolshevization of the country and organized — in a rather naïve way, without much hope for a final success — several movements and organizations on a national or only Prague scale. Since the Fall of 1947, I expected a communist *coup d'état* to take place before the elections scheduled for May 1948. My extracurricular activities brought me in close contact with some of the cultural and political personalities in Prague and Bratislava. Among the young communists I was searching for people who would be able to see the danger of suppressing democracy and could help us to stop it in time. Needless to say, that did not save the country but might have helped my insight into their problems and motivation. I left Czechoslovakia in August 1948. My bias, hopefully, is for objective truth, humanism, and democracy only.

actions. At this meeting most of the communists present did not oppose a proposal to send a telegram of support to President Beneš, asking him to solve the governmental crisis in a constitutional manner. (The crisis was started when most of the non-communist members of the government tendered their resignation in protest against the continuing takeover of the police by the CPC and hoped to force an early election.) But the dean of the philosophy faculty of the Charles University, Professor J. B. Kozák, talked and talked at such length that the telegram was never sent. Thanks to Kovárna and Peroutka, and to communist hesitation or embarrassment, Professor Kozák was not allowed, as he wanted to, to proceed from the meeting as Cultural Union's spokesman straight to a convocation of prominent people, selected by the Communist Party, to take part in the founding of a Supreme Action Committee in charge of the "revolution" led by action committees as organs of the revolutionary seizure of power. J. B. Kozák, a protestant with international connections, especially in the U.S.A. where he had spent the war years, was until then considered the main native philosopher of democracy and protector of T. G. Masaryk's humanist heritage. Later, defending his action, he explained to me that a gigantic fight was going on in the world between two blocks of ice, as he put it, and that he hoped to join the Soviet side as soon as possible in order to, at least, "dress the wounds of the victims." As I have predicted, his name was only misused for a short time by the communists and he himself was dropped the moment he was of no use to them any more. As I was told by the President's brother, Vojta Beneš, the desertion of J. B. Kozák hurt Dr. Edward Beneš as much as Fierlinger's treason. (Fierlinger was a former Czechoslovak Ambassador in Moscow who helped the communists liquidate his own Social Democratic Party. George F. Kennan already in 1945 considered him "to all intents and purposes a Soviet agent."[7]) The President named the two as the major traitors of the democratic cause in 1948.

The fear of the attacking communists was too great even before they won the conflict. Just a little example: as a continuation of the Cultural Union's meeting, the heated discussion spilled over to our office in the Mánes building. The future Minister of Culture and one of the most stubborn and dogmatic communist intellectuals, Professor Ladislav Štoll, was upset by "the youth's" opinions and, in order to convert, had used several of the usual Leninist clichés, such as "During a flood waters get dirty" and "When you cut down trees, chips fly" on the address of "the youth" that replied, "Not all dirty water is a flood." Finally, he promised that he would intervene in order to get those students released who had been arrested by the police during demonstrations in Prague in support of the President and democracy.

Professor J. B. Čapek, another of the leading men of Protestant culture in Czechoslovakia, during the debate kept quiet but from the background pulled the sleeve of the arguing student, and whispered: "Be careful, don't destroy yourself!" In his lectures at the University, talking about the Renaissance or Czech poetry,

---

[7] See his *Memoirs, 1925–1950* (Boston: Little, Brown, & Company, 1967), p. 254. Marcia Davenport, a close friend of Jan Masaryk, found Beneš "cold, oracular, . . . a pygmy, . . . his mind devoid of wit, grace, or flexibility;" she particularly disliked Fierlinger: "Rat, I thought; I have never seen a human being whose face was so rodent-like." *Too Strong for Fantasy* (London: Collins, 1968), pp. 314 and 317.

he belonged, both before and after the *coup*, to a small group of humanists who kept warning, in an indirect and highly sophisticated fashion, against the extremes of political barbarism masked as progressive, but in an actual revolutionary situation preferred fearful cautiousness. Although that was understandable for his generation that just went through six years of Nazi terror, in the aftermath of World War II, it helped the communists into power.

My next example comes from the Castle. In my attempt to join some forces that would defend democracy, when I could not meet the President, I went to see another prominent representative of Czech culture and democratic socialism, writer Josef Kopta. He was well known for his novels of the World War I, for which he had used his own memories of the Czechoslovak revolutionary corps on the Russian front. I visited him in his capacity as director of the President's cultural office. Again, he tried to "calm me" and I remembered the sentence which expressed his way (and surely not only his way) of gracefully accepting what was then happening: "We Czechs have always been for socialism." There was no way, at least not on that day, to persuade him that the question then was not socialism but a *coup d'état* and an end to democracy without which there is no socialism. On the way out of his office, in the corridor, I could see members of the new government, just accepted by President Beneš, in his capitulation, helping each other after the audience into winter coats.

According to his own admission, Dr. Petr Zenkl, leader of the second largest party in the ČSR, the Czech (National) Socialists, was in hiding, and instead of organizing a defense of democracy spent hours driving through Prague in a taxi. When he heard about the acceptance of the new government on the radio, he burst into tears.

During the *putsch*, the Social Democratic daily reported a speech of the party chairman, Bohumil Laušman, under large red headlines: "Let's Not Fear a Putsch!"[8] A black headline under it proclaimed: "Masaryk's Nation Can Go to Socialism Only the Masaryk Way", which was probably right but in the situation did not help much since another Minister of the Party, Václav Majer, the day before was not even allowed to speak on the radio.

Even the Minister of Foreign Affairs and son of T. G. Masaryk (founder of the Republic), Jan Masaryk, who was very popular with the people of his country, before he was found dead on the pavement under his windows on the courtyard of his Ministerial palace, pronounced a few sentences which show the mistaken beliefs that helped to lose the contest. He said — and it was widely reported in the press — that he would never go against the people (at a moment when the Communist Party claimed to be leading the people's revolution), that he would never go against the Russians (who ordered and supported the *coup d'état*), and that he was looking forward to governing together with the communists.

"At the critical moment, not a single leader from any political party suggested active measures for handling the situation."[9]

[8] *Právo lidu*, 22 Feb, 1948, p. 1.
[9] Otto Friedman, *The Break-up of Czech Democracy* (London: Victor Gollancz, 1950), p. 94. For another good short history of the *coup*, see Pavel Tigrid, "The Prague Coup of 1948: The Elegant Takeover," *The Anatomy of Communist Takeovers*, ed. by Thomas T. Hammond (New Haven: Yale University Press, 1975), pp. 399-432. There is a basic bibliography in footnotes on pages 399 and 400.

The communists were victorious. Surprised by the easiness of their success, they felt the exhilaration of it. Especially the young generation of communist intellectuals cast itself in the role of a historical savior of the nation and of its proletariat whose majority could not care less. Only gradually, they lost their illusions. I believe that case studies could best evoke the changing perspective and motivation of some of the future heroes of 1968.

Chapter 2.

"We are charlatans who passed ourselves off as surgeons"

PAVEL KOHOUT, born in 1928, was author of the July Manifesto of 1968 — the document signed by hundreds of thousands of Czechs and Slovaks, which entreated members of the Czechoslovak Politburo to hold steady and not to give in to the Soviet counterpart at a meeting in Čierna. He tried to recapture his feelings and activities of 1948 in his autobiographical novel, *Diary of a Counter-Revolutionary*, written, at least in part, after the invasion of August 1968.[1] In this case study I will complement it by other sources.

During the February days of 1948, Kohout wished to be like John Reed.[2] He made a decision: "As soon as possible I will become a poet. In my heart and pen the Revolution will always have a reliable weapon ready to shoot at all times." He left home with a note to his (bourgeois) parents: "Will come back after the revolution. Your comrade son."[3] The 20-year-old Kohout offered his services to Klement Gottwald, chairman of the Communist Party and Prime Minister of the Czechoslovak Republic: "What should I do?" — "We need you in the Youth Association!" Kohout then proposed and organized the Theatre of the Revolution — FRONTHEREV. On the Old Town Square, listening to Gottwald's speech during the pseudo-revolutionary staging of the *coup d'état*, he felt great:

> I had a sensation of certainty: yes, my hope that once, in desperation, I looked for in God and then in Love, is here, in that human mass which set out to search for justice, and in this man (Gottwald) who is leading them into the decisive battle. That is the CENTRUM SECURITATIS that Comenius tried to find in vain and I have now found.[4]

Impressionable young men did not see through the staging; for them the show represented reality. Kohout's enthusiasm was sentimental and rather cheap: "Perhaps a revolutionary composer will soon create a 'Gottwald's Concert for Sirenes and Proletarian Choir' in order to celebrate this day yearly."[5] He then encouraged a group of communists to physically attack the secretariat of the Social Democratic Party. He participated in the brutal manhandling of several party members — some of them old — who were present. At least one of them (in his

---

[1] Pavel Kohout, *Aus dem Tagebuch eines Konter-Revolutionärs* (trans. Gustav Solar and Felix R. Bossonnet, Luzern: Verlag C. J. Bucher, 1969). English and French translations appeared later. Throughout this thesis I will quote from the first German edition in my own translation. Later quoted as "*The Diary* . . .".

[2] *Ibid.*, p. 80.

[3] *Ibid.*, p. 83.

[4] Kohout is not addicted to understatement and all the capitalizations are his. *Ibid.*, p. 83.

[5] *Ibid.*, p. 84.

9

eighties) was pushed down the stairs. "And I have the magnificent impression that for the first time my words became acts."[6]

A romantic revolution needs a romance. In the evening, in company of other revolutionaries, Kohout entered a villa. "The villa looked like a castle. A typical fortress of the Prague bourgeoisie."[7] Here the self-appointed proletarian (son of a rich family) meets another destiny — a girl. What a remarkable dialogue! "For the first time I drank Scotch. . . . 'You are so revolutionary that I am afraid you might be impotent.' — 'And you are a typical daughter of a class that can't produce other values but money.'" He gets drunk, vomits but the dialogue between classes continues: "What frightens you? The Revolution, that's also me! If you want to I will stay with you and teach you everything. I will teach you how to live." — "Then in exchange I'll teach you how to make love!"[8] And the happy revolutionary adds:

> I didn't have any idea that only on the other side of bashfulness the wide land of love begins. . . . FIVE DAYS THAT SHOOK CZECHOSLOVAKIA AND ONE NIGHT THAT SHOOK ME!. . . In the morning I will ask B. to marry me. It doesn't matter that she is five years older than I. On the contrary — that's ingenious: mutually, we will be teacher and pupil to each other. She will make a man out of me. I will make a revolutionary out of her. . . . For you, my Party. For you, my love.[9]

Touching? Or childish? But people of this caliber were playing their "historical roles" and for decades deciding about their country and fate of millions of men.

After the double *coup* of Kohout came first disillusions. A girl-friend of his was not allowed to study or work because of her bourgeois origin and she and her boy-friend, a real proletarian, left the country together. Another friend explained to him that sentimentality during the revolution and the liquidation of the class enemy does not pay. "The revolution is a profession."[10] The Leninist determination to act decisively against class enemies even if "masked as workers" had to be learned by every revolutionary.

On the Workers' Holiday, 1 May 1950, during an official mission to Moscow (Kohout served there for a few years as cultural attaché), he wrote in his diary:

> I don't want to deny that sometimes my heart feels heavy. I am not a diplomat. I find it difficult to talk in the language of the protocol with people whom I would rather embrace. I don't like it that I can't visit them in their homes: they are still defending themselves against spies and traitors.[11]

But there are great compensations for the hungry heart: "The biggest experience of my life . . . finally, today, I caught a glimpse of Him [Stalin]!"[12]

As we know, most of all, Kohout wanted to be a poet of the revolution. His poetry was probably the worst of its kind — stupid adulation of Stalin and Gottwald, or hateful condemnation of Slánský and other "traitors" alternated with encouragement to workers to work harder and, as much as possible, just for the glory of it. The regime opened all doors for him. At the beginning of the 1950s,

[6] *Ibid.*, p. 88.
[7] *Ibid.*
[8] *Ibid.*, p. 91.
[9] *Ibid.*, pp. 91-2.
[10] *Ibid.*, pp. 100-3.
[11] *Ibid.*, p. 114.
[12] *Ibid.*, pp. 114-5.

he became the most published poet in Czechoslovakia. Another Czech writer had this to say: "Pavel Kohout entered literature with poems and verse-plays in which the 'temporary' insanity of his time reached an unusual degree of concentration."[13] Most of the poets kept quiet either voluntarily or otherwise. Many disappeared in prison or went into exile. A few committed suicide. Small talents were making great careers.

In 1953 came the shock of Stalin's and Gottwald's death. "We are like an army which on the eve of the battle lost both commanders-in-chief. . . . We admired and loved Stalin and Klement Gottwald so much that we had no idea of their mortality. . . . Sometimes it seems to us that everything is finished."[14] But, naturally for Kohout, everything had to be expressed poetically. This is a sample of his constructive poetry for public consumption, published 10 March 1953, in the main daily of the CPC, *Rudé právo*:

> The natives ask it on their drums,
> The world's poor send cablegrams:
> "Stalin was the light in our night,
> What will become of us if it died? . . .
>
> World's poor, believe me,
> The Sun Stalin will not die,
> And in our bossoms burning
> Will produce light amazing . . .[15]

Privately, Kohout's mental state was not as optimistic as his public stance. After Gottwald's death Kohout, in military service, was throwing hand-grenades and "constantly was tempted to keep them three seconds longer in his hand."[16] Three years later, Khrushchev's "secret" speech marked "the end of security. I was convinced that a world collapsed."[17] I recall that somewhere else Kohout wrote that he spent his nights crying.

But his doubts about the absolute righteousness of the system started to awaken earlier than that. Often the military service brought young Party intellectuals in close contact with the reality of the Soviet order and resulted in permanent damage to their propagandistic idealism. At the beginning of the 1950s, the armed services of Czechoslovakia were going through a strict sovietization. Of his service, Kohout has this to say:

> The critical years of '52 to '55 I lived through in the army. . . . Daily contact with the army reality, which bore specially conspicuous traits of the times, brought about a fateful change in my literary activity. That is to say, for the first time I met people of my *own* generation and of my *own* conviction who were nevertheless wronged. And I met other people of my *own* conviction who committed the wrong, and what's more, insisted on it . . . dogmatics. . . . It was clear: these were not exceptions but a norm.[18]

[13] Josef Škvorecký, *All the Bright Young Men and Women . . .*, p. 188.

[14] Pavel Kohout, *The Diary . . .*, pp. 44–5.

[15] In my translation the naïveté and clumsiness of the poem were reproduced from the Czech original as faithfully as possible.

[16] Pavel Kohout, *The Diary . . .*, p. 145.

[17] *Ibid.*, pp. 44–5.

[18] "What I Was . . .," *Literární noviny*, 21 Mar. 1964, p. 3.

Kohout began to write satirical short stories and received a prize but he had difficulties with his play *September Nights*. The main theme was that a man who committed unjust acts, though objectively honest, could not remain as commander. Following Soviet example, the Party was then encouraging limited criticism, but the Minister for the Defence, Dr. Alexej Čepička, one of the main manipulators of the Slánský and similar trials, who had created a special cult of his own in the army and in the theatre, felt personally attacked. One year before the Twentieth Congress of the Soviet Communist Party, the play created a stir. The public liked it but the Party leadership was shaken up.

Kohout had his share of success and troubles. Typically, experiences of personal wrongs, suffered for criticism, were pushing him further and further to the side of the opposition. In 1956 he was supposed to get a state prize, his pictures were already taken, but then his name was crossed out because at a plenary meeting of communist writers he opposed some views of President Zápotocký. Kohout commented that state prizes were also given to writers for keeping their mouths shut.[19] When in 1956, at the Second Writers' Congress, some communist poets, especially Hrubín and Seifert, promised that they would stop lying about reality and would represent the conscience of the nation, Kohout asked himself: "When and where did I lie? Did we really know so frightfully little?" Still, he refused to accept the ugly truth about the regime from the mouth of real poets who spoke up, "because they offended my idiotic innocence!"[20] Because of strengthened censorship one of his plays, *Poor Thing*, was never produced. Since then, all his plays discussed "the ethics of our society." They became popular but had growing difficulties with censors. For instance, his repeatedly postponed play *Such a Love* was, in its filmed version, criticized for condemning for cruelty to man the whole society as "an inhuman organization."[21] A Party screening was initiated against him but he passed it mostly unharmed since "after the revolution he fulfilled all the tasks of the revolutionary constructive movement."[22]

In the 1960s, a little like Yevtushenko in the U.S.S.R. in the same period, Kohout continued fighting on two fronts — on one side against Western imperialism and capitalism, and on the other against "deformations" of socialism at home. Both types of activities — in poems, plays, and films — were most probably genuine, although the first necessity was paying for the second luxury. In his verses Kohout celebrated the immortal Lenin and Gagarin or heroic Cuba, and attacked the Americans: "In winter and heat / up to New York our rockets can meet."[23] Even such enthusiastic support for the Party line had its problems: in the general scarcity of many non-military supplies. He could not obtain paper to complete some work till a friend, an atomic physicist, stole paper for him.[24]

At the Third Czechoslovak Writers' Congress in 1963, Pavel Kohout, matured, complained about poor living standards, protectionism and unlawful

[19] Pavel Kohout, *The Diary* . . ., p. 169.
[20] *Ibid.*, p. 176.
[21] Miloš Fiala in *Rudé právo*, 8 Oct. 1959.
[22] Quoted from the record of the Party screening, which took place on the 10 October 1960, by Josef Sobotechý, "August August August," *Tvorba*, 27 May 1970, p. 16.
[23] Pavel Kohout, "Stop, Amerika," *Večerní Praha*, 6 Jan. 1962.
[24] See Kohout's letter in *Kultura*, 3 Aug. 1961.

arbitrariness. He discussed "the shaken confidence of a part of our citizens in socialism in general or, at least, in its morality," and called for admission of guilt by those guilty of "administrative measures" [a euphemism for police actions] as well as for "very severe punishment of people who participated in inflicting suffering and death and who belied the Party."[25]

Kohout's successful dramatization of the novel *Good Soldier Švejk* was based on his "conception that it concerns a fight against blockheads and that švejkism is a historically conditioned defence of a helpless citizen against an organized force which has all the power."[26] The class concept of life and ethics did not seem important any more. Enemies of the oppressed citizens were the State and its ruling class.

In a great public confession in the Writers' Union weekly, Kohout answered attacks by reforming communists who did not trust him and reminded him of his ridiculous poetry on Stalin:

> I was born 1928 .... For my generation the arrival of Russian tanks was a real miracle. ... The perspective of a socialist revolution seemed to be the only starting point .... Our enemies wanted to restore capitalism. Most of all, I liked to be the poet of the revolution. It was an era of great faith that around the corner was the time when the best ideals of humanity will be realized. I am not ashamed of that faith whatever I called it, Stalin or else. The poet — unlike judges — has the right to believe.[27] Also a citizen has the right to believe. Trust is an indispensable part of democracy. So much greater is the historical responsibility of everybody who disappointed it. Whoever he is, Stalin or else.... Unfortunately, just then the proposition resounded on the sharpening of the class conflict when the enemy penetrated our own lines. That sealed the tragedy .... Anyway, I am not apologizing ... Rather it will never stop grieving me that the years which I then considered to be "the best years of our life" were for so many others the cruellest ones — and for a good many the last. I can never forgive those who willfully brought it about. But also for myself I will not have a full feeling of my own dignity till I came to terms with the tragedy of the nation and revolution at least partly by a creative act.[28]

Such a creative act was probably his television play *Obžaloba* [*Accusation*, 1966] in which he defended himself as an accused for the crimes of the 1950s. The older generation was guilty. For Kohout and some of his colleagues it was primarily a conflict of different generations of communists. But also by courageous activities Kohout clearly tried to justify his revolutionary ideals and the purity of his involvement. At the Fourth Writers' Congress in June 1967, when the communist

---

[25] *Kultúrny Život*, 1 June 1963.

[26] *Mladá fronta*, 9 Dec. 1963.

[27] Unfortunately, the self-stylization does not fit. Kohout never was a poet but at best a versemonger. Even other communists thought so, among them literary critics of the official Party daily. In a review of his book of poetry *Time of Love and Struggle*, they praised his aim "not to allow an atmosphere of carelessness and of blunting the hatred towards enemies. He shakes hesitant hearts .... Kohout attempts to show the face of the enemy who penetrated the Party." But the reviewers castigated his limited vocabulary, declamatory style, declaratory superficiality, sentimentality, and boisterous phrazemongering. (See A. Jelínek and M. Schulz, "On Pavel Kohout's Poetry," *Rudé právo*, 12 Dec. 1954.) *Slovník českých spisovatelů* [*The Encyclopedia of Czech Writers*], published in Prague in 1964, had this to say: "Kohout entered literature by political and love verse which then won great popularity; they expressed and bore out the first, essentially yet naïve notions of 'victors' children' on life in socialism; however, it soon appeared that in their political alertness and even in interest in sentimental life of the youth they often were shallow, mentally sterile, and in places banal."

[28] Pavel Kohout, "What I was ... , *Literární noviny*, 21 Mar. 1964, p. 3.

intellectuals publicly clashed with the Party leadership and challenged its right to decide everything, Kohout sharply criticized from a moral point of view the foreign policy of his government, primarily its anti-Israeli aspects in the Middle East. He demanded free access to information for everybody and the right to publish views that might differ from official policies. Later he read from the tribune to the assembly of hundreds of writers an unpublished letter of Alexander Solzhenitsyn to the Soviet Writers' Congress which had suppressed it. (A few Soviet writers pleaded with their Czech colleagues to have it read in Prague. Also liberal influences were coming sometimes from the East.) Kohout was punished by a strict reprimand with warning by the Central Committee of the Communist Party of Czechoslovakia, but — among others — President Novotný intervened in order to save him from the proposed expulsion from the Party. In a letter sent the 5th October of 1967, Kohout stressed that "our contributions to the congress had a single aim: to help heal the wounded revolution." The next day he read it at the actif of communist writers.[29]

During his conflict with the Party leadership, Kohout still professed quite a few of the attitudes that have formed his perspective since the 1940s. In an interesting exchange of letters with the West German writer Günter Grass, first published in journals on both sides of the border and later collected in a book, Kohout still acted as a devoted believer in communism in its Leninist form and as someone who has been initiated into higher wisdom that escapes the comprehension of his partner. In spite of his growing knowledge of the West where he witnessed some fifty or sixty of first nights of his plays he still felt alienated there and kept stressing the need to fight against non-communists and against the bourgeoisie. The world for him was still divided into two camps. Although he did not abstain from reminding Grass of "the immense multitude of crimes" committed by the German nation, he defended Lenin's and Stalin's terror as necessary in the "state of siege." An understanding of the substance of Soviet reality was still lacking. He defended the *coup d'état* of 1948 as a genuine revolution but later did not like the means used: "We knew that the victors always have to surround themselves with power in order to lead the victory to fulillment. But we did not foresee that to that end we would use exactly the ways that we had ourselves condemned before."[30] Because of the humanist content of their aims, claimed Kohout, almost all great personalities of the Czech and Slovak arts actively supported the efforts of the CPC. "It was and is our revolution. Our team-generation has only one alternative: to renew the continuity of the revolutionary process that in our country from the foundation of the Communist Party had above all a democratic character."[31] Grass did not press the point that Kohout obviously did not seem to thoroughly know the history of his own party, but it was easy for him to win the argument that the Munich Agreement was not typical for the bourgeoisie and that socialist states do not often act differently. But Kohout did not give up and insisted that his revolutionary way was a realistic one:

---

[29] The letter was published in Paris in *Svědectví*, vol. ix, no. 33 (winter 1967), p. 107.

[30] Günter Grass and Pavel Kohout, *Briefe über die Grenze: Versuch eines Ost-West Dialogs* [*Letters Across the Frontier: Attempt at an East-West Dialogue*] (Hamburg: Christian Wegner Verlag, 1968), pp. 13-14.

[31] *Ibid.*, p. 14.

It seems to me that my participation in this combat is less Utopian than your fight for cleanliness and effectiveness of the parliamentary democracy . . . . I do not agree with your opinion that the Czechoslovak development is a confirmation for the believers in evolution. It should not be forgotten that the revolution in Czechoslovakia took place immediately after the war when the bourgeoisie was forced to give up its economic and political bases for their positions. That created a classless society.[32]

Early in 1968, the Party organization of the Writers' Union elected Kohout as its chairman. Esteem for Kohout among fellow communist writers was clearly rising, although his fighting qualities might have been considered important too.

During the Prague Spring, Kohout committed himself completely from the beginning to the process of purification of his Party and society. He wrote: "Monday, 18th March 1968. Weekly average: three hours of sleep a day . . . . Now I am doing politics at my own cost. I have a feeling that I owe it to somebody."[33] The obedient collectivist who used to follow Party orders blindly changed into an individualist serving the community according to his own conscience: surely an unexpected but rather typical result of twenty years of indoctrination and experiences with the results of Party policies.

Kohout who in 1952 had celebrated in verse the legal murder of Slánský, the general secretary of the CPC, now helped his widow to publish her anti-Stalinist memoirs, *A Report About My Husband*.[34] In an interview for West German readers (he had theatre engagements there quite often) he said: "If this Party does not prove itself true, we'll have to seek another road."[35] The reform of the Party was the first goal but the Party was not absolute any more.

His activities reached a climax in his July Manifesto of 1968. Finally, he was able to feel accepted by his writer colleagues, some of whom used to feel contempt for him, and by his Party and people. Josef Smrkovský, one of the "big four" of the communist leadership of the ČSSR in 1968, praised his effort later:

Our journey [to Čierna] attracted the attention of the entire nation. A manifesto appeared at the time. I think its author was Pavel Kohout. It gave our delegation a mandate of confidence such as few Czechoslovak delegations have had for foreign negotiations, but it also set limits for our transaction. It stressed that we should hold to and defend four postulates of the Czechoslovak Socialist Republic, namely socialism, alliance, sovereignty and freedom as the program of our country, of our people![36]

The naïve versifier of his twenties, at forty became a spokesman for his nation and for the revolution. But how different was this revolution from the *coup d'état* of 1948! It was not staged and manipulated but genuine and humanist both in its conception and means.

A few weeks later, the second apparition of Soviet tanks in the streets of Prague did not seem to represent another miracle, and Kohout summed up his career:

---

[32] *Ibid.*, pp. 38–9 and 85–6.

[33] *The Diary. . .*, p. 73.

[34] See an interview with Mrs. Jozefa and Miss Marta Slánský in *Borba*, 12 May 1968. He encouraged her writing since she showed him the manuscript after his speech at the Writers' Congress in 1963.

[35] Jürgen Serke, "Interview," *Die Welt*, 27 Mar. 1968.

[36] Josef Smrkovský (an unfinished conversation), *The Story of the Czechoslovakian Invasion of 1968, As Told by an Insider* (An *Australian Left Review* pamphlet, Sydney: Red Pen Publications, 1976), p. 20.

It could be said that then, long ago, perhaps we were idiots but certainly not criminals. Since 1956, since the Twentieth Congress of the CPSU, we know everything, we know that there was no question of socialism . . . . After twenty three years, for the first time, I have the sensation of belonging to a nation.[37]

In a discussion with a Czech communist friend in Rome the question of guilt came up again:

He: "We were pure . . . . We could not suspect that the proved leaders of the revolution would transform the class war in an inquisition!"
I: "That is the question."[38]
He: "Do you want to say that we were criminals?"
I: "I want to say that we were no Marxists and if one day we should be punished, then more than anything else for our crimes against Marxism. We are charlatans who passed ourselves off as surgeons."[39]

It is interesting to note that his devotion to abstractions did not leave him: a creative act or Marxism seem to be more important than massacred people. In order to finish his personal history of a revolutionary between 1948 and 1968 as we began, that is *in flagranti* with a girl (naturally, again of bourgeois origin), here are her words from an Italian bed in 1968, after his boasting that he "for twenty years fought for the purity of the revolution":

Always did you pigheadedly fight for something that was basically ridiculous. In twenty years you managed to achieve an enormous victory: gloriously, you brought us to a point where we were twenty years ago. And you expect us to thank you for the good chance.[40]

I met Kohout only once — several months before the *coup d'état* of 1948 — in a studio he recited a poem from a program I had prepared for the Prague radio. He did it so well that I inquired about and remembered his name. He was then member of a famous Czech vocal group. He was a good performer and among his gifts the theatrical was clearly the most obvious. Because he often acted without inhibitions, he was sometimes described as an exhibitionist. Kohout himself qualified his enthusiastic participation in his Party's efforts between 1948 and 1954 as activities of an idiot and charlatan. His conscience suffered but not too much since his *naïveté* could be ascribed to his youth and deception by the elders leading the Communist Party of Czechoslovakia or supporting it as mature artists and writers.

Even if we cannot accept Kohout's thesis that his crime, if any, was only in his *naïveté* and trust of elders, since he and other activists of his age personally participated in violent deeds and cruel handling of their non-communist contemporaries, it has to be admitted that both the cultural and political élites of the nation — with rather rare exceptions — were guilty of a lack of humanist leadership and must accept responsibility for their large role in creating the nationalistic and other myths which helped to undermine democracy and welcome the Soviet prestige and influence.

But if young communists could also quite honestly claim that they did not

[37] Dieter E. Zimmer, Interview with Pavel Kohout, *Die Zeit*, 30 Aug. 1968, p. 10.
[38] In the German, original publication, in English.
[39] *The Diary*. . . ., p. 46.
[40] *Ibid.*, pp. 15 and 17.

know the criminal history of the Soviet Union, they have no excuse for transgressing moral and behavioral precepts normal in a civilized society. They had many warnings which they refused to heed. After all, an almost free press still existed till 1948 and polemics with fanatical and undemocratic communists were held everywhere — among students, workers, and in cultural societies. They disregarded all such admonitions because they believed that it was the class enemy speaking, the class enemy who had to be defeated or eliminated, that the class struggle was necessary and the class enemy was already condemned by history and science. This belief was among the hardest ones to abandon since it puts the believer among the "chosen people." Some of them kept it even after the Soviet invasion of 1968, since the whole Soviet reality, if needed for the preservation of faith, can be dismissed by a believer just as a temporary deformation of otherwise valid premises. It was one of the most difficult steps for them to take — to acknowledge that throwing old Social Democrats down the stairs or eliminating thousands of students from further studies and sending them to work in mines, under the pretext that they were of bourgeois origin, were also criminal activities.

The pathological foundation of this feeling of belonging to the victorious proletarian class is manifest in the fact that most of the accusers were of the same bourgeois origin as their victims, but they decided to join the chosen class of workers by a mental exercise, without any material or social disadvantages to themselves. On the contrary: like Kohout, for their role as liquidators they were able to advance and to join the ruling class with, at least temporarily, great material and social advantages for their benefit. Therefore the basic belief in a class struggle without mercy is surely one of the roots of the problem. It can be considered a formative feature of an aberration or mental sickness extremely dangerous to the healthy development of a society which should be able to defend itself while there is still time, before the dangerous patients and psychopaths seize power. It is wonderful when a psychotic youngster manages in twenty years to grow into a decent human being but the social cost of such a benevolent transformation has in the meantime been extremely costly.

After the Soviet invasion in August 1968, Pavel Kohout quickly completed his belletristic — but I suppose quite truthful — *Diary of a Counter-Revolutionary*. In the design of the title, spread over two pages, the Swiss publisher managed well to convey the author's obvious intention to always be considered a revolutionary, with the epithet "counter" supplied only by the Soviet invaders together with their domestic collaborators, and accepted by Kohout (and other Czechoslovak reform communists) just as a sad joke. The *Diary*, never published in Czechoslovakia, is much more interesting for the insights into the psyche of a modern Leninist follower than as a successful novel which it is not. It is arty in construction, sentimental, banal, and often painful to read. The major gift of Kohout, after all, was and remained theatrical, and too much depth should not be expected. But in his political pronouncements and journalistic articles Kohout achieved much higher levels: often they are well written, witty, to the point, and courageous.

Kohout ridiculed the pro-Soviet arguments then being used that "anti-popular pressure groups" were responsible for continuing crises. Using the typical official jargon, among such groups he mentioned the:

shameless activization of the well-known bastions of the Czech and Moravian bourgeoisie such as — without any doubt — to name only the most glaring examples, the factories Škoda Works in Plzeň or Gottwald New Metallurgical Works in Kunčice. Old agents of international imperialism, many of whom have, in their trickiness, as early as in 1921, founded the Communist Party of Czechoslovakia, and others who have already for decades been carrying on their sordid intrigues in the Kladno coal pits or at the Silesian blast-furnaces, now quite obviously want to weaken the government of working people. It is sufficient to read the documents from the Metalworkers' Trade Union Congress to grasp the moral quagmire of this pressure group of no fewer than 950,000 obstinate enemies of socialism who stoop to nothing by putting on the mask of workman's overalls.

The source of power in our country is, of course, the people, but not any people. There is a difference between a people who respect this power without opposition, and a people who constantly requests something. It should not be forgotten that in question is people's power. A people who criticizes its representatives is basically anti-people.[41]

This piece of journalism in which Kohout successfully paraphrased the pro-Soviet style and logic — at a time when the workers' opposition to Soviet "normalization" was at its height — closed by revealing "this ridiculous handful of several million people" as the "pressure group ČSSR."[41]

At public meetings with young people, Kohout tried to spread humor and optimism. So, for example, on the 15th of January 1969, he acknowledged that the following joke was suppressed by the censorship of *Listy*, the writers' weekly: "Two men are standing in front of a factory bearing an inscription 'With the Soviet Union forever.' One says to the other: 'Gee, how time flew!'"[42] At the same meeting, which was later strongly criticized as a show of counter-revolutionaries, the question "Are you still convinced that socialism will conquer?" was answered by Kohout: "I think, yes. I think that socialism will win even in the Soviet Union".[43]

During Husák's period of "normalization", Kohout proved to be one of the most courageous and outspoken oppositionists to the new wave of sovietization of Czechoslovakia. He refused to be pushed into emigration which he was offered:

In my opinion, a writer should leave his own country only if he has reason to fear for his life. In recent years I have had to undergo many terrible things, many abuses, actions, and gestures that were almost insupportable. The more I think about it, the more I am convinced that the

---

[41] Pavel Kohout, "Sebetritika" [Self-criticism], *Práce*, 4 Jan. 1969, p. 2. I wonder if Kohout knew a poem written by Bertold Brecht after the June 1953 uprising in East Germany:

After the rising of the 17th June
The Secretary of the Writers' Union
Had leaflets distributed in the Stalinallee
In which you could read that the people
Had lost the Government's confidence
Which it could only regain
By redoubled efforts. Would it in that case
Not be simpler if the Government
Dissolved the People
And elected another?

See Martin Esslin, *Brecht: The Man and His Work* (Garden City, N.Y.: Anchor Books, Doubleday & Company, Inc., 1961), p. 183.

[42] Jan Šroubek, "Testimony of a Jest," *Tribuna*, 11 Mar. 1970, p. 15.

[43] *Ibid.*

time has gone when it was possible to cut open a knot with a sword. . . . Naturally, I want to continue being able to speak with absolute frankness to those who, among other things, have tried to demonstrate that there can be a union of writers from which the majority of writers is excluded.[44]

Repeatedly, Pavel Kohout was detained by the police and threatened with a trial in case he refused to go into exile.[45]

During a violent campaign which continued in the press into 1974, Kohout was repeatedly compared with Judas since "he received money for his treason."[46] This Czech journalist reminded his readers of the sentence Kohout coined in his Stalinist youth and which has often been quoted after 1968 to discredit him: "With one hand I write verse, in the other I hold my gun."

In spite of these and many other harassments, Kohout insisted on his right to have a passport valid for re-entry and to have his foreign earnings — his only means of existence during a total ban on his work at home — legally recognized.

He finally succeeded, first in going to another communist country, Hungary,[47] and in August 1975 to Lucerne in Switzerland for a *première* of his new play *Roulette*, a comedy about an aborted revolution, and later to West Germany and Austria for the same purpose.[48] In a very limited application of the "spirit of Helsinki" Kohout was among the first and the few who were allowed to travel abroad with the right to return home. With great danger to himself, he had to fight for this natural right for six years. His victory was of a very short duration. When in October 1976 his play *Poor Murderer* had a *première* on Broadway in New York, he was not allowed to go there under the pretext that he did not have the necessary foreign currency, although his Western publishers and the Broadway producers of his play had stated in writing that they would be responsible for all expenses incurred by him and his wife.[49]

His persecution continued especially after the publication of the Charter 77 which bore his signature. The police took away his car registration certificate, his driver's license, and his identity card. He was also told that he would have to take a new driving test. He was evicted from his Prague flat and ordered to stay away from the capital city. A new violent campaign was mounted against him in the press and on television, but that did not stop his criticism of the violation of human rights in Czechoslovakia.

On 9 January 1978 Kohout received the $10,000 Austrian prize for his contribution to European literature and the next day in an interview on Austrian Radio he declared that repressive practices "cannot go on in the long run."[50]

We do not know what are his opinions about Leninism or Marxism but all his

[44] Quoted from Kevin Devlin, "Plight of Czechoslovak Intellectuals: 'Espresso' Interviews Kohout and Others," *Radio Free Europe Research* paper, no. 1836, 5 July 1973, p. 6.

[45] In the Fall of 1973 Kohout's country house started to burn — according to the local police, with many suspicious traces of deliberate arson. See *Listy*, vol. iv, May 1974, p. 19; *UPI*, Prague, 31 Oct. 1973, and *Süddeutsche Zeitung*, 28 Sept. 1973.

[46] Jiří Svoboda, "Betrayal for Sale," *Rudé právo*, 9 Mar. 1974, p. 3.

[47] *Index on Censorship*, vol. 4, no. 2 (summer 1975).

[48] Situation Report/Czechoslovakia, no. 48, *RFER*, 10 Dec. 1975, p. 10; and *Svědectví*, vol. viii, no. 50 (1975), p. 198.

[49] *The Times*, 11 Nov. 1976, p. 8.

[50] *International Herald Tribune*, 11 Jan. 1978.

public pronouncements testify to a great belief in the importance of human rights. Asked about his political opinions, Kohout said on 26 September 1973 in a program of the Austrian television:

> I am a convinced supporter of socialism. . . . For me socialism is a system in which socialization of means of production under public control creates a basis for the full development of freedoms that humanity has been endeavoring after for centuries — freedom of opinion, freedom of artistic and scientific activity, freedom of movement, etc. socialism is unthinkable without these freedoms.[51]

In Kohout, the "poet of a revolution" became its victim and a pathetic caller for rights and freedoms which his generation of young communists had helped to destroy. He did learn his lesson but too late for himself and for his nation.

Even his intention to bear the drastic measures of the "normalization" and to continue fighting against the suppression of human rights in Czechoslovakia till the end was not fulfilled. He was allowed, "in the spirit of Helsinki," to leave Prague on 28 October 1978 on a one-year exit visa, in order to work as a special adviser to the Vienna *Burgtheater*. When he attempted to return home less than one year later, he was not permitted to enter his country. After some other intentionally humiliating procedures, he was finally told at the Czechoslovak embassy in Vienna that he was deprived of his citizenship.[52]

---

[51] See *Listy*, vol. iv, no. 1 (Feb. 1974), p. 27. With the exception of the last two pages, this chapter as well as the next one were finished and given their final form already in 1975. Therefore I was not very surprised when I discovered that Pavel Tigrid in his latest book, *Amière révolution*, published in Paris by Albin Michel in 1977, out of the Czechoslovak dissidents had selected Pavel Kohout and Ladislav Mňačko; by a strange coincidence, his choice of material from Kohout's *Diary*. is similar to mine.

[52] *New York Times*, 7 Oct. 1979.

Chapter 3.

"We have learned from our own blunders"

OTHER examples might help to confirm the fact that, to a large degree, Kohout's thoughts, attitudes, and behavior were typical of young communist intellectuals of the era.

Ladislav Mňačko, born in 1919, is a Slovak writer whose fighting spirit and career in many points resemble Pavel Kohout's.[1]

Very much as his Czech counterpart, he was full of enthusiasm for the "building of socialism" and the erection[2] of many constructions inspired by the Communist Party in order to get cheap labor and to send young people away from home doing voluntary work. For long periods of time they could be detached from their families and indoctrinated as supporters of the regime. Of great propagandistic value for these Party purposes were Mňačko's many reportages, poetry (or rather versemongering à la Kohout but in Slovak), and a play, called symbolically *Mosty na Východ* [*Bridges to the East*], for which he received the State Prize in 1953. In 1954 he became a candidate for membership in the Central National Committee in Bratislava.[3]

In the 1960s, again like Kohout, Mňačko in his publications kept fighting on two fronts. For a disappointed but disciplined communist, Nazism and Fascism always presented a safe and ready-made target. Under the pretext of abhorring old Nazi crimes they warned against similar communist practices. In 1959 Mňačko published a successful novel, *Smrt sa volá Engelchen* [*Death Named Engelchen*], for which he obtained a prize from the Czechoslovak Writers' Union and five years later the Klement Gottwald State Prize for a film scenario of the same name.[4] He

---

[1] In an autobiographical collection of short stories entitled *Marxova ulica* [*Marx's Street*], published in 1957, he described his youth as a son of a mailman in a workers' settlement in Martin. Before World War II he came close to the Communist Party. During the war he twice tried to get away from the successor States of Czechoslovakia, but was caught both times, first in 1939 by Hungarians and a year later by Germans on the Dutch border. He spent four years in German prisons, concentration camps, and on forced labor but at the end of the war, in 1944, was able to join a partisan unit. This experience was the basis for his first drama *Partisans,* produced in 1945. The same year he started work as a communist journalist in the main Party organ, *Rudé právo,* and later, till 1953, in the Slovak C.P.'s *Pravda*. Most of the preceding information comes from, or is corroborated by, Josef Sobotecký, *Tvorba,* 1 July 1970, p. 16.

[2] One is, naturally, reminded of sexual symbolism explored in politics generally by William Reich and for Stalinism especially by the Yugoslav movie director Makavejev in his film *W. R. or the Power of Organism*.

[3] *Mladá fronta,* 17 Apr. 1954.

[4] *Rudé právo,* 30 Apr. 1964.

was present at the trial against Eichman in Israel and published a book on it called *Já Adolf Eichman* [I, Adolf Eichman].[5]

Only in 1963 did it become known how bitter Mňačko had been at least since 1956 and how much discipline as well as censorship was needed in order to suppress angry expressions of disappointment. On 22 April 1963, at the Conference of Slovak Writers in Bratislava, Mňačko read a contribution which he had written seven years before for a Slovak cultural weekly but which was then not allowed to be published. In it he criticized Kopecký who had long been (until his death) the head of "our ideological front"[6] for "ill-will" and "declaratory, non-literary, and often rather vulgar criteria" of his interference with literature, "like the ill-famed actif of communist writers in Bratislava in 1951, which for a long time paralyzed the work of Slovak writers."[7] At that meeting in 1951 a prominent Slovak poet and communist, Laco Novomeský, was stigmatized as a "bourgeois nationalist" and together with Slovak politicians of the same deviation, Gustáv Husák and Vlado Clementis, disappeared in prison. Clementis was hanged, Husák tortured but spared, and Novomeský twelve years later was welcomed back at the Conference in 1963 in the Union of Slovak Writers. He made a speech in which he reminded his listeners that Vlado Clementis, a few hours before he was executed, in his last two letters asked the addressees "never to doubt the truth and correctness of socialism, always to follow it and live for it, even after what was going to happen."[8]

In obedience to this commandment, not unusual in movements that claim to know the absolute truth, Novomeský, Mňačko, and other communist intellectuals who devoted their lives to the cause, continued to believe in socialism and in the Communist Party, in spite of everything, but wanted to cleanse it of "deformations" and get rid of political representatives who had committed some of the crimes. The year 1963 saw Dubček's coming into power in Slovakia, a power which was limited by Novotný's stranglehold on Czechoslovakia but which allowed the Slovak intelligentsia greater freedoms and political influence than was enjoyed by their counterparts in Bohemia and Moravia.

In April of 1963 Mňačko published an impassioned appeal to abolish the "Iron Curtain" that existed, as he said, between communist countries. He complained that communist writers and artists had been completely isolated in their own countries without any possibility of knowing either about developments in Western Europe or in other socialist states. He condemned the "complete isolation" as "absurd" and blamed the authorities for having deliberately created it.[9]

His speech at the Third Congress of Czechoslovak Writers in May 1963 was courageous and very critical: "Our country finds itself in an un-rosy economic, political, and moral situation. Our Party is picking up courage to put an end to the abuses and remnants of the personality cult. In such a situation our first duty is to lead the way and not to wait and see how it all ends." He called for "a battle between the new and the old . . . which is actually just beginning" and "will not be

---

[5] *Večerník*, 15 Nov. 1961.

[6] My well-educated recitor-friend in 1948 defended this little Machiavelian as a man who is "so far ahead that we cannot even grasp his vision!"

[7] *Kultúrny život*, 4 May 1963.

[8] *Ibid.*

[9] *Plamen*, no. 4, Apr. 1963, p. 104.

easy. Excuses of mousetraps come from fear. There is no time for cautiousness and mistrust." Mňačko admitted both a collective and personal guilt for the show trials of the 1950s:

> All of us who sit here did condemn Slánský, London, Clementis, Novomeský . . . . We all screamed in some kind of mad zeal — stone them to death! . . . This realization, this fact will forever remain a stain on the name of every one of us and in this case even the proposition is not valid that ignorance cannot commit sin.

Mňačko called on Ladislav Štoll, who was present, not to keep silent any more but "without a flagellant striptease" to admit in a "manly" way that his book on Czech poetry. *Thirty Years of Struggles,* had had "very negative results and consequences" [meaning destruction of careers and lives of many poets]. "All right, I too had written, at that time, that a certain man should die. But I found no peace and worked for ten years to make good my misdeed, and as to a public confession, I have already written it." After that appeal, Ladislav Štoll was only willing to say that although he might phrase some of his judgments in a different way, basically he was right.[10]

Mňačko's courage and fighting spirit were rewarded by the writers who elected him to the committee of the Union of Slovak Writers[11] and to the board of directors of the Czechoslovak Writers' Union.[12]

Beginning in 1963, Mňačko published a series of reportages that really created a sensation. One of them, for example, took the form of an interview with a former Czechoslovak member of the British Royal Air Force during World War II, who along with his colleagues, after February 1948, was persecuted as a potential enemy. He denounced the Party cadre policies, its concept of class war against almost everybody, police brutality, and especially the all-pervading fear created by the system of terror.

> You have produced a general psychosis of fear. Everybody is afraid. . . . Everybody fears for something and everybody is afraid of somebody . . . . Look how ridiculous it all is. Everywhere class aspects are applied. Origin is everything . . . . Show me a person who is not fed up, intimidated, and afraid, who has not been accused of the basest deeds, who has not been suspected, who has not been brutally kicked, who has not been insulted, to whom nobody has done anything![13]

Many approving and some disapproving letters reached the author or the editorial office. In an interview Mňačko stressed the purpose of all his "Delayed Reports":

> The question of justice appears to me to be one of the most important ones, and not only in the legal sense, which our society must deal with. A sense of lawlessness caused in our country a decline of the initiative of individual citizens right down to the freezing point; how can socialism blossom without the initiative of every citizen?[14]

[10] Ladislav Mňačko, "Pasca na myši" ["Mousetrap"], *Kultúrny život,* 1 June 1963, p. 1, and *Literární noviny,* 1 June 1963.

[11] *Kultúrny život,* 27 Apr. 1963, p. 1.

[12] *Literární noviny,* 29 June 1963, p. 2.

[13] "Nočný rozhovor" ["Night Talk"], *Kultúrny život,* 8 June 1963, p. 7.

[14] *Kultúrny život,* 22 June 1963, p. 6.

Before the year 1963 ended Mňačko added to justice another moral value; namely, the truth: "A nation does not need to be led across the crossroad of history on a string like little children from a nursery. . . . A mature nation . . . needs something else — the truth, however harsh it may be."[15]

At the end of 1963, the Czechoslovak Writers' Union decided (unanimously, through its central committee) to propose Mňačko's *Delayed Reports* (with reference to his previous work) for a State Prize. The Party leadership did not agree but, in a typical compromise of the times, gave it to him in 1964 for his old and much less controversial film scenario, *The Name of Death Is Engelchen.*

When an unsatisfactory translation of Mňačko's *Delayed Reports* was published in West Germany, the author took the publisher Jakub Habner to court, won the case in Cologne, and the German book had to be withdrawn since Mňačko contended that his intention was to correct deformations in his country and not to feed the sensationalist press in the West. He made a big fuss about it, spoke at press conferences in Vienna and Bremen, and started to exchange public letters with the well-known German dramatist Rolf Hochhut, creating another similarity with Pavel Kohout. Mňačko's sincerity as a "believer in the communist faith" — as attested later even in attacks on him during the period of "normalization"[16] — was beyond any doubt, but at the same time avid readers in Czechoslovakia had a rare occasion to read opinions from the other side of the border. As a result of his travels on the *Autobahns* of Western Germany, Mňačko was able to slightly open another window to the West by publishing his observations from much better roads than in the ČSSR, in his book entitled *Dlhá biela prerušovaná čiara* [*The Long White Interrupted Line*].[17]

Between 1962 and 1966 Ladislav Mňačko was considered to be a personal advisor of President Novotný and an extended arm of the ideological department of the CPC. In 1966 he received the Distinguished Artist Order and it was announced that he had completed a new novel, *Jak chutná moc* [*The Taste of Power*].[18] Its publication was promised by the publisher Molden in Vienna for the spring of 1967[19] but — for the time being — not in Czechoslovakia.[20] Looking for causes where he could serve communism with good conscience, Mnačko departed as a war correspondent to Vietnam.[21] At a press conference held at the Czechoslovak Embassy in Hanoi he declared that he had concluded that Americans in Vietnam gained only hatred: it was a conflict between demoralization and morality.[22] He became a member of the Lord Russell's Committee for Investigating American Crimes in Vietnam.[23] It was much easier to feel like a good communist in Hanoi than in Prague. There he was in trouble. His book *The Taste of Power* could not be

---

[15]   Ibid., 21 Dec. 1963, p. 1.
[16]   See *Tvorba*, 1 July 1970, p. 16.
[17]   Bratislava: Slovenský spisovatel, 1965.
[18]   *Plamen*, no. 8, 1966.
[19]   *Frankfurter Allgemeine Zeitung*, 13 Oct. 1966.
[20]   *Ibid.*, 21 Oct. 1966.
[21]   *Literární noviny*, 24 Sept. 1966, p. 2.
[22]   Radio Prague, 29 Nov. 1966.
[23]   *Večerní Praha*, 28 Jan. 1967.

published since President Novotný recognized himself in the book as the evil hero. Mňačko after a few years of close contact with President Novotný described him as a power-hungry simpleton who had been responsible for most of his country's troubles and crimes. What many people then only suspected Mňačko confirmed later, during the Prague Spring, at his press conference in Rome.[24]

Such a personal challenge could not remain unpunished. Although the Party organization of the Slovak Writers' Union, instead of the demanded expulsion, supported him in February 1967, one month later, the Presidium of the CC of the CPC punished him by a reproof with warning[25] (exactly as would happen to Kohout a few months later). For some time the warning seemed to have its effect since at the Czechoslovak Writers' Congress in June 1967 Mňačko distanced himself from rebellious Czech writers.

Therefore, it came as a real surprise when a few weeks later Mňačko left the Republic and on his way to Israel declared in a statement, first published in West Germany, that by his dramatic gesture he wanted to protest against the anti-Semitic and anti-Israeli policy of the ČSSR: "Not even by silence do I want to support a policy whose aim is the annihilation of a nation and liquidation of a State." Mňačko, who is not Jewish himself, but whose wife is, made it clear that by his unusual protest he hoped to stop government encouragement of anti-Semitism in Czechoslovakia and speed up the process of regeneration: "If we want to have a socialist, humane, and healthy State we must change the whole system."[26]

This sentiment played a large part in the preliminaries of, and during the, revolution of 1968. The humanist tradition of T. G. Masaryk, who quite successfully had tried to immunize his nation against anti-Semitism, was incited by forces that attempted — for the second time in sixteen years — to bring over from the Soviet Union the spirit of the pogrom. Mňačko in his interview stressed the fact that similar tendencies were again appearing in the official press, just as during the early 1950s when the majority of the Party leaders condemned and hanged in the so-called Slánský trial were denounced as "dirty Jews." For the nation and for the communist intellectuals who had been trying to de-Stalinize their country and did not want to see the horrors repeated, it hit a very sensitive nerve. And it was a moral nerve.

The reaction by the authorities was swift. A violent press campaign was launched against Mňačko.[27] The presidium of the Union of Slovak Writers in an official statement, requested by the Party leadership, called him "a political adventurer and anarchist."[28] The Presidium of the CC of the CPC expelled him from the Party and the government deprived him of his citizenship and all his awards and decorations.[29]

Mňačko was able to return to Czechoslovakia in May 1968 but the shock of the Soviet invasion in August led him into a new, and more permanent, exile. He

---

[24] Radio Prague, 5 Apr. 1968.
[25] J. Sobotecký, "Delayed Reporter," *Tvorba*, 1 July 1970, p. 16.
[26] *Frankfurter Allgemeine Zeitung*, 11 Aug. 1967.
[27] See, for instance, *Kulturní tvorba*, 24 Aug. 1967.
[28] Radio Bratislava, 15 Aug. 1967.
[29] *Tvorba*, 1 July 1970, p. 16; and *The Times*, 17 Aug. 1967.

described the crucial events of the occupation as witnessed by him in a new book.[30] It was also an indictment of the whole era from 1945 up to the invasion. In the middle of October 1968, at a press conference in Vienna, Mňačko declared that even in emigration he would remain a communist and predicted the third destruction of the Czechoslovak intelligentsia (the first in 1939-45, the second after 1948), Mňačko could no longer continue his fight at home and as many other Czechoslovak communists he could see his years of "building socialism" and later years of reforming efforts in ruins. An era of hope was finished. He acknowledged it by giving permission for a German translation of his *Delayed Reports* which he so vehemently refused to allow in 1964. His new introduction to the book explained the reasons for his change of mind: the *Reports* should warn against future attempts to repeat the ugly past. It all served as a basis for a new violent campaign against him in the Czechoslovak media.

In an interview with *Sláva Volný*, (born in 1928, another well-known communist who was deprived of his Slovak citizenship after 1968), which was published in an exile monthly, Mňačko talked about his participation in the twenty-year experiment and made the following conclusions:

> We have lost something, we have definitely lost something. We will no longer be able to set forth to the nation anything and attempt to give it some impulses. . . . [I have in mind] first of all the communists of my generation, these people who were mature and adult in the year '48 and who instead of thinking and acting as Marxists plunged into a blind faith and in the name of this blind faith were willing to agree with filthy deeds. Even to commit such filthy deeds that they ruined the Republic. I myself have since then been living with a conscience of guilt which cannot be made good . . . . We have to admit to ourselves: We have brought it upon ourselves. We have brought it by our *naiveté*, by our naïve faith, we have brought it upon ourselves by our character defects. In the end we have tried to free ourselves of it. I think that a lot of communists during the process of regeneration opened their eyes.

At this moment the interviewer interjected: "I agree with you. The whole Czechoslovak Spring was in fact, to a certain degree, an attempt to make restitution of our wrongdoings in the past." Mňačko consented: "Yes, it was, therefore our generation carried it. We already knew, we were enlightened, we had already learned from our own mistakes, injuries, and blunders."[31]

---

[30] *Die Siebente Nacht: Erkenntniss und Anklage eines Kommunisten* [*The Seventh Night: Verdict and Accusation by a Communist*] (trans. Adolf Maldess, Vienna: Verlag Fritz Molden, 1968.)

[31] "Rozhovor s Ladislavem Mňačkem: Zavinili jsme to sami" ["Interview with Ladislav Mňačko: We Brought It Upon Ourselves"], *Text 70*, no. 1, Jan. 1970, pp. 1-2.

Chapter 4.

From a blockhead to a human being

ALTHOUGH many Communists claimed not only in 1968 but also in 1948, and in between, that their intentions were maybe naïve but pure, some comrades developed an even stronger feeling of personal guilt than Mňačko. It helps to explain their actions. Sometimes courting a disaster in a fashion provocative for a police state, they showed symptoms of suicidal impulses, similar to frustrated romantic lovers who have been deceived by their loved one.

One of the major heroes of the "illegal" broadcasting during the first hectic days of Soviet occupation, Luděk Pachman, born in 1924, an international grand master of chess, is a case in point.

Pachman became a member of the Communist Party in May 1945 and during the years of illusions and terror served his Party well as an organizer and propagandist; for instance, for years he systematically helped to change free workers' labor unions into Party transmission belts of manipulation:

> The battle against remnants of capitalism in people's minds is one of the basic tasks in the construction of socialism, one of the unavoidable conditions for the final victory of this construction. . . . The revolutionary labor movement, following the example of Soviet labor unions, sets out on a journey that will make out of it a school for masses of millions of builders of socialism.[1]

He wrote for and edited several communist journals, among them the main Party daily, *Rudé právo*. Later, at the end of the 1960s, during the time of revelations, Pachman commented on his work with a self-critical humor:

> During the years of 1949-1952 I even stood at the head of the department in charge of labor union education. Already at the age of twenty-five I was then supposed to educate our workers' class. I attempted to inculcate in their minds philosophical wisdom from a well-known pamphlet written by the genial leader and teacher [Stalin]. . . .

> At the end of 1952, however, I decided to leave the arena of politics and preferred to devote myself fully to the less demanding game of chess. . . . I have found it hard to understand the necessity of completing the class war with the help of hanging hemp ropes. . . . Nevertheless, for years I developed loyal activities in a new field. ("Hold fast by the [Party]line, comrades!" my editor-in-chief used to say with predilection.) In my reports on Western countries I succeeded in discovering obvious signs of capitalistic pauperization, and on the other side of the world I was always impressed by proofs of an immense growth in the standard of living. And so I was getting on well in my work and only three years ago [1966] in a brotherly paper I was labeled as a model communist.[2]

[1] Luděk Pachman, *Tvorba*, 30 Aug. 1950, pp. 838-40.
[2] *Zítřek*, 5 Mar. 1969, p. 1.

A few years later, in his autobiography, Pachman had this to say about his propaganda in the beginning of the 1950s:

> We schooled, belched out fine sounding phrases about exploitation and a happy future, and tens of thousands at the same time wandered to prison, the existence of hundreds of thousands was being ruined.... No one revealed it to me since the persecuted ones simply did not trust us communists. To say today that I did not know [about it] sounds very untrustworthy but I cannot say anything else if I want to tell the truth. Ignorance, of course, is no excuse.[3]

After several minor conflicts with the authorities of his own Party, Pachman found his first major cause for disagreement in the 1967 Middle East war. Three days before the important Congress of Czechoslovak Writers' Union, Pachman wrote a letter (also signed by writers Arnošt Lustig and Jan Procházka) to the Central Committee of the CPC in which he sharply criticized the foreign policy of the socialist camp. The following sentence expresses the quintessence of the protest: "The politics of socialist countries should not start from great power interests but from genuine principles of justice and progress corresponding to the noble ideas of a socialist society."[4]

The letter played its role in the deepening crisis of Czechoslovak communism when Party secretary Jiří Hendrych, responsible for the ideological "front", attacked it at a meeting with the Party organization of writers as an example of wrong intellectual thinking. To his surprise, among many of them he provoked a strong reaction which then spread to the Czechoslovak Writers' Congress. Czech intellectuals, in their majority, sympathized with the Israelis whose difficult position and small size reminded them of Czechoslovak problems with Hitler and the Munich Agreement of 1938. Together with other arguments for his stand, Pachman in his letter underscored the fact that communist parties were not allowed to exist in Arab states whose leaders, "politicians of a semi-fascist type, have on their conscience also persecution and assassination of genuine Arab patriots, such as the chairman of the Communist Party of Lebanon, comrade Helu."[5]

After that incident Pachman was not allowed to write on any other topics but chess. In the meantime, his mental development continued, as he described in his "ironic self-portrait of a transformation of a blockhead into a human being:"[6] "At that time, in my thoughtlessness, I have considered prohibition of a Communist Party a sin against democracy."[7]

But even during the early parts of the Prague Spring, while Pachman taught chess at Puerto Rico, he sent an article to the Czech journal for official humor *Dikobraz*, protesting against the growing popularity and acceptability of the

---

[3] *Jak to bylo: Zpráva o činnosti šachového velmistra za období 1924–1972* [*How Was It: A Report on the Activity of a Chess Grandmaster from 1924 to 1972*] (Toronto: 68 Publishers, 1974), p. 68. This book was later published in English under the title *Checkmate in Prague* and in other languages. All quotes are from the Czech original in my translation.

[4] *Ibid.*, p. 15.

[5] *Ibid.*, p. 114.

[6] For that statement of progress, see the publisher's leaflet announcing the Czech publication of the book. Undated.

[7] *Jak to bylo . . .* , p. 118.

emigrants of 1948.[8] As was already demonstrated in Kohout's and Mňačko's histories, it was difficult to get rid of the ingrained and easy dichotomy of "us" and "them".

After his return from San Juan to Prague in May 1968, Pachman soon felt the reforming enthusiasm of his colleagues and the gratifying warmth of the public response. As he reveals in his book and as he mentioned in several articles and interviews with foreign journalists, Pachman believed that the only viable way out of the sharpening conflict with the Soviet Union and its allies was to throw the conservatives out of the Party leadership, arrange a fast Congress of the Party, and declare, after a partial mobilization, that the frontiers of Czechoslovakia would be defended in all circumstances.

During and after the Soviet invasion, Pachman belonged to the most active spokesmen of the opposition against concessions to Soviet pressures. He wrote many articles and letters to both domestic and foreign officials, addressed public gatherings,[9] talked to foreign correspondents, visited many factories (repaying his intellectual debts from the 1950s when he helped to fool the workers) and universities, helping to cement the unity of thought and action among the intellectuals, students, and workers. Pachman was not only trying to expiate his own feelings of guilt but was worried about the usually unheroic willingness by the majority of his nation to accommodate itself to the unpleasant realities of the situation. "Not for everything in the world, in no circumstances should we walk in fear."[10] By showing lack of fear he hoped to encourage others to a similar fearlessness. "L. Pachman said that he is afraid of only one thing — fear itself. Many begin to yield to fear. But to yield to fear, said L. Pachman, means to lose everything."[11]

When the student Jan Palach publicly burned himself on the main square of Prague and died, the highest authorities in the land asked Pachman to address himself on television to an anonymous group of students who planned to create further "human torches" if Palach's demands (end of censorship and of distribution of the Soviet armed forces publication in Czech, *Zprávy*) were not fulfilled. Clearly, Pachman had a moral creditability and a trust by young people that almost nobody could match.

In the key novel on the actors of the Czechoslovak Spring of 1968, based on facts and written by a non-communist, though socialist, author and participant in the events, Josef Škvorecký (living now in Toronto, Canada), Pachman takes on the name of Bukavec but remains international grand master of chess. He and the famous Czech writer, whose novel *Zbabělci* [*Cowards*] created a sensation in the late 1950s (and was then violently denounced as a decadent work in an article written by Luděk Pachman), used to go to school together and then met again at a party which was given in 1968 by Dubček at the Hradčany castle in Prague. In the

---

[8] *Ibid.*, p. 123.

[9] "In eight days from 17 to 24 November [1968] altogether I spoke at seventeen public meetings." *Ibid.*, p. 158.

[10] From an article by Pachman in *Mladý svět*, no. 5, 1969, as reproduced in *Jak to bylo . . .*, pp. 167–72, quote on p. 172.

[11] *Mladá fronta*, 22 Mar. 1969, supplement, p. 2. F. D. Roosevelt's famous statement on fear was widely reported in Czechoslovakia after World War II.

novel, Bukavec-Pachman begs Škvorecký to forgive him all that he has done against him during the period of fanatical communism:

> "I am now remembering everything. Sometimes I think I will go mad. If one could do something for penance. . . . I have done wrong to so many people! I was young and stupid but that's no excuse. I was a dirty pig, you know." Tears gushed from his eyes. . . . "Or my denunciations!" He named his former colleague who during detention on remand died as a consequence of falling on his head on a wall: "I testified against him that at a tournament in Casablanca he had private contacts with Freddy Cohen. They told me that Freddy Cohen was an agent of CIA and I believed it, I fool! What, a fool? I am a murderer. . . . I was culpably idiotic! Culpably idiotic!" With clenched fists he began to beat his temples so that I grew frightened he could finish in front of my eyes like his colleague.[12]

It might be interesting to note that at the end of this chapter, still at the party above, we can also meet, as I suspect, Pavel Kohout, renamed Vrchcoláb:

> Youthfully running, Vrchcoláb passed by chasing the most beautiful young woman writer of Central Europe, Eliška Obdržálková. [In real life, I guess, Linhartová, and really beautiful.] "Look," I called the chase to the attention of the tortured Jarda Bukavec. "He doesn't take it as badly as you. No penance. He believed everything — as you did — and he counts it as absolution!" — "He's a different character," sobbed the grand master.[13]

In 1969, in a more dangerous situation, at least once, Pachman condemned himself publicly for his denunciations (among them of three labor union employees who praised Hemingway as a writer, which was then enough to lose a job or get into a concentration camp) and in vain entreated his listeners to spit on him.[14]

And Pachman almost met the same end as his former colleague. A few months after the party at the Prague castle (which clearly entered the world literature as a vision of Kafka's novel of the same title), it was reported by several sources that during detention on remand, during which Pachman staged a few hunger strikes and lost 34 kilos in the process, he wounded himself critically by battering his head against a wall of his prison cell and for months remained unconscious.

> Luděk Pachman's in the Pankrác prison hospital with a cracked skull and brain injuries. His condition is serious and he does not recognize anyone. The official explanation of his injuries is that he himself battered his head on his cell wall. The prison doctors let it be understood that his injuries could not possibly have been caused in this way.[15]

Pachman spent more than six months in a prison section of a mental hospital.[16] He mentions that altogether eleven psychiatrists refused to declare him mentally ill. No Serbsky Institute in Prague?

First, it looked like a usual police report about one of their victims but Škvorecký's memoirs suggest a possibility of penance by expiation. Pachman's eagerly awaited autobiography does not help much to clarify the crucial event of his first confinement since during the critical night everything for him was and remained foggy. After he found himself in a prison hospital bed in pain with a cracked cranium and seriously wounded spine, he was told that he smashed his

[12] Josef Škvorecký, *Mirákl* [*Miracle*] (Toronto: 68 Publishers, 1972), vol. 1, pp. 202–3.
[13] *Ibid.*, p. 204.
[14] *Ibid.*, vol. 2, p. 158.
[15] *The Times* (London), 17 Jan. 1970, p. 8.
[16] *International Herald Tribune*, 24 Dec. 1970.

head against the prison wall.[17] Naturally, Pachman might have been influenced by depressant drugs whose use in Czechoslovak prisons has been reported quite often. But according to his own account, during his second detention in 1972, he tried to kill himself at least twice by jumping on his head, once from a table and once from a bed:

> More and more it kept occurring to me that in fact I do not have any right to live. I have spoilt my whole life by selfishness and maybe only by death could redeem myself. The idea flashed through my head that if I died something could be saved. I also thought about Jan Palach and so on.[18]

Pachman probably believed that through self-sacrifice he could attempt to wake up the nation to courage the way Jan Palach tried.

The human drama of protagonists caught between the West and the East, between their own illusions about the Soviet Union and their gradual discovery of the truth, was complicated, painful, and in many instances tragic. The crisis was not just political but philosophical and existential as well. In the prison where Pachman on two occasions spent since 1969 altogether almost eighteen months without trial, often marked by extremely humiliating and agonizing experiences during which the state of his health was repeatedly critical, he began to read the Bible and to pray. Pachman had left the Church in 1946 but now returned to Catholicism. Repudiating the materialism of his youth he became profoundly spiritual.[19] After his discharge from confinement, Pachman remarried his wife in church, at the occasion of the twenty-fifth anniversary of their civil wedding. He remained a confirmed Christian.

Since the Soviet Union is also a great power in chess, the last part concerning the international grand master Pachman should be devoted to this important aspect of his active life. He is quite well-known in chess circles around the world, especially as the author of fourteen outstanding books on chess theory.

In 1968 Pachman publicly apologized to the Hungarian chess grand master Szabo whom he met before in Moscow at a tournament in 1956 during the Hungarian revolution and to whom he then, in a heated argument, declared that only a few Soviet divisions could save the Hungarian situation. He also admits that after his return from this Moscow tournament he lectured at a meeting about lessons to be learned from Hungarian events and boasted about his foresight.[20]

The second episode shows the genuine feelings of a Soviet grand master but is also interesting for the way the Soviets kept using their Czech colleagues internationally [Cubans, beware!] as only too willing and loyal servants. Pachman writes about the Great Grand Master Chess Tournament in Moscow in July 1967 as part of the celebrations of the Great October Socialist Revolution:

> At the festive assembly, as always, I spoke in the name of foreign participants. Naturally, less on chess and more on revolution, ending with a few sentences about peace, democracy, and

---

[17] *Jak to bylo* . . ., chapter 19, entitled, in Czech, by the prison names "Ruzyň and Pankrác," esp. pp. 212-14.

[18] *Jak to bylo* . . . , pp. 314 and 317.

[19] For details, see *Jak to bylo* . . . , chapter 12, entitled "You must always belong to a party," a reproach to him by Ludvík Vaculík.

[20] *Jak to bylo* . . . , p. 249.

socialism, all according to a deep-rooted routine. A completely unconventional address by Michael Tal [previously world chess champion] created sensation. He said more than I did but my speech was applauded and his accepted by an uneasy silence. He said verbally: "We in the Soviet Union always play memorials. First a memorial of famous Tchigorin, then of famous Alekhin, and now we have just finished a memorial I don't even know of what.[21]

The third event described in his autobiography happened after the invasion. Pachman left Prague for a trip abroad in September 1968 and although he refused to play in the Chess Olympiad for the Czechoslovak team, boycotting international contacts with the occupiers' representatives (like almost all other Czech and Slovak intellectuals or sportsmen at that time), he went to Lugano, where the Olympiad was taking place, in order to denounce the Soviet occupation of his country. At a dinner in Hotel Arizona he was invited to join the eleven member Soviet chess delegation. The political leader of the group, Sherov, asked Pachman about his press conference and inquired about the reasons for the boycott. In the following discussion most of the Russian players supported Pachman, whom they all knew well, but not Sherov who became — according to Pachman's narrative — very nervous. When Pachman said that the Czechs have to insist on their rights since it concerns not only them but other nations as well, Boris Spassky, another chess world champion, declared: "*Pravilno*, the Czechs are fighting for us too."[22] After that both Tal and Spassky could not travel abroad for some time.

After Pachman described his meeting in Lugano at a public re-encounter in Prague, he become the target of sharp Soviet attacks. Various Soviet journals assailed him as one of the leaders of the "creeping counter-revolution" in Czechoslovakia. His troubles with prison confinements followed.

In January 1971 Pachman received a letter from the Czechoslovak Chess Association telling him that by his "attitudes and declarations" he "excluded himself from the ranks of State representation."[23]

The last game in Prague that Pachman played, invited by the chairman of his Prague club, was against a visiting team of the Moscow University. He even helped his club with a gift: "At home I had a picture in a pretty frame, nowadays superflous — Lenin playing chess with Gorky. They will give it to our guests."[24] But the day after the match, the Soviet Ambassador to Prague, comrade Chervonenko, called the secretary of the CC of the CPC Kempný, condemned Pachman's start as a provocation, and demanded strict consequences to be drawn. Two chess functionaries lost their positions and Pachman was not allowed to play any more even in a club. "A thirty-year-long chess career seemed to be completely closed."[25] Nothing helped, not even three requests to Dr. Euwe, chairman of the International Chess Federation. No reply at all was received from Amsterdam and no action taken against a chess federation acting against the rules.[26] Dr. Euwe was known for his great efforts to remain on good terms with Soviet chess authorities but such a coexistence means fully accepting Soviet terms.

[21] *Ibid.*, p. 111.
[22] *Ibid.*, pp. 154–6.
[23] *Ibid.*, p. 241.
[24] *Ibid.*, p. 250.
[25] *Ibid.*, p. 251.
[26] *Ibid.*, p. 253–4.

Since Pachman's other, especially political, activities could only endanger his friends, without any hope for success, he decided to leave Czechoslovakia. Some members of the leadership were willing to accept a deal. He managed to leave Czechoslovakia in November 1972, on his fourth attempt.

But that was not the end of his troubles. The Soviet chess power is great and follows Pachman almost everywhere. In 1973 he was able to take part in only one contest, in Israel. "He is not being invited to international events as the organizers fear that his presence might lead to a boycott by the Russians and by other East European chess federations."[27] Some rare individuals claimed that the world chess organization, F.I.D.E., should condemn "such inhuman persecution,"[28] but without any result. When Pachman could not be refused participation at a zonal tournament in Barcelona, which forms part of a selection of a chess player eligible to challenge the world champion Karpov for the title, six East European players had to withdraw on orders of their national chess associations. "It is tragic that discrimination in this way against one man can be allowed to persist," commented a British participant in his report on the tournament.[29]

At least in Pachman's case, chess stopped being only a simulated battle. And the moral of the story? It would seem that in certain countries it is easier to live as a blockhead than as a human being. Moral considerations, respect for truth, honesty, and courage make life difficult if not impossible. And still, these societies create heroes who are willing to risk everything since they come to the conclusion that only such values make life worth living and that they should give an example of courage and determination.

[27] *Index*, vol. 3, no. 2 (summer 1974), p. 75.
[28] *Chess*, vol. 40, nos. 721-5 (May-June 1975), p. 244.
[29] *Chess*, vol. 41, nos. 735-6 (Dec. 1975), p. 88.

Chapter 5.

"Without the benefit of humanism and justice"

AS suggested by a few case studies — to which I would like to add some shorter ones in order to show how widespread was the moral indignation and what were its major sources — almost all of the heroes of the Prague Spring of 1968 went through painful experiences and a similar change of heart. Almost all of them committed smaller or bigger crimes, first, against non-communists and then against their own comrades; almost all of them participated in systematic campaigns of propaganda against the bourgeoisie, American imperialism, cosmopolitanism, Titoism, Zionism, Slánskýism, or other deviations as determined by the changing Soviet liquidation labels. Often this was followed by physical destruction of victims. Almost all of them had to lie or support lies, terrorize others, and be in turn terrorized themselves.

Quite a few of them were tortured by other communists and some of them were later able to write and publish their testimonies; for instance, one of the three high communist officials who survived the Slánský process, *Artur London.* He belonged to the generation of mature communists since he was born in 1915 and spent some ten years in service of the Bolshevik Party, especially in Spain during the civil war and then in France. A few months before he himself was arrested, London was in favor of the death sentence for the Hungarian communist László Rajik. In his book of detailed descriptions of personal experiences with the Party fabrication of show trials, we can follow this scene in a Prague prison:

> Commander Smola strangles me and screams full of hate: "You and your dirty race, we'll know how to annihilate you! You are all the same. Not everything that Hitler did was good but he destroyed the Jews and that was a good thing to do. Too many escaped the gas chambers. What he did not finish we will terminate. . . . We will bury you and your dirty race ten meters under the earth!" These words are uttered by a man who in his buttonhole carries the Party insignia, in the presence of three others in uniform who approve by their silence! What can be common between this anti-Semitism, this spirit of pogrom, and communism, Marx, Lenin, the Party? That's the first time in my adult life that I am insulted as a Jew, that I hear reproaches of my birth as a crime, and that by a member of the security police of a socialist country, by a member of the Communist Party![1]

In his book London affirmed many times his old faith that socialism could be built in Czechoslovakia by democratic means[2] and that the barbaric methods used after 1948 were brought to his country by Soviet specialists.[3]

Later, alone in his cell, after months of torture, he meditates about his wife's and his own:

unlimited confidence in *the Party which can never be wrong* and in whose apprenticeship I have been here for almost six months and which showed me the puerility of my unconditional faith in an abstract idea of the Party, leading to an alienation of the thought. The Party, yes, it is possible to have trust in it when one considers it as it should be, that is an emanation of masses of Communists, but never when it is a narrow, bureaucratic *apparat* which abuses qualities of devotion, of trust, of sacrifice of its members in order to draw them in to a perverted path that does not have anything in common with the ideals and the programme of a Communist Party.[4]

To a nonbeliever in the sect, the unlimited faith in the Party led by a mass murderer is hard to accept, especially since London could not possibly have been as naïve as he sounds. He had served the Party in secret missions in Spain during the civil war and later in France. The conspiratorial work usually required not only skill and devotion but also severity. For that reason as well, reading the book can be a painful experience.

Prior to 1948, Professor Vondráček in Prague, during his lectures on psychiatry, used to illustrate his points on delusions of megalomaniacs by presenting as patients typical cases of communists who professed to change man and the whole world completely, blindly believing in Stalin and his Party. Could he do it after 1948, I wonder?

When London at the show trial admitted his "guilt" — most of the accused in the Slánský process blamed their treasonal activities on their Jewishness and bourgeois origin — his wife denounced him in a public letter to President Gottwald as a traitor and divorced him: "My husband isn't a victim, but a traitor to his Party, to his country!" Listening to the daily broadcasts of the Slánský trial, it was clear, at least to me and other people as well, that it all was a put-on propaganda show with multiple purposes and that the "actors" recited, in a monotonous voice, their roles which they had to learn by heart — but it was not obvious to relatives of the victims who remained faithful to the Party! — London's life was saved only by repeated interventions by the Communist Party of France.[5]

---

[1] Artur London, *L'aveu. Dans l'engrenage du Procès de Prague* (Paris: Gallimard, 1968), p. 53. The book was published in Czech as *Doznání [Confession]* by Československý spisovatel, 1969. Here it is quoted from the French, in my own translation. It is interesting to note — because of the resemblance to Czech communists' attitudes — that when a film, based on London's life-story, was made by Costa-Gavraz and shown in Yugoslavia, at a press conference in Zagreb, Simone Signoret, who played London's wife, speaking also for her husband both in life and in the film, Yves Montand, said that in the past he and she held certain incorrect, Stalinist, views, but that they are not sorry for them, "because we were sincere. . . . We see only now that these views were wrong." She added that this was one of the main reasons why they decided to appear in the *Confession*: "You must understand us. Yves and I have felt it our duty to make this film. It was debt due to our consciences." See Slobodan Stankovic, "French Film on Stalinism in Czechoslovakia Enthusiastically Received in Yugoslavia," *Yugoslavia*, no. 0657, Radio Free Europe Research, 16 July 1970. In this polycopied paper of 7 pages, there are substantial quotations from *Vjesnik u srijedu* (Zagreb), 15 July 1970.

[2] For instance, on p. 298.

[3] For example, on p. 82–3 and 377–9.

[4] *Ibid.*, pp. 178–9.

[5] See the series of long articles written by the famous French writer and member of the Central Committee of the CPF, Louis Aragon, for *Les Lettres Françaises* in February and March 1969; and Věra Veverková's article in *Práce*, 19 Mar. 1969, pp. 4–5.

London finally understood that "the guilty one is Stalin and the monstrous 'apparat' he had created," but he "asked himself in vain: Why?" without finding an answer.[6]

It took years before London managed to have his case reopened. He quotes one of his friends commenting on the leadership of the CPC: "They don't pardon us for their own blunders."[7] In 1955 he completed a long report on his own pre-trial investigation and torture. It contained 400 pages; his wife helped by typing it and presenting it to both Czechoslovak and French leaders. Again, his report was a confession of faith in the Party:

> Those comrades who say: "You should have held out!" I remind them that I was in the hands of the Party, accused, judged, condemned by it . . . In such conditions, how can one fight if the enemy in front of you is the Party and Soviet advisers and if *every fight is considered a fight against the Party and the Soviet Union?*

With a typical twist of a fanatical believer who does not give up his faith in a Party (or Church — after all, liberal Catholics did not give up hope that the Vatican would come closer to ideals of Christ after almost 2,000 years of disappointments), London has found new strength for his hope:

> When I heard about the condemnation of Beria and his accomplices, about the denunciation of illegal, terrorist methods, used by the services of the Soviet Security against honest militants of the Party, then I comprehended that I have been, as so many others, a victim of Beria and his zealots . . . With the understanding of the problem, I regained my confidence in the Party and the U.S.S.R.[8]

After his slow and partial rehabilitation, London had to undergo a long treatment abroad in order to restore his shattered health. A few hours after his return to Prague, his "sentimental education" continued; he became witness of the Soviet invasion:

> So there was this chapter in my life, from the moral point of view maybe worse than anything I have already known: the first [?] aggression in the history of the workers' movement against a socialist country by other socialist countries. Against a socialist country guilty of having wanted to restore the trust of its peoples in socialism.[9]

London admired the behavior of his nation during the invasion and had the impression that the dream of his whole life — revolution, socialism, and freedom — was being finally realized in his country.[10]

It is a rather sad, if not really tragicomic, proof of the falseness of premises on which London and other communists in Czechoslovakia hoped to create socialism. The picture of a realized dream crushed under the tanks of allied armies might excite by its tragedy and martyrdom but it surely does not speak for realism on the part of the main protagonists. Their whole system of beliefs and hopes was wrong from the beginning of the 1920s and it took them a long time to grasp the truth. Many of them needed the second coming of Soviet tanks to Prague and other

---

[6] A. London, *L'aveu*, p. 329.
[7] *Ibid.*, p. 439.
[8] *Ibid.*, p. 445.
[9] *Ibid.*, p. 449.
[10] *Ibid.*, p. 450.

Czechoslovak cities to fully understand the fact that there was no chance of building democratic socialism with the help of the Soviet Union whose leaders in such attempts saw only a provocation to their absolute power.

Why did so many intellectuals of Jewish origin join the Communist Party and for so long, in spite of everything, associated all their hopes with it? Artur London does not give an answer but the widow of another victim of the Slánský trial, Rudolf Margolius, chief in the cabinet of the Minister of Foreign Trade, Mrs. Heda Kovály-Margolius, described the reasons persuasively in her autobiographical part of a book, published after her departure from the ČSSR.[11]

During the early 1950s, when many communists started to disappear, she asked Rudolf Margolius: "Isn't it strange that there are so many Jews among those who've been arrested?" — "For God's sake," Rudolf reacted nervously, "are you going to think that the Communists are anti-Semites? What utter rot! That shows you still don't understand anything. You need to do much more reading."[12] Instead of more reading, Mrs. Kovály-Margolius now believes they should "have collected our few belongings, packed them in a bundle, and run as fast as we could before the light from the East would change, ever more rapidly, into a conflagration."[13]

A few weeks before her husband's arrest in 1952, they had their last political discussion:

> "I cannot believe," I told him, "that something good could turn into its very opposite like this, just because of a few mistakes or personal failures. . . . Look what has become of all those idealists who asked nothing but to work for the good of others. Half of them in jail, the other half shuddering every time the doorbell rings. It is all a fraud, a trap for the trusting." . . . "Heda, . . . I have given up everything I loved. But there is one thing I cannot give up. I cannot give up the conviction that my ideal is essentially good and right, just as I simply cannot understand why it failed as it has. I have to believe that this failure is just a passing crisis. Don't you see, if you were right, if it all really were a fraud, then all I have done would make me an accomplice in a monstrous crime. If I let myself believe that, Heda, I could not go on living . . . and I would not want to."[14]

One of the main reasons why many Jewish intellectuals joined the Communist Party was that it seemed to them to be the only force totally opposed to Nazism and which promised to build a humanist society without racial or national discrimination. Especially at the end of World War II, when some survivors were coming back from the Nazi concentration camps, they wanted to devote themselves to a movement guaranteeing that "bourgeois" democracy, which allowed the Munich Agreement and Nazi victories, would be radically changed and Nazi horrors would not be repeated again; "The devil of it is that communism

---

[11] Heda Kovály and Erazim Kohák, *The Victors and the Vanquished* (New York: Horizon Press, 1973). The Czech original version, with her part the same but Professor Kohák's part different was entitled *Na vlastní kůži: Dialog přes barikádu* [*On its Own Skin: A Dialogue Over the Barricade*] and published in Toronto by Publishers 68 in 1973. I am quoting from the English version.

[12] *Ibid.*, p. 100.

[13] *Ibid.*, p. 74.

[14] *Ibid.*, pp. 101–2.

appeared to many of us the one system under which this could 'never happen again.'"[15]

People who were able to survive the war often felt that they should sacrifice themselves to the reconstruction of society. They experienced guilt feelings for the past and wanted to serve unselfishly:

> When a person became a communist, he wanted to be a *good* communist. We believed that, while we were building upon the ruins of a system that had failed, we were still deeply marked by that system and were still burdened with a great deal of obsolete prejudice and weakness. Most of all weakness — why didn't we stand up to Hitler? Why did we let ourselves be locked up in concentration camps and prisons, why did we die on gallows and in crematoria? Because we were weak, degenerate, spoiled. If we want to achieve something, we must be willing to be transformed. Communism, we believed, is the eternal, perennial ideal of humanity. If we want to be reborn, we must not doubt the ideal — only ourselves. . . . Were it not for the war and that irrepressible need for change and negation, damning all that had been, including ourselves, we would have seen through it easily. But when a person despairs over the world and doubts everything, it means first of all that he doubts himself — and the Party was prepared to provide the certainty and assurance we lacked. While the democrats asked us to trust in ourselves, the Party offered us the chance to put our trust in someone and something we did not have to doubt.[16]

By now social scientists know that feelings of personal helplessness and of crumbling societal orders can be easily used by demagogues who build their movements and empires on frustration and false millennial hopes. The trouble is that the hope is eternal and there are always new ways to present the latest sure-proof model of salvation. Especially the experience of the collapse of the Czechoslovak Republic and later horrors in the concentration camps prepared some Jews for their role after the war. "It felt like the end of the world. It seemed to us we were living through a complete break in the evolution of mankind, through a total collapse of man as a rational being."[17] Therefore, "they wanted change — radical, fundamental change."[18]

It needed Stalin and his anti-Semitic, anti-Israeli policies of the 1950s to show them the terrible mistake they had made. (Since then, by the way, I have suspected that Soviet communism lost its battle for the world by antagonizing an extremely important and intelligent part of humanity, which, until then, to a large degree, worked for or was willing to tolerate its enterprise.) Communist adoption of postures reminiscent of Hitler also shocked many non-Jewish intellectuals.

The nation was not fooled by the fig-leaf of "anti-Zionism" which was supposed to distinguish the Soviet campaign from similar Nazi policies and which later would win for the U.S.S.R. majorities in the United Nations. It was already shown that the anti-Israeli foreign policy of the Novotný government following the Soviet line, helped to trigger the resolute criticism of the Party leadership by Czech writers and by the Slovak writer Mňačko. But not only the foreign policies of anti-Zionism antagonized large sections of the population, the domestic pogrom atmosphere of the trials of the 1950s influenced the developments in a similar way.

[15] *Ibid.*, p. 60.
[16] *Ibid.*, pp. 62–3.
[17] *Ibid.*, p. 64.
[18] *Ibid.*, p. 65.

It became one of the major factors in the demand for radical reforms of the system and finally led to the revolution of 1968.

The prominent historian of the show trials in Czechoslovakia, *Karel Kaplan*, first created a name for himself by his books and articles celebrating communist victories in his country.[19]

He was a fellow of the Historical Institute of the Czechoslovak Academy of Sciences and later its deputy director as well as chairman of its Party organization. In 1966 as a faithful Party propagandist he still believed that the February *coup* was just and necessary, although the title of one of his contributions to its celebration sounded rather defensive: "There Was No Other Way."[20] Even at the beginning of the Prague Spring in 1968, in a round table discussion with a title "What Does February Mean for You Today?", Kaplan expressed himself like a good *apparatchik*: "When members of the People's Militia marched we almost cried how powerful we all were . . ."[21] But a few weeks later, in the same journal of reformers — he was a member of its editorial board — he supported the democratization program.[22] He became a member of a team preparing the Party Action Program, as well as secretary to the commission of the CC of the CPC in charge of the rehabilitation of victims of the 1950s.[23]

Kaplan's career in the 1960s is a good example of the politically split personality of an active communist intellectual: publicly, all his works carefully served the established Party lines but, hidden from the public eyes, a much more important development was taking place. As a historian and trusted Party activist he became secretary to the CC of the CPC commission for the rehabilitation of the victims of political trials of the 1950s and obtained almost unlimited access to Party archives. His study of documents from meetings of the Communist party leadership, responsible for the trials, came as a terrible shock:

> I went through a bitter period when I found out, some time ago, the details of what happened in the 1950's. That was a time of inner suffering, heavy depression, and estrangement, which were further exacerbated by constant and pressing questions from the ranks of the younger generation and by their justified disgust, their reproaches, and accusations against us of the

---

[19] In February 1948 he served his Party as district secretary of the CPC in Vysoké Mýtó. . . . In the 1950s he worked in the Pardubice regional council of the CPC. In 1961 he became a member of the editorial board of the Party journal for history, *Přípěvky k dějinám KSČ* [*Contributions to the History of the CPC*], and in it, as well as in other journals, published a long series of studies devoted to the contemporary history of his Party, especially successful and cruel manipulation of the peasants. In 1961, at the Institute for Social Sciences of the CC of the CPC, Kaplan successfully defended his candidate's dissertation entitled "The Communist Party — Organizer of the Farmers' Movement between 1945 and 1948 in Bohemia." He brought together his researches and Party propoganda in a book *Utváření generální linie výstavby socialismu v Československu: Od Února do IX. sjezdu KSČ* (Prague: Akademia, nakladatelství ČSAV, 1966). [*Formation of the General Line in the Construction of Socialism in Czechoslovakia: From February to the Ninth CPC Congress.*]

[20] *Svobodné slovo*, 23 Feb. 1966, p. 1. He also wrote another article on 1948 for *Literární noviny*, 26 Feb. 1966.

[21] *Reportér*, no. 7, 17-21 Feb., 1968, beginning on p. 1.

[22] Karel Kaplan, "Jak dál v demokratizaci" ["What Next in Democratization?"], *Reportér*, 3-10 Apr. 1968, pp. iii-v.

[23] *Práce*, 23 July 1968, p. 3.

older generation for our lack of courage. . . . In the trials socialism failed in its mission, it suppressed what should have been the most typical of it — humanism.[24]

Kaplan, the historian of successful though deceitful Communist Party tactics used to achieve absolute power and to keep it, now became the historian of its crimes. His study of the Slánský trial, published in the summer of 1968 in three parts, became one of the most important documents available to the public in 1968. What until then was known only to a limited, although steadily growing, circle of Party intellectuals and activists, entered the public domain. The old Communist Party leadership was revealed as a murderous gang of plotters who followed orders and advice not only from the Soviet leadership and its secret police agents but also from Polish and Hungarian officials like Rákosi, who supplied long lists of names of those Slovaks and Czechs who should be arrested (for instance, of many Slovaks who might have provoked his displeasure by their participation in the transfer of the Hungarian population from Southern Slovakia into Hungary after World War II). Kaplan wrote:

> These were the largest political trials in postwar Europe, not only in their scope but also in the number of extreme punishments awarded. . . . In the history of Czechoslovakia they represent a singular, unorganic, and unnatural phenomenon. . . . They were mainly directed against Zionism. . . . The political trials deeply influenced the whole life of society . . : . A serious social consequence of the political trials was the atmosphere of fear and suspicion they created. Mistrust penetrated ever deeper into human relationships.[25]

The author of some ninety pages of historical records and analyses which read as an accusation not only of individuals responsible for the long series of crimes but of the whole political system that made them possible, was preparing a book on the trials and in December 1968 delivered the manuscript, under the title *Procesy* [*Trials*], to the publisher. The setting up of type for printing was finished in 1969 but the new Party leadership under Husák ordered the presses to be stopped for its "negative political influence." It requested that the author repay the cost involved and excommunicated him from the Party. He was also blamed for the publication of the so-called *Black Book* or *Seven Days of Prague, 21–7 August 1968*, containing documents on the invasion of Czechoslovakia. His criticism of Soviet interference in Czechoslovak affairs was especially singled out for condemnation.[26]

Although he was not able to see his major opus in print, Kaplan kept warning, even after the Soviet invasion, against a repetition of the crimes and of the atmosphere of the 1950s. He published an excellent analysis of the mechanism of political trials as imported from the Soviet Union,[27] and in February 1969 another general survey of the disastrous consequences of the trials:

> The political trials . . . were among the most extreme distortions which affected negatively the humanistic essence and purpose of the postwar development. . . . The trials were a classical

[24] Karel Kaplan, "Zamyšlení nad politickými procesy" ["Thoughts About the Political Trials"], *Nová mysl*, no. 6, June 1968, p. 765. The best historical review of the trials, especially of the most important one, against Rudolf Slánský and "his group", was published in three installments: 1. *Ibid.*, pp. 765–94; 2. *Ibid.*, no. 7, July 1968, pp. 906–40; 3. *Ibid.*, no. 8, Aug. 1968, pp. 1054–78.

[25] *Ibid.*, 1054, 1056, 1062–3.

[26] *Obrana lidu*, 25 Apr. 1970, p. 4, and 1 May 1970, p. 4.

[27] "Železná logika procesů: Zamyšleni nad padesátými léty" ["The Iron Logic of the Trials: Contemplating the Fifties"], *Život strany*, no. 29, 27 Nov. 1968, p. 8.

example of political manipulation . . . of citizens. . . . This activity was inhumane and was in conflict with the sense and aim of socialism. It grew out of lies and it misused thousands of honest and trusting citizens. This was one of the causes of the future social crisis, because the discovery of truth turned confidence into mistrust of both individuals and policy . . . . The internal crisis of the people and society grew, little by little, proportionately to the truth as it became known.[28]

Lost in the contradictions between their original illusions and the realities they gradually discovered, communist intellectuals in Czechoslovakia step by step found their way out of the moral morass of their own making. As Mňačko said, "There are people in our country — and I am one of them — who regard the current situation in Czechoslovakia not as an economic but a moral crisis."[29] Since their feelings of what is proper in society were deeply hurt, they reacted with indignation and the freely accepted iron discipline of the Party was finally questioned. The Soviet import proved to be alien to their nations' traditions and outlook.

The connection between the Slánský trial and Middle Eastern policies of the Party, together with moral problems and questions of humanism, were well symbolized by *Eduard Goldstücker*. Professor at the Prague University since 1958, he was born in Slovakia in 1913, joined the Communist Party in 1948, and from 1949 till 1951 served as Czechoslovak Ambassador in Israel. When the original pro-Israeli policy (Czechoslovakia had supplied arms and armed contingents in support of the young Israeli State) changed into its opposite, Goldstücker was recalled and in 1953 condemned on trumped-up charges for perpetuity as a "Jewish bourgeois nationalist." He was released in 1956 and in 1963 helped to launch the famous campaign for the rehabilitation of the Prague Jewish writer Franz Kafka. From this time comes his statement expressing the core of his own and other intellectual communists' basic discovery: "If the history of our time has proved something beyond a shadow of doubt, it is that it was fatally wrong to believe that a new and higher social order could be created without the benefit of humanism and justice."[30]

During "two decades of bitter experience" (the denomination comes from Ota Šik about whom more will be said later), Czechoslovak communists passed through several stages of (1) illusions and enthusiasm both before and in 1948; (2) "building of socialism" and the accompanying terror against "bourgeois class enemies"; (3) Soviet bolshevization of Czechoslovakia through discoveries of "foreign spies, Titoists, Zionists, nationalists", etc., in the ranks of the Communist Party itself; (4) successive waves of de-Stalinization and re-Stalinization; (5) gradual acknowledgement of the inhuman face of Soviet "socialism" and slow but systematic attempts to recapture the thrown-away moral values of truth, justice, human decency, and courage; and, (6) the final effort to overcome the "distortions

---

[28] "The Political Trials and the Present Day," *Doba*, 13 Feb. 1969.

[29] See his letter published in the *Frankfurter Allgemeine Zeitung*, 11 Aug. 1967, previously quoted.

[30] "The Problem of Franz Kafka," *Literární noviny*, 16 Feb. 1963. Both during 1968 and after the invasion, Goldstücker had to face a dirty campaign organized against him as a Jew by Soviet supporters. He published one of the letters addressed to him which began: "Mr. G., gangster and Zionist hyena!" See E. Goldstücker, "Občané, pozor!" ["Citizens, Beware!"], *Rudé právo*, 23 June 1968, p. 3.

of the past" and to establish, in the difficult conditions of 1968, a pluralist and humanist, social democratic system. Although their participation in numerous crimes, committed against both democrats and communists, varied, and although the degree of guilt, felt or admitted personally, is also variable, almost all of them in contradiction to their initial position, rediscovered moral values and placed them high above class or historical context.

It represented not only their personal or group victory. It helped to create a national revival. Active intellectuals returned with a renewed vigor to its humanistic beliefs and traditions since the two decades of experimenting with a different system confirmed their validity. It was encouraging to see that people can learn from their political experience in order to overcome dangerous illusions and change their criminal practices. Jules Benda's *la trahison des clercs* is not a dead-end street; there are happy returns. The country was again united and the split of the nation's workers and intellectuals into democrats and communists, which was started in the ČSR in the 1920s and which grew after World War II, was healed.

For the nation and its intellectual élite, T. G. Masaryk, the moralist, decidedly won over V. I. Lenin, the tactician of class war.

Part II
Economic problems and social history

Chapter 1.

The ČSR: Workers and intellectuals in a Soviet economy

ALTHOUGH Czechoslovak developments of the 1960s, obviously, did not have only moral but, among others, economic causes, what can a non-economist add to the thorough descriptions and analyses published by economic writers who often took part in the reform movement and therefore have the benefit of personal experiences? Maybe a study of changing motivations by some of the leading economic specialists as well as some observations, though important, rarely if ever mentioned can be helpful to the understanding of the revolutionary process. For instance, the connection between the workers' and the intellectuals' opposition has been mostly neglected or interpreted one-sidedly; namely, as intellectuals influencing workers only and not — if warranted — the other way round. After a survey of the conflict between the Soviet and Czechoslovak moral and political culture, a similar, and very much interconnected, conflict between the economic and social traditions and models of both countries should be examined.

1. Cast of actors

Selected topics will be discussed often, but not exclusively, with the help of written contributions by a few of those Czechs and Slovaks who actively participated in the public debates of the 1960s and who were prominent in various aspects of the economic controversy. For the purpose of this study the main four actors are:

Eugen Loebl, born in 1907 in Slovakia as son of a merchant, studied at the School of Economics in Vienna, then worked for an international insurance company, joined the Communist Party in 1934, and in 1939 left for England where he worked as economic adviser on the U.N.R.R.A. to the Minister of Foreign Affairs, Jan Masaryk. Later he became head of the Ministry of Economic Reconstruction of the Czechoslovak government in exile. In the resurrected Czechoslovak Republic Loebl acted as the Deputy Minister of Foreign Trade and belonged to the influential Presidium of the Economic Commission of the Communist Party of Czechoslovakia. He was arrested in 1949 and in 1952, together with Rudolf Slánský and twelve others, condemned on trumped-up charges of espionage, high treason, and sabotage; they were hanged, he was sentenced to life imprisonment. He was released from prison in

1960, partly cleared in 1961, and two years later, when Dubček came to power in Slovakia, Loebl was rehabilitated and made Director of the Slovak State Bank in Bratislava. Many of his articles and several books showed his reforming zeal. He knew especially well the economy of the United States. He represents here the older generation of communist economists, influenced by pre-war democracy, and eliminated soon after the *coup* of 1948 which they helped to prepare and organize.

At the time of the February seizure of power Loebl was forty, *Radoslav Selucký* was not yet eighteen years old. First he served his Party as a propagandist and published articles celebrating the "building of socialism." After his studies at the university in Leningrad, where he graduated as an economist, he became a lecturer in economics at the Technical University in Prague and published quite a few articles and books. His knowledge of the Soviet Union and of its economic development was rather exceptional. He is quoted here for the young generation of economists educated by the system and by their experiences with it.

The man who was often called the Father or the Architect of the Czechoslovak economic reform of the 1960s, *Ota Šik*, participated in the communist seizure of absolute power in 1948 as a young man of twenty-eight. Born in Teplice, of a mixed Czech–German family of a textile merchant, Oswald Schick, Šik joined the Communist Party when he was thirteen. He went to German schools but left the secondary level in 1935 before graduation, because of bad marks, as was maliciously revealed after the Soviet invasion in a campaign to destroy his charisma.[1] He became an electrician. Šik spent four years in the German concentration camp Mauthausen. Soon after the war ended, he entered the Communist Party *apparat* and as an external student completed his university education in political economy. Beginning in 1946, he published many studies, following the Party line, and lectured at its schools. In 1951 he left the *apparat* and became the head of the faculty of political economy at the CPC Institute. At the same time, Šik continued his studies of Marxism and helped to translate Marx's *Das Kapital* into Czech.

A steady flow of Stalinist writings continued throughout the 1950s. Since 1958 he worked as Professor of the Institute for Social Studies at the CC of the CPC, in 1961 became Director of the Prague Economic Institute, and one year later — as the first in the ČSSR — obtained the title of the Doctor (Soviet type) of Economic Sciences. Some of his books from the 1960s were also published in English and other languages. His role in the preparation and introduction of the economic reform as well as in the toppling of Novotný was important. In 1968 he became Deputy Prime Minister but was not coopted to the CPC Presidium.

Jan Štern — a student at the time of the *coup* — at the end of the 1940s and at the beginning of the 1950s was very active as an aggressive poet and as a sectarian journalist, being one of the editors of the main Party weekly *Tvorba*. He seemed to enjoy an easy access to inner Party circles. Although he never achieved any

---

[1] See Jiří Leša, "Tečka za emigrantem Otou Šikem" ["Full Stop Behind the Emigrant Ota Šik"], *Tribuna*, 18 Mar. 1970, p. 3. The title was premature: innumerable articles attacking Šik have been printed since.

scientific specialization as the other three men, at the end of the 1960s, in the workers' union's daily *Práce,* he was one of the most outspoken and systematic fighters against sectarianism and for genuine working men's rights. Štern has his place in this study and in this chapter as the type of a Leninist conspirator whose inspiration comes from literary images that only in time are replaced by recognition of real workers.

All four of our protagonists were thrown out of their Party in the post-invasion purge as prominent "revisionists."

2. Fears, hopes, and illusions (1945-8)

Although the Czechoslovak Republic did not create the major problems of the depression of the 1930s, its "capitalist democracy" was blamed for them after World War II. Many economists and workers felt that a radically different system was needed. For instance, the Slovaks remembered that "in the winter of 1932-3 about 300,000 were out of work in Slovakia. With their families, this meant that about one-third of Slovakia's population had no regular income."[2] However, poverty and a perennial lack of job opportunities had been a Slovak problem long before 1918. Since 1870 till the end of the Austrian-Hungarian Monarchy, one million Slovaks had to leave their country in order to look for work abroad.[3] The Czech part of the Republic did not inherit similar difficulties but in 1932/3 one million Czechs could not find work and until 1938 the recovery proceeded at a slow pace.[4] The older generation remembered their own and their fathers' humiliations of the 1930s and quite a few adherents to the communist program were led by fears of another depression or Western fascism. "When I came out of Mauthausen I was an absolute fanatic wanting to put the world right."[5] Only much later could Šik's Slovak comrade, Eugen Loebl, observe in a more detached way:

> Let us recall the economic crisis of the 1930s. We all thought that it was a crisis immanent to the system but in fact it was a crisis of thinking in the field of monetary theory. My generation of intellectuals believed in the leading role of the proletariat and saw the role of the intelligentsia in the service of the proletariat.[6]

Loebl returns to this generational shock again and again; for example, in his book *Conversations with the Bewildered:* "Experiences of my generation cultivated in us a deep scepticism to existing forms of democracy."[7]

[2] Victor S. Mamatey, "The Development of Czechoslovak Democracy, 1920-1938", in *A History of the Czechoslovak Republic 1918-1948,* ed. by Victor S. Mamatey and Radomír Luža (Princeton University Press, 1973), p. 143.

[3] *Pravda,* 25 Mar. 1972, p. 6.

[4] Mamatey, *Ibid.*

[5] Adam Oliver, "What Went Wrong" an interview with Ota Šik, *Manchester Guardian Weekly,* 22 Apr. 1972.

[6] See his article "Paběrky z USA: O společnost s lidskou tváří" ["Gleanings from the USA: Towards a Society with a Human Face"], *Literární listy* (a special issue published in exile on the occasion of the second anniversary of the occupation), no date, but probably Aug. 1970, p. 11.

[7] The book was published in George Gretton's translation in London by Allen & Unwin in 1972. Quoted from Ferdinand Peroutka, "Kritika kritiky čs. demokracie" ["Critique of a Critique of Cz. Democracy"], *Hlas domova,* XXIII, 10 (14 May 1973), p. 5.

The distrust of democracy and capitalism, based on the experiences of the 1930s and half of the 1940s, acted as a strong motivational force for people like Šik and Loebl (or another economist, Margolius, discussed in the last chapter). It was a *generational trauma* which led to an attempt to create a new reality with the help of communism and the Soviet Union. When during the war in London democratically oriented economists and politicians warned that following the Soviet example might be dangerous, they heard expressions of the hopeful belief that the Czechoslovak path to socialism would be different:

> Loebl then still objected that cooperation with the Communists as the largest party would be a national duty, that in the National Front all parties would be equal, and that therefore there is no reason to fear in Czechoslovakia similar developments as in the Soviet Union.[8]

Even among the democrats the trust in Western democracy had been shaken by the twin horrors of the Great Depression and victories of fascism — both resisted or mastered by Western democracies rather poorly and late. Also the expectation prevailed that the Soviet Union would move towards democracy and would behave in Czechoslovakia in a decent way, without interfering in its domestic evolution. The Communist Party was able to persuade the democrats that they had to cooperate and hope for the best. They clearly expected that it was possible to moderate their communist colleagues who often sincerely believed that it would be up to them to develop the promised special Czechoslovak way to socialism. A communist historian later wrote:

> Especially between 1945 and 1948 in the Party a creative searching and independent attitude triumphed when specific conditions of our country were observed and national policies pursued, without forgetting class and international principles which form the basis of the Communist movement.[9]

Even after the February *coup*, for some time the leading economic and political personalities of the Communist Party believed that they could proceed with the revolution according to local conditions and preferences. The Economic Commission of the Central Committee discussed the intended extent of the proposed further nationalization of private property. As a result the newly adopted Constitution of 1948 contained the paragraph 158, guaranteeing "private property of small and middle-sized enterprises with up to fifty employees." In a similar way, small and medium-sized peasant holdings were guaranteed by the Constitution. Describing these developments, Loebl added: "It was beyond dispute that small private enterprise should be allowed. We consider it self-evident that *nationalization of small plants did not have either economic or political sense.*"[10] At the same time, the communist economists (and politicians) wanted to continue trading with the traditional Western partners of Czechoslovakia and to develop local production of mostly light industry and consumer goods for which

---

[8] Ladislav Feierabend: *Soumrak československé demokracie* [*Twilight of Czechoslovak Democracy*] (Washington, D. C., 1967), p. 70.

[9] Václav Vrabec, "Concerning the Level of Responsibility: The Mill and the Millers," *Reportér*, 24–31 July 1968, p. ii.

[10] Eugen Loebl, "Small Enterprises and Socialist Market," *Hospodářské noviny*, 6 July 1968, p. 1. Loebl's emphasis.

both the domestic traditions and world hunger for goods after the war were propitious.

3. Stalin's hand

But Stalin had different intentions. Soon after the February *coup*, through decisions made by the Cominform or in personal meetings he persuaded Czechoslovak communist leaders that "the Soviet model of building socialism is the only correct and possible one and therefore classical and binding and that any deviation from it is considered an expression of bourgeois nationalism." The decision was made 28 June 1948 (a day before the publication of the Bucharest resolution of the Cominform) by the Politburo of the CPC. "The Party reoriented itself to fulfillment of directives from Moscow."[11]

In September 1948 Gottwald met Stalin in the Crimea and accepted further instructions for the implementation of the Cominform resolution. The 9th of the same month, the Czechoslovak CP Politburo decided to start a "sharp class war against reaction."[12] The need for making a law establishing concentration camps of forced labor was recognized. Some members of the Politburo indicated that such camps already existed in Slovakia and in other regions and that the experiences were good. Among the inmates were many workers.[13]

There was no longer any chance of implementing the fresh Constitution and defending small enterprises. Loebl commented: "Under the influence of the Soviet model it was proceeded to an absolute directive planning of the economy."[14]

Foreign trade also had to be accommodated to Stalin's wishes. In the summer of 1948, in order to improve mutual trade relations with the United States, discussions took place. They were to continue in December 1949. Loebl wrote: "I was appointed head of the Czechoslovak delegation. But in November I was already in jail, and the Soviet Security Police considered this to be my 'crime'. The Soviets wanted to condemn Czechoslovakia for seeking economic independence by — among other things — trading with the West." For a similar crime; namely, discussing trade with Great Britain on Gottwald's orders, Margolius was condemned in the same trial of Slánský and "his conspiratorial group." Loebl finally concluded: "In reality Gottwald and the whole leadership of the Party and of the government had been condemned." The Soviets installed their advisers

[11] Vrabec, "Mill and Millers," p. ii.

[12] "All ideas of a specific road to socialism came to an end in this country." Karel Kaplan, "The Class War After February 1948: A Contribution to the Process of Forming the General Line of the Construction of Socialism," *Příspěvky k dějinám KSČ*, 3, 1963. See more on Kaplan in Part I, chapter 5.

[13] Vrabec, *op. cit.* The author states that at the beginning of the 1950s there were 422 such camps in Czechoslovakia! "It was possible to send a citizen even to a forced labor camp without a court order. Blameless people, too, including workers, were sent there." Václav Vrabec, "The Relationship of the CPC and the Public to the Political Trials of the Early Fifties," *Revue dějin socialismu*, no. 3, July 1969.

[14] "Small Enterprises . . . ," p. l.

everywhere: "Their domination was absolute. Everything that did not please the Soviets was a crime."[15]

According to Loebl, the cause of this "avalanche of tragedies" was that "the leadership of the Party and of the government delivered the Republic to Beria's agents."[16]

The Soviet Union was determined not only to prevent any possible political opposition in its East European satellites but also to use them fully in order to augment its own production of heavy industry and armaments in preparation for an expected war. In this economic strategy the highly developed and industrialized Czechoslovakia was to play a major role. That was *one of the reasons* why so many prominent communist economists figured in the Slánský and other trials of the 1950s. Ota Šik later commented:

> The show trials of the 1950's served in Czechoslovakia (as in the other "People's Democracies" of the day) to stamp out any independent thinking on economic and political matters and to ensure that only those willing to toe the Moscow line would be allowed a say in the running of the country. These preliminaries cleared the way for adapting all branches of the Czechoslovak economy to the Soviet model.
>
> The product was a monolithic monopoly that left neither freedom of operation to producers nor freedom of choice to the buyer. . . . And for the people of Czechoslovakia the consequences were little short of disastrous.[17]

The *second reason* is less known but very important. The regime needed scapegoats for the failing economy and drastic lowering of living standards. The Party had promised that with the departure of democratic ministers from the government, the economic situation would rapidly improve once the "enemies of socialism and of the people" lost power. When exactly the opposite happened there was a need for a new set of such enemies. This time, since no one else had any power, they had to be found in the Party itself. Already on 8 December 1948, the Secretary-General of the CPC, Rudolf Slánský, declared that "behind the various so-called objective difficulties is hidden tricky work of the enemy." And in March 1949 he was more specific: "The most dangerous enemies are those who are hiding in our ranks."[18] A communist historian stated in his study of this development: "Gradually, the cause of all difficulties and shortcomings was seen only as the result of the activity of the class enemy who was suspected everywhere and especially in the Party."[19] It was a double process: the Communist Party was being attached to the Soviet Union and detached from its own people. A reversal would be attempted in 1968.

---

[15] Eugen Loebl, "Superstalinism: The New Soviet Foreign Policy," *Interplay,* June–July 1969, p. 22.

[16] *Práce,* 15 May 1968, p. 4. Loebl narrated the whole story of his economic controversies with Soviet leaders, especially with Mikoyan, and of his trial investigations, involving systematic torture, in his book *Svedectvo o procesé s vedením protištátneho sprisahaneckého centra na čele s Rudolfom Slánskym* (Bratislava: VLP, 1968). In Maurice Michael's translation, it was published in New York by Grove Press in 1969 as *Stalinism in Prague: The Loebl Story.* See also his *Sentenced and Tried* (Elek Books, 1969) and *My Mind on Trial* (New York: Harcourt Brace Jovanovich, 1976).

[17] *Czechoslovakia: The Bureaucratic Economy* (White Plains, N.Y.: International Arts and Sciences Press, 1972), pp. 4–5.

[18] See Vrabec, "Mill and Millers," p. ii.

[19] Kaplan, "The Class War," p. 31.

4. Workers' opposition (1948-53)

The discontent among the working population was so prevalent that the Party desperately needed a lightning rod to better withstand the threatening storm. An unusual study of the phenomenon — a study based on rarely accessible and very rarely used CPC archives — was published during the first summer of Husák's administration (not necessarily with his blessing since for scientific journals the delay between editing and printing usually amounted to several months).[20] According to this important study, the economic situation in Czechoslovakia deteriorated very fast:

> In fact, it was precisely the first six months following February [1948] which witnessed the lowering of the standard of living of urban dwellers. The shortage of elementary human needs especially burdened the workers; the workers' earnings grew, but the chance to utilize them on the market deteriorated. The reduction of the food rations reached the lowest possible degree. The prices on the black market rapidly rose. . . . The question of the food supply was generally at the forefront of daily problems. In many cases, the Party organizations sent resolutions with categorical demands directly to the central offices. Some resolutions contained the threat of strikes, and in some cases strikes did occur.[21]

The author named some twenty towns, among them the major ones like Prague, Brno, Bratislava, and Ostrava where between 1 July and 6 September strikes and demonstrations were reported.

This report is corroborated by a historical study, published five years earlier, which was also based on Party archives documentation and, describing the situation, often used the strong word "panic":

> In the summer of 1948, some negative tendencies began to grow stronger in the internal life of our state. Supply difficulties became more and more marked. . . . There were snags with the procurement of agricultural products and the rations remained low and insufficient. Serious difficulties were again frequent as far as the textile situation was concerned. The demands and claims were far from being satisfied. In such circumstances, the black market assumed unusual proportions. . . . In some towns, the supply difficulties were particularly grave and a critical state arose in Slovakia. . . . Inflationary tendencies were growing stronger. . . . Dissatisfaction was engendered and grew among the working people. . . . In some factories it reached such proportions that resolutions were sent off containing demands . . . and sporadically signs of no confidence in the Government even appeared. . . . General panic and dissatisfaction were spreading.[22]

The alarmed leadership of the Party took several steps to ease the tension. It released bread, flour products, and potatoes from the list of rationed goods and controlled their gradually lowered prices. Between May and July 1950, it arranged thirty-six major trials against the democratic "enemies of the people" — the main one in the capital against a highly esteemed lady, Dr Milada Horáková, and other

---

[20] Vrabec, "The Relationship. . .," as previously quoted in footnote 13.

[21] *Ibid.*, pp. 20-1 of the polycopied translation. Based on CPC CC Archives, File 02/1, ref. 132, and File 100/24, ref. 927.

[22] Archives of the CC CPC, File PUV 132-76, meeting of the CC Presidium on 9 September 1948; J. Frank's report; and File OS-67-46, meetings of the Organizational Committee on 20 August 1948; also, conference of the secretaries of regional CPC committees, September 1948 — all quoted in Karel Kaplan, "The Class War," pp. 16-17.

prominent Czech personalities. The rest was spread, for maximum impact, in the regions. Altogether "639 persons were accused, of whom ten were sentenced to death (among them Dr M. H.) and forty-eight to life imprisonment. Further terms of imprisonment, totaling 7,850 years, and allied to confiscation of property and fines, were imposed."[23]

At the end of 1950, together with a major trial of members of the Catholic hierarchy, "enemies of the people" started to be discovered in the Communist Party itself and a steadily growing avalanche of arrests of prominent Party members began with the arrest of the Brno regional secretary, Otto Šling.

Since the large membership of the Communist Party showed strong democratic impulses, they had to be curbed and the Party turned into a totalitarian body fully manipulated from above. Paradoxically, Šling was partly condemned for his dictatorial methods and for his disregard of the people.

According to the Party historian, the highest standard of living was achieved in 1950. But some tensions remained, also because it still was much lower than in 1948:

> In the ranks of the workers, partial conflicts and moments of resistance were also reported (especially on the question of strengthening the output norms and wages). Inside the Communist Party, dissatisfaction grew with the limitation of internal democracy, with bureaucracy, and the dictatorial methods then prevailing.[24]

At the end of 1950, on orders coming from Moscow, the Czechoslovak government decided to further step up the production of heavy industry, to restrict the consumer industry, and to increase free market prices of food. It was hard to buy bread. Other supplies disappeared in a buying fever. "These measures . . . caused considerable nervousness, a definite change of mood, in towns, villages, and mainly in factories, and raised a number of questions as well: Who is behind this?; Is this the work of reactionaries?"[25]

The lowering of the standard of living continued at least till the end of 1952, if not till Stalin's death, as is shown by this estimate of real spending income of workers in Czechoslovakia:

1948	100
1949	80·3
1950	84·8
1951	81·8
1952	72·7
1953	73·2[26]

Throughout the year 1951, one harsh measure followed another. In February rationing of bread, flour, and pastry was reintroduced. Prices of food and industrial products went up steeply:

---

[23] Vrabec, "The Relationship. . .," p. 3.

[24] *Ibid.*, p. 22.

[25] *Ibid.*, p. 24.

[26] Gregor Lazarcik: *Comparison of Czechoslovak Agricultural and Non-agricultural Incomes in Current and Real Terms, 1937 and 1948–1965* (New York: Columbia University, 1968), Table 14.

The prices of industrial products increased so much that these products became quite inaccessible for a number of categories of employees. Sales of these goods started to drop sharply. On October 1, potato rationing was also reintroduced. Simultaneously, the issue of supplementary food rations for workers was also limited. And toward the end of November, further measures were also announced: the abolition of Christmas bonuses for a large part of employees . . ., the reduction in the allocation of ration stamps.[27]

Large sections of the peasantry, including the collectivized agriculture, lost their coupons for rationed food and consumer goods. Pauperization of the country increased.

Although the plenary session of the CPC CC in February 1951 added Švermová and Clementis to the list of "uncovered saboteurs, conspirators, and traitors," and reported that "after crushing this enemy base, the way to more rapid progress toward socialism was opened," the mood of the working population did not improve since the havoc was continuing. Strikes took place repeatedly in many regions, another great buying fever hit the dwindling supplies, and at the end of 1951 large demonstrations by tens of thousands of workers threatened even the stepped up armaments production, since especially in their centers; namely, in Brno and Plzeň, the strikes and street demonstrations developed in large proportions. The discontent continued unabated throughout 1952:

> Protest delegations from some districts arrived in Prague and the breaking up of public meetings was reported from various country regions (the Olomouc, Brno, Plzeň, Karlsbad regions). In some cases, the "speaker had to leave the meeting because he was threatened." . . . In many basic organizations protests also took place: "Things were better under Hitler than they are today," "The Party keeps the people under its thumb by using beautiful phrases, and at the same time fleeces them.". . . "We have worked like blacks without result, we have felt it, but didn't those on top realize this?" . . . "Where are we going, where are our leaders taking us?" . . . "The Party has betrayed its mission," "We are worse off than before," etc.[28]

The separation of communist workers from those who refused to enter the Party gradually disappeared. During many work-slow or sit-down strikes, solidarity prevailed, and in quite a few instances the communists, especially those from the unions, took leadership in the confrontation with the government:

> The distinction between the Party and the masses began to become obliterated and the moods of the masses found their direct reflection in the life of the Party. At that time, dissatisfaction even affected Communists and the organizations, some of which were in the throes of panic. These signs even penetrated as far as to the ranks of the party officials.[29]

The CPC information media mounted a campaign and during the years 1950 and 1951 the Party press was full of attacks on the "opportunists" who instead of enforcing the Party line and defending it against the "seduced masses" became spokesmen for the workers. The example of Adolf Zídek, chairman of the workers'

[27] Vrabec, "The Relationship. . .," p. 23.
[28] *Ibid.,* pp. 24–8.
[29] Kaplan, "The Class War," pp. 17–18. Kaplan quotes from the Archives of the CPC CC, File OS-67-46, meeting of the Organizational Secretariat on 20 August 1948: "Nervousness is beginning to make itself increasingly felt, as well as panic, and they affect our Party and our officials. Our people spread panic and our officials are even sending deputations."

union in the Stalingrad Iron Works in Lískovec, became famous since he used to say: "I represent thousands of slaves of this factory."[30]

The First Five Year Plan had disastrous consequences for the population but, since it was not yet tamed and frightened enough, also for the system of the "proletarian dictatorship" which was fast losing its power base. Therefore the indictment of the arrested "conspirators" was pushed further towards economic crimes against the Republic. Rudolf Slánský, Secretary General of the CPC, who was unpopular for his ruthless Stalinism, was denounced as the head of a "conspiratorial center" which supposedly caused economic damage worth billions and thus substantially lowered the people's standard of living:

> The institution of criminal proceedings against a number of leading officials of the Party, state and the economic apparatus as evil doers and saboteurs of the people and of the development of the new social system played the part of an instantaneous safety valve for strong social tension.[31]

Unfortunately for the instigators of this typical Stalinist shock treatment, it did not work in Czechoslovakia as well as in the U.S.S.R. People were much more civilized and skeptical. The shock worked just for a few days or weeks but soon backfired as an open admission of guilt and gross mismanagement by the whole Party leadership:

> The shocking character of the scope of the indictment also stimulated thoughts about the system. . . . After the first enthusiastic approval of the trial, many citizens began to ask questions: How is it possible that Slánský and the rest could cause such great damage, how is it possible that "so much money was wasted, without the leading officials of the Party and of the government noticing it?"[32]

Workers at factory meetings and Party organizations demanded resignation of many government ministers and sometimes of the government:

> Toward the end of 1952, there occurred a crisis of confidence so far as all personalities and offices responsible for the control of the State and society were concerned. . . . In many cases, the crisis of confidence evolved into a consideration of the whole political system. . . . Many people, even within the ranks of the Communist Party, started to express doubts about a system in which "Gestapo agents" and "imperialist agents" could climb to the leadership of the Party and State. . . . There was a lot of talk about democratic centralism and control from below.[33]

The disapproval of Party policies and methods went through much of the ruling system itself. Regional and district CPC officials and even Members of parliament protested and also refused to go to the villages and defend there the policy of forced collectivization. Antonín Zápotocký confessed: "We had a revolution in our parliamentary faction."[34]

---

[30] For documentation on this and other cases, taken from the Czech Communist press, see Confédération Force Ouvrière: *Tchécoslovaquie: Les Ouvriers Face à la Dictature, 1938–1948–1968* (Paris, 1969), pp. 160-1. Later quoted as *CFO: Tchécoslovaquie*.

[31] Vrabec, "The Relationship. . .," p. 29.

[32] *Ibid.* "What all the comrades perpetrated together, they now blame on Slánský, stated the workers of Avia in Čakovice", p. 11.

[33] *Ibid.*, p. 30.

[34] *Ibid.*, p. 26.

The system was bankrupt both economically and politically, in towns as well as in villages. Further trials were conducted in 1953 and 1954 but the proceedings were not publicized and there was no attempt made to provoke mass reactions of approval. Contrasting with this modesty is the fact that after the Slánský trial, four-and-a-half million brochures were published, one for each adult resident of the country.[35] The Soviet method of show trials worked only to a certain extent, creating conditions of fear necessary for a totalitarian government, but at the same time pinching the strong democratic nerve of moral and political as well as economic traditions of the country. The damage done was permanent:

> The ideological current which originated in the "crisis of confidence" about certain individuals in power and progressed to doubts about the whole political system, and democratic demands also never disappeared. It is a fact that later, after further social and political shocks which followed the monetary reform in 1953 and changes in the Party policy in the years 1953-4, a gradual renewal of confidence in a number of leading politicians, whose prestige had been shaken, was achieved, but the demands for the renewal of democratic principles in respect to the Party, State, and the whole political organization of society penetrated ever more strongly, took center stage.[36]

Both nations, Czechs and Slovaks, were humiliated and enraged in their entirety but, interestingly enough, the complaints and demands for change were coming especially from two groups — workers and members of the Communist Party. They felt privileged since they were supposed to be the masters of the country and beneficiaries of the new order, and had much less to lose than other sections of the population who always could be demoted, as a punishment, to the rank of manual workers. (This type of punishment, rather incongruous with the official doctrine that workers were the chosen class of people selected by history to create communism, was always hanging over people in white collar jobs. The situation was reminiscent of German concentration camps with their signs. *Arbeit macht frei* [Work Makes one Free,].) That was one of the reasons why the Party considered it important to show manual workers and its own members that they also could be downgraded by removal into concentration camps or into forced labor batallions. But workers in crucial occupations, that had a marked lack of apprentices or of new people eager to be employed in hard and demanding jobs, like in mines, heavy industry, and in construction, remained adamant and dared to voice their disappointments louder than other people. Finally, it erupted in prolonged strikes, demonstrations, and some local attempts at a rebellion (in June 1953) in several major industrial regions, mainly in Plzeň and Ostrava.

The violent reaction of the workers was provoked by the so-called monetary reform. Everybody lost a lot of cash on the exchange of the inflated crowns (at rates varying from 5:1 to 50:1) and even if salaried employees were not hurt as much as other people by the confiscation of all saving banks accounts, the workers forfeited

---

[35] *Ibid.*, pp. 31 and 14. Based on CPC CC Archives File 018/17, ref. 83.
[36] *Ibid.*, p. 32.

almost all of what they had managed with difficulty to save.[37] It was an economic catastrophy but the workers' anger rapidly turned into political demands for freedom and a change of the regime. Strikes started on the same day (30 May) as the measures were announced and on the first and second of June developed into mass-scale riots, especially in the West Bohemian industrial town of Plzeň,[38] and two days later in the North Moravian (or Silesian) mining and industrial region of Ostrava where street demonstrations were complemented by a general strike. All other important industrial centers experienced strikes and demonstrations, although on a less rebellious scale. In some instances, workers' militias and army units refused orders to use arms against the striking demonstrators. The government succeeded in breaking the rebellion only by encircling the ities, cuting them off from the rest of the country, and crushing the revolt by special police and army forces brought in from elsewhere. In many instances the local Party and state officials sympathized with the insurgents; naturally, a purge followed.[39]

In one of the best-informed surveys of the evolution which led to the revolution of 1968, we can read this summary concerning the period of 1948 till 1953:

> The development of the economies of the individual [communist] countries was progressively organized for the preparation for war. . . . The enormous overstraining of the forces of the country, the people, and the Party, caused ever more frequently by pressure of power in the years 1951-2, created serious social and political difficulties in the country. The dams of accumulated dissatisfaction were burst by the currency reform which was introduced on 1 June 1953. Strikes and demonstrations, some of them ending in street riots, created pressure for a critical revaluation of the political line and practice of the CPC.[40]

When two weeks later even more serious insurrection spread over large areas of East Germany, including East Berlin, a temporary reprieve in the form of a New Course was initiated by Moscow and gradually introduced also in Czechoslovakia.

[37] "The adjustment of prices combined with the monetary reform hurt also a considerable part of workers. . . . In the following days the situation, especially in great industrial centers, began to change dramatically and discontent kept growing. Embitterment of the workers was increased also by some wrong measures taken by factory management just prior to the monetary reform, by unthoughtful and insensible interferences, by a lack of discipline of state and economic organs. A role was also played by the fact that Party activists till the last moments before the monetary reform denied contentions about planned monetary measures . . . which caused a discreditation of functionaries." Jaroslav Žižka, "Boje a sláva dělnické Prahy: obtíže roku 1953" [Struggles and Glory of Labor Prague: Troubles of 1953], *Večerní Praha,* 17 Oct. 1975, p. 6.

[38] "Workers marched through the town with verve, calling 'We will not allow to be robbed!'" . . . When the chairman of the national committee began to talk about a workers' government, they started to scream 'Down with the government! We want a new government!'" Then they took over the local seat of government. For this quote from an eyewitness account, see Ivo Ducháček, *Svědectví,* ii, 3 (1958), p. 238.

[39] During the 1950s, excellent documentation and analysis of developments in Czechoslovakia, especially among the workers, were systematically provided by a Paris-based, polycopied sheet, *Masses-Information Tchécoslovaquie,* edited and mostly written by Paul Barton (psued.); the events of May-June 1953 were described in detail in its issues of May-June and July 1953. The riot in Plzeň was best described by a local judge who later left Czechoslovakia, Otto Ulč, in his article "Pilsen, the Unknown Revolt," *Problems of Communism,* xiv, 3 (May-June 1965).

[40] Vojtěch Mencl and František Ouředník, "Jak to bylo v lednu" ["What Happened in January"], *Život strany,* second installment, no. 15 (July 1968), pp. 11 and 12.

5. Intellectuals' collaboration (1948–56)

All available evidence seems to indicate that in Czechoslovakia at least until 1953, and most probably, until 1956, there was no united front of workers and communist intellectuals. Certainly, the riots of June 1953 did not have any such leadership. To most of the communist intelligentsia the disturbances must have come as a surprise since they tended to believe their own propaganda about the prospects of a supposedly proletarian dictatorship in a mythical workers' state. But there were also other reasons for this separation of interests and experiences.

Between 1948 and 1953, every social group felt the pressure in a different way. Workers saw their working conditions steadily worsening — norms getting tougher, working hours longer, with week-end "voluntary" shifts adding to their burden; sanitary and safety measures in their working-places deteriorating and provision of food and consumer goods becoming desperate. Their standard of living markedly declined. Their unions were gradually changed from helpful protectors into enforcing and policing agents. The disappointment was great and came fast. The workers were supposed to be masters but became slaves. They did not have at their disposition the sophisticated delusions of the intellectuals. Harsh reality was experienced directly and could not be easily disguised by ideology. All propaganda gradually lost its persuasive force. Disillusioned workers started to defend their interests and fight back against their oppression and exploitation.

At this time many young Party intellectuals saw their living standards going up. Their salaries increased substantially, they obtained plush offices with pretty secretaries, made fast careers since so many "defeated enemies of the people" had to be replaced. They moved into their villas and large apartments; cars, then still a great luxury, were at their disposition; chauffeurs included. They obtained great power over their democratic adversaries and purging them gave them a lot of pleasure. For them, it was a successful revolution. The Party used them against the workers, too — they had to "educate" them (see the Pachman case in Part I, Chapter 4) and make "new men" out of them, unselfishly working for the benefit of their new master, the communist state and its bureaucracy. "The appeal of Communism to the intelligentsia is understandably powerful. It appeals both to their desire to serve the people and to their desire to dominate it."[41]

Workers and intellectuals often found themselves on the opposite side of a barrier. The ones had to do all the hard manual work, the others encouraged them to make even greater efforts, singing to it their ideological poetry or declaiming their propagandistic prose. They were busying themselves by inventing the rosy blueprints of progress and planning the glorious future that had to go through difficult periods of early troubles since the working class, as the party dogma explained, was still full of remnants of trade unionism, material interests, selfishness, and other sins inherited from bourgeois capitalism.

That is one of the reasons why in the writings of our four selected protagonists (and their colleagues as well) from this period we cannot find documents which would show that they realized the fraud perpetrated on the workers and their

---

[41] Hugh Seton-Watson: *Nationalism and Communism. Essays 1946–1963* (New York: Praeger, 1964), p.219.

suffering. The other reason is that soon after the early period of eager collaboration, some of them became victims of systematic campaigns against nationalism, cosmopolitanism, Titoism, Zionism, etc., which made it impossible for them to publish. They either disappeared in prison or lost their access to the heavily censored publication media. But some of them (Štern) would soon return to their propaganda with renewed vigor for fear that they would lose all if they did not follow *any* Party·line faithfully. Others (Loebl) would try to learn from their mistakes. Let us survey their activities as far as we can ascertain them.

Eugen Loebl represents the middle-aged generation of well-educated communist economists who experienced the democratic Republic between the two world wars, with all its great benefits but also shortcomings, especially the economic crisis of the 1930s with large unemployment and the following defeat by German Nazism. First, Loebl shared his Party's dreams and took a leading part in its anti-democratic surge to power in 1945-9. Towards the end of 1949 he disappeared in prison and with him the cream of the Party's economic brain trust, both theoreticians and practitioners, people like Otto Fischl, Josef Frank, Ludvík Frejka, Ivan Holý, Pavel Hrubý,* Rudolf Margolius, Eduard Outrata, and many others. Most of the large trials took place after 1953 — long after they ended in other "people's democracies" — and were devoted to "economic crimes."[42]

After the working-class riots of June 1953, many Social Democrats, in and out of the Communist Party which one-third of them joined in 1948 in a forced amalgamation, were blamed as scapegoats for the riots, since they supposedly influenced workers by social democratism and "Masarykism." But even before their turn, the communist economists with Western contacts went down with the hopeful "bridge" of East–West cooperation.

In prison Loebl seriously tried to rethink the problem and to discover what went wrong. In the 1960s, he published several books based on his thoughts of this period; a local admirer wrote on the occasion of the first one in print:

> His work is a triumph of a communist — a fighter. It was born where the author not only did not have at his disposal any literature, statistics, newspapers but not even any paper or pencil. He was alone with his thoughts and kept them firmly in the part of the brain which we call memory. . . . Everybody fights with the weapons at his disposition. . . . In a prison cell . . . wins the intellect of a communist over those for whom every idea was suspect and a creative one was equal to treason.[43]

When Loebl was again allowed to publish, he reminisced about the period of arrogant certainty: "Armed with eternal truths we could safety condemn everybody who came with different opinions as an ignorant person or even as an enemy. . . . But man, an individual, is more than a society. Society should serve man!"[44] On another occasion he wrote:

*No relative of the author.

[42] "Many had been sentenced on grounds of economic 'crimes', with accusations ranging from direct sabotage and subversion of economy and finance . . . to such 'crimes' as conducting propaganda for economic Trotskyism." Vladimir V. Kusin, *The Intellectual Origins of the Prague Spring* (Cambridge University Press, 1971), p. 89.

[43] Edo Friš, *Práca*, 13 May 1967.

[44] Eugen Loebl, "Večný smäd po poznaní" ["Eternal Thirst for Knowledge"], *Kultúrny život*, 19 Mar. 1965, pp. 3 and 8.

> When in 1945 I returned from emigration I visited the Sudetenland. I saw German citizens with armbands. They lived on the level of "Jewish rations" [of the Nazi occupation time] and were deprived of all human rights. I was horrified by this victory of defeated Fascists. During my detention on remand and then in prison, I have found out that their spirit by far did not die out. We should proceed by a different, much more human road and morally defeat those who, no doubt, ruled by a socialist phraseology but in fact by Fascist methods.[45]

The moral element became his major inspiration for further economic and political activities:

> In such conditions [long years of imprisonment in isolation] man does not want to *be* right but he only wants to *discover* what's right. . . . I carried on a controversy with myself. . . . Humanity stands in front of an alternative to coexist or stop existing. . . . This was the starting-point of my thoughts: how is it possible that all that happened what is now being called — with an exaggerated taste for euphemism — the era of the cult?. . . The exclusion of the element of humanism, led, not by accident, to the exclusion of the element of science. . . . The real sense of human history and of our days is the fight for the freedom of man.[46]

For Loebl, in a communist prison, the humanistic and democratic influences of his own country and its Western heritage of culture reasserted themselves and led to a rebirth of creative energies and a revival of public activities in which he would mainly try to communicate his recognition of mortal dangers to humanity, stemming from socialist and revolutionary trends without humanistic, democratic, and liberal practice. For Loebl moral considerations became more important than economic illusions of a collectivist miracle. Such a process of recognition lasted longer for his younger colleagues who personally did not experience the basic decency of the pre-war Republic and the depth of the Sovietized regime's depravity.

Jan Štern was a son of an old Social Democrat but around the year 1948 almost nothing suggested that twenty years later he would be playing the role of the most unionist minded journalist. He was then interested in literature that would be useful to the Party as an educational and propagandistic instrument. He radiated an aggressive but, at the same time, carefree and jovial attitude of a determined and initiated Party activist, marching to an inevitable victory over bourgeois capitalists. At a congress of young writers which took place three weeks after the *coup* Štern described capitalism as a "sinking ship"[47] and talked about the need to destroy "everything old." He also outlined some features of the "future man of communism" who would be capable of sacrifices in the name of the future.[48]

Throughout 1949, Štern was regularly appearing in the pages of the CPC cultural weekly *Tvorba*, both as a Mayakovskyan poet and as a sharp propagandist,

[45] *Smena*, 5 Mar. 1968, p. 4.

[46] Eugen Loebl; *Úvahy o duševnej práci a bohatstve národa* [*Essays on Intellectual Work and the Wealth of Nation*] (Bratislava: Vydavateľstvo Slovenskej akadémie vied, 1967), pp. 8, 9, 12, 14, 45. His emphasis. The Slovak work was published later in German as *Geistige Arbeit - die wahre Quelle des Reichtums. Entwurf eines neuen sozialistischen Ordnungsbildes* (Düsseldorf: Econ Verlag, 1968) and in English as *The New Source of Wealth: The Revolution of the Intellectuals* (trans. Maurice Michael; New York: Grove Press, 1970).

[47] *Svobodné noviny*, 21 Mar. 1948.

[48] Sergej Machonin, reporting on his speech in *Svobodné noviny*, 16 Mar. 1948.

writing on all subjects in the same drastic way. The main target of his attacks was then the U.S.A. and "bourgeois thinking."[49]

A conception of enormous human masses was very impressive for an adolescent who wanted to merge with them or rather march in front of them: "Hundreds of millions of people, gentlemen imperialists! And we, the Czechoslovak people, are marching in the first rows of these immense masses. Forwards, to socialism."[50] His style was full of clichés that used to be considered typical for nationalist and bourgeois journalists of the previous century but its bombastic *naïveté* corresponded with the primitive content of his triggered mind. Discussing a novel he wrote: "We inscribe 'Anna the Proletarian' with golden letters on the banner of socialist literature."[51]

Encouraging to hate mercilessly was part of the vocation: "Every fault of yours, comrade, turns against these children. Every weakness of yours against the class enemy assists their murderers. Therefore, *beat mercilessly* your own faults and the class enemy, comrade. Mercilessly."[52] Stalin's designation of erstwhile supreme communist leaders as class enemies and their merciless liquidation was swallowed as eagerly as the rest. In an article in which he talked about the "Anglo-American man-eaters" he wrote: "The fifth column of reaction received in this country a decisive blow in February. The experiences of the U.S.S.R.,the disclosure of Tito's clique, and the trial of Rajk make it possible for us to prevent a surprise and finish of the criminal once and for all."[53]

When he thought about workers at all then, it was in order to encourage them to work and work: "In the Ostrava engine shed the work, in spite of all the hardship, begins to be a pleasure. The storm-troopers' movement took hold of them with full strength."[54] But he must have seen their real mood: *"The workers complain, criticize — but they don't complain in a selfish interest but for the sake of work, because of delays in work."*[55]

His contributions to the Party cultural weekly were becoming less frequent as many of his comrades were being swallowed by communist torture chambers. His last two contributions that I could find before the official closure of his weekly were both devoted to "sister Korea" that was "chasing the Moor [!] away and defending us from the bandit's paw" against the "U.S. occupation."[56]

From the end of 1949 till the end of 1951, a search has been going on for the

---

[49] Jan Štern, "Měšťácké svědomí" ["Bourgeois Conscience"], *Tvorba*, 30 Mar. 1949, p. 308.

[50] Jan Štern, "Přehlídka mírové armády" ["Review of the Peace Army"], *Tvorba*, 4 May 1949, p. 413.

[51] Jan Štern, "Epopej českého proletariátu" ["Epopee of the Czech Proletariat"], *Tvorba*, 27 Apr. 1949, p. 391.

[52] Jan Štern, "Řecké děti" ["Greek Children"], *Tvorba*, 6 July 1949, p. 634. Emphasis added.

[53] Jan Štern, "Na stráži proti zradě" ["On Guard Against Treason"], *Tvorba*, 12 Oct. 1949, p. 965.

[54] Jan Štern, "Staré dílny nových lidí" ["Old Workshops of New People"], *Tvorba*, 19 Oct. 1949, p. 994. The title tells more than intended: the regime invested much more in propaganda than in modernizing old workshops.

[55] Jan Štern, "Plán jsou lidé: Ze staveništ Ostravska" ["Plan is People: From the Ostrava Constructions"], *Tvorba*, 26 Oct. 1949, pp. 1019–20. Emphasis added.

[56] Jan Štern, "Jsme s tebou, Koreo!" ["We Are with You, Korea!"], *Tvorba*, 2 July 1950, p. 643; and "Země se brání" ["A Land Defends Itself"], *Tvorba*, 18 Oct. 1950, p. 1003.

Czechoslovak major "traitor" and Titoist, and all the influential Party people were tense and worried. The year of 1951 was the year of suicide for several prominent communist artists, Biebl, Machov, and Teige among them. Antonín Novotný started to climb to the top. Then Slánský was arrested in November 1951. As one of many victims, even the Party main cultural weekly, *Tvorba*, was closed down and managed to protest only by a strange and sad epitaph. Among its editorial staff was André Simone who would be executed the next year together with Slánský. Party activists who in spite of their aggressive loyalty could not boast of an Arian grandmother were in deep trouble. Since Slánský and some of his co-defendants, such as Geminder, or literary *agitpropchiks,* such as Štern, could not only provoke anti-Semitic sentiments but were often hated as especially sharp and merciless Bolsheviks, there was an attempt being made to use their unpopularity for blaming them (and not the Party) for all the "sectarian" excesses in economy as well as in other fields and to change the direction towards more domestic traditions. For example, in the literary press some writers condemned Štern and others for their arid and dull poetry and denounced their writing style and themes as "barren." At the beginning of 1953, the central committee of the Czechoslovak Writers' Union called for a "struggle against Slánskýism" in literature.[57] And so Štern will reappear in our survey only during the second part of the 1950s, again as a "schematic sectarian" but at the end of the 1960s, as an anti-sectarian and pro-unionist writer.

Radoslav Selucký did not show Štern's literary ambitions but actively participated in propaganda articles extolling young people's involvement in revolutionary processes. In 1949 he celebrated a special Party program in which for a day young people took over the administration of Brno, one of the largest Czechoslovak cities,[58] an action for which later the local CPC secretary, Otto Šling, would be blamed as seeking notoriety. Selucký's pronouncements on the future of socialism belong to the category of wishful thinking of typical dreamers promoting Party plans in the early years of the "building of socialism": "In a socialist society there are no expropriators and no expropriated. . . . There are only free working people . . . with enthusiasm they are building steps to an even more perfect and more beautiful Communist way of life."[59]

Selucký would be able to visit the Soviet Union several times. He will study economics in Leningrad and get to know the system inside out.

More than fifteen years after the quoted report he would comment on his early uneducated enthusiasm and later loss of arrogant certainty in a review of a book published by his colleague Loebl: "Our aim: to think afresh about questions that once seemed to have been solved for ever."[60]

Ota Šik has the dubious distinction of being the most attacked of Czechoslovak

---

[57] See *Literarní noviny,* 24 and 31 Jan. 1953.

[58] R. Selucký and D. Hamšík, "Mládež vede Brno" ["The Youth Leads Brno"], *Tvorba,* 18 May 1949, p. 470.

[59] Jaroslav Vojtěch and Radoslav Selucký, "Vodní schodiště: O stavbě průplavu Volha-Don" ["Water Stairway: On the Construction of the Canal Volga-Don"], *Tvorba,* 22 Nov. 1951, pp. 1122-3. This article was the fourth and fifth part of a series on constructions built mostly by slave inmates of concentration camps, a fact probably unknown to authors.

[60] *Kultúrny život,* 2 May 1967, p. 3.

reform communists. The number of pages published after 1968 by Husák's "normalizers" against him personally and criticizing his economic policies seems to be much higher than similar output produced against any one of the others. I think that this is due to the qualities of leadership displayed by Šik not only in matters of economics but also in the political crisis of the 1960s, which was to a large degree provoked by economic pressures. Several times, especially in 1967/8, Šik showed that he would have been the natural replacement of Novotný and, maybe, also a capable leader able to get the country and its Communist Party — if anybody could do it — out of its troubles. That might be a reason why Brezhnevian *agitpropchiks* concentrated their fire so heavily on him.

It was not easy since without any doubt Šik connected his whole economic and political career with the CPC and always tried to serve it more energetically and devotedly than anybody else. To a large degree, he also represented the theory and practice of the economic community that could work after the purges of the late 1940s and early 1950s. Therefore, it was extremely hard to cut him retrospectively off the body of official Party policies. Most of the normalizing propagandists did not pay attention to it and (following Soviet models) presented him as a villain and traitor from the beginning of his career. They provoked a series of more thoughtful studies whose authors attempted to separate the "good Šik" from the "bad Šik" and thus serve Husák's professed determination to salvage from the economic reforms its "sound basis." (More will be said about this later.)

According to one of these critics, all Šik's publishing and educational activities were, at least till 1956, not only Marxist but talented and exemplary.[61] In the *first period* of his active participation in the Communist Party's attempt to take over Czechoslovakia, he concentrated his attention on problems of workers, middle class officials, and clerks whom the CPC did not want to antagonize but rather win for its promise of democratic changes. In 1948 Šik followed the Party's changed tactics and started to vigorously attack the middle class and democratic theories of socialism. Šik faithfully fulfilled all of his Party's propagandistic tasks in political economy. Actually, after the disappearance of so many older Party economists, he led the effort and made a career. In a similar way as Kohout, Mňačko, and others, described previously (in Part I), his career was made quickly out of nothing with little to back it up, except loyal fanaticism and narrow-minded partizanship. He was then also teaching and very much appreciated for his services: "Thousands of former Party University students recognized him already then as an outstanding lecturer and suggestive speaker."[62] Šik then sincerely believed in, and propagated all, the Stalinist economic theories and practices. As the title of one chapter of his study stresses, *central planning* was one of the basic laws of the new system: "Plan as the supreme law of socialist economy."[63] In another article he wrote optimistically:

[61] See Květoslav Roubal, *Nová mysl*, no. 1, Jan. 1971, pp. 63-84. For much of the following bibliographical data concerning Šik's early publications I am indebted to this study. Roubal wrote: "It is not true that what comes from Šik, *eo ipso* comes from the Devil, and that everybody who merely brushed past Šik should be burned. Such tendencies which exist could only harm the Party." *Ibid.*, p. 65.

[62] Jaroslav Fidrmuc, *Smena*, 25 July 1970, p. 6.

[63] See his brochure *Prednosti socialistickej hospodárskej sústavy pred kapitalistickou* [*Advantages of a Socialist over a Capitalist Economic System*] (1951) as quoted by the same source. (Roubal gives 1952 as the publication date of this brochure.)

"Productivity grows much faster than under capitalism not only because all the technical progress in fully utilized but, first of all, because the enormous initiative of the people is awakened. To mobilize this initiative, that is the task of the plan."[64]

But according to "normalized" Doc. Ing. Jaroslav Fidrmuc, CSc., Šik was sinning by "his zeal in services to the then idols and ideals:" "Instead of deducing his theoretical conclusions from factual economic developments he deduced them from higher authorities, often without regard to reality. This is basically a subjectivist-idealistic methodology."[65] In contradiction to this condemnation of Šik's early period of writing, Květoslav Roubal started to seriously reprove Šik *ex post* only when in 1962 he criticized Stalin "without entitlement" since "Stalin surpassed Šik by several heads."[66] As can be seen, there was no unity in judgment of Stalin's and Šik's respective economic sins and merits, which corresponded to the unsolved problems of neo-Stalinism or economic as well as political reforms. Clearly, the exact science of Marxism-Leninism has its problems with economic laws.

Following CPC policy, soon after the February *coup*, Šik concentrated on a systematic and often violent rebuttal of the so-called "revisionist and bourgeois economists," especially of M. Stádník, K. Engliš, and J. Macek whose influence in Czechoslovakia was strong. "He was then thrashing them head over heels as imperialist lackeys." Roubal has high praise for it: "Even today Šik would not have to feel ashamed of these products of his theoretical youth. (Therefore, it was a shame when in 1968 as Deputy Prime Minister he apologized for them to Stádník at a public meeting of the CPC basic organization in the Economic Institute of the Czechoslovak Academy of Sciences.)"[67] Since exactly the same superficial and hateful approach to "imperialist economists" prevailed in Czechoslovakia after 1969, the youthful, immature Šik is to be preferred to the mature, experienced one. Roubal wrote: "It is necessary 'to see every problem from a class point of view — which means consistently in a scientific way.'" This principle, so actual today, Šik then admonished and repeated exactly. "What a pity that later he has forgotten it so shamefully."[68] Although Roubal castigates Šik's style "full of needlessly strong words and naïve," he values his "then still sincere revolutionary ardor, that up to this day impresses upon these essays, the indelible stamp of the young author's devotion to Marxism."[69] In other words, it does not matter if you are stupid if, at the same time, you are stupid sincerely and with ardor.

Šik was also highly praised for his attack on economic theories of the social democratic Professor Josef Macek who favored socialism based not on class hate but on humanist ideals of cooperation: "In his polemics with Macek, Šik not only stood up for a Marxist standpoint but defended it firmly and with a fighting spirit, and for that time manifested entirely unusual talent for independent application of

[64] *Nová mysl*, 1949, p. 188.
[65] Fidrmuc, *op. cit.*, p. 6.
[66] Roubal, *op. cit.*, pp. 77 and 80.
[67] Roubal, *op. cit.*,
[68] *Ibid.*, p. 73.
[69] *Ibid.*, p. 71.

Marxism in criticism of bourgeois theory." Especially after the invasion of August 1968, Šik must have enjoyed this praise of his twenty-year-old ephermeral effort: "He unmasks Macek's anti-communism and anti-Sovietism."[70]

Šik's polemical style and scientific level at that time, in a truly Leninist vein, can be appreciated from a sample [to be found on page 396 of *Nová mysl,* 1949] of his writing: "In the case of Macek we do not have to deal with a scientist who is sincerely looking for objective truth but with a bourgeois obedient domestic who, on the contrary, in the interest of his bread-givers, always purposely distorted the truth in a tricksy way."

Since Roubal comes to the conclusion that "Šik of the period 1948 correctly refutes Šik of the period 1968" it is hard to believe that he can be completely serious and that at least some malicious *švejkism* is not involved in such paradoxical observations, especially since he himself admits that "experiences with the socialist construction so unpleasantly were crushing all naïve conceptions" and that "the rise in Šik's scientific qualities" between 1962 and 1968 was "without any doubt considerable and obvious."[71] It rather seems ridiculous to attempt bringing back the old times of naïve illusions and return the country and Šik to slogans and attitudes which have been proved wrong and failed miserably. Today, after the bitter experience, they cannot be resurrected since the naïve belief of "innocent youth" is gone.[72]

In the *second period* (1951–6) of his economic and educational activities (he obtained the professorial chair of political economy at the CPC CC Institute — "University"), Šik devoted himself more to elaboration of theoretical bases for the socialist economy of Czechoslovakia. Again, he published many brochures and wrote many studies for magazines. "They distinguished themselves positively from the so-called dogmatic average."[73] Through extensive quotations Roubal proved that Šik was then writing as a Marxist-Leninist-Stalinist and exactly as the Party expected. His growing influence was connected with Novotný's rise to power. A few quotes might demonstrate what kind of views Šik would overcome in a few years and start his economic reforming plans from completely different premises; for instance, stressing the need for competition between socialist enterprises in a market. Still, in 1955 he wrote: "Competition is one of the laws of the development of private and especially capitalist production of goods. Competition and planning are then mutually exclusive. . . . From socialist economic conditions follows the impossibility of competition."[74]

The main reason why so many economists (and also non-economists influenced by them) joined the communist Party after the experiences with the economic crisis of the 1930s, or sympathized with it, was the conviction that since economic crises of major proportions are endemic to capitalism, only a planned socialist economy could overcome them successfully. Ota Šik, together with quite a few other

[70] *Ibid.,* p. 75, in a discussion of Šik's essay "Reformismus o politické ekonomii" ["Reformism on Political Economy"], *Nová mysl,* 1949.

[71] Roubal, *op. cit.,* pp. 78, 80, 83.

[72] Roubal, *op. cit.,* p. 74.

[73] Roubal, *op. cit.,* p. 68.

[74] Ota Šik: *Zákon plánovitého proporcionálniho rozvoje národniho hospodářstvi* [*The Law of a Planned Proportional Development of National Economy*] (Prague: CC CPC, 1955), pp. 6, 8, 11, as quoted by Roubal, *op. cit., p. 68.*

communist economists in Czechoslovakia, clearly still in 1955 strongly believed to be on steady ground with this theorem and could not imagine that many obvious economic troubles had other than temporary and superficial causes.

6. The New Course and hesitant de-Stalinization

The Soviet New Course was applied in Czechoslovakia much more modestly than in Poland and Hungary. In a Czech replica of the dualist Malenkov–Khrushchev Soviet leadership, dubbed "collective," President Antonín Zápotocký competed for power with the First Secretary of the CPC, Antonín Novotný.[75] On 1 August 1953, Zápotocký, hesitatingly, announced the New Course in his speech at Klíčava dam but coupled his permission to collective farmers to leave the kolkhozes, to which they had been previously forced, with a warning that they would probably have to return to them again.[76] The leadership of the CPC was not united behind this policy since during the same month the Minister of Agriculture, Nepomucký, criticized the peasants who left the collectives.[77] Due to this uncertainty, only 15 per cent of all collectivized farmers left, to be driven back in a renewed collectivization drive in 1955. President Zápotocký was sharply attacked in the Party Politburo since several of his speeches devoted to the "Thaw" were not discussed and approved by this body:

> A. Zápotocký was accused of infringing on the principle of collective leadership and of creating the personality cult of Zápotocký. The dispute was solved by a CPC delegation with representatives of the CPSU in Moscow. . . . This conflict within the leadership of the CPC could not end otherwise than in the political defeat of A. Zápotocký.[78]

Zápotocký placed his bet on the wrong competitor for power; namely, Malenkov.

Towards the workers the New Course was a little more beneficial and longer lasting, but only after a new clash occurred in the summer of 1953. When the workers responded to the monetary reform by strikes and riots, the government postponed a prepared strict measure against absenteeism and unauthorized changes of jobs from the 3rd till the 13th of June, but even then the workers refused to accept it. This time threat of a massive withdrawal from the official unions forced the regime to cancel the measure just one week after its promulgation. When the Party leadership lost that conflict, in order to divide the united front, it decided to use different tactics. Mass arrests and trials of ancient Social Democrats and workers of bourgeois origin were complemented by a series of price reductions of selected consumer goods and by some wage rises. The real income of workers slowly

---

[75] "In the leadership of the Party a sharp conflict existed between A. Zápotocký and some other members of the leadership led by A. Novotný." Vojtěch Mencl and František Ouředník, "Jak to bylov lednu" ["What Happened in January"], II, *Život strany*, no. 15, July 1968, p. 10.

[76] See *Rudé právo*, 2 Aug. 1953.

[77] S. P. Lyon, *The Communist Party of Czechoslovakia*, background information of 28 Mar. 1958, *RFER*, p. 49. The doyen of the Party intellectuals, Professor Zdeněk Nejedlý, who was becoming senile and in his regular radio talks often said more than was officially normal, commented: "There is no doubt that there hangs in the air we breathe a sort of question mark — an uncertainty as to what or, better, how to continue." Radio Prague, 18 Oct. 1953, quoted in Ivo Ducháček, "Czechoslovakia: New Course Or No Course?", *Problems of Communism*, vol. iv, no. 1 (Jan.-Feb. 1955), pp. 12-19.

[78] Mencl and Ouředník, *op. cit.*, p. 13.

but gradually began to climb, especially thanks to above-the-tariff-bonuses, till in 1959 it achieved, and even slightly passed, the wages of 1948.[79] It took ten years of hard work to reach the pre-communist level of real income. Not much of a success, but it meant a reversal of the previous downward trend.

In May 1955 the CPC confirmed its devotion to Stalinism by the erection in Prague of the largest monument to Stalin in the world. In June of the same year it definitely left the New Course, embarking upon a new campaign of terror in the villages by its decision to complete the collectivization of farm land before the end of the 1950s. Still improvement in workers' standard of living was allowed to continue. That it was part of a deliberate policy becomes clear when we realize that a decision of the CPC state conference from the spring of 1956 to "gradually remove shortcomings in the wage system, especially to correct the tariff system of workers' wages" was postponed both in 1956 and 1957 and began to be applied only in 1958.[80] Together with another, the fifth, decrease of retail prices, it helped the leadership of the Party to weather the storm of 1956 by successfully separating the majority of workers from some rebelling Party activists, students, and intellectuals.

Following the revelations of Stalin's crimes at the Twentieth Congress of the CPSU, a few Czechoslovak writers, mainly František Hrubín and Jaroslav Seifert, at the Congress of their Union in April 1956, protested against censorship and demanded more freedom as well as release from prison of their imprisoned (mainly Catholic) colleagues. They were concerned about the general situation of lies and terror in the country but did not seem particularly worried about the condition of the prestige class of workers.

Soon after students in Prague changed their traditional May ("Majáles") celebration of spring, love, and poetry into demonstrations against the government, and demanded abolition of censorship, political freedoms, travel abroad, and access to foreign books and journals. They manifested much more political acumen than their elder writers by questioning the adulation of the Soviet Union and its exploitation of Czech uranium resources. They hired airplane taxis for fast communication between the Czech and Slovak capital cities, and kept motor cycle connections of the Charles University with major factories, in order to coordinate their demands and actions. The police and workers' militia, composed of the most Bolshevik guards, suppressed the students' movement brutally.

Some communist journalists successfully used all available targets in order to express the popular discontent. When one of the most unsympathetic leaders, Dr Alexej Čepička, Klement Gottwald's son-in-law and Minister of Defence, was recalled from all his functions, as a scapegoat, at the CPC CC session of 19–20 April 1956, his behavior and life style, so typical of almost all communist (and Fascist) leaders, became the target of press attacks which showed the depth of class hatred

---

[79] See Lazarcik, *op. cit.*, Table 14.

[80] The leading article in *Rudé právo*, 5 Sept. 1958, added to this information the following explanation: "The unsatisfactory development of wages in 1956 and partly also in 1957 showed itself by a high overdrafting of the plan of wage funds, amounting to hundreds of millions, delayed the carrying out of these changes."

against the *nouveaux riches* masters of the proletariat, as is apparent from this sample:

> Called by the workers' class to rule, he procures for himself with the money of this workers' class a villa, a country house, and in addition to official motor cars also his own automobile. He then fortifies this villa and equips it with armed guards, evidently to protect himself against the workers' class.[81]

Some journalists did not criticize just one selected member of the government but the whole "new class": "Why do higher functionaries have so many Sunday 'official trips' by car and squander national wealth? Why don't their children go to school like other youths but have special teachers and educators as it used to be under the monarch?"[82] The antagonism between the people and its masters was described quite graphically:

> We also have a nobility. They don't make a step on foot. They dance from the club to a reception and from the reception to a club, but about the 'needs and moods of the people' they write and speechify for eternity. People laugh at it and sometimes also are mad about it.[83]

A congress of Czechoslovak journalists was scheduled for June 1956 but was cancelled by the Party, worried about the concerted criticism and demands by students, writers, and journalists.

In addition to these professional expressions of dissatisfaction the turmoil in the CPC organizations far surpassed the intended activization of the party membership by the shock treatment of Khrushchev's "secret" speech. The demand for convocation of an extraordinary Party Congress that would be able to change both the communist leadership and its policy was overwhelming but simply was not allowed to succeed. The storm blew itself out, since the Politburo did not support a rebellion against itself — Zápotocký's and Široký's attempt at a de-Stalinization was already rebuffed at its meeting on 29 February.[84] The regional Party secretary in Hradec Králové called such local demands "somewhat hysterical"[85] and the Central Committee secretary, Bruno Köhler, refuted "gross errors committed by a number of comrades" of a Prague organization by using a few sophisticated explanations of their basic rights:

> Censorship does not hinder reliable people. When everything is all right, the censor of the press has nothing to do. Unfortunately, that is not always so, even with us. . . .
> You argued that the Party statutes give Party organizations the right to demand the convocation of a special Party congress. Yes, you had the right to ask for the convocation of a special Party congress. But what matters is using that right wisely. That you did not know. . . .
> When the Central Committee of the city or district committee and their functionaries advise you, it does not mean that the rights of basic organizations are interfered with. Nevertheless, some comrades accepted such advice unwillingly and took it for inadmissible meddling in the activities of the organization. However, it was a help to your organization.[86]

---

[81] *Literární noviny*, 28 Apr. 1956.

[82] *Svoboda*, 27 Apr. 1956.

[83] *Květy*, 10 Jan. 1957.

[84] See Mencl and Ouředník, *op. cit.*, iii, Aug. 1968, p. 18.

[85] František Kraus in *Pochodeň*, 30 Jan. 1959.

[86] See *Život strany*, Mar. 1957. Sydney Gruson reported from Prague about the speech in *The New York Times*, 9 Apr. 1957.

Although the communist intelligentsia — still very much divided in a conflict of loyalty to lofty ideals or to the dictatorial regime that claimed to represent them — could not make a common front with the working people. They considered the ideological and intellectual challenge to be of prime importance. A systematic attack on the Party intellectuals would be accented and continue in full strength until the beginning of the 1960s.

In order to avoid future repetition of conflicts with Party and union leaders who in 1953 and 1956 often sided with the workers, a continual purge took place among the functionaries. At lower levels, energetic people were replaced by comrades who most of all wanted to stay out of trouble. In the higher ranks, pre-war communist representatives had to make place for young intellectuals, mainly lawyers, economists, and sociologists or *apparatchiks* who lacked democratic or unionist experience. They were willing just to pass down orders from above, shuffle papers, fill in questionnaires, and prepare false but acceptable reports on multiple "resolutions" to work harder and harder.[87]

7. Popular roots of revisionism: Workers in a "workers' state" (1956-9)

After the events in Hungary and Poland in 1956 confirmed the hopelessness of open clashes with the government, many workers retrenched to passive resistance, stealing from factories and collectives, pursuing personal interests and, generally, trying to avoid open conflicts with the authorities. Practically, it meant passing resolutions which no one intended to fulfil and almost no one bothered to control. To the constant regimentation and exhortation by a neurotic regime always demanding more and more, the population, in self-defence, responded by švejkian behavior, well expressed in a slogan that before the 1950s ended could be seen everywhere: "To chce klid!" It could be translated: "Take it easy!", "Keep calm," or "Leave me alone." Needless to say, such a generalized attitude sapped the energies and achievements of the system most effectively, and was bound to frustrate the propagandists.

Since there was a lack of workers available to be hired, some managers tried to keep those they had or attract new ones by unofficial bonuses, soft norms, and by closing their eyes to pilfering, unused work hours, short work weeks, regular "sicknesses" mainly Mondays and Fridays, and similar devices that made it possible for capable workers to augment their incomes substantially by illegal private work during extended week-ends on the widespread black market of services. Thus the many-sided corruption of the working force, on one hand, blunted the system's effectiveness but, on the other hand, by avoidance of sharp conflicts, helped it to survive, although in a slightly paralyzed state. Party spokesmen kept complaining about this "lack of enthusiasm" of the workers, occasionally tried, in vain, to stir them to greater efforts but mostly accepted the *modus vivendi* as the only possible balance of mutually hostile forces.

The tug of war was going on all the time. Not everybody was willing to give up

---

[87] See CFO: *Tchécoslovaquie*, pp. 165-6.

and the game had to go on. Party leaders claimed that only foreign propaganda could be blamed for lack of discipline or revisionist ideas but the official press was full of complaints that demonstrate the real character and domestic origins of the conflict which foreign propaganda could possibly influence but certainly not create. A few samples should prove the point.

A member of the editorial staff in the main Slovak trade union paper, Mrs Ruppeldtová, once described how isolated and alienated workers felt from the supposedly workers' government:

> At a large plant one day I talked to a group of workers and mentioned production conferences. "What is it?" asked an intelligent looking young welder who received an award in a competition in production economy in which he participated without knowing exactly what it was all about. . . .
> When I asked about organization of socialist competition and norms, another man, also a welder, gave me a surprising reply: "Those in charge write it on paper. Then they come here and read it to us and ask who is for it and we vote for it." Once this has been done no one seems to care any more. . . .
> Cannot the workers submit their suggestions? Have they no opportunity to make recommendations to improve the work? Can they not ask questions? Only one found it worth while to react to my questions. He just waved his hand. . . .
> The result is that people are frank when they talk to each other and not when they should be frank, namely at the meetings with those criticized. It also leads to a lukewarm attitude to the Party trade union movement. "Just inquire at the works council," they told me, "they will tell you how many people have stopped paying the union contributions." So this is the weapon!. . .
> It would serve no purpose if I said in which enterprise I found these conditions; similar experiences could be made in many other factories as well.[88]

The theoretical premise that the state belonged to the workers was in strange contrast to their feelings of absolute inability to claim even minor rights. The following example is taken from the Czech edition of the same trade union daily. The editor Škodová wrote about the difficulties which the workers often had to face in factories that according to theory were theirs:

> "They transferred me to another working place and I do not know why!"
> "Recreation was promised to me but someone else was selected and they did not tell me why."
> "They lowered my pay and nobody explained to me why!"
>
> We have been getting a lot of similar letters at our paper. The majority of them end like this: "Well, am I not worthy of an explanation?" — "I no longer know where to turn," we often read in letters by our readers. Complaints are different: the plant is in disorder, the director is a dictator, the workers' council did not stand up for somebody, etc.[89]

The publication of articles similar to those quoted above could demonstrate that occasionally the workers who still cared and did not give up any hope found people ready to serve their cause but it was all part of a game that rarely led to any satisfactory results. Fulfillment of production quotas depended, to a large extent, on workers' contentment. Some functionaries were paying attention to workers' demands but often lacked means to redress the situation. They found themselves to be the target of Party leadership that regularly made the lower-placed officials

[88] *Práca*, 6 May 1958.
[89] *Práce*, 29 Jan. 1958.

responsible for its own shortcomings. They were then under a twofold and contradictory pressure: from the regime, and from the people. The meaning of such campaigns of encouraged but limited criticism against lower-placed functionaries was that the policy of the government was sound but its implementation of it by some officials was inadequate. After repeated use, this maneuver ceased to work, some of the officials lost their temper, and were tempted to give the game away. The pressure from both sides was getting on their nerves and government ingratitude made them resentful. The author of our last quotation described the attitude of these unhappy officials, thrown into the arena to do the dirty work and then to do penance for the sins of the government: "I'll give it up! They pester me all the time and criticize me! I'll give it up! Let someone else come and try instead of me."[90] Every such case was a victory for the oppressed population because another of their drivers was driven to despair. The regime in its Machiavellism was losing loyal servants and creating additional oppositionists every time it cheated.

In one way or another, functionaries transmitted popular demands and dissatisfaction to their superiors. At all Party conferences officials who had contact with the people spoke in a manner quite different from the Ministers and Party secretaries from the center who had no contact with the grass roots. From their speeches it was clear that it was much easier to make plans and write directions in the secretariat in the capital than to implement them in factories or mines.

The continuing identification of some Party and trade union functionaries with the demands of workers is apparent in the following quotation from a speech by Bohumil Bělovský, secretary of the CPC regional committee in Ostrava, an important industrial city:

At present, hostile elements center their efforts on the economic field. This is indicated by *mass pilfering* of national property, by acts of sabotage, by violation of *working morale,* and by similar misdeeds. . . .

However, the decisive battle is fought in the field of ideology. By diverse theories, e.g. the theory of people's capitalism, national Communism, class harmony, and the like, imperialist propaganda strives to deceive the workers' class in their respective countries, and at the same time, to influence the people's mind in the countries of the socialist camp. The bearers of these hostile ideologies are chiefly the remnants of the exploiting classes and their collaborators, of whom many are active directly in the workers' class, where they try to exert their influence. The petty bourgeoisie, especially the peasantry, too, is receptive to hostile ideologies and tends to waver. . . . *Nor is the workers' class immune from hostile ideologies.* . . .

Wage problems are still the main topic of discussions at our places of work. Efforts to reach higher wages regardless of work productivity are not merely isolated phenomena. This dogmatic adherence to unjustified *demands for wage increases,* to outdated norms, the drive for equalization, are to be traced to social-democracy.

These efforts, of course, find attentive ears among less responsible workers, are rather *popular,* and cause unjustified unrest and, in some instances, even *strikes.* . . .

The *bearers of such tendencies* are not always necessarily the members of the former Social Democratic Party. Even today we can observe such efforts on the part of *trade union officials* as well as *Party officials and members.*[91]

[90] *Ibid.*
[91] *Nová svoboda,* 7 Sept. 1957. Italics are mine.

Workers clearly were dissatisfied. In some places union and Party officials supported workers' demands. Where the workers' consciousness was higher than average, the government had to cope with solid opposition.

It was difficult, if not impossible, to win workers for self-sacrifices when all they could see was chaos in production, constant lack of basic supplies, and cheating in shabby socialized services. An encyclopedia could be put together of complaints published in newspapers. A few more samples should show the scope of daily problems and the resulting mood of discontent.

Most of the workers had to eat in institutional cafeterias. The service was mostly appalling and cheating was widespread, even according to an official survey:

> The Slovak Ministry of Commerce carried out recently a check of the workers' canteens. 126 establishments were checked, on average 21 in every district. The results were startling. In 77 out of the 126 canteens the prescribed weight of the portions was not kept. The people catered for were deprived of 18 per cent of meat, 24 per cent of potatoes, 37 per cent of dumplings, and of 30 per cent of pastry. Not only this: some enterprising managers and chefs prepare the meals of low quality material. . . .
>
> The workers who are hit by this mismanagement believe that it is part and parcel of our system. The unscrupulous managers and chefs of work canteens become willy-nilly helpers of the reaction and of the class enemy who systematically tries to spread *dissatisfaction among the masses and the feeling that it will never work in our country,* that our standard of living does not rise adequately, etc. . . . It is said that love goes through the stomach. If it is so then many of our canteens are not doing their best to evoke the love of our people for the system.[92]

A check of textiles available in Czechoslovak stores revealed that "65 per cent of the checked merchandise was defective and should not have appeared on the market."[93]

Young workers especially did not have any illusions about the system and did not care about the exhortations of older communist workers who became part of the new ruling class through their white collar managerial positions or of their educated intellectual helpers. The secretary of the district council of the youth organization ČSM in Ostrava complained about it and in the process revealed some interesting figures:

> Many, especially in schools. . . see in the association's card a permit to the school-leaving examination or to the university. . . . Almost half of young people are not members of our association. It is puzzling that these are mostly young workers and farmers. . . . In the majority of mines in our district the number of members does not surpass 40 per cent. And there exist enterprises where the number of organized youth not only does not grow but, on the contrary, is falling. It is best proved by the example of our famous motor-car factory Tatra. In 1956 there were in the ČSM 65 per cent of young people and today only 48 per cent.
>
> Many functionaries show aversion to founding of organizations, especially at places where it is known beforehand that the task would not be easy.[94]

The Deputy Minister of Education and Culture, writing about the relations between young workers and the regime, admitted:

> A part of the workers' youth shows lack of interest in social problems in enterprises, leanings

---

[92] *Pravda,* 9 Oct. 1957. Emphasis added.
[93] *Rudé právo,* 18 Aug. 1959.
[94] *Mladá fronta,* 23 Aug. 1958.

become apparent towards individualism and towards an egotistic interpretation of duties at work places, a disrespectful relation to older workers and to their experience exists, and the Western way of life is falsely admired. ... The danger remains of the influence of bourgeois and petty-bourgeois egotism on the youth.[95]

Treating the dislike of the communist system by young workers who grew up in it as a contagious bourgeois disease was not only poor Marxism but did not help either. Obviously, the class conflict between the bureaucracy and workers also had its generational aspect.

8. White collar reaction to pressure from below

Quite a few communists tried to develop their organizations into equal organs of power with the Party in a pluralist system. It would have made their life more bearable. The following quote condemns these attempts and so reveals them:

> It is not just by chance that comrade Strouhal, delegate from Horní Maršov, was the first and, unfortunately, not the last to mention something about the necessity of "cooperation" between the Czechoslovak Youth Federation, the trade union movement [ROH], and the Communist Party. Perhaps one might be inclined to think that it was a slip of the tongue. Unfortunately, comrade Kálalová from the railroad station Svoboda-Jánské Lázně had similar ideas as regards "cooperation" between the Party organization and the ROH. Also comrade Pithart of the district health institute praised the "cooperation between the basic Party organization and the institute."
>
> Similar false theories were voiced by a number of other comrades. This proves only that some comrades of the Trutnov region — unfortunately, even some functionaries with serious Party schooling — have not yet realized what they are doing when they put the Party on a level with any other social organization.[96]

The top leadership was well informed about the rebellious mood of many of its representatives and propagandists, reflecting the workers' dissatisfaction. Jiří Hendrych, one of the most powerful men in the ČSR, talked about it in his address to the CPC CC meeting on 13 June 1957. He condemned labor unions for "wrong opinions" and "unjustified demands." His Leninist class contempt for manual laborers showed in his talk about "unconscious workers" and the working-class' "principle 'snatch what you can!'": "An atmosphere of inadmissible indulgence toward negligence and minor transgressions is a nourishing ground for stealing in extensive quantities which was discovered in a number of factories, in construction, railroads, and on collective farms." Hendrych criticized "petit-bourgeois liberalistic and anarcho-radicalist tendencies" of Party intellectuals who in a mistaken "fight against imperialist and Stalinist reaction" elevate "the most backward states of mind of certain parts of the working class" to justification even of the Hungarian "counter-revolution." He complained that such "platforms" were created in some institutions of higher learning and in various central institutions.[97] This was one of the very rare instances where a connection was made between workers' unhappiness and intellectuals' reflection of it.

A vigorous campaign was mounted against a few selected comrades, most of

[95] Václav Hendrych, "Tasks in the Sector of Specialist Education in the Fight for Completing the Building of Socialism," *Pedagogika*, no. 4, Aug. 1959.

[96] *Pochodeň*, 21 Mar. 1958.

[97] *Rudé právo*, 19 June 1957, supplement of 24 pages, pp. 16, 8–9, and 12.

them coming from economic institutions or closely connected with production. Their condemnation was supposed to frighten everybody else. A Party spokesman complained that "all basic forms of modern revisionism could be found in our country" and among warning examples singled out the typical "cases of Kuhnl and Kusín at the Prague School of Economics, or Zdeněk Dubský at the School of Mining Engineering at Ostrava."[98]

Ostrava, the most important coal-mining and iron industries center in the ČSR was a particularly sensitive town. Its exposed situation near the northern frontier with Poland, with thousands of Polish workers daily commuting to work across the border, aggravated the tension created by exaggerated requests of stepped-up production of minerals needed in the overstretched five-year plans of heavy industrial expansion. At that time, Polish workers were used to a much freer atmosphere of Gomułka's post-October 1956 liberalization.

Before coming to the local case of comrade *Zdeněk Dubský*, it should be pointed out how difficult it was to work there and how the Party's uneconomic methods generated unproductive chaos. Not only workers but also top level personnel suffered from abnormal turnover since no one was able to solve the problem of antiquated methods and miners' opposition:

> Fluctuation of manpower poses a grave problem to our national economy and causes considerable moral and material damage. It is particularly the Ostrava–Karviná coal basin (OKR) where this problem is very acute. However, very few realize that a similar situation prevails in the leading positions as well, and that the damages inflicted there by fluctuation are far greater. What is the real state of affairs?
>
> At the 22 OKR mines, 131 directors and 137 chief engineers, respectively deputy directors, have been exchanged between May 1945 and mid-1957. . . . Nineteen directors had been exchanged in 1951 and twenty-one engineers a year later. . . . Already during the first half of 1957, five directors and five chief engineers have left the enterprise. There are seven mines at which directors were exchanged twice a year, three mines (i.e. "Fučík", "Zárubek", and "Urx") where such a change took place three times a year for two successive years, while the mines "First May" and "Gottwald" had three different chief engineers in a single year. . . .
>
> Mines with the most frequent changes of directors and chief engineers have always been, or still are, notorious non-fulfillers [of targets]. This applies particularly to "Fučík" and "Urx" with eighteen changes each, "Zárubek" with seventeen, and "Zápotocký" with sixteen changes in leading positions.[99]

It is not surprising that in such a managerial mess it was hard for teachers of Marxism-Leninism to believe that socialism was being successfully built in Czechoslovakia. In a paper intended for circulation in the inner circle of Party functionaries, a member of the CPC works' organization at the Graduate School of Mining Engineering at Ostrava, in denouncing Dubský revealed some of his ideas and the difficult process of combating them:

> Dubský worked at the School from 1951. In his capacity of special assistant at the chair of Marxism-Leninism he came forward in the period following the Twentieth Party Congress in Moscow with wrong anti-Marxist, revisionist opinions. . . . He spread erroneous theories about "liberalized Stalinism."
>
> According to his "theory" the Leninist conception of the dictatorship of the proletariat is obsolete and it is necessary to replace it by a new form of dictatorship "of a wider coalition of

---

[98] Jaromír Sedlák in *Rudé právo*, 10 June 1958.
[99] Jaroslav Klečka, "One Cannot Be Silent!", *Hospodářské noviny*, 27 Oct. 1957.

classes," i.e. including the bourgeoisie. He attempted to lower the importance of the leading role of the Party in the building of socialism in our country. . . .

Bureaucratic tendencies in Party work do not have their origin in the non-compliance with Leninist norms of Party life, according to Dubský, but in the fact that "the Communist Parties assume rights which do not belong to them." Dubský meant by these "rights" the leading role of the Party in the State and its organizational part in the building of the new society. His ideas on the building of the Party and particularly on the leading principle in the organizational structure of the Party, i.e. democratic centralism, were in the same vein.

Apart from his erroneous opinions in questions of theory, he was found to have serious shortcomings in practice as well. Thus, for example, he refused to accept a Party function on the ground that he would have to enforce many decisions and measures of higher Party organs with which he did not agree.[100]

Dubský's mistake was to advocate postulates which just a few years later would be embraced by Khrushchev in the slogan of an "all people's State." Other articles expressed more openly the major demand of Dubský and other "revisionists": return to "internal democracy" and "free discussion" in the CPC as well as rejection of strict Party centralism with its complete subordination of local organizations to top leadership's commands.[101] From the long procedure described as necessary to censor comrade Dubský it follows that the Party leadership found it hard to suppress "wrong opinions" locally:

Dubský's serious shortcomings were the subject of an investigation by a members' meeting of the Party organization at the Graduate School of Mining Engineering as well as by the district, town, and regional Party committees in Ostrava. Dubský rejected any kind of criticism of his opinions. The School administration, therefore, released him from his post of special assistant and dismissed him from its services. The general meeting of the Party organization decided to punish him by reprimand and warning. The Party district committee changed the decision to expulsion from the Party.

However, this did not conclude the case. Dubský continued to persist in his opinions. . . .

Dubský's case demonstrated to us that *the fight against revisionism is a difficult one* . . . difficult because *most of us Party members* are as yet inexperienced in the conduct of this fight.[102]

Clearly, the courage and self-confidence of dissenting Party members was much greater than it had been some years before. The number of meetings where this case was presented as damnable and had to be debated suggests that it was not easy for the Party hierarchy to get agreement from the lower organizations for strong measures against Dubský. This view is corroborated by the punishment changed by higher echelons of the Party and especially by the last paragraph of the article which, translated from the usually modest understatement of resistance encountered, should read, to be true: "Most of us Party members do not *want* to know how to fight against revisionism."

But not all functionaries and intellectuals supported the unhappy working masses. When the future fighter for workers' rights, *Jan Štern*, attempted to refute the conflict of generations he did not yet think about workers and addressed himself, instead, to fellow writers:

[100] Ludmila Geierová in *Život strany*, no. 22, Nov. 1957.

[101] See, for instance, František Doktor writing in *Pravda*, 18 July 1957; or the leading article entitled *"Democratic Centralism and Party Discipline"*, in *Život strany*, no. 11, June 1957.

[102] Geierová, *op. cit.*

Young generation? Well, yes, but what is its program? Does it adhere to the program of that group of young poets and reciters who appeared in the "**Práce**" theater with the attractive slogan "Tired Heroes"?. . .

There are young artists who, in my opinion, view reality in about the following, textbook-like schematized fashion: From what they say, socialist art cultivated till around 1948 can be accepted. Thereafter commenced the domination of the personality cult and everything that arose was trash, schematism, dull realism, pseudo-art and, in the best case, the master's artistic error.[103]

Štern well represents the rough but naïve and idealistic young communists who during the second half of the 1940s dreamt about the future communist paradise not at work places but in coffee-houses, bars, and at CPC meetings. They did not know the real workers, except as targets for propaganda. Their inspiration for a revolution was not coming from factories but from literary works. Naturally, Štern is interested in his own self-defence:

I wish these 20-year-old Know-Alls were at least once in their life inspired by those thoughts and emotions which filled the sails of our art [[103]] in the spring of 1948. Indeed, that was not bad inspiration! And not proud of himself but ashamed of himself should be everybody today who then, as artist, remained indifferent. We should criticize and not elevate as an example of artistic scrupulosity him who was silent then because he had nothing to say, because his soul was perplexed by the revolution which paralysed him. We, on the contrary, present such people as an example to the artists who at that time set to work unconditionally, endeavoring to resolve at once the problems which we shall yet cope with for decades to come.

It shall remain the pride of many of us that we neither collaborated nor flirted with the revolutionary time, but that we lived it.[104]

Another time, although writing in the official daily of the workers' union, Štern still full of his enlightening mission, bombastically attacked those who were upset by the exploitation of his country by the Soviet Union, as many workers were. He reprimanded those who suggested that the ČSR should defend its own interests, as well as those who demanded more freedom and claimed that "the socialist bloc is only a military bloc:"

Freedom of man in our, socialist, conception means to behave in such a way that my acts are in agreement with the historical necessity, in agreement with progress. . . .

Against national selfishness, against Philistine indifference we are proudly raising the flag of comradely international cooperation and mutual help![105]

At that time, *Selucký* was studying in the Soviet Union, *Loebl* was in prison contemplating his early mistakes, and *Ota Šik*, according to his own account, found himself at a crossroad:

I faced a choice — either to leave the Party or to try to help to change the system through long-term, patient, and purposeful work. Together with a few closest friends who were of the same opinion we decided for the second possibility. And so in 1957–1958 began my searching for new thoughts and new ways.[106]

---

[103] "Generation Or 'Generation'?", *Květen*, no. 9, May 1958.

[104] *Ibid.*

[105] *Práce*, 24 Aug. 1958, p. 4.

[106] *Der Dritte Weg* [*The Third Way*] (Hamburg: Hoffmann und Campe Verlag, 1972), as quoted by Vladimír Gerloch, *Tvorba*, 9 May 1973, p. 7. In the German text the quotation is on p. 11. Its English translation by Marian Sling can be found on p. 9 in a slightly different version (*The Third Way*, London, Wildwood, 1976).

Here a historian faces a problem which is hard to solve since in a state governed by a totalitarian party with conspiratorial and secret police methods, the opposition cannot work openly and by necessity must combine public pretension of strict loyalty with careful and secret pursuit of its own aims, as much as possible trying to present them as fulfillment or rightful extension of party policies. By external observation of pronouncements and writings it is impossible to decide what was genuine and what merely tactical. Such activities make the inner opposition in communist parties highly vulnerable; when convenient, its representatives can be accused of false double-dealing and of masking their true intentions by untrue expressions of support for official party lines.

After 1968 Ota Šik was often attacked for such "hypocrisy" in the "normalized" press. One of his articles, published in March 1957, "therefore at a time when Šik, according to his own words, occupied himself with intensive searching for 'new thoughts and new ways',"[107] ridiculed those who imagined that decentralization would mean an end to central planning and that it would give enterprises power and the responsibility to decide about their own production, shopping for materials, and selling their products. Šik saw in such decentralization "danger of return to capitalism" and "general anarchy in production."[108] Since Šik was then busy officially planning a limited, and unsuccessful, decentralization it is hard to say if he was playing a game and trying to achieve the maximum possible at the time, or was still defending strictly centralized economy and believed in it.

On another occasion, at an international forum, Šik defended Stalinist economy so vehemently that he would be praised for it even after the 1968 invasion. In March and April of 1958, UNESCO sponsored a meeting in Turkish Bursa of economists from the East and the West "On Peaceful Co-operation and International Understanding". Ota Šik's criticism of Western economy was considered exemplary by his critics even in the 1970s and his old report, published after his return home,[109] was acceptable even under Husák's leadership although Šik, defending the communist system and attacking Western economists, tried to stress the need to study "contemporary bourgeois economy" and to stay in contact with the economic thinking all over the world. Although Šik in 1958 "subjected the concept of the so-called 'democratic socialism' to crushing criticism"[110] his major message *pro domo sua* seems to have been the freedom of scientific study and the need of international contacts. Under the innovating and ambitious regime of

[107] See Gerloch, *op. cit.*, pp. 7 and 17.

[108] Ota Šik, "Oč jde při decentralizaci" ["What Is the Aim of Decentralization"], *Tvorba*, no. 13, 28 Mar. 1957, as quoted by Gerloch. In 1957 Šik was in official favor as proved by his nomination as assistant professor of political economy at the CPC CC Institute of Social Sciences in Prague.

[109] Ota Šik, "Proti některým názorům soudobých buržoazních ekonomů" ["Against Some Opinions of Contemporary Bourgeois Economists"], *Nová mysl*, 1958, as quoted extensively by Květoslav Roubal, "O umění metati kozelce aneb Ota Šik — teoretik" ["On the Art of Turning Summersaults or Ota Šik — Theoretitian"], *Tvorba*, 17, 24, and 31 Mar. pp. 3, 15, and 14–15, respectively.

[110] See Roubal, *ibid.* 24 Mar. p. 15. By the way, Roubal's copious verbal denunciation of some old Šik's theories could be easily suspected of serving the same purpose of liberating the economists from closeted adhesion to clichés and of renewing contacts with both Marxist and non-Marxist economists of the West, as Šik's article in 1958 advocated. The art of hiding the positive message in a lot of negative verbal garbage for the benefit of the censors, did not die in 1968 and is endemic to the Soviet system of censored publications.

Khrushchev such an attitude was possible and was, to a large degree, part of the official policy, although conservative communists did not trust the trend and applied brakes whenever they could.

The major mistake of Khrushchev was that he ambitiously and confidently believed that through coexistence communism would win in the world. However, history has proven, in both the case of Šik and Czechoslovakia, that the Moscow type of communism was not the wave of the future and was bound to lose in competition, at least as far as contest of ideas and scientific standards is concerned. It was unable to coexist in social sciences without being influenced by the West to a very decisive degree.

Very much as in Russia, the decentralizing attempts of 1957 in Czechoslovakia[111] ended in 1959 by a strict re-centralization. With a new wave of steeply stepped up production orders coming from Moscow, the next economic plan till 1965 stipulated "maximally mobilizing"[112] targets. The half-hearted attempt at decentralization of 1957/8 was "swept away"[113] by this trend:

> According to the State Statistical Office the number of industrial enterprises (excluding local and cooperative industries) decreased after the reorganization from 1,417 to 929. The average number of workers per enterprise increased at the same time from 1,244 to almost 1,900.[114]

Even *Ota Šik* — the future prophet of market competition in socialism — can be quoted as a defender of the return to rigidity; he participated in a renewed campaign of attacks on Yugoslav economic experimentation:

> If Yugoslav Communists call it [the central planning] in their program "monopolization" then we consider such "monopolization" historically more progressive than competition. . . . Freedom consists in recognition of the necessity. . . . To improve the planned management of socialist production demands not at all weakening but, on the contrary, strengthening and still more consistent unification of central administration.[115]

The new shock of exacting industrialization of an overstretched and unbalanced economy, depending on disgruntled workers, could only aggravate the crisis.[116] The government attempted to reduce workers' wages by a

[111] For a devastating picture of the failure of the Czechoslovak economy and for a subsequent Party decision to decentralize its management, see, for instance, the address of the Politburo member of the CPC in charge of economy, Jaromír Dolanský, at the meeting of the CPC CC on 27 February 1957, as published by *Rudé právo* in a supplement of 16 pages.

[112] Antonín Novotný addressing the Eleventh CPC Congress on 18 June 1958, *Rudé právo*, supplement of 23 pages, no date, p. 9.

[113] Mencl, Ouředník, *op. cit., Život strany*, no. 16, p. 20. Engineer Jan Jirásek in his analysis of the twenty years of communist economy in Czechoslovakia wrote: "Some economists recognized the negative trends of the economic development relatively soon; in 1957 they obtained even a name: raising the effectiveness. And the first attempt at changes in economic conditions of industrial management began. The attempt failed early and completely: normative rules were deduced from the Third Five Year Plan which was so exorbitant that it collapsed the first year." See his article, *Doba*, no. 15, 17 Apr. 1969, p. 10.

[114] *Rudé právo*, 26 Feb. 1959.

[115] "Proti nemarxistickým teoriím 'decentralizace' řízení" ["Against Un-Marxist Theories of 'Decentralization' of Management"], *Tvorba*, 15 Jan. 1959, pp. 57-9.

[116] "During most of this period [1945-60] we lived in a state of tension which many would probably label as a crisis. It was not so much a crisis in terms of growth but in terms of shifting bottle-necks, shortages, disproportions and henceforth of popular dissatisfaction." Jaroslav Krejčí in Kusin, ed., *Cz. Reform*, p. 231.

new attack on "soft norms" but it was not easy to fool the workers any more as shown by a sample letter from a welder in the Lenin (Škoda) Works: "I work in Lenin Works, shed No. 47. Many of my fellow-workers are distrustful of the changes in the wages and tariff structure. They consider it to be an attack upon the wages."[117]

A campaign against "revisionism" and against "workers lacking class consciousness" continued: "For a certain part of the *less thinking working people* revisionism is attractive due to its apparent Marxist cloak. . . . *A battle for the mind of the people* must be our foremost duty."[118]

Both Jan Štern and Ota Šik — along with many other communist intellectuals participated in this continuing campaign at least till the end of the 1950s. Only much later did they express publicly what most of the workers already felt then; it took them a long time to learn from the workers about the causes of "an unheard of wastage of capital and production resources:"

> The basic problem is that wage earners are interested only in increasing their wages. . . . It is an important discovery that the nationalization of the means of production by communist states has in no way overcome the alienation of the workers from the factories but has even deepened it because of the extraordinary bureaucratization of management. Capital has been taken over by the state, not by society. The system has become state capitalist, or state monopolistic, not socialist. . . .[119]

In a few years, Šik clearly realized the awful consequences of state monopolization of all resources.

9. Conclusion

The extreme Soviet demands on Czechoslovak production and the accompanying totalitarian methods, taken over as part of the Stalinist model, brought the country into a deep and lasting crisis. Although the pressure and persecution applied mainly against the peasantry and non-communist middle class, the workers by their continuing resistance and unending urgent demands from below as well as by many ways of slowing down or pilfering the economy, using their theoretical prestige in Marxism-Leninism and practical working power, undermined the effectiveness of the whole system. The system, however, to a large degree and for quite a time, was supported and helped by the activities of the communist intelligentsia. But both Soviet demands and Soviet methods, in the end, antagonized many activists who were working for the Party and who were constantly faced with the workers' opposition.

At the Reading Conference, professor Seton-Watson expressed the generally accepted opinion when he said: "So the workers played a leading role in Poland from the beginning, in Hungary only in the crisis itself, but in Czechoslovakia

---

[117] Ladislav Panc in *Pravda* (Plzeň), 27 Jan. 1959.

[118] František Kraus (secretary of the CPC regional committee in Hradec Králové), *Pochodeň*, 30 Jan. 1959. Emphasis added. A detailed discussion of some of these questions pertaining to the 1950s can be found in Edward Taborsky: *Communism in Czechoslovakia, 1948–1960* (Princeton University Press, 1961).

[119] "Dr Ota Šik on the conflict between capital and wages: the Maudling memorandum: a communist critique," *The Times*, 4 Oct. 1972, p. 14.

they were, so to say, a supporting element, rather than an initiating element in the story."[120] For observers, looking mainly at the developments of 1967/8, this seems to be obvious, but a longer-time perspective, as suggested by this chapter, does show, how to a large degree, the communist intellectuals were much slower than the workers in comprehending the failures of the system. Often, on one side, were the intellectuals with their illusions and loyalty; on the other, the workers with their sense of reality and distrust of those in power. From a Marxist point of view, for the workers the communist intellectuals were not recognizable from the exploiting masters to whose class they belonged. And not only that: the constant refusal of workers to be fooled by one campaign after another and their successful attempt to safeguard for themselves at least a certain acceptable mode of life, in a system both economically and politically bankrupt, gradually exhausted many of the intellectuals who cooperated with the hated exploiters and willingly served as their "engineers of the soul," trying in vain to create an ideal "new socialist worker" who would forget his needs and would sacrifice himself for the benefit of the Soviet and satrap leaders. It can be said that here lies the basic tragedy of Marxism-Leninism. In the name, but climbing on the back of the workers to absolute power, the Marxist-Leninist intelligentsia idealizes the workers that it needs for its ascent. But once in power it wants from workers only two things: hard work and complete obedience. Therefore the ideal worker must be created as an idiotic robot who would slave happily and be rewarded by great parades, a lot of speeches, and occasional recitation by the masters of some verses of "workers' power". When such change of a normal worker into an ideal slave proves to be impossible, some members of the upper strata start wavering and eventually give up their useless drive. Some even rebel as part of the totalitarianized proletariat. Basically, Marxism-Leninism not only misuses but also misunderstands the worker. Therefore, genuine workers never last long in the leadership. People like Gottwald and Zápotocký, to name just two, can pose as workers' representatives since they belonged to the group for a very short time, but a closer look at their careers reveals that they did not like to remain workers and used the first occasion to organize other workers and to get above them.

At the end of the 1950s it was becoming clear to the managing class that there would be no great success achieved with the Soviet extensive and wasteful type of economy. It was not suitable for a small country with limited resources, especially since it had to struggle against the "lack of enthusiasm" displayed by the working people. It was mainly the working youth who were lost to the Party. Even the Party intelligentsia and some *apparatchiks* had, if not rebellious, or reformist and revisionist attitudes, then at least serious doubts about the whole system. It had to be radically changed although the approach of the Party bosses was cautious and hesitant. They still needed the shock of the economic failure of the early 1960s to open the closed gates to substantial reforms.[121] Propagandists (à la Šik) realized

---

[120] See Kusin, *Cz. Reform*, p. 97.

[121] "The hard lessons of the 1960s had yet to be learned to make the party leadership, technocrats, and theoretical economists realize the limitations imposed by the material forces of production on political decisions relating to allocation of productive factors and undertaken without rational economic calculations." Professor M. Bernasek in his paper presented at Reading. See Kusin, *Cz. Reform*, p. 209.

that exhortation to workers on moral grounds and official over-optimism about the blissful future, did not work and that at least a minimum of real "gulash" advantages and consumer goods would have to be produced.

Therefore, in the first phase, from 1948 till 1960, workers persuaded the intelligentsia and the *apparatchiks*, especially those in contact with the masses, that the system must be changed, that there was no way to improve it substantially just by pressing the workers harder and harder. We can come to a justified conclusion that the Party intelligentsia reacted to the stresses and debacle of Sovietization of Czechoslovakia in a slower and less radical way than the workers who at places acted violently in 1953 and 1956 but who sapped the strength of the system, especially its economic effectiveness, at all times between 1948 and 1960, in sabotaging the planners' and propagandists' dreams and by taking care of their own needs by helping themselves everywhere they could in a systematic, though unorganized, way. The push for changes came more from below than from above. Also it can be said right now that one of the reasons for the workers' slow acceptance of the reform movement in 1968 was not only their fear that in an efficiency drive they would lose some of their hard won (and often illegal) advantages, but their understandable conviction that they could not trust the Party intellectuals, who not long before participated eagerly in so many efforts of the regime to fool them and get more out of them for less and less. Without the workers' slow but very effective undermining of the exhortative and exploiting economy, there would have been no exhaustion and despair of the propagandists and the consequent realization that the system must be changed would have come even slower than it did. The working class can then be compared to a Samson who by its strength and position shook the palace of the ruling class to its foundations. Anyhow, the communist intellectuals belonged to the ruling class and when the palace started to shake they tried to save it by reforms and themselves with it, since the image of a revolution with communists burning and hanging from lampposts as in Budapest in 1956 had, at least for some of them, an obsessive warning quality.[122]

---

[122] In his recent book Zdeněk Mlynář, one of the important men in the *apparat* of the CPC till 1968, confirmed my old suspicion: "At the end of 1956 . . . we communists lived in fear. . . . There was present a fully concrete image of a crowd lynching the communists and hanging them on lampposts." See his *Mráz přichází z Kremlu* [*The Frost Comes from the Kremlin*]* (Cologne: Index, 1978), p. 52.

Chapter 2.

The ČSSR: Economic reform and scientific-technical revolution?

ALMOST as a reward for its successful weathering of the troubles of 1956 with the population, the CPC was allowed to declare in a new Constitution that socialism had been achieved in Czechoslovakia and that the path leading to the ideal era of communism was entered into. The Czechoslovak leaders, proud and flattered, kept repeating Khrushchev's statement that Czechoslovakia was marching to communism, together with the Soviet Union, as a vanguard of the world proletarian movement.

This boastful self-confidence was soon shattered by the fiasco of the Third Five-Year Plan (1961–5).

1. Economic failure and intellectual power

In the first half of the 1960s, the Czechoslovak production, until then the envy of other socialist countries, showed signs of depression and even disintegration. A series of partial reforms at the end of the 1950s did not help much, and the ensuing recentralization of the economy made matters worse. The Party felt obliged to accept a plan for a complete overhaul of the national economy.

The economic stagnation, and between 1962 and 1963 a retrogression, strengthened the hand of a group of young communist economists who were preparing a new model of economic management which became one of the major factors of change. Threatened by a complete failure and bankruptcy of the whole economy, several economically minded members of the Presidium were won over to the program of change. But the new economic model was only a part of a substantial reform which was step by step emerging in cultural and scientific magazines and which united a large group of specialists, scientists, and other members of the intelligentsia.

It is worth noting that Novotný's regime helped to prepare its own grave-diggers. Supposedly, after his meeting with President Kennedy in Vienna, Premier Khrushchev suggested to Novotný that he should create, for his own use, a brain trust similar to that which impressed him in America.[1] And so in the preparation of the Twelfth and Thirteenth Congresses of the CPC (1962 and 1966, respectively),

---

[1] Ota Šik claims that he was giving Novotný the same advice: "I used to tell him: 'Why don't you pick up the best brains in the whole country, why don't you create for yourself some committee of advisers? To be sure, no one demands that you be an expert on everything. Why don't you surround yourself by the best brains?'" See an interview with Šik by Marcel Brožík, *Kulturní noviny*, 29 Mar. 1968, pp. 1 and 3.

many specialized committees were formed. Scientists were asked to study the situation and prepare new programs for discussion by the Congresses. These committees were kept throughout the 1960s and were gradually enlarged. Because of this partly genuine and partly snobbish ambition of a Party that claimed to be led by scientific knowledge of the laws of history and society to really study it, several groups of capable reformers obtained necessary facilities, access to secret statistics or archives, and to forbidden domestic and foreign scientific literature. They also enjoyed at least a partial protection for their "revisionist" activities. The results of the study groups were supposed to remain secret or limited to scientific institutions and leading organs of the Party, but soon started to filter into public media. Thus the new model of "socialism with a human face" was born with the help of Party *apparatchiks*.

But as a typical bureaucrat of the Stalinist school, Novotný basically looked for autocratic remedies to the deteriorating state of the economy: "Central management must be strengthened and responsibility and state discipline must be improved at all stages."[2] Nevertheless, the "Twelfth Czechoslovak Party Congress decided that henceforth all proposed economic measures must be carefully examined and subjected to public discussion. Thus an atmosphere was created in which progressive thought could flourish."[3]

The planned targets of production were not nearly met and in fact the national income in 1963 fell even below the poor 1962 level.[4]

> "How could we," asked a prominent Czech economist rhetorically, "the most highly industrialized nation in Eastern Europe, have taken the Stalinist system of highly centralized, nonspecialized planning which sets the same broad quantitative norms for all fields of production — a system devised to increase radically the basic, heavy industrial plant of a backward nation — how could we have been so stupid as to take such a system and impose it lock, stock and barrel on our economy? It's incredible."[5]

The plan failed miserably. It was scrapped in August 1962. Today, after repeated failures and difficulties that Western economies suffered in the 1970s, it does not seem to be such an exceptional catastrophe as Czechoslovak economists thought it was in the 1960s. But then Western economies were blooming and for comrades who associated annual growth rates with the victorious building of socialism the shock of seeing the graphs and numbers declining was horrifying. It was a sufficient reason to rethink the whole system and eventually to change it. Even leading Party politicians, who during the 1950s proved to be among the most Stalinist and conservative in Eastern Europe, were willing to listen to reform economists and risk some changes.

---

[2] *Rudé právo*, 5 Dec. 1962.
[3] Harry G. Shaffer, "Out of Stalinism," *Problems of Communism*, xiv, 5 (Sept.–Oct. 1965), p. 35.
[4] For a good contemporary description of "unrelieved squalor" and of the crisis in Czechoslovakia of 1963, see George Bailey, "Kafka's Nightmare Comes True," *The Reporter*, 7 May 1964, pp. 15-20. It was reprinted in Irwin Isenberg, ed., *Ferment in Eastern Europe* (New York: H. W. Wilson Company, 1965), pp. 130-40. Bailey's reported verdict: "Sixteen years after the great experiment of Communist planning began, all are agreed that it has resulted in an almost unqualified failure." *Ibid.*, p. 134.
[5] *Ibid.*, pp. 134-5.

2. Workers opposed, intellectuals changing

To use Marxist terms favored in Eastern Europe and at some Western universities, the whole problem of reforms, however, concerned only the ruling superstructure of the Czechoslovak society. The technocrats pressed for reforms only when shocked by economic failures. Most of the workers did not trust the regime, did not believe that it could reform itself, and wanted to be left alone.[6] They either conformed only externally, trying to get the best possible deal for themselves by unconventional means,[7] hoped that it would collapse, or rebelled against it by running away from it (many refugees from Czechoslovakia were of workers' origin). Many even attempted to prepare a revolution. Trials of clandestine groups became quite frequent and publicity was given to workers' participation, as can be seen from the following example.

The author of an article about a group of workers on trial started by lamenting the fact that "only ten years ago everything was simpler." Enemies could be easily identified; they were of bourgeois or petit-bourgeois origin: "These times are gone!" Then she proceeded to describe a case tried in Prague. Five young workers, born between 1944 and 1947 — that means between the ages of eighteen and twenty-one — four of them bricklayers and one apprentice of Town-cleaning, during the months of March and April of 1962, distributed hundreds of leaflets, printed with the help of a child's toy printing press. They called for an uprising against the regime. The authoress stressed that their parents also belonged to the working class. Already in 1961, one of the masons was telling the others that "in the ČSSR there is no freedom for the working people but only slavery." He used to hear from older bricklayers that "once, out of a single season's earnings, it was possible to live for a whole year." According to the writer, the mason also heard that "America is a country of unlimited opportunities . . . where every worker has a car." In Czechoslovakia, "he did not enjoy anything."[8]

The last sentence does not exaggerate. From surveys of responses by Czech and Slovak refugees to questioning by American and European public opinion specialists, I remember the usual, and mutual, surprise when the refugees almost always answered the question about what they liked in communist Czechoslovakia by a single word: "Nothing!" Only some of them, being dragged to it, unwillingly at the end, tried to please their interrogators by finding at least something positive in a system which for them represented an absolute negation of life. It could not be enjoyed but only suffered.

---

[6] "At one meeting in a factory we put a leading question to the young people: 'What do you want us to do?' After a long silence, someone said quietly: 'Nothing. Just leave us alone.'" *Rudé právo*, 12 Jan. 1964.

[7] "On 29 May, 1968, BBC-1 Television showed a report by their *24 Hours* team from Czechoslovakia including interviews with ordinary Czech men and women. A woman told the reporter that the Czechs would have to learn again how to be honest because the inefficiency of the previous system was such that everybody had to be ruthless and dishonest to provide for himself and his family. Everybody was on his own, people did not dare to talk to each other. Other interviewees explained how they had been stealing things from their offices or workshops because these things could not be obtained in any other way. Stealing was considered normal." Ljubo Sirc, *Economic Devolution in Eastern Europe* (London: Longmans, 1969), p. 63.

[8] Olga Šulcová, *Kulturní tvorba*, 30 May 1963, p. 8.

In the élite's superstructure, in order to reform the system, a whole setup of mental images and slogans had to be changed first. To workers the problem seemed to be clear long before, as one of the main Party propagandists admitted: "The common sense of the working class long opposed arguments about the irreplaceability of heavy industry."[9] For the political economists who began to attack some of the basic beliefs of Stalinism in Czechoslovakia, we can start by quoting from an article *Radoslav Selucký* published in 1962. He wrote that propagandists who for years kept talking about harmonious development of a socialist society,

> are now mildly horrified when instead of angelic conflictlessness and perfect harmony of interests they see real life, full of discord and contradictions. . . . It is very difficult, and not seldom even painful, to replace faith in an ideal world by really scientific recognition and especially comprehension of its real substance.[10]

After careful consideration of communist leaders' sensitivities, Selucký came to the aim of his appeal: "The roots of the daily conflicts" are not in survival of capitalism in people's minds but in "the low level of economic management and planning." Only "hopelessly naïve cultural workers" can be upset about manual workers demanding better pay and higher standard of living:

> If people on a mass scale desire to satisfy their needs, it is impossible to brand these needs as manifestation of petit bourgeoisie, a luxury, expression of egoism, and to recommend to them modesty and sacrifice. . . . For example, the mass desire of people to have a modern and comfortable apartment is not luxury but a natural, objectively existing, and legitimate need of a socialist man. . . . The claim of tenants to have their dwellings heated in winter is not a mark of over-indulgence but an expression of basic human needs. . . . If a broken water-tap is running and I cannot live to see communal service, I might be hundred times persuaded of the immorality of illicit work, finally I will call for it. . . . So far no one was ever able to get rid of a black market (or illicit work) . . . only by declarations, appeals, and punishments without eliminating their real causes, namely eliminating the lack of certain goods or services. . . . At many meetings I witnessed how some people saw the main condition exclusively in the education of a new man and, at the same time, underestimated a condition which is much, much more important: there must be absolute abundance of everything.[10]

For people used to freedom such enumeration of the basic ABC probably seems to be superfluous but after fourteen years of the Soviet system in Czechoslovakia, even such an article as this was daring and Selucký would soon provoke the ire of the highest authority in the State, since he was undermining the ideological pillars of the dictatorship.

A few months later Selucký continued his attack on some of the basic articles of faith that were part of the ideology of the ruling group. He summed up his criticism of the entire set of Stalinist economic dogmas as "the cult of the plan:"

> This latter gradually brought about a situation in which the measure of people's merit ceased to be their concrete socially useful work, having been replaced by another, purely administrative one — the fulfillment of the planned indexes. The pursuit of indexes became the leading idea of society. . . ., the plan was elevated to the status of a moral code. What should have only been an instrument had become the goal! . . . What good does it do if the railroads fulfill all their indexes regarding transport, when the transport of many products is itself

---

[9] Jiří Sekera, *Nová mysl*, no. 1, Jan. 1963, pp. 1–11.
[10] *Literární noviny*, 20 Oct. 1962, pp. 6–7.

unnecessary? What good does it do if productivity is higher in the case of washing machines than in the case of refrigerators, when the stores are full of the former while people are queuing for the latter?

According to Selucký, workers became "victims of a planning mania."[11]

This hit a sensitive spot. President Novotný felt obliged to answer publicly and accused Selucký that "he would like to make anarchy and chaos prevail in our economy."[12] A few days later, in an authoritative editorial, written by Jan Fojtík (who after the Soviet invasion continued to function as one of the highest Party propagandists), the Party daily declared that the only permissible area of discussion was "how to increase the authority of the plan, how to improve the planning of our national economy."[13]

3. The decisive year 1963: From economic stagnation to economic discussion

During the year of 1963 the economic situation grew steadily worse, intensified by bad management.[14] The need for a radical change was consequently felt with increasing urgency. Novotný's government — losing its unity — was willing to permit a thorough study and discussion of economic matters but, at the same time, hated to see some basic sacrosancta of Stalinism attacked and ridiculed.

Authors in scientific and literary journals, which were open to scientists and economists as well, demanded taking a different road to socialism. They wanted a consistent democracy that would protect the individual from intimidation, an application of science in planning and management. They hoped for new scope to be given to qualified economists to apply their science in practice. They requested an end to "barracks" form of collective life, higher level of university teaching, return to humanism, and protection of human interests that were lost in bureaucratic machinery.[15]

The Leninist argument that the leading role of the proletariat was represented by the Communist Party, came under review in an article which hit another sensitive target:

> The dogma of the immaculate origin of the proletariat has persisted for so long that the proletariat has been looked upon as the most progressive element there is. . . . The law of social origin has become equal to the law of heredity. While we know how to deal, say, in biology or in pedagogy with the pseudo-scientific overrating of heredity, when it comes to proletarian origin, we have known nothing but sheer idealism. With enthusiasm and with a kind of

[11] See *Kulturní tvorba*, 7 Feb. 1963; parts translated in *East Europe*, xii, 5 (May 1963), pp. 13–14.
[12] *Rudé právo*, 24 Mar. 1963.
[13] *Ibid.*, 29 Mar. 1963.
[14] An unusual exercise in public relations, called "Free Forum," a radio and television program, during which citizens could ask questions and various state and Party officials answered them, was dropped after eight weeks since it showed that shortcomings were too many and were widespread: in consumer goods, especially children's clothing, dairy products, beef, pork, sauerkraut, non-alcoholic beverages, women's stockings, synthetic fibers, coal, chinaware, teaspoons, repairs, etc. See *New York Times*, 11 Aug. 1963.
[15] Excerpts from the Czechoslovak press·in *East Europe*, xii, 11 (Nov. 1963), pp. 20–4.

flagellant exstasy, we have stepped aside in order to make room for those we were sure would never falter.[16]

The author of this revealing essay concerning one of the basic articles of faith also attacked those who kept using the formula in order to cover up their enslavement and exploitation of workers. He reminded them of, and compared them with, the "wrecks of society" in Engels's discussion of the *Lumpenproletariat*. Many a Party activist must have recognized himself as "the petit-bourgeois disguised as a worker" or as one of the "elements with a murky past who demagogically boast of their proletarian origin and of their dislike of education." And Rašla added: "This mercenary *Lumpenproletariat* is ready to join (or to elbow its way into) any movement which gives it any hope of spoils. ... These 'revolutionaries' will join any movement proclaiming a change of the existing order." He expressed the hope that the workers would be able, in time, to dissociate themselves from "the rapacious and parasitic elements." Sigmund Freud would have been pleased to see how violent a reaction this article provoked.[17]

A conference of leading Czechoslovak economists took place in Prague in November of 1963 and was allowed to publish its devastating criticism of the old economic system and its call for a radical change in the direction of the economy. Individual speakers condemned the "cult of the plan," and requested the introduction of a price system based on the law of supply and demand. They stressed that "it is necessary that we begin to criticize socialism as a social order," and deplored "completely irrational foreign currencies and exchange relations," the low standard of Czechoslovak economy as a science, the lack of access to relevant facts, non-availability not only of books by Keynes and Lange, but even of Soviet authors of the 1920s and 1930s, as well as the low educational level of factory managers and executives who "often find it difficult to multiply simple fractions."[18]

Out of the conference came a resolution calling for reversing the established order of things: it is not the Party that should lead the economists but rather the scientists who should provide the basis for Party economic policy. It was a new and radical proposal for an end to the claim that the Party has the right to lead everybody in every field, enlighted by its mysterious knowledge of historical and social laws. (Gradually, scientists and professionals in other disciplines challenged the totalitarian system, too.)

At the end of the crucial year 1963, the Central Committee of the CPC met and announced its decision. The main speech was made by the chairman of the Ideological Commission of the CC, Vladimír Koucký, who criticized writers for their views but, at the same time, accepted many of their observations. The Party decided to permit economic discussion to go on and promised to allow

[16] Anton Rašla, *Kultúrny život*, leading article, 16 Nov. 1963; excerpts in *East Europe*, xiii, 2 (Feb. 1964), p. 24.

[17] See, for instance, František Havlíček, "Socialism Ensures the Free and Active Development of Everybody," *Rudé právo*, 7 Dec. 1963. Havlíček, after a career as a propagandist in the Party *apparat* was then deputy to the chief editor of the main Party daily. He acknowledged, however, that "dishonest and unworthy people may find their way into the Communist Party, into the apparatus of the socialist state."

[18] *Hospodářské noviny*, 8 and 15 Nov. 1963.

experimentation, but to limit the exchange of views to professional circles and to use administrative measures against cultural magazines. Economic reforms were considered necessary but the freedom of journalists was judged to be exorbitant.

In the field of economy proper, Koucký acknowledged that "leading executives in the economy . . . possess rather scant political and economic knowledge and vision" and that "established production lines are continued, regardless of whether society needs them or whether they spout poor-quality merchandise which is not only of no use at home but which also damages our good name abroad." He announced an end to the levelling of remuneration — one of the main demands of the intelligentsia. He welcomed "the constructive contribution of the discussion regarding the enlistment of the help of science in planning and management" but refused a "general criticism addressed to planning" because "it could lead to indiscipline." Profit, profitability, and credit might be introduced into the economy but "in harmony with the principle of planning." In the more directly ideological field of his responsibility, Koucký called for a counter-offensive of Party hardliners against what he called "a doubtful uniformity of cultural journalism."[19]

This Party policy, as announced by Koucký, of chasing two hares at the same time, of reform but little or no change, was followed till the end of 1967.

The December plenum of the CC also heard a speech of a much more forward looking character. *Ota Šik* defended principles of market economy that should replace central planning, as practised till then, and criticized those bureaucrats who are unable to "overcome a simplified, schematic, and stiffened method of thinking that all of us more or less absorbed during the long years of the Stalinist cult. . . . There are people who are afraid that through new methods and suggestions they could lose their present positions and comfortable life." It was a direct challenge to Novotný's leadership and to Party bureaucrats entrenched in high positions. In his CC address Šik outlined a new system of socialist economy based on market relations and profitability, and stressed that even the Soviet Union sooner or later will have to embark on such a program. Czechoslovakia, without Russia's reserves of manpower and its relative self-sufficiency, "must eventually take the lead and begin to solve a fundamental issue which has not yet become so urgent in other socialist countries."[20]

At the end of the year 1963, several authors gave expression to the general feeling among the country's intellectuals that the ice of Stalinism finally started to crack and the floes to move. In Prague a communist poet wrote: "There have been years of stagnation, years of dilemma. . . . [The year of 1963 was] a good year. . . . Thinking has revived, the will to express views without impediment has strengthened; a principled, unyielding attitude has taken root."[21]

In Bratislava, where Dubček was already in charge, a Slovak writer spoke of the year 1963 as one of "rebirth," of "antidogmatism," and of a new kind of socialism: "Socialism has acquired characteristics and attributes known before only in medicinal doses. It has become human, it has humanized itself."[22]

[19] *Rudé právo*, 21 Dec. 1963.
[20] *Rudé právo*, 22 Dec. 1963.
[21] Jiří Šotola in *Kulturní tvorba*, 22 Dec. 1963.
[22] Pavol Števček in *Kultúrny život*, 21 Dec. 1963.

At least for the moment, Masaryk started to win over Lenin; ideals of democratic socialism over totalitarian import. Czechoslovak communists attempted to humanize Soviet communism. The economic failure and obvious need for reform facilitated the attempt. Between 1963 and 1968, the ambitions of the reformers remained constant and consistent but it took them four more years to dislodge Novotný from power.

4. Problems of the New Economic Model

Figures for the performance of the national economy continued to be alarming. Not even the modest target of a 1 per cent increase of gross industrial production was attained in 1963 and it actually fell below the 1962 level.

The Central Committee of the CPC met again on 21–2 January 1964, to consider the serious economic depression. The secretary of the Party in charge of economic matters, Drahomír Kolder, enumerated many failures of the economic policy, and announced that the change must be radical. The production of unusable goods continued to plague the Czechoslovak economy. In a country with a large unsatisfied demand for consumer goods, Kolder reported:

> The number of rejects in production continued to grow, . . . stocks increased to seven billion crowns [one billion US dollars]. . . . One of the most serious problems of our foreign trade is the poor quality of products, their unsatisfactory technical standard, and their insufficient adaptation to market demands abroad.[23]

Prime Minister Jozef Lenárt talked about the same problem on the radio on 7 February and said that the number of rejects rose nearly 12 per cent in 1963, despite the fact that the industrial output declined.[24] A few months later, the total value of accumulated and unusable inventories was estimated to amount to almost one-quarter of the national income![25] These figures persuaded almost everyone that in an economy of scarcity to continue with such waste of investment in capital, labor, and material would not make sense. The production for production's sake had to stop.

Professor *Ota Šik* prepared himself well for the coming task. After the premature cancellation of the mini-reform of the economy at the end of the 1950s, he withdrew from public activities and worked on his doctoral thesis which won him the first

---

[23] *Rudé právo*, 26 Jan. 1964.

[24] Quoted in *East Europe*, xiii, 3 (Mar. 1964), p. 31.

[25] *Hospodářské noviny*, no. 12 (1964), p. 31. The problem of accumulating and unsellable stocks, however, continued to plague the Czechoslovak economy. As a Polish economic writer, Stanislav Albinowski, reported in *Tribuna Ludu*, 2 Sept. 1968, in 1967, out of the fifteen billion crowns of growth in national income over 1966, about eleven billion (that means more than 73 per cent!) went toward adding to the stocks of unsold products. By the end of the first half of 1968, the accumulated unsold inventories were valued at two hundred billion crowns, a sum equivalent to the entire Czechoslovak national income in 1967! Quoted from Harry G. Trend, "Pre-August Trends in Czechoslovak Economic Organization and Policy — III," *Radio Free Europe Research*, 18 Nov. 1968, on p. 7 of 30 polycopied pages.

Ph.D. (Soviet style) in Marxist economy in his country.[26] At the Party Congress in 1962, Ota Šik was elevated to full membership of the Central Committee of the CPC.

At the turn of 1962/3, at a special seminar at Liblice under the aegis of the Socialist Academy, Šik, for the first time, presented to a gathering of almost three hundred economic specialists (both theoretical and practical) a rounded conception of a new economic model of management. His speech was then widely distributed.

In 1963 he became Director of the Economic Institute of the Academy of Sciences. Since the end of 1963, he was chairing an official governmental commission of experts, composed originally of twelve economists and managers but later substantially enlarged. The commission prepared a draft, containing 500 pages, of a new economic system.[27] The basic idea of their work — how to fight against the built-in-the-system waste of resources — was well expressed in one of Šik's books:

> Under the old administrative planning, the main interest of the enterprises in setting up the plans was to gain as much capital as possible for investment and all the manpower they could, with as low production targets as possible and to this end they subordinated all the required planning data and information. But if there is consistent utilization of market relationships, they will be interested in such investments and future production conditions (capacities, manpower, etc.) that will enable the enterprises to achieve the highest effect with the relatively lowest volume of factor inputs.[28]

The Presidium of the CPC returned the proposal several times for amendments but finally the Central Committee formally adopted its principles at the end of January 1965.[29] Capital investment was curtailed and consumer needs stressed. The year 1965 was declared to be a year of experimentation in selected enterprises. By April one hundred enterprises were operating according to the new plan but with fixed prices still in force. The main branches of the economy would use the New Economic Model in 1966.

Two problems continued to disturb the economic reformers: fixed prices (on some 1,500,000 different categories of goods) and politically appointed managers of enterprises. The economic reform did not have any chance of success without a radical change in those two crucial categories. Many studies and articles were published during 1964–5 in favor of such a change but the leadership of the Party strongly objected since two important levers of centralized manipulation were involved — administration by directives and cadre policies. Ota Šik and

---

[26] It was published in 1963 under the title *Ekonomika, zájmy, politika: jejich vzájemné vztahy v socialismu* [*Economy, Interests, Politics: Their Mutual Relations in Socialism*]. Two years later this book would be published in Moscow in Russian. In the preface to its second, revised edition in 1968 Šik wrote: "The most important aim of the book was to contribute to a refutation of some basic Stalinist theoretical axioms that have served . . . for generations as a theoretical system unreservedly accepted."

[27] *Volksstimme*, the Austrian Communist Party daily, 12 Jan. 1965.

[28] *Plan and Market Under Socialism* (Prague: Academia, 1967), p. 356.

[29] *Rudé právo*, 30 Jan. 1965. In 1965 Šik published in Prague another programmatic book, *K problematice socialistických zbožních vztachů* [*On Problems of Socialist Market Relations*].

others kept stressing the all-important role of prices in an efficient allocation of productive resources, but with little success.[30]

The January 1964 resolution of the CPC CC provided that priority must be given to capable managers without regard to their party affiliation, but no radical change in top managerial positions took place. Drahomír Kolder publicly interpreted this policy as meaning that existing managers should change their views; they themselves do not have to be replaced by new people.[31] But almost one-third of the directors of the Czechoslovak enterprises and plants (exactly 31.4 per cent) did not possess more than an elementary education.[32] Again, Selucký was not alone in attacking this dangerously weak point in the economy, but to no avail. With economic simpletons in charge of large enterprises it was extremely difficult to introduce scientific methods. Much of the struggle in the country was between loyal, but retarded communists, and the more intelligent ones.[33]

Eugen Loebl, provoked by dogmatic theories, published mainly in the Slovak press a series of articles on the problem of economic management.[34] He stimulated a discussion during which he was attacked from all sides.[35] Even Ota Šik thought that Loebl went dangerously far.[36] After more than one year, Loebl could return to his criticism that material incentives should not be overestimated as the only medicine needed. At the beginning of 1965, he attempted to show the difference between the old type of personal management and the more modern management by a board of specialists using an American example. This way he could denounce abhorrent dictatorship at home while not hurting native tyrants' sensitivities:

> [During World War II] Ford deliberately managed his enterprise as the property of one person and he alone made every important decision. It was actually a dictatorship of one man, who had at his disposal a perfect system of spies, his own secret police, with whose help he was able to control every employee. He fired everyone who made an independent decision or failed to follow his wishes to the letter. Thus he gradually lost his best people. The new management adopted a fundamentally different system.

Then Loebl attacked the Party managers for a system based on command and fear, and their usually very poor character. He tried to show the connection between intellectual plus moral problems and economic deficiencies:

> Under certain conditions it is possible to increase the profitability of an undertaking substantially, without any investment, without new technology, without the introduction of more modern equipment. . . . The fact that the system of directive planning simply negates the

[30] For a survey of some other economists' writings, see H. Gordon Skilling, *Czechoslovakia's Interrupted Revolution* (Princeton, N.J.: Princeton University Press, 1976), esp. pp. 57–62 and 119–25.

[31] See his article "Party Management of National Economy," *Nová mysl*, no. 8 (1966).

[32] Radoslav Selucký, *Mladá fronta*, 21 Nov. 1964.

[33] A Slovak editor wrote: "In quite a few factories the director has not even the qualifications of a foreman, in quite a few enterprises the executives are hardly fit to hold any job at all. No wonder such people hold onto their jobs tooth and nail." Vladimír Ferko, *Predvoj*, 28 Mar. 1968. The lack of qualifications also marked people in high positions.

[34] See especially his article "On Dogmatism in Economic Thought", *Kultúrny život*, 28 Sept. 1963, p. 6. Also in *Hospodářské noviny*, 15 Nov. 1963.

[35] Milan Kodaj in *Pravda*, 18 Nov. 1963; Vladimír Gerloch and Milan Plachý in *Hospodářské noviny*, 29 Nov. 1963. On Loebl's reprimand by the Central Committee, see *Rudé právo*, 3 Apr. 1964.

[36] "How Antidogmatism Should Not Look," *Kultúrny život*, 2 Nov. 1963, p. 3.

intellectual abilities of man, deprives the economy of the very element which is, to a decisive degree, its source of wealth. . . . Creative thinking cannot be simply commanded. . . .

It is also possible to calculate the worth of character. . . . What damage was caused to our national economy by bad character traits of, unfortunately, quite a few of our chiefs of enterprises. . . . We would find that without making any investments, we would save hundreds of millions by the mere dismissal of such bosses.[37]

For the dogmatists, and also for some of the reformers, Loebl's direct and ethically motivated criticism was too provocative. The author, however, clearly enjoyed solid backing by the Slovak Communist Party leader Dubček and also by his friend Gustáv Husák who acted as a strong political figure behind the Bratislava scene.[38] And so Eugen Loebl continued his publications in which he dared to denounce even the "repressive *apparat* that mercilessly liquidated everybody who would voice criticism and often his family members, too."[39] Touching upon the question of state police power (backed by Soviet specialists) was probably going too far even for Zdeněk Mlynář, prominent among the reformers, who attacked Loebl's "deeply naïve idealistic opinions."[40]

Loebl's major work was devoted to an attempt at a modern revision of Adam Smith's exploration of the wealth of nations.[41] It was published in 1967 and was based on his solitary thinking in Czechoslovak communist prisons. Some of the basic ideas should be quoted here rather then transcribed since they give ample proof of the basic change in Loebl's philosophy, away from materialist determinism to spiritual and organic freedom:

Natural forces mastered by human intellect in a steadily growing measure carry out work instead of man. (p. 23)

A machine represents intellectual contribution contained in applied science. (p. 62)

A harmonious evolution of a society in general and of the economics in particular depends on a harmonious evolution of the total intellectual level. Interruption of such an evolution brings disharmony and a crisis situation. (p. 82)

For the growth of wealth will be responsible, first of all, the class of intellectual workers. (p. 87)

If in an economy based upon empirical thought and thus on the human working force the wealth of a nation was directly proportional to the amount of exerted physical work, for a modern economy a different principle is valid which we would formulate as follows: the wealth of a nation is directly proportional to the share of mental and indirectly proportional to the share of physical work. (p. 90)

What is the source of wealth in a modern economy? . . . . The applied natural sciences. (p. 163)

For his model of a "lucractive economy" Loebl then postulated two basic "bipolar" principles: (1) "The purpose of the economy is production for

---

[37] *Kultúrny život*, 16 Jan. 1965.

[38] "From 1963 onwards Bratislava was teeming with political and intellectual activity. The most active were the historians, economists and philosophers. . . . He [Husák] soon became the most influential man in Bratislava intellectual circles." Eugene Steiner, *The Slovak Dilemma* (London: Cambridge University Press, 1973), p. 122.

[39] *Kultúrny život*, 19 Mar. 1965, pp. 3 and 8.

[40] *Rudé právo*, 6 and 8 Apr. 1965.

[41] *Úvahy o duševnej práci a bohatstve národa* [*Reflections on Mental Work and National Wealth*] (Bratislava: Vydavatelstvo Slovenskej akadémie vied, 1967).

consumption, respectively for the consumer," and (2) "The wealth of a nation is directly proportional to the intellectual level of the production process and its regulation."[42] Both principles come together in a consumer-oriented production based on application of science. The accent on both must be understood in the context of a system which for two decades negated basic needs of both consumers and scientists:

> The model of a lucrative economy is based on the recognition that science is becoming in a decisive manner a wealth-creating factor and that the whole economic system must be organized in such a way that the application of science serves the consumer.[43]

Radoslav Selucký, reviewing Loebl's book, welcomed his stimulating ideas but criticized its second, practical, part where he found his essays "surprising by their naïvety and utopianism." He also objected to Loebl's stress on consumption as the purpose of production.[44]

Although *Ota Šik* held some positions necessary for an active and decisive role in the introduction of the New Economic Model, his power to do so was very much restricted. Like other economic reformers he tried to win the battle of wits through publications and to put pressure of public opinion, as much as it could assert itself, on the Party and managerial bureaucracy which hindered his work. Again and again he returned to the problem of unsatisfied consumer demand and of state production for production's sake which was filling warehouses with useless stocks worth billions of Czechoslovak crowns.[45]

Early in the year of 1966, Šik published a three-part analysis of the difficulties met in implementing the new economic system. As one of the major problems he singled out the failure to revise wholesale prices in time and the fact that monopolistic trusts, because of their authoritarian habits, instead of taking the new "orientation indices" accept them as the old "directive indices" as absolute orders from above. Also some workers had shown displeasure at the introduction of the New Economic Model because they have been accustomed to an easy life.[46]

The *workers' wages* were generally low and they complained about many other things. The department of sociology at the J. E. Purkuně University in Brno conducted in 1967 a nation-wide public opinion poll and some of the results were published in the daily press. According to this survey, 76% of those questioned claimed that better results could be achieved at their places of work if they were to receive a better remuneration. Forty-seven per cent considered the amenities at their plant insufficient, 54% complained about the lack of showers, 62% about excessive noise, 55% were dissatisfied with the facilities for taking their meals, 47% were unhappy about the poor organization of work. Only fewer than two-thirds were employed in the branch for which they were trained, and more than one-half of those interviewed would have liked to change their occupation because they were dissatisfied with their prospects of higher pay or of advancement in their work.[47]

[42] *Ibid.*, pp. 207–8.
[43] *Ibid.*, p. 208.
[44] *Kultúrny život*, 2 June 1967, p. 3.
[45] See his *Economic Planning and Management in Czechoslovakia* (Prague: Orbis, 1965).
[46] *Rudé právo*, 18, 22, and 23 Feb. 1966.
[47] See *Práce*, 25 Aug. 1967.

At the same time, their *standard of living* remained poor even according to other criteria. The Slovak microcensus of 1967 revealed that only 6.39% of workers had satisfactory houses or apartments with running water, electricity, bathroom, and a water-closet. And 11.12% lived in apartments considered dangerous to health. Although the author claimed that the answer the workers gave to the question of their own ranking of themselves in society showed their "great self-confidence" in their "high social self-classification," the figures quoted do not support this view: selecting their rank according to participation in management of the society and their position in it out of six possibilities, workers mostly placed themselves in the low fourth or fifth category, 34.27% or 24.50%, respectively. The first, highest, rank attracted only 4.25% of answers but the sixth, the lowest, 6.62%. The second position selected 11.5% workers and the third 19.21%. Most of the workers clearly did not consider themselves to be masters of their own "workers' state" or to rank in their socialist society very high.[48]

Ota Šik kept returning to the problem of workers' unhappiness and of their low wage levels as well as to the uselessness of campaigns which bombarded them with exhortations to work harder and more just for the glory of their masters. In a book published in Prague in the 1960s he chose his words cautiously:

> The distaste of dogmatists for using economic instruments orienting the labor of people and their preference for moral stimuli comes, for the major part, from the fact that it is much easier and simpler to pronounce political appeals, slogans, moral entreaties, general criticism, and so on.[49]

Six years later, in an interview in exile, he was speaking about the same problem but more clearly:

> We had a situation where no one had any incentive to work harder or to improve his qualifications, because neither hard work nor a diploma could help him better his personal condition. . . . This was an invitation to apathy, conformity, mediocrity, idleness and a general reluctance to tackle anything but the easiest and least responsible jobs. People accepted the fact that they earned little and their answer to this poor reward was to give very little in return. We discovered after two decades of bitter experience that at this particular phase of the development of society the majority of people will not work harder or better unless they get more money for their work, and unless the goods they want to buy with their money are available. Ignore this rule and you can be sure that your economy will be heading for ruin.[50]

The reformers hoped that the change would lead the workers to perform better. But the workers could not be sure that it would not remain the only result of the reform, since it obviously appealed to conservative Party leaders who expected to frustrate other, more popular, parts of the reform. And so, at the beginning, most of the population did not trust the New Economic Model and considered it just another governmental trick to give people less money for more work.

If at first the new system of economic management provoked more problems than advantages, it started to win friends where it mattered most — in the highest

---

[48] See František Taský, "The Workers' Class in Slovakia After the Victory of Socialist Revolution," *Sociológia*, no. 1, Feb. 1973, pp. 17 and 27.

[49] See his *Plan and Market Under Socialism* (Prague: Academia, 1967), p. 364.

[50] George R. Urban, "A Conversation with Ota Šik," *Survey*, vol. 19, no. 2 (Spring 1973), pp. 256-7.

organs of the CPC. For instance, Drahomír Kolder, Head of the Party Economic Commission, seemed to be constantly moving closer to the ideas of the reformers. At the Thirteenth Congress of the CPC (31 May–4 June 1966), he declared: "This reform is of the utmost importance and must be carried out with utmost urgency."[51]

At the Congress another important member of the Presidium (often considered only second to Novotný), Jiří Hendrych, defended the economic reform on ideological grounds and as necessary for technological progress.[52] Although Ota Šik announced his intention to speak President Novotný did not want to give him the permission. It was Kolder who finally persuaded him that Šik should be given a chance to address the gathering. Novotný has regretted it ever since.[53] Ota Šik later commented: "I came on after all, with only one speaker left to go, and I expressed radical ideas. The result was extraordinary. The clapping went on for fifteen minutes. On the platform Brezhnev sat ice-cold and tight-lipped."[54]

Novotný's stubborn resistance to the New Economic Model proved to be one of the main reasons for his defeat two years later. But as long as he stayed in power he could repeatedly frustrate the economic reform.

A Viennese paper quoted a current joke from Prague: the New Economic Model resembles an imaginary order to taxi-cab drivers in Prague to test — for the sake of a compromise — a new circulation plan by a switch to driving on the left, while the rest of the cars would continue driving on the right. And the reporter added:

> "My plan," said Professor Šik, "has met a similar fate. They strangled it by 'testing it' only in individual plans and in matters that are atypical and of small import." . . . Czechoslovak experts with whom I talked recently seemed more skeptical than they were a half-year ago. The Šik plan, they say, is already being strangled.[55]

There was no hope for a successful economic reform without previous political changes. "The subordination of economics to politics in the non-market model is almost absolute."[56] Until 1966 Ota Šik and many other economic reformers

---

[51] Quoted from *Rudé právo* in "A Congress of Organizers," *East Europe*, xv, 7 (July 1966), p. 42. Ota Šik later wrote: "Members of the Central Committee saw the growing criticism and discontent from below." See his interview in *Kulturní noviny*, 29 Mar. 1968, p. 3.

[52] *East Europe*, as in footnote 51.

[53] "Comrade Kolder told comrade Novotný that Šik also should take part in the discussion. . . . An overwhelming majority of the congress delegates expressed agreement by an almost demonstrative applause; comrade Novotný, however, flew into a rage and said to Kolder: 'Certainly, I shouldn't have allowed this Šik to speak. You've forced me into it.'" Interview with Ota Šik, *Kulturní noviny*, 29 Mar. 1968, pp. 1 and 3. For this important glimpse of gradually shifting alliances in the Party leadership, we have also Novotný's testimony from his address to the graduating cadets of the Military Colleges on 2 August 1967: "We have permitted Šik to write and say things here, and even at the Thirteenth Congress to give, as the last speaker, a stormy speech about democracy. Naturally, when this was discussed at the Congress, the writers also caught on, and all stormed: democracy! democracy!" This quote from Novotný's address was used by Mencl and Ouředník as part of a motto in their series of reports "What Happened in January," *Život strany*, no. 14 (July 1968), p. 22.

[54] See Ota Šik's interview in *Manchester Guardian Weekly*, 22 Apr. 1972.

[55] *Die Presse*, 5 Oct. 1966; English excerpts in "Šik versus Schweik in Czechoslovakia," *East Europe*, xvi, 2 (Feb. 1967), pp. 21–2.

[56] Radoslav Selucký: *Economic Reforms in Eastern Europe: Political Background and Economic Significance* (Trans. Zdeněk Eliáš; New York: Praeger, 1972), p. 20.

believed that decentralization of the economic sphere would be followed by a political democratization. Although, for obvious reasons, in a political dictatorship they did not push this expectation to the forefront of their public pronouncements, it was present in many of their writings. Ota Šik at the Thirteenth CPC Congress stressed that the economic reform would "mean a great step towards the democratization of our society." His speech at the crucial Central Committee meeting in December 1967 contained concrete proposals for a democratization of the CPC and of the State.[57] Later, Radoslav Selucký made this comment:

> Thus the attempt to marketize the Czechoslovak socialist economy comprised from the very beginning a very important political implication: a decentralized economic basis was to influence the political superstructure, an abolition of the command *economic* system was to initiate the weakening of the command *political* system. . . . It is evident that the concept of marketization resulted from both economic and socio-political analysis of the failing command system in Czechoslovakia.
>
> The Czechoslovak leadership of the day did not accept *this* concept of the economic reform, however. As soon as 1966 it became quite evident that political change and reform will have to precede, rather than follow, an economic reform.[58]

The decision of Czechoslovak economists to work for the democratization of their country was one of the main causes of the profound changes in 1968. Politics again proved to be more important than economics; after all, this should be considered a genuine part and lesson of Leninism since 1917.

5. Political and social conditions of the scientific-technical revolution

> People are getting impatient. . . . How long is this going to last? people ask. Will our troubles ever cease?. . . For the public the new system has become synonymous with the need for change. . . .
>
> As 1967 opens, we are obviously on the threshold of a major ideological battle over the consistent application of the new principles of management and the threshold of decisive conflicts between the old and the new, . . . between traditional ideas and progressive, scientific methods of economic management — with all their economic, social, and collective implications.[59]

Exactly one year before Novotný's replacement by Dubček, although probably overestimating the unity of the public concerning the new economic system, the author of the above quote previewed well the year of continuing conflicts at all levels, up to the Presidium of the Communist Party.

In a developed, highly industrialized society, with well-educated and large groups of scientific workers, it had to happen sooner or later: the party that wanted to rule the society and manipulate separately all of its different strata was in turn surrounded and penetrated by them, each of them demanding its share of power and influence. The intellectual core of the Party, its different scientific commissions, developed their solidarity with members of their professions outside of the corps of *apparatchiks* or even incorporated some of them. (For instance,

---

[57] Vladimír Bernard in *Tribuna*, 6 Jan. 1971, p. 4.

[58] See the first paper presented at the Reading Seminar, in Kusin, ed.: *The Czechoslovak Reform* . . . , p. 6. Emphasis in the original.

[59] Jiří Kantůrek in *Kulturní tvorba*, 5 Jan. 1967.

several reforming writers became members of the Ideological Commission and some of the economists were co-opted to the Economic Commission.) And what's more, these "Party scientists" had the professional ambition to use the tools of their disciplines (very often sharpened by new scientific developments in the West or even in some communist countries, especially Poland) and rule "scientifically."

When for economic reasons encouraging *tourism* became official policy, a number of visits permitted both to the Soviet Union and the West had exactly opposite effects. Visitors to Moscow and other Soviet centers became disillusioned and shocked by prevalent economic and social backwardness. Jan Procházka, future chairman of the Writers' Union and a member of the Central Committee of the CPC, wrote at the beginning of 1967:

> Some time ago, it used to be said that the U.S.S.R. is something like the Gethsemane Garden. . . . It was constantly demanded that we should learn from the U.S.S.R. even in branches in which we enjoyed world primacy but we have reached it by old-fashioned bourgeois customs. . . . In Czechoslovakia there is a higher standard of living than in the U.S.S.R. It has always been. Even when the opposite was claimed. Czechoslovakia . . . was a highly industrialized country at a time when in Russia they started to build their first high chimney.[60]

Until the second half of the 1960s, visits to Russia were as much restricted as to the West. But now, when many more comrades could travel to the Soviet Union, the shock of discovery of the truth had a sobering effect on most of them. They could not see the radiant future of humanity there, as used to be claimed by poets and politicians alike, but the distant Tsarist past still present. *Radoslav Selucký* was able to explore the U.S.S.R. from one end to the other. As a sequence to his popular book that was published in Prague in 1964, *Západ je Západ* [*West Is West*], he serialized his impressions from the Soviet Union in the weekly *Reportér* in 1968 and later in his book *Východ je Východ* [*East Is East*]. His thoughts well expressed both the positive attitude to the Russians and the negative influence of first-hand experience:

> God knows why I have always loved *Russia* and wished it a nicer fate than that assigned by history. But there was nothing here that could evoke in me a pinch of optimism or at least of conviction that there is any hope. . . . [Ideology] is good only *pro domo sua* to cover the old Tsarist system functioning under a new label. . . . As can be seen, people can be kept on leash either by ecclesiastical hymns and candles or by slogans on the building of communism.[61]

Visitors to Western countries were surprised by their high standard of living and modern facilities. Comparative statistics started to be published and shattered the carefully built illusion of a communist paradise:

> We are astonished to learn from a comparison of the health expenditures of twenty-three countries that Czechoslovakia was next to last on the ladder — ahead of Tanganyika. . . . We have noted in the present decade that there is only one country in Europe in which housing

---

[60] *My 1967*, no. 1 (Jan. 1967); quoted from his collected articles in *Politika pro každého*. (Prague: Mladá fronta, 1968), pp. 118–22.
[61] Radoslav Selucký, "Východ je Východ" ["East Is East"], *Text 72*, vol. 4, no. 3 (32), 30 Mar. 1972, p. 8. Emphasis in this fragment from the book is in the original. The book was published in Cologne by Index in 1972. The original articles appeared under the title "The Socialist World As Seen by a Czech Economist," i–x, in *Reportér*, nos. 6–16 (1968).

deteriorated between 1950 and 1961, and that country was Czechoslovakia. . . . The discrepancy is especially marked when we compare the time that a Czechoslovak worker had to expend in order to earn the means to buy a produce type that his Western colleague, for example, can acquire in an incomparably shorter period. (TV set 470:133, Sewing Machine 287:88, Transistor Radio 117:12, 1 kg chocolate 10.5:1.5 working hours, etc.)[62]

The fear that Czechoslovakia would definitely lose its once prominent place in the world and would never be able to catch up with the fast advancing Western countries became one of the main motives of demands for reforms which finally turned into a revolution. In the 1960s it was no longer a fear that economically Czechoslovakia was badly lagging behind other industrialized countries but also that the country would completely miss the new *scientific and technical* (or, as often called, technological) *revolution.*

It was one of the motivations for the activities of Ota Šik:

> We started to hear timid references to the scientific and technological revolution in our country at a time when the industrially advanced countries had long been swimming in the current of these changes in civilization. The guardians of our ideological purity labelled cybernetics as a bourgeois pseudoscience at a time when the Western world was busy installing hundreds of computers. Czechoslovakia has taken only the first steps in automation, while the production of plastics, synthetic fibers, and fertilizers is still in its infancy.[63]

The concept of the scientific-technical revolution came to Prague relatively late since the "Program of the Communist Party of the U.S.S.R."[64] already not only contained the term itself but stressed science as the "key growth factor of social productive forces" and announced that "the role of the scientific community in deciding on research must increase."[65] The Soviet State committee for the Coordination of the Scientific Research (established in 1961) was renamed the State Committee for Science and Technology in 1965 and Premier Kosygin declared to the Twenty-third Congress of the Soviet Communist Party in March 1966: "The course of the economic competition between the two world systems depends on the rate of development of our science and on the scale on which we use the results of research in production."[66]

Various aspects of the scientific and technological revolution have been studied and some of the results published in Czechoslovakia since the late 1950s. The year of 1963 saw a few publications devoted to the overall concept of the scientific and technical revolution, among them one written by *Radovan Richta (Man and*

[62] Ota Šik, *Czechoslovakia: The Bureaucratic Economy* (White Plains, N.Y.: International Arts and Sciences Press, 1972): An English translation of his June and July 1968 television talks (their Czech publication began in *Květy*, 3 Aug. 1968, pp. 4–9). This book was published also in other languages, e.g. *La vérité sur l'économie Tchécoslovaque* (Paris: Fayard, 1969) and *Fakten der Tschechoslowakischen Wirtschaft* (Vienna: Molden, 1969).

[63] Ota Šik, *op. cit.* (U.S. edition), pp. 55–6. In his polemical attack on Ota Šik, a Soviet author, A. Sobolev, committed at least two gross errors when he criticized his model of market socialism for ignoring the scientific-technical revolution and for putting up his reform against the conception of an economic reform prepared by the Party. See his article reprinted from the Soviet *Partiinaya Zhiznj* in *Život strany*, no. 6, 18 Mar. 1974, pp. 12–15.

[64] *Pravda*, (Moscow), 30 July 1961.

[65] According to Eric Moonman in the book he edited, *Science and Technology in Europe* (Penguin Books, 1968), p. 17.

[66] Quoted from R. W. Davies and M. J. Berry, "The Russian Scene," *Ibid.*, p. 124.

Technology in the Revolution of Our Time). In 1965 he became head of a large research team made up of specialists in many scientific branches in order to study "Social and Human Implications of the Scientific and Technological Revolution." In 1966 the result was published and helped to influence and streamline thinking of many Czechoslovak reformers.[67] The third, expanded, edition was published in 1968 and its English version in 1969 together with translations in several other languages. The book, *Civilization at the Crossroads*, lists collectively sixty authors and expresses thanks to many other specialists who were consulted.

Though uneven in quality, it is an impressive work. Its terminology, basic ideas, and principles were adopted by many reformers in Czechoslovakia, including Ota Šik and Radoslav Selucký.[68] It helped to put the economic reform into a much wider perspective of the scientific and technical revolution which supposedly would end the industrial revolution with all its obsolete concepts of class struggle, workers' class, division of labor, and alienation of workers in both capitalist and socialist societies. The authors carefully surveyed all available literature on modern developments of our civilization and used recent American, British, French, German, Polish, Russian, Yugoslav, and other sources. The special importance of the work for Czechoslovak developments was in its thoroughly Marxist elaboration of the necessity (as claimed) in an advanced society to overcome *extensive* development of industry and to liberate scientific and cultural forces because without their freedom socialism could never reach the stage of contemporary capitalist production and high level of applied scientific research. Since modern management was seen as the key to the full use of all potential innovation and planning of research, and since democracy with all its basic freedoms is an absolute necessity in the new era, the authoritarian government, prevalent in communist societies, was denounced as a requisite of past ages and a hindrance to progress. All this was done in an elegant, positive way and Marx, abundantly quoted, never sounded so humanistic and democratic as in this book. Its prophetic tone of absolute certainty about stages of development, expressed in Marxist terms, must have appealed to people who all their adult lives believed that they have found absolute truth in Marxism-Leninism-Stalinism but were more and more puzzled by strange discrepancies between the prophesy and actual developments. In Richta's synthesis they could find another Bible which revealed Marx as a contemporary who had expected the enormous rise of the importance of science, and which, at the same time, led them out of the morass of chronic daily problems to the promised land of plenty, humanism, and democracy. There was no need, not yet, to give up the old and almost forgotten ideals of brotherhood and

[67] *Civilizace na rozcestí: Společenské a lidské souvislosti vědecko-technické revoluce* (Prague, 1966). In a review Eugen Loebl contradistinguished the Chinese "Cultural Revolution" from the scientific-technical revolution in *Kultúrny život*, 16 Sept. 1966, and translated in German for *Volkszeitung* (Prague), 7 Oct. 1966, p. 7, and 14 Oct. 1966, p. 7. Loebl's book, quoted previously on pp. 275-6, was published a year later and was, to a large degree, based on a similar reading of statistics from highly developed and less developed economies. Over 50,000 copies of Richta's book were sold till 1968.

[68] R. Selucký, for instance, the last day of 1967 wrote: "In the coming scientific-technical revolution . . . doors leading to the new system [of management] opened a little. . . . In this sense the year of 1968 is for the citizens of our Republic a year of expectation and hope." See "Open the Doors Wide," *Svobodné slovo*, 31 Dec. 1967.

happiness in communism. All that was needed was to push Novotný aside and open the doors wide to democratization of the Party and of the State, to scientific and technological revolution with its promise of plenty of consumer goods and improvement of services. The book was an expression of the prevalent optimism of the 1960s, inspired by Western successes in all spheres of human life, and viewed the liberated future almost everybody wished for. The message was individualist:

> In contrast to industrialization, which originally shaped the technological base of socialism — within boundaries that do not permit steady mass progress of human power — the scientific and technological revolution represents a process of civilization that not only allows of, but makes imperative, the steady and all-inclusive expansion of abilities and powers in every individual.[69]

The basic Marxist tenets, which made Richta's work acceptable to his communist readers not only in Prague but in Moscow as well, are responsible for some serious flaws. History did not work the way it was supposed to. As claimed in the book, socialism *should be* more suitable than capitalism to the development of creative sciences, technological progress, and the liberation of every human being. Unfortunately for the authors, they have to admit that *"theoretically*, the social groundwork capable of carrying out the scientific-technological revolution thoroughly in all respects (while avoiding any disastrous alternatives) is to be found in the advance of socialism and communism in their *model* aspect."[70] Rather unscientifically, they then must add some magic — which is, after all, also Marxist in a way:

> Naturally, the course of the scientific and technological revolution is not a simple copy of a logical pattern; it is refracted by the prism of mediation that is typical of industrial civilization, whereby causes and effects are always made to appear inverted. [!]
>
> Hitherto many scientific discoveries and technological achievements have undoubtedly made their first appearance in capitalist countries. Contrary to the model patterns, most socialist countries have so far been passing through the phase of industrialization.[71]

It is a handy "science" that permits itself to use the *opposite* of its claim to be cited as a proof of its validity. I suspect that at least some of the authors, writing or reading passages as this one, must have kept their tongues in cheeks or remembered their Švejk with his lesson on how to make ridiculous statements seriously.

Radoslav Selucký was much more frank when he wrote in 1964:

> We shall have to adopt a scientific procedure because the issue is not only that we should work more but that we should work more efficiently, effectively, and productively; it will not be so much the strength of our hands and muscles that will help as the strength of reason, science, and brains! . . . Our eyes were closed to the fact that *capitalism is applying the results of the scientific-technical revolution much more quickly and consistently than we are doing* and that many products of Western firms are of a considerably higher technical standard than ours and that they are less expensive, more perfect, and better for their purpose than ours. . . . At present the most important condition of qualitative progress is not the number of factories or the amount of tons of coal or steel produced, but the number and standard of scientists, technicians, and highly skilled workers.[72]

---

[69] R. Richta *et al.*, *Civilization at the Crossroads* (White Plains, N.Y.: International Arts and Sciences Press, 1969), p. 53.

[70] *Ibid.*, pp. 56–7. Emphasis added.

[71] *Ibid.*, pp. 59–60.

[72] *Kulturní tvorba*, 23 Jan. 1964, p. 1. Emphasis added.

As can be expected in a collective work at its best, published in a police state with vigorous censorship, Richta's book alternates between brilliant passages, which in their liberating aspects were extremely well suited to the situation in Czechoslovakia during the second half of the 1960s, and doubtful generalizations on modern capitalism and its future prospects in the era of the scientific and technological revolution. It is hard to say if all corresponded to the opinion of the authors or if they just had to be there since the book was originally written in a difficult period when every writer felt the scrutinizing eyes of the police censor. Usually, they seem to be on a much lower level than the rest of the book, which is outstanding. It helped to unify a large segment of the communist intelligentsia in Czechoslovakia behind a program that seemed to be offering both a Marxist and humanist perspective.

6. Workers' activism before and after the invasion

Much more is known about the activities of intellectuals and politicians in 1968 than about the workers whose rather slowly growing support of the political and economic reform is usually accepted as a disappointing but more or less understandable fact.[73] Throughout this and the preceding chapter I have tried to show that the workers did not, and could not, easily create a common front with communist intellectuals whom they did not trust. Their fight against, or accommodation with, the regime had a different history as well as forms than the longer collaboration and gradual but slower disillusionment of the communist intelligentsia with the regime they so much helped to establish and propagate. The active participation of workers in regenerating democratic practices was significant. It sometimes started early and lasted long, especially after the invasion. At places where the intellectual or political stimulators of the "Spring" thought about contacting workers, the results of this cooperation were obvious. I would like to give a few examples and follow them with glimpses of special contributions by the few selected protagonists of this and the previous chapter.

The first concerted action by a large group of workers in defense of their sectional interests occurred among the *railwaymen*. Locomotive engineers in the Czech lands had a relatively long history of unionism. Their first Union of Engine-drivers was created in 1896 and in the remaining twenty-odd years of the Austrian-Hungarian Monarchy fought successfully for its members' rights. In 1921 it changed its name from Union of Czechoslovak Engine-drivers into Federation of Locomotive Engineers in Czechoslovakia and became a model of a union with high standards of

---

[73] See, among others, Galia Golan, *The Czechoslovak Reform Movement* (Cambridge, 1971), pp. 283-7; H. Gordon Skilling, *Czechoslovakia's Interrupted Revolution* (Princeton University Press, 1976), pp. 433-43 and 579-85; Alois Rozehnal, "The Revival of the Czechoslovak Trade Union," *East Europe*, vol. 18, no. 4 (Apr. 1969), pp. 2-7; Vaclav Holesovsky, *Planning and Market in the Czechoslovak Reform* (New Haven: Yale University Press, 1972); V. V. Kusin, *Political Grouping in the Czechoslovak Reform Movement* (London: Macmillan, 1972), pp. 9-43; Alex Pravda, "Some Aspects of the Czechoslovak Economic Reform and the Working Class in 1968," *Soviet Studies*, xxv, 1 (July 1973), pp. 102-24; A. Oxley, A. Pravda, and A. Ritchie, eds., *Czechoslovakia: The Party and the People* (London, 1973), pp. 149-218; and Karel Kovanda, "Czechoslovak Workers' Councils (1968-1969)," *Telos*, no. 28, summer 1976, p. 36-54.

performance and discipline.[74] After the end of World War II, under the slogan of unity of all trade unionists, the communists managed to federate all workers, employees, and students in a giant association ROH, manipulated by the Communist Party. When after the *coup* of 1948 the unions gradually changed into one-way transmission belts for state policies and completely stopped protecting the workers against management, attempts to return them to their usual role were rarely successful and even then only locally and for a short period of time. Expressions of anger by railroad workers finally led to the preparation of new pay scales in 1967 but their implementation was postponed again and again.[75]

Before the first signs of a political thaw became clear in 1968, locomotive crews of the depot Prague-Centre at several turbulent meetings decided to create an independent union of their own. Their representatives soon managed to contact colleagues at all other important railroad centres throughout Czechoslovakia and gained their enthusiastic support. The organizers sent a deputation to Josef Smrkovský who was among the first communist leaders to publicly encourage reforms. He told them: "How many are you? After all, twenty thousand! So what are you waiting for? Act!"[76]

The new Federation of Locomotive Crews was established at the end of April 1968 when 282 delegates from the whole country attended a two-day meeting. It soon associated in its ranks 24,000 railroad men, chiefly locomotive engineers.[77] The Federation demanded a shorter working week of thirty-eight hours, abolition of one-man attendance of locomotive engineers on express trains, retirement age at fifty-five with a pension of 80 per cent of average income, etc. "They based their demands on some data from the pre-Munich Republic. . . . It is natural that these demands were popular among many railway workers."[78] The example of the First ("bourgeois") Republic was serving as a model and goal in the Socialist ("workers") Republic.

The local organizations of the Federation were very active both before and after its establishment in matters that irritated them. For instance, the Prague-Centre requested the dismissal of an unpopular chief officer who obtained a high distinction for his services to the regime, Order of the Twenty-fifth February. They expressed their distrust of the functionaries of the CPC district committee and when the chairman of the local branch of ROH refused to criticize higher organs of the labor union movement, forced him to step down. They revoked a formal patronage by the Moscow railroad depot *Moskva Sortirovochnaya* because they did not agree with its initiative of free Saturday work. As one of the members of the preparatory committee expressed it: "For us it must be equal to establish relations with the Chinese, Germans, Americans, or Russians."[79] The "normalized" authors of 1970 kept calling similar spontaneous and democratic actions, taken by the Prague-Centre and all other depots of Czechoslovakia, expressions of "hysteria."

[74] See K. Vajc, M. Kolář, *Tribuna*, 19 June 1970, p. 9.
[75] *Práce*, 8 July 1970, p. 4.
[76] K. Vajc, M. Kolář, *op. cit.*
[77] *Lidová demokracie*, 18 Mar. 1969.
[78] *Práce*, 21 Feb. 1970, p. 4.
[79] K. Vajc, M. Kolář, *op. cit.*

In 1968 the official Party representatives did not stoop to refer to workers' demands in such a way. After the Federation threatened and used passive resistance friendly discussions followed quickly. Some requests were accepted immediately and some postponed for future, more appropriate, times. The Ministry of Transportation recognized the Federation as the exclusive representative of locomotive engineers and its Deputy Minister ordered railroad depots to discuss all unresolved issues with local organizations of the Federation and achieve amicable solutions. In a few days, the railroad labor unions — since other workers, encouraged by the success of the engineers, followed suit — achieved for themselves a change from a totalitarian dictatorship into a social welfare democratic system. The Ministry even started proceedings about establishing a special "fund for cultural and social needs" for the railwaymen, as demanded by the Federation.[80]

Railroad strike actions were repeatedly taken in 1968 and since the government was vitally interested in a smooth operation of its railway system (not only for the sake of domestic production, but especially since the transportation of goods into the Soviet Union was being threatened), the railwaymen usually achieved their aims very fast.

The most spectacular strike occurred in Žilina, an important Slovak depot. The local workers repeatedly complained about the behavior of several state managers and labor officials, but without success. Finally, on June 5, at 3 a.m., six express trains and forty-two freight trains were kept standing till 9 a.m. when all the workers' demands were accepted. In Slovakia the political Spring was coming late but the well-executed strike alarmed the officials. The independent Federation was officially recognized, unpopular managers were replaced, work reorganized, and welfare care improved.[81]

In a similar way, the organized railwaymen were able to enforce compliance with their demands almost everywhere. Wherever they operated the totalitarian structure was paralyzed. Engineer František Mottl, economic deputy of the chief officer on the Southwestern Railroad in Plzeň, complained about it after the situation became "normalized":

> How active was the Federation of Locomotive Crews in our place? It caused the activity of the Party to be, moderately speaking, completely stopped not only in the locomotive depot Plzeň but also in the locomotive depot České Budějovice. . . . Political, labor unionist, or economic functionaries were . . . dismissed from their functions.
>
> The preceding twenty years of our State and Party work were absolutely negated as a loss of twenty years of life. . . . I do not hesitate to say that the Federation of Locomotive Crews was by its acts in many cases an organization hostile to the State.[82]

---

[80] *Práce*, 9 July 1970, p. 4.

[81] Although even during the later period of the liquidation of independent labor unions in 1970 it was recognized that the workers in Žilina had for years suffered by mismanagement, disorganization of work, bad working conditions, dictatorial bosses, and so on, the Party newspapers blamed social democratism and denounced organizers of this strike by names in order to hunt them down and frighten the rest. This report was based mainly on two articles: *Práca*, 20 May 1970, p. 4; and *Pravda*, 22 June 1970, p. 4. The first article claimed that the damage done by the strike amounted to more than 170 million crowns, some 24 million U.S. dollars.

[82] See his article "Co byla Federace lokomotivních čet?" ["What Was the Federation of Locomotive Crews?"], *Tribuna*, 28 Jan. 1970, p. 7.

During the first days of the Soviet invasion of Czechoslovakia, railroad workers managed to slow down and finally bring to a complete stop a special train that was bringing to Prague sophisticated equipment for tracking down "illegal" radio and television stations. Where a loyal communist, who did not change his ways even then, broke the solidarity of his comrades and colleagues, he became a target of a concerted campaign. For instance, Antonín Mikula, chief officer of the railroad station Moravičany, who worked for the ČSD [Czechoslovak State Railroad] for forty years and for twenty years was the secretary of the local CPC organization, ordered the Soviet train to be released after the railwaymen, in spite of the protests of the Soviet transport commander, halted and side-tracked it. Mikula was then denounced as a "collaborator with the army of occupation" and as a "traitor to his nation." For a week Mikula had to hide with his wife in his locked apartment, did not dare to go out shopping, and his nerves suffered when his colleagues kept singing under his windows the refrain of an old Sokol song: ". . . and to him who turns renegate, in the treacherous chest with a blade."[83]

Throughout 1968 not many workers showed such a decisive and sustained initiative as the railroad men. None had such easy access to important means of transportation which were so crucial for the economy and for deliveries of goods to the U.S.S.R. But in many instances the workers took the situation in their hands and achieved at least partial successes. Some of their actions became mutually coordinated and the longer the year 1968 lasted the more widespread and organized they became. After the invasion added the element of nationalism to other interests, it became a mass movement.

We can follow some of the developments in one of the largest concerns in Czechoslovakia, *ČKD Praha* [Česko-Moravská Kolben Daněk] which in 1968/9 was sixth in the ČSSR according to production and third by its number of employees [40,470].[84]

Changes started to take place in 1966 when comrade Dalibor Dorn became responsible for the personnel department. As part of the New Economic Model, in order to improve the qualification of leading managers, he was able to get rid of some of the loyal but inefficient communists and replace them by people who had to pass through professional selection by competitive applications. In this effort he was supported by both the CPC local chairman Januš and ROH's plant chairman Kulíšek.[85] As almost everywhere, in 1968 it was difficult, but necessary, to dislodge conservative communists from their entrenched positions. When at the end of January, the chairman of the Czechoslovak Writers' Union, E. Goldstücker, defended on television the Slovak writer Mňačko for his demonstrative departure for Israel the previous year, the district committee of the CPC in Prague 9 (the location of the ČKD Sokolovo plant) invited him to explain his statement at a meeting. He came with twenty-two other writers and journalists and although the official Party and ROH representatives almost unanimously condemned him (with strong overtones of anti-Semitism) and his personal reforming zeal, after a report in the daily *Práce* and after an intervention by workers from Kladno's SONP

[83] *Tribuna*, 22 Apr. 1970, p. 20.
[84] *Svět hospodářství*, no. 10, 23 Jan. 1970, p. 1.
[85] *Rudé právo*, 24 July 1970, p. 5. In December 1967 Dorn refused to accept a decoration on the occasion of the twentieth anniversary of the *coup* in February 1948.

(the seventh plant in Czechoslovakia according to both production and number of workers), it became a starting-point for a concerted action during which many of the dogmatists lost their prominent positions, among them even the general director of the ČKD and alternate member of the CPC CC Presidium, Engineer A. Kapek (who would play a major role after the invasion as a "normalizer"). The progressives were elected into all-important jobs in both the factory CPC and ROH local organizations. The local labor union committee had among its twenty-one members only six communists.[86] It clearly reflected the opinion of ČKD workers but came as a shock to Party conservatives who without proper elections until then found it easy to coopt themselves into positions, stick to them, and to believe that they had a "historical" right to be there as workers' representatives.

Beginning with the January meeting, the Prague 9 Sokolovo plant of ČKD became an important centre coordinating activities of workers and writers. Students also established good contacts with them.[87] Among the regular journalist visitors to the ČKD in Prague 9 was one of the editors of the daily *Práce*, *Jan Štern*. Together with CPC leaders Císař, Smrkovský, and Slavík, he was credited with the "transformation of one of the revolutionary bastions of the working class into one of the bases and directing centres of Rightism which influenced not only other factories in Prague 9 but also in the whole Republic." The factory journal *Kovák* [*Metal-worker*] "far exceeded the factory's scope."[88]

The communist organization of the ČKD Locomotive plant supported the "Two Thousand Words Manifest" and in a joint resolution with the Medical Faculty of the Charles University called for an early convocation of the Fourteenth Party Congress. When the "friendly invasion" took place in August, the plant CPC organization demanded "immediate withdrawal of the army of occupation" and dismissal of all "collaborators and traitors." Many other factories then joined this appeal.[89]

During the invasion the Red Corner of the factory became a studio for the "illegal" Czechoslovak radio broadcasting. It was well provided with technical equipment supplied by another factory, specialized in radios, *Tesla Hloubětín*. The operation was helped by several ambulances and supply trucks labelled *Potraviny* [Foodstuffs].[90] The workers from different enterprises managed to cooperate beautifully both among themselves and with the intelligentsia from the public media.

In April of 1968 a campaign was initiated in Ostrava in order to create *workers' committees for the defense of freedom of the press*. Fearing that the Party would reintroduce censorship, some forty workers in the Ostrava Nitrogen Factory (MCHZ) founded the first of such committees. The local daily, *Nová svoboda*, published on 26 April a proclamation of fifteen workers from the second guild of the Nitrogen Factory:

> In the rapid development of political life in Czechoslovakia towards democracy a decisive role was played by stoppage of the censorship. . . . We believe that in the contemporary

[86] *Rudé právo*, 21 July 1970, p. 5.
[87] *Ibid.*
[88] *Ibid.*
[89] *Ibid.*, 23 July 1970, p. 5.
[90] *Ibid.*, 24 July 1970, p. 5.

situation it is of utmost importance to create workers' committees for the defense of freedom of the press as a basic civil right. . . . These committees for the defense of freedom of the press would, in case of necessity, initiate in a decisive way such actions which would clearly demonstrate that suppression of freedom in Czechoslovakia was always done against the will of the working class.

The appeal from the chemical factory was quickly followed by creation of similar clubs for press freedom by rolling-mill workers in Lískovec, NHKG in Kunčice, iron-works in Vítkovice, and in all major works in the Ostrava region. In May it spread to Prague, Plzeň, and other industrial centres, so that by June it was estimated that hundreds of such workers' clubs existed. At the same time, police investigators began to pay special attention to forty workers active in the original committee in order to frighten them.[91]

The important *První brněnská strojírna* [First Machine Factory in Brno] went through a development similar to that of the ČKD Locomotive Works in Prague 9, described previously. Even post-invasion critics of the "Brno Spring" admitted the real causes of the upheaval by answering their own question "How can one explain that the personnel fully backed up the opportunist policies" as follows:

> Already before the year 1968 the Party organization was led incorrectly. Political attitude to people was replaced by an administrative, bureaucratic method of direction of Party work. Gross blunders were committed also in the management of the factory. . . . Therefore in 1968/9 the Rightists could quickly transfer the Party organization to "progressive forces" that pressed for a reverse in the CPC, for a break away from the U.S.S.R. and other socialist countries. The employees trusted them because these functionaries managed to make full use of previous blunders in order to act against the Party and honest workers of the *apparat*.[92]

Communists who still supported the old system lost their positions, hated cadre materials (Party and police files on all employees) were burned. Social Democratic Party cells began to function, and there was a great interest in creation of workers' councils. Several resolutions accepted by workers supported progressive public policies. The appeal of "Two Thousand Words" was welcomed. New works rules stipulated that Party organs and functionaries should have no more right to make decisions concerning personnel matters which should be henceforth decided by the management in agreement with the unions. "The employees must not have the feeling that their rights are restricted by Party actions." In another document the right of the CPC to a leading role was denied and the National Front (of all parties and interest groups) recognized as a base of all political life.[93]

Political activism radiated from the factory into the whole town. Before the city conference of the CPC met to elect delegates to the Fourteenth Party Congress, the factory workers published a statement which supported decisive reforms and influenced the meeting. When Škrabal, a worker from the forges, spoke first the conservatives complained that the "town conference moved in the wrong direction." The progressive intellectual leaders of the CPC in Brno, Špaček, Šabata, and Černý often became guests of the factory and the influence was, as we can suppose, mutual.

---

[91] For these and other details, see Ivan Kubíček, *Reportér*, 26-3 July 1968, pp. 9-11.
[92] *Rudé právo*, 30 July 1970, p. 3.
[93] *Ibid.*

The machine-shop workers were "shocked" by the invasion and immediately created an emergency force "in case of an intervention by the allied armies against the enterprise." Two one-hour strikes took place on the second day of the invasion and the factory established contacts with seventeen other major enterprises in Brno. It became the centre for their "coordinating action groups."[94]

In Slovakia the evolution in factories was slower than in Bohemia or Moravia. When in 1968 Dubček moved to Prague and was replaced in Bratislava by Vasil Bil'ak, the leadership of the Communist party of Slovakia was in the hands of conservatives. There was no support from above for changes in the bureaucratic system. It can be seen, for instance, in the developments in the enterprise *Stavoindustria* [Building Industry] PZ PSV in Banská Bystrica-Král'ová where in March 1968 the pressure mounted to call a new annual meeting in order to replace the old committee by a newly elected one. The most unpopular functionaries had to go and moderates were selected on 29 May. It became fully progressive only after the invasion, by elections in October 1968, and again in March 1969. During the first days of the occupation, two national flags were hoisted at half mast and a black flag at full mast as signs of mourning. The workers organized a strike in protest against "the illegal invasion of our country by occupation armies."[95]

But even in Bohemia changes sometimes took place only after the invasion. Although in May 1968 the director of the national enterprise *Dioptra* in Turnov, since 1955, Heřman Capoušek, was criticized for many faults in Party and factory activities, he was allowed to remain in his position and to lead a vacation trip of apprentices to Rumania between August 12 and 24. When they arrived back many of the participants in the journey criticized his behavior, especially when on the way home during a stop in Budapest, on hearing the news of the invasion, he declared: "There are no occupation troops but only troops that came to liberate us." In the evening of the day of his return, the director was summoned to an emergency meeting of the factory organization of the CPC and, although it was Saturday, it lasted from 10 p.m. to 3 a.m. of the 25th, met again from 7 to 11 a.m., but without reaching a decision. After an intervention from the local section of the National Front, a larger and less Stalinist group of union and Party representatives met and decided to ask comrade Capoušek to resign his function which he did. A carefully objective document on these meetings was presented to workers of all workshops in *Dioptra* and the decision put to the vote. The expression of mistrust of the director by employees was unanimous. The next month the district committee of the CPC in Semily confirmed the action of the workers and recalled comrade Capoušek from the function of enterprise director in Turnov.[96]

Similar developments occurred in many, if not all, factories in Czechoslovakia — with the usual distinction between Czech or Moravian and Slovak patterns — the cooperation between workers and technicians was very good. At the beginning it took them some time to dislodge the entrenched power holders who were often backed from above and by the police. In many towns the factories became the centre and fortress of the pressure for changes.

[94] *Ibid.*

[95] *Pravda*, 22 July 1970, p. 5.

[96] Jiří Mareš (chairman of the CPC, Turnov), *Tribuna*, 18 Feb. 1970, p. 20; and Oldřich Jarušek, *Tribuna*, 3 June 1970, p. 20.

In institutions where the large part of employees belonged to the category of white, rather than blue, collar workers the evolution proceeded along parallel lines, as a sample will show.

The *Institute for Nuclear Research in Řež* was the largest scientific establishment of the ČSAV [Czechoslovak Academy of Sciences]. Very soon after the CPC leadership changed in January 1968, its employees started to push for radical reforms both in their own place of work and in the whole country. Interestingly enough, the plant's committee of the centralized unions, ROH, served as the nucleus for this breakthrough. On the 20 February it returned sixty badges which had been delivered for the twentieth anniversary of the February *coup* of 1948. They explained that "among employees there is no interest in such actions" and demonstrated disgust with the anniversary just as the Czechoslovak Writers' Union did distancing itself from the official celebrations attended by Brezhnev.

In the Institute a "Standpoint of the establishment's union on contemporary political situation" was prepared which presented a well-thoughtout program of necessary changes in the system of government. It demanded postponement of May elections since "the majority of the population is intimidated and until May would not be able to get rid of obstructions . . . in order to develop a pre-election fight." The limitations imposed on political activities must disappear: "It is necessary to reckon also with other socialist parties that would bring into our life an element of competition of opinions." Employees of the Institute gave their approval to this statement. The Standpoint was sent to many other institutions as well as to progressive politicians, among them Ota Šik. Such points of view were often elaborated in the basic organizations and flooded the offices of public figures, exercising a strong democratic pressure from below.

The Řež Institute also devoted a lot of attention to the mission of labor unions and in its "Report on the activities of the ZO ROH [establishment's union of the Revolutionary Labor Movement] during the period from April 1967 to March 1968" presented a set of principles that should lead to a replacement of the Soviet imposed totalitarian unions by a democratic system in agreement with Czechoslovak democratic traditions. The leading role of the Communist Party was absolutely denied and the separation of the labor unions from the National Front was requested since "the unions as an interest organization cannot cooperate with a coalition of political parties, especially in a situation when in this involuntary coalition they became executors of the *governing political minority*, often against the will and in conflict with the interests of their members." The document declared the usual duties of unions in a Soviet system (expanding work initiative, political education of workers, etc.) as absurd, invented by "higher organs," and stressed that "the only and principal task [of the unions] has always been to defend the interests and needs of their members against interference by economic and state organs." The employees also expressed their satisfaction that "for the first time after twenty years we have a chance to express ourselves openly."

In these and other documents the unionists from the Institute criticized "the excessive union *apparat*," demanded a thorough democratization, and exercized strong pressure in order to change the unions' state leadership imposed by the Party. Although there were 30 per cent communists in the Institute, out of thirty-three elected works councillors representing the scientific departments in

1968 only one communist passed the democratic test. The slogan "unions without communists" became very popular, although the workers probably did not know that they had reached the same conclusions as rebels in Kronstadt and Budapest had before them.

There was a widespread tendency to remove communists from the unions so that they could never be used by them again for Party machinations. At least local elections at Řež proved that the claim expressed by the Institute that a minority was ruling the country had some merit.

In April the Institute began to take part in activities of both the K 231 (Club of persecuted victims of Stalinism) and KAN (Club of Engaged Non-party People) whose initiative to support clubs for the defense of citizen's rights led to the creation of a "union commission for the defense of human rights" in Řež. The cadre materials on employees were destroyed.[97]

It is known from the Soviet Union that atomic scientists are among the most politically minded and progressive people in the realm. The Czechoslovak experience with the Institute in Řež seems to be confirming this vital sense of social responsibility of atomic scientists and crucial importance attributed by them to democratic methods and human rights as safeguards in a world standing on the edge of a possible nuclear catastrophy.

7. The intelligentsia in 1968

During the "abnormal" times between January and August of 1968, the solution to issues connected with the New Economic Model and the scientific and technical revolution was almost fully concentrated on political reforms and creation of basic freedoms necessary for the development of both.

Soon after the January changes in the CPC leadership, when the Slovak Communist Party in Bratislava was led by the conservative Vasil Bil'ak, *Eugen Loebl* involved himself in the fight for renewal, speaking at Party meetings and writing articles. On the third day of a tempestuous Party gathering of the city committee in Bratislava, his address was greeted with a "stormy applause." He talked about the proposed federation of Czechoslovakia from an economic point of view — he clearly preferred creation of a united economy — and had high praise for the young intelligentsia since it was not burdened by dogmatic thinking.[98] A few days later he took an active part in a stimulating discussion on democracy in the university information club (*Informklub*).[99]

His attention was devoted to the necessity for an economic reform[100] and he was among the first to get involved in spirited but rather counter-productive polemics with Soviet commentators. These polemics did, however, help to bring about a national unification for the defense of a hoped-for political and economic sovereignty:

> I did not want to believe my own eyes when on the 5th April I read the reflections of the

[97] For all the details concerning this scientific institute, see A. Zázvorka, *Svět práce*, 24 June 1970, p. 5. Emphasis added.

[98] See *Pravda*, 18 Mar. 1968.

[99] *Pravda*, 22 Mar. 1968.

[100] *Večerník*, 27 Mar. 1968.

candidate of philosophical sciences, V. Kozlov, concerning the specific way to socialism. . . . He reaches the conclusion that "excessive emphasis on national peculiarities, that lead necessarily to the interpretation of a specific way to socialism and some sort of special form of Marxism," is not Marxist. I have heard exactly the same formulations in 1949 in detention on remand in Ruzyň, although then the spokesman was not some university lecturer "on a generally philosophical level" but a Beria-type collaborator on an extra-ordinarily ground-floor level. The form might have been different but the content was exactly the same.

After a few quotes from Lenin and from the Declaration of Communist Parties dated 30 October 1956 [after which came the Hungarian massacre! — didn't they see the difference between words and tanks?!], Loebl came to this conclusion: "Typical for the revolution of 1917 was the specific way taken by Lenin and the Bolshevik Party."[101]

Loebl did not forget to entertain contacts in the West. German *Die Zeit* (of April 1968 on page 14) published a chapter of his book on the new wealth of nations and the book itself soon appeared in a German edition.[102] His book on the Slánský trial and Loebl's experiences with it as one of its victims was also published in German.[103] Its Slovak publication was followed by an interview in which Loebl did not hesitate to blame the Soviet Union for the excesses of communist terror in Czechoslovakia in the 1950s:

> For me it is clear that what we had was not socialism. Always I have considered it mutilation of socialism. . . . It could not have happened without the Party and State leadership's sellout of the Republic to Beria's agents. . . . It is good to realize that every time, under whatever enticing title, a State gives up its own sovereignty or places other interest above its own, an avalanche of tragedies follows. . . . The whole horrible system was an effective wholesale manufacture of weak characters. And it changed decent people into indecent. . . . Between Gottwald and Slánský or between Gottwald and Clementis there did not exist any basic differences. What operated was pressure from abroad. Instead of Slánský in the prisoner's dock Gottwald could sit as well, but Slánský was more convenient because he was an intellectual and a Jew. . . .
>
> What we have now are consequences of a dictatorship when a man was the property of the ruling circles exactly like a machine. He was likewise subject to manipulation. There existed a live-stock and a dead-stock inventory. Live-stock inventory included not only horses and cattle but also man.

In this important interview he spoke in favor of democracy but with limitations: no "temporary majority" should be allowed to change the socialist character of the Republic; as a true Leninist, Loebl still spoke about "bourgeois democracy" with hate and contempt.[104]

In a long essay written for an economic weekly, Loebl returned to his pet idea that the market needed between 100,000 and 200,000 small enterprises which could be put into operation immediately and thus show that the Party really intended to go a new way, tapping the initiative and enterprising spirit of the population. Forcefully, he defended the New Economic Model as necessary for

[101] *Pravda*, 12 Apr. 1968.

[102] *Geistige Arbeit – die wahre Quelle des Reichtums: Entwurf eines neuen sozialistischen Ordnungsbildes* (Düsseldorf: Econ-Verlag, 1968).

[103] Eugen Loebl and Dušan Pokorný, *Die Revolution rehabilitiert ihre Kinder: Hinter den Kulissen des Slánský-Prozesses* (Vienna: Europa Verlag, 1968). In Slovak the title, without D. Pokorný's co-authorship, was *Svedectvo o procese s vedením protištátneho sprisaheneckého centra na čele s Rudolfom Slánskym* (Bratislava, 1968).

[104] *Práca*, 15 May 1968.

using the intellectual potential of the nation and for realizing the scientific-technical revolution. His examples were again taken from American experiences with the coexistence of gigantic concerns and complementary small enterprises. Bitterly he complained about the mistaken nationalization of small-scale trade and production after the seizure of power in 1948.[105] But the Dubček government did not follow his advice.

During the critical month of August, Loebl continued his polemics with the Soviet mentors, defended such a federalization of Czechoslovakia which could not serve the interest of those Slovak communists who wanted to use it only as a pretense for their refusal of a thorough democratization of the country, and kept attacking unnamed Slovak and Czech communists who in the situation acted "as a potential fifth column."[106] He was upset that "a few states in an ultimatum asked a sovereign state to abolish freedom of speech and to introduce censorship." He also bitterly complained that "socialist governments, whose sincere allies we have been, characterized as good and brave communists just those whose conscience is burdened by crimes of the 1950s, who discredited socialism, and who became an ideological prop of the European reaction."[107] In this article Loebl suggested that institutional forms should be given to friendly relations with Rumania and Yugoslavia who before World War II formed with the ČSR the Little Entente.

Following the personal history of *Ota Šik* between January and August, we can discern how even in 1968 the new economic reform remained far from realized and had to face many hindrances.[108] Although some of the leading conservative figures were willing to get rid of Novotný they did not want to substantially change the system.

Before President Novotný lost his position in March, he attempted to gather the conservative forces in factories by playing on their fear that the economic reform would mean a loss of social security. Ota Šik engaged himself fully in a counter-attack, spoke at meetings and wrote articles, in order to stress progressive and beneficial features of the new system in the long run. His main argument was that even if some workers could experience temporary difficulties of adjustment, all would benefit from a healthier climate in economy and politics based on democratic principles.[109]

His personal advancement proceeded under a special cloud. Before he could become a full academic (corresponding) member of the ČSAV two meetings had to take place. At the first one, 14 March 1968, Šik obtained a minority, five out of fourteen votes in the ČSAV presidium. Only two weeks later, 27 March 1968, after a strong appeal by the Academy's chairman, František Šorm (he used to be a dogmatic Party man), did he master thirteen positive votes against one negative.[110]

At the beginning of April, in the reorganized Party leadership, Šik was not

---

[105] *Hospodářské noviny*, 6 July 1968, pp. 1, 6, and 7.
[106] *Kultúrny život*, 16 Aug. 1968, pp. 1 and 10.
[107] *Ibid.*, 9 Aug. 1968, pp. 3 and 6.
[108] For a good detailed record, see H. Gordon Skilling, *Czechoslovakia's Interrupted Revolution*, pp. 412–50.
[109] See his articles in *Mladá fronta*, 21 Feb. 1968; *Pravda*, 27 Feb. 1968; *Zemědělské noviny*, the same date; *Práce*, 5 Mar. 1968; *Rudé právo*, 15 Mar. 1968; etc.
[110] *Rudé právo*, 22 July 1969, p. 3.

elevated to the Presidium, although in the debate several speakers suggested it.[111] Among the progressive journalists, who judged the situation to a large degree by Šik's position on the political barometer, there was great disappointment when in the new Oldřich Černík government, announced on 8 April, Šik was not made directly responsible for the implementation of the economic reform. Although he was named as one of 5 deputy prime ministers (together with Gustáv Husák) and as such was especially charged with the theoretical aspects of the New Economic Model, its practical implementation was in the hands of another deputy prime minister, conservative Lubomír Štrougal, who also became chairman of a newly formed Economic Council. Šik was only a member. The man in charge of the economy and heavy industry in the CPC CC Presidium, Drahomír Kolder, was also an old conservative. So were several other comrades, able to brake the reform from various economically decisive state and Party positions.[112]

"Šik, although a member of the government, was still critical, lamenting that after a decade of struggle for economic reform, they were still at the very beginning of a transition to the new system."[113] He went on making speeches and writing articles[114] but to no great avail. His major and successful attempt to mobilize public opinion came in a series of six television talks at the end of June and beginning of July.[115]

When the Party leadership decided that a foreign loan, amounting to some 500 million U.S. dollars, was needed for modernizing the industry, Šik went to England and between the 10th and 17th of July held talks with responsible British statesmen concerning a supposed loan of 200 million British pounds.[116] The Soviet leaders opposed it, although they refused to extend their own credits to a government they did not trust.

In the domestic confrontation, Šik often advocated rather moderate and considerate measures. In at least two of his articles he appealed to workers not to proceed with indiscriminate dismissal of managers[117] and his original proposals for workers' participation in management could be described at best as technocratic rather than proletarian or radical.[118] But faced with the stubborn opposition of bureaucrats to many aspects of the political and economic reform, as well as by constant prodding by radical intellectuals like Karel Kosík and Karel Bartošek or by some workers' collectives, Ota Šik gradually moved away from a technocratic conception of an expert body to the idea of workers' councils. In a speech to the Czechoslovak Economic Society's annual conference, he included democratization of factories as a necessary condition of further progress and proposed the

---

[111] *Rudé právo*, 2–5 Apr. 1968.

[112] For details, see Skilling, *Czechoslovakia's Interrupted Revolution*, pp. 225–6 and 419–22.

[113] *Ibid.*, p. 422.

[114] For instance, *Rudé právo*, 7 Apr., 16 and 26 May; *Kulturní tvorba*, 2 May; *Mladá fronta*, 26 June; *Práce*, 7 July 1968; etc.

[115] See footnote 62.

[116] *Rudé právo*, 9 July 1970, p. 6.

[117] *Rudé právo*, 7 Apr. and 22 May 1968.

[118] In his talk on Radio Czechoslovakia I, on March 27, Šik advocated for self-management of factories a "collective expert organ" composed mainly of specialists. See A. Pravda, "Some Aspects . . .," *Soviet Studies*, July 1973, p. 116.

formation of working people's councils.[119] Even then the government and also factory workers — with some notable exceptions — did not show any haste in implementing them, till the time of foreign invasion when they would become very popular.

During the mounting tension between Czechoslovak and Soviet (as well as Polish and East German) authorities, Ota Šik left his statesmanlike reserve and defended "socialism with a human face" quite frankly:

> To many of our opponents we will be hardly able to explain that Czechoslovakia, a country with democratic traditions, endured with great difficulty restrictions of basic human rights. . . . And many an economist will not understand our despair over a development which under the pretext of planning prosperity led to unimaginable anarchy, to squandering of human work and of spiritual potential. . . . Many countries of the socialist world live in completely different conditions than we — somewhere so different that simply the fact of other possible, so far unknown, socialist developments can hardly penetrate there. . . . We want to accomplish all that's needed for building in our democratically oriented and industrially well-developed country a socialism measuring up to the standards of our century.[120]

Both exact and social scientists, in their majority, participated in the liberalization of the regime and at least once attempted to influence the progress publicly as an interest group by a collective statement published in the main Party daily. This time a seventy-five-member-strong "interdisciplinary team of scientists for the exploration of societal and human connections of the scientific-technological revolution" signed a fundamental analysis and program of the New Czechoslovak Model of Socialism. There was no trace in it of the unreal, pseudo-scientific Marxist-Leninist jargon that at times marred the earlier book produced by the team. As one of the strongest indictments of the Soviet regime imposed on Czechoslovakia after 1948 (to be quoted in the next chapter), it is probably the best systematic expression of the basic ideals and intentions of the anti-bureaucratic revolution of 1968. It was dated 28 June 1968 but the editor-in-chief of the main Party daily, Oldřich Švestka, himself a dogmatic *apparatchik*, published it only with delay, after the district and regional Party conferences were over; they were electing delegates for the Fourteenth Party Congress. He clearly feared that they might have been influenced by the document.[121]

Six weeks later, on the same day that Moscow *Pravda* titled a long article "Defense of Socialism — the Highest International Duty" (its last sentence, "This duty is for us above everything," reminded me of Eichman's claim at the Jerusalem court that always, even during his help with the murder of millions of Jews, Kant's categorical imperative was his life principle), on the same day, a Russian officer, doing his part of the fraternal duty, posted the following order on the door of the seat of Czechoslovak scientists in Prague:

> *Order.* I, the representative of the Army of the Warsaw Pact, First Lt. Yuri Alexandrovich

---

[119] *Rudé právo*, 22 May 1968, p. 3. He said; "Above the management of enterprises there should arise workers' councils composed, depending on the size of the enterprise, roughly, by ten to thirty members. A decisive part of these members would be elected by workers from their own ranks." His speech was also reproduced in *Bulletin Československé společnosti ekonomické*, no. 3, 1968; there the quote can be found on page 53.

[120] *Rudé právo*, 27 July 1968, pp. 1 and 3.

[121] *Rudé právo*, 10, 11, and 12 July 1968.

Orlov, order all workers and members of the Presidium of the Czechoslovak Academy of Sciences to stop work and leave all rooms of the Academy of Sciences of Czechoslovakia on August 22 by 1300 hours. Signature.[122]

It well symbolized the military attempt to end a humanist revolution in whose preparation and content scientists played their part.

8. Human versus Soviet face of socialism

No one bothered to post such an order on the gates of one of the largest factories in Prague and so the same day, 22 August, when they found the entrance to their building barred, a number of the scientists could take part in the clandestine Fourteenth Party Congress of the Czechoslovak communists which was assembled in an emergency session. The delegates talked about matters that seemed to be more urgent than the fate of the scientific and technical revolution, but the materials that were prepared for the regular meeting planned for September are in the book devoted to this really extraordinary Party Congress. There could be no doubt in the reader's mind that the communist scientists who participated in their preparation were completely serious in their intentions to democratize the system and open doors wide to the coming scientific and technical revolution and to what they considered its main condition — democracy. Quite a few members of both Šik's and Richta's teams took part in the formulation of the program and their participation was acknowledged. In the proposal of a long-term Party program we can read, for instance:

> If we want to orient socialism to modern trends of civilization's progress, towards the scientific and technological revolution, we have to rely upon men with high intellectual capacities and with developed senses and feelings, with a dynamic willpower, and with sensitivity for human values. . . .
> Socialism must be founded on free, autonomous, and completely unhindered development of science and research.[123]

A similarly determined spirit is manifested in other documents, especially in the proposed new Party statutes, and in a historical outline of Party development since the last congress. Clearly, the scientists were able to take over the intellectual and conceptual leadership of the CPC, replace the uneducated and uncultured professional organizers, and lead the Party along a completely different path of democratic socialism which would be in accordance with most of the country's humanistic traditions.

Although *Radoslav Selucký* during the "Prague Spring" did not participate in critical exchanges of opinion with Soviet commentators — "During the year of 1968 I personally was doing all possible in order not to speed up this process

---

[122] *Encyclopedia Moderna* (Zagreb), Nov.–Dec./Jan. 1969 issue, as translated by Slobodan Stankovic in "Russian Lieutenant Commanding Czechoslovak Academicians," *RFE Research*, 17 Jan. 1969.

[123] Jiří Pelikán, ed. *XIV. mimořádný sjezd KSČ. Protokol a dokumenty* [*Fourteenth Extraordinary Congress of the CPC: Minutes of Proceedings and Documents*] (Vienna: Europa Verlag, 1970). Quoted from this Czech edition of my translation. With an eye on police censors of the mail but also with a sense of humor, this edition was being sent to, and distributed in, Czechoslovakia with its title-page funerally printed in black on white: V. I. Lenin, *Spisy* [*Works*], xiv.

excessively, in order not to inflame passions"[124] — in the fateful month of August, he published a clear statement separating the Czechoslovak "European, democratic, and humanistic" model of socialism from the Soviet "monolithic centralist" version:

> The Soviet model of socialist construction much more naturally followed Russian national forms of the nineteenth century than European forms of the mid twentieth century which should have been, often were willingly, followed by some central European socialist countries.... After Lenin's death and after discussions and inner conflicts, an industrializing and collectivizing model of socialism was established, based on administrative, centralist, bureaucratic-dirigist methods. Stalin, who led this process as a theoretician and also as its practical realizer, usurped the monopoly not only of interpreting Marxism but also of interpreting Leninism. . . .
> Experiences with the whole existing development of socialism prove that the *Stalinist* interpretation of Leninism must not be a monopoly interpretation and that especially in the conditions of a central European country that is traditionally well-developed, industrially efficient, democratic and humanist, it is necessary to interpret a Marxist conception of a socialist evolution differently than Stalin did in Lenin's name. . . . It is necessary to consider the historical development of socialism in the U.S.S.R. not as general but particular. . . . It is a country which did not pass through the phase of a civic society, did not absorb the intellectual trends of antiquity, Roman Christianity, Renaissance, and Enlightenment, a country taking over Marxism without the experience of its original sources and interpreting Marxism first of all from the angle of its internal needs and state interests.[125]

Selucký's basic refutation of the validity of the Soviet model for Czechoslovakia in the theoretical journal of the CPC was followed immediately in the same issue by *Michal Reiman* (one of the founders of the CPC was his father, Pavel Reiman). He stressed similar differences between the Russian and Czechoslovak economic, social, cultural, and political setup:

> Stalinism . . . means yielding to the Russian reality, especially where it was undeveloped, immature, and unsuitable to socialist construction. . . .
> . . . Czechoslovakia belongs . . . into an entirely different cultural sphere than Russia. . . . The working class and peasantry, especially in the Czech lands, differed substantially from similar classes in Russia. . . . No small place belonged to traditions of political democracy. . . .
> The consequences [of the Stalinist monopoly mutation of Leninism] were tragic. . . . A political system was built that was in sharp contradiction with the whole previous national history and tradition.[126]

The CPC and together with it the ČSSR were being returned to the magnetic field of Western liberal and social democratic trends.[127]

The Soviet invasion and occupation followed, in order to pull them back into the Soviet orbit. Without a sufficient amount of illusions, of intellectual fools, of political collaborators available (as in 1948), without the active backing of large sections of the working class, only the armed power could stop the natural

---

[124] V. Valenta's "Interview," *Telegram* (Toronto), 5/III, 15 Jan. 1973, p. 2.

[125] *Nová mysl*, no. 8, Aug. 1968, pp. 1021–6.

[126] *Ibid.*, pp. 1027–33. In 1968 he published *Ruskárevoluce* [The Russian Revolution].

[127] In his conclusions at the Reading Seminar, *Selucký* said: "The Czechoslovak attempt was to express an alternative to the command socialist system of the Soviet type. It was based fully on humanist Marxism — its main task was to overcome the contradiction between economic improvement and humanization of the lot of a man. The old command system is both economically inefficient and undemocratic." See Kusin, *Cz. Reform . . .*, p. 12.

tendencies displayed in 1968 by Czechs and Slovaks, including this time the majority of communists.

Ota Šik summed up the loss of his own and other people's "post-war illusions" as follows:

> Centralist-bureaucratic planning and control of economic activity together with liquidation of basic economic functions of the market, is not the precedence of socialist economy ... but the result of application of some state-capitalistic forms from Wilhelm war Germany in conditions of backward economy of post-revolutionary Russia, and their Stalinist absolutization and preservation. . . . For the industrially developed Czechoslovak economy, vitally dependent on expanded foreign trade and on superior, inventive, and highly productive work of its population, this system of primitive planning became a gravedigger.[128]

Most of the communist economists in Czechoslovakia were united in this condemnation and many of them thought that the original "Czechoslovak way to socialism" should not have been interrupted in 1948. *Selucký* expressed it when he said:

> "January" [of 1968], naturally, was a consequence of "February" [of 1948] — without "February" there was no need for anything offered by "January." Personally, I feel that January offered what would have developed in our country without February 1948 by a completely natural way. When February came about, I was eighteen; personally, I imagined then that February represented something very similar in content and form with the January program. I think that "January" was, for a large part, self-criticism of one generation of communists for "February" and the 1950s, and, besides, this self-criticism was positive and honest.[129]

Eugen Loebl went even further than that when he compared the February *coup* with the Munich appeasement and denounced his Party as traitorous to its country:

> I consider "February" as one of the most tragic events in the history of our Republic. . . .
> [For me the central question is that] the CPC, being in power, gave up the independence of Czechoslovakia, handed the Czechoslovak Republic to the Soviet Union, created a new Munich, after which a new March followed, the first occupation which gradually came after February and officially manifested itself by the trials of the 1950s. The occupation of 1968 was just a reprise. . . .
> Only after 1949 when the Communist Party *de facto* delivered the Republic to the Soviet Union, did the Soviet specialists seize also the economy, changed the plan endorsed by the government, and established directive planned economy that proved to be the major brake on development. . . .
> For thirty-seven years I was a member of the CPC before resigning from it because it changed into a collaborationist party and because I cannot remain member of a party that betrayed the nation and its own program.[130]

---

[128] *Literární listy*, "Special edition published on the occasion of the second anniversary of the occupation of Czechoslovakia by the armies of five countries of the Warsaw Pact," p. 1.

[129] Valenta, "Interview," *op. cit.*

[130] See his written contribution to the First European Conference of the Czechoslovak Society of Arts and Sciences in America which took place in Horgen near Zürich in Switzerland, 26–8 June 1970. See the polycopied record, pp. 78, 79, 81. Loebl characterized the Soviet Union as originator of the Cold War and as the cause of the division of Europe.

9. Abnormalizing the normal (intellectuals)

The following history of the gradual abandonment of the Czechoslovak economic reform can be seen either as a perfect example of the use of the proved "salami tactics" by the Soviet government or as a result of its hesitations and a tug of war between Soviet dogmatists and Czechoslovak reformers trying to save (with actual or hoped-for help from some Soviet leaders) as much of their freedom of decision and of the reform as possible. We cannot say if it was cunning trickery, irresolution, or a mixture of both because the archives where an answer probably could be found are not accessible. We can only observe the tortured path of persistent illusions. It was hoped that out of sheer self-interest the Soviet leaders would allow the economic reform to continue. As its vital condition the Czechs and Slovaks considered some democratizing measures. It was only slowly realized that all hope of a reasonable (and not treasonable) cooperation with the Russians had to be given up.

During the time of invasion, *Ota Šik* was vacationing in Yugoslavaia. He felt reassured by meetings at Čierna and Bratislava that no such threat existed. Since the top leaders of the Party and of the government were kidnapped by the invaders and for a few days kept incommunicado, it was his prerogative as Deputy Prime Minister to empower the Minister of Foreign Affairs, Dr. Jiří Hájek, to protest at the United Nations against the armed intervention. Later he would be blamed for it by Soviet leaders and their local collaborators. His numerous speeches at meetings in Western Germany, Italy, Switzerland, and France would also be held against him.[131] Among the personalities the Soviet leaders demanded to be demoted from their positions, Ota Šik's name figured prominently. He resigned as Deputy Prime Minister in early September 1968.

On 13 September 1968 the National Assembly heard a governmental declaration that it was essential to adhere to the program which had been outlined in the new system of management of the national economy. Two statements signed by prominent economists followed. The first one contained thirteen Czech names and the second was approved by fifty Czech and Slovak economists. Both supported the decision to continue with the reform and attempted to save it from its identification with the proscribed name of Ota Šik which made the Soviet leaders see red:

> The new economic management system of our national economy, on whose elaboration academician Ota Šik participated in a substantial measure, was not only his work but a result of innumerable discussions of prominent Czechoslovak economists and managers. . . . For the Czechoslovak economy it is even henceforth the most effective way of development.[132]

The second, much longer, statement, ended with these words:

> If our country is to become a dignified part of the modern economic development of the world and if it is to contribute to the fulfillment of the historical role of the world socialist

---

[131] Jiří Leša, *Tribuna*, 18 Mar. 1970, p. 3. Leša based his relevant information and quotes mainly on an interview with Ota Šik by Manfred Beer in *Die Welt* of 20 Oct. 1969.

[132] *Rudé právo*, 16 Sept. 1968, p. 2.

system, the basic principles of economic reform must be the guide-lines for our entire economic policies.[133]

It is doubtful that strictly colonialist policy could be averted by such appeals to ideals not necessarily shared by cynical Soviet leaders who decided to obtain technological innovations directly from the U.S.A. and other Western states and with their indirect help, keep closed the avenues to democratization in their empire.

A violent vituperative campaign was going on in the Soviet and allied press against Ota Šik (and Jiří Hájek). The Presidium of the Czechoslovak Academy of Sciences strongly protested against it and asked the government to do likewise.[134] But these brave words were not supported by tanks.

A few months after the invasion, *Radoslav Selucký*, still in Prague, wrote an article calling attention to the gulf between "beautiful words about faithfulness to the post-January course" and "practical acts which are in sharp contradiction to the Action Program." He was very pessimistic about the economic and political outlook and asked rhetorically:

> Will we have as much freedom as our Hungarian neighbors enjoy realizing their reforms? Will we be able, by freeing the initiative of small enterprises, to start from the situation that exists in the German Democratic Republic? Will we be able, expanding external economic contacts with the West, to count on actions customarily used by the Soviet Union? Where begin and where end limits for our search for solutions?[135]

Since members of the government and leading Party personalities kept reassuring the public (and themselves) that the economic reform will be continued, even *Ota Šik* tried to hold his options open, did not consider himself to be an emigrant (although 16 October 1968 the Swiss government offered him asylum), asked his government to legalize his stay in Switzerland "for study purposes," and was willing to return to Prague under certain conditions (an exit visa).[136]

But he also explained to his friend Hübl that if needed he would stay abroad:

> I think that in addition to necessary and direct endeavors at home, which are forcibly limited by compromises, there must also exist a possibility to develop our designs without limitations, without tactical and other regards. I would like to try doing that although I know that it is a long-term affair.[137]

The Dubček government was still in power but had to share it with Soviet

---

[133] *Rudé právo*, 24 Sept. 1968.

[134] See the *Věstník ČSAV*, no. 5, Oct. 1968.

[135] *Práce*, 3 Dec. 1968, p. 5; see also Osgood Caruthers, "Czech Economist Warns of 'Catastrophe'," *International Herald Tribune*, 4 Dec. 1968.

[136] See his letter in answer to Milan Hübl, chancellor of the University for Political Science in Prague, who publicly asked him to return to Czechoslovakia in order to frustrate attempts of conservatives to achieve his political liquidation. Both letters were published in *Práce*, 16 and 23 Dec. 1968. See also Ota Šik's son's letter and editorial comments, both in *Práce*, 18 and 22 Dec. 1968.

[137] *Práce*, 23 Dec. 1968.

interventionists[138] and in order to accomodate them was doing some dirty work of "normalization" no one else could do without provoking a strong reaction by the population. The illusion was entertained that it could save at least some parts of the Action Program. In order to help, Ota Šik from Basel and Eduard Goldstücker who was in England returned to Prague for a short time to be sworn into the new Czech regional parliament. They listened to the governmental address, which included modified economic reforms, and then returned to their "commitments to foreign universities."[139]

The campaign against Šik continued. In Czechoslovakia it was spread publicly by the newspaper distributed free by the occupation forces — and hated by all.[140] When the Soviet TASS picked up a funny report by some Lebanese paper claiming that Šik and Goldstücker participated in an alleged secret "Zionist meeting" in London and for "Zionist money" organized from abroad a conspiracy against socialism in Czechoslovakia, Šik defended himself against these "lies and calumnies" and added:

> It is somewhat painful when a communist has to answer such racially colored lie to a communist press agency. And it is entirely shocking that German fascists, by whom I was imprisoned for four years in the concentration camp in Mauthausen for illegal activity in the communist movement, did not consider me a Jew even according to their own racial laws. Obviously, "head of the counter-revolution" (as I was labeled until now) does not work any more and therefore the search is on for a new variant of a rather rude sort, reckoning with the basest instincts, according to which I am even a Zionist.[141]

The Soviet occupation paper then called on the CPC CC commission to stop postponing its decision on Šik and go ahead "in a principled way."[142]

Although the economic reform in Šik's conception was clearly doomed when on 17 April 1969 Husák replaced Dubček as the leader of the CPC, Šik was (supposedly asked by Gustáv Husák) working with several aides from the Economic Institute in Prague on an economic analysis as a basis for the implementation of his reform.[143] But at the next meeting of the CPC CC Šik was ousted from it in a purge of "opportunist elements."[144] Also in June, Šik resigned as director of the Prague Economic Institute and as chairman of the academy's economic collegium. It was announced that he would continue as a member of the senior staff of the Economic Institute and that economist Karel Kouba, who

[138] There was a minor consternation in Prague when the journal *Zprávy*, published and distributed by the "allied armies" in Czechoslovakia, announced in its twenty-fifth number that "marshal of the Soviet Union Andrei Gretchko, temporarily charged with the function of the Minister of Defense of the Czechoslovak Socialist Republic" took part at a meeting in Moscow. The daily *Práce* asked the editorial board of the allied armies to publish a correction, without really expecting any. See the notice "Do We Have a New Minister of National Defense?", 5 Nov. 1968.

[139] *International Herald Tribune*, 24 Jan. 1969, p. 1.

[140] See, for instance, *Zprávy*, 8 Mar. 1969, p. 3.

[141] *Reportér*, 27 Mar. 1969, p. 12.

[142] *Zprávy*, 19 Apr. 1969, pp. 1-2. The author claimed that Šik returned to Prague at least twice before and that he was probably there again.

[143] *International Herald Tribune*, 30 May 1969. Three years later it was revealed that "as late as in the first half of 1969 there was in the Institute elaborated for the benefit of the Party and state leadership a theoretical contribution *Outline of a Basic Conception of the Development of the economic reform*.... fully from the position of market socialism." *Politická ekonomie*, no. 9, Sept. 1972, p. 814.

[144] *International Herald Tribune*, 2 June 1969.

signed both declarations in support of the reform, was appointed to both vacated positions.[145] Obviously, the reformers, in spite of the military occupation, did not mean to give up anything that they did not have to, except under extreme pressure. Confirming the supremacy of the Party Presidium over the government, the First Secretary of the Slovak CP CC, Štefan Sádovský, revealed:

> The Presidium had several times urged the federal government to submit its concept to the Party organs, and the government has several times submitted it; but each time we have rejected it in the Presidium. . . . We then became convinced that a considerable number of the comrades who work in this sphere are still subservient to Šik's influence on the management of our economy.[146]

During the summer of 1969, together with reports about the disastrous state of the economy which was, naturally, made even worse by dislocations caused by foreign armed forces and by the popular resistance they provoked, further assurances were given that the reform must go on. Andrej Lantay, director of the Economic Institute of the Slovak Academy of Sciences, first stressed the great economic problems in production and distribution as well as in foreign trade, and then wrote:

> In our country today hardly anyone doubts . . . that the economic reform is not only possible but is absolutely necessary. Without it we could not overcome fundamental causes of our contemporary difficulties nor guarantee a steady development to our economy. The program of consolidation for next years will be carried in the spirit of the economic reform. . . . Contemporary economic hardships provoke in many people pessimism and a feeling of uselessness.[147]

Some of the problems were openly discussed by Vladmír Kadlec, Professor of the Economic University; Karel Kouba, director of the Economic Institute of the Czechoslovak Academy of Sciences; and Miroslav Koudelka, deputy minister for finances of the ČSSR. They all complained about the high level of inflation and individually about lack of hard currencies that would allow buying modern, efficient machines abroad; about ineffective "over-employment" whose solution would create "difficulties for several hundreds of thousands of people;" about continuing nivelization of wages and enormous subsidies to inefficient enterprises (60 per cent of the total); about an obsolete price structure; about the drastic, hidden devaluation of the national currency (although officially one U.S. dollar was equal to seven Czechoslovak crowns, as a *target* for reproduction of a dollar thirty-one crowns were mentioned); about the impossibility of creating an economic plan; and about the lack of attention the government was paying to economic consequences of the "political normalization."[148]

The uncertainties and hopes were dispelled when, during the same summer, on 17 July, the CPC CC Presidium decided to "renew the leading role of the CP in society, . . . enforce a unitary and planned direction of the economy, enhance the

---

[145] *Ibid.*, 27 June 1969.

[146] *Pravda*, 9 Oct. 1969.

[147] *Život*, 9 July 1969, p. 7. Due optimism was shown by a loyalist spokesman when he wrote: "The hope of our science mainly consists in people who by far did not achieve in science what they could achieve." Jiří Smrčina, " 'Pistoleers' in Science," *Rudé právo*, 22 July 1969, p. 3.

[148] *Nová mysl*, no. 7 (July 1969), pp. 847–57.

authority and influence of the Party in this field, and strengthen the role of the State and central organs in the economic management." At the same time, it was stressed that "economic propaganda must be improved and wrong opinions about economic questions overcome." The document complained about "anti-Soviet and anti-socialist manifestations, that appeared in a vast array of places."[149]

Simultaneously, *Ota Šik* became the target for a new series of concerted attacks. In three consecutive issues of the main Party daily he was especially blamed for destroying "socialism" by his denial of a decisive role of the State in the economy. The reforms were derisively called "the so-called Czechoslovak economic model of socialism."[150] Ota Šik was expelled from the Party on 13 Oct. 1969.

Although the moderate reformers still hoped that they would be allowed to follow at least the Hungarian pattern of reforms,[151] the East German system (with some limitations, for instance, no encouragement of small private enterprise) would become their prescribed model.[152] The economic plan for 1970 was confirmed by the government on 23 December 1969. Although the document in its introduction admitted continuing lack of consumer goods with accompanying surplus of unsaleable stocks in other industrial products, also "high consumption of raw and other materials, low utilization of the working force, growth of unfinished construction, low productivity, bad quality, inflation," etc. (all the old troubles caused by the dirigist management), the government again and again stressed the need to return to the "authority of the plan." Although the authors of the proposed plan complained that "needed sources of energy and demands on coal deliveries" were not provided for, they ordered for 1970 a fourfold acceleration of the 1969 rise in exports of machinery (mainly to the U.S.S.R.). These "demanding tasks"[153] showed that the temporary help which in 1969 COMECON countries provided in consumer goods was ending and the habitual role of an industrial workshop was again imposed on the Czechoslovak colony.

The clock was turned back. A few months later, *Ota Šik* commented in Basel:

> There is now less economic, political and ideological freedom than there was in the last years of Novotny. I have lost all my expectations for a little more freedom in Socialist society.... The ideological obstacles are very strong, always returning the economy to the strongest centralization. And so you have a very clear contradiction between the needs of the economy and ideological hindrances. What will win? It is difficult to say. For the time being in Czechoslovakia the political pressures are greater. But in the long run, without liberalization and use of market functions, the Socialist economy cannot win. So over the long run I think our ideas will come through.[154]

---

[149] At least some of these incidents will be mentioned later. See *Zpravodaj KSČ*, no. 22, 6 Aug. 1969, pp. 4-7.

[150] *Rudé právo*, 23, 24, and 25 July 1969.

[151] For instance, the Slovak CP Secretary and a noted economist, Viktor Pavlenda, went to study it in Hungary and then praised it in *Pravda*, 19 July 1969. The economic weekly, *Hospodářské noviny*, in its issue of 25 July 1969 published a long interview with Rezso Nyers, economist and Secretary of the CC of the Hungarian Socialist Workers' Party, entitled *The Hungarian Economic Reform*. Its English translation in RFE Research: *Czechoslovak Press Survey*, 17 Oct. 1969, contains no less than 54 pages.

[152] See contributions by B. Frost on p. 227, by Ludek Rychetnik on p. 233, and by Jiri J. Kosta on p. 234 of Kusin's *Cz. Reform*.

[153] *Rudé právo*, 29 Dec. 1969, p. 5.

[154] *International Herald Tribune*, 16 Mar. 1970, p. 4.

In May it was announced that Šik was appointed lecturer for economic planning in theory and practice at St. Gallen College of Economic and Social Sciences. For years to come, there was no question of his return to Czechoslovakia. In his numerous foreign publications he attempted to disseminate his and his comrades' experiences with Soviet economic planning and methods; for instance, as in his widely translated book, *Czechoslovakia: The Bureaucratic Economy.* *

Together with *Loebl* (at Vassar College) and *Selucký* (at Carleton University, Ottawa), *Šik* returned to education, the traditional occupation (beginning with Comenius) of Czechoslovak intellectuals in exile, hoping that other people could learn from their mistaken beliefs and painfully won insights.

10. Abnormalizing the normal (workers)

As on several occasions in these two chapters, let us now turn away from observing primarily the communist intellectuals and focus on workers, their unions, and the growth and doom of the workers' councils.[155] The normalizers first concentrated on the seats of intellectual power, on opinion formulators, and only later turned their malevolent attention to factories, in order to destroy the accumulated power of the workers' class. It proved to be a difficult task. They did not have to deal with predominantly communist intelligentsia but with masses of people among whom loyal communists formed only a tiny minority.[156] "The Party lost influence upon factories."[157]

Quite spontaneously, the factories became centres of opposition since the occupying armies were much more interested in storming the *offices* of the Party, of the radio and television, of literary and scientific establishments than in taking over the blue-collar working places.

The invaders did not only want to be feared, but they also wanted to be loved! [Oh, the Russian soul!] Only a few typical reactions by workers will be documented although almost all attempted to do at least something.

In many factories working on deliveries to the Soviet Union, the employees decided to stop such production. In the *Locomotive Factory ČKD-Sokolovo* in Prague it was decided to discontinue assemblage of locomotives CME3 for the U.S.S.R. When Soviet representatives wanted to visit the plant in order to create comradely relations, "as late as during the summer months [of 1969] some provocations occurred that on the part of Soviet comrades, in spite of all their efforts to calmly judge the events they have witnessed, could not evoke anything but sincere astonishment and indignation."[158]

---

* When this book was published in White Plains, N.Y., by IASP in 1972, it was already available in eight languages, including German, French, and Japanese.

[155] These were often called (in Czech) "councils of the working people" or "enterprise councils" since they also included white-collar workers. For a discussion of implied differences, see Skilling, *Czechoslovakia's Interrupted Revolution*, pp. 436-7.

[156] The next chapter systematically explores the relative strength of the CPC in these two crucial sections of the population.

[157] So declared an official document, entitled "Why Was Alexander Dubček Expelled from Party Ranks?" Although the blame for this was laid by the CPC, led by Husák, not on the era of 1948-67 and the invasion but on Dubček, the CPC admitted that "workers' aversion to the Party was [previously] getting constantly clearer." See *Rudé právo*, 18 July 1970.

[158] *Rudé právo*, 24 July 1970, p. 5.

When in May 1969 a celebration of the twenty-fourth anniversary of the liberation of Czechoslovakia by Soviet armies was planned for a large hall in the *Czech ship building-yard* in the Libeň district of Prague, the workers called a meeting, went on strike, refused to allow any Russians or their sympathizers to enter the enterprise, and forced the cancellation of the meeting at which the celebrated Soviet Army Corps was supposed to participate.[159]

At a meeting in the small town of Kamenice pod Vtáčníkom (Central Slovakia) the police broke up a riot of workers protesting the playing of the Soviet national anthem. "The rioters were pacified with the use of truncheons."[160]

Elsewhere, workers refused to take part in similar manifestations organized in order to revive pro-Soviet sentiments of 1945 that were so successfully killed in 1968.[161] It reminds me of a typical Russian Tsar in a typical Russian opera, desperately crying over the dead body of his son whom he previously murdered.

Many collectives protested against the distribution of the propaganda bulletin of the occupation armies, *Zprávy*. Because of the lack of power possessed by the legal government, it is pathetic to read in one of these resolutions: "The enterprise council requests an appropriate intervention and punishment of the culprit."[162]

There were not many workers left who in spite of everything still believed in the Soviet Union. An old lady comrade in the Prague textile industry, *Pragoodēv*, bitterly complained that out of three and a half thousand employees in 1968 only four remained "faithful to the Soviet Union" although all the others made a laughing stock of them.[163]

The treatment of pro-Soviet collaborators was often much harsher. Especially when Husák's regime, at the first anniversary of the invasion, began to use tough methods in order to prove that Soviet armies were no longer needed for suppression of street demonstrations, workers often terrorized those who participated in the brutal police actions:

> In AZNP Vrchlabí a list was posted of militiamen who took part in the actions in Prague. . . . In Prague 8 the enterprise union council . . . dealt with a "complaint" against People's Militia. An appeal was distributed in order not to allow members of the militia entry in the factory. This appeal was delivered also in Kladno. In *Tesla Radiospoje* a leaflet appeared condemning militia's behavior, an appeal not to let its members back to work, eventually to punish them.

According to this source, in Brno militiamen found pictures of gallows on their lockers, in Ostrava their windows were broken, etc.[164]

Workers defended the freedom of expression as long as they could. Miners in the coal belt around Ostrava, in northern Moravia, formed a united front with journalists to preserve freedom of speech and ensure more trade union and economic news in newspapers, radio, and television.[165] After the government managed to reintroduce strict censorship in public media and sacked most of the

[159] *Svět socialismu*, 11 June 1969, p. 6. Paul Hoffman reported on it in his dispatch to *New York Times* from Prague on 28 May 1969.
[160] An AP dispatch from Prague on 31 July 1969, quoting the Bratislava newspaper *Smena*.
[161] See, for example, *Tribuna*, 18 Feb. 1970, p. 20.
[162] *Svět práce*, 24 June 1970, p. 5.
[163] *Hlas domova*, xxv, 3 (3 Feb. 1975), p. 3.
[164] *Rudé právo*, 27 Aug. 1969, p. 2.
[165] *Mladá fronta*, 3 Feb. 1969.

journalists, for some time factory magazines openly defied the censors and continued printing material considered damaging to Soviet prestige and interests. The journal of the First Machine Factory in Brno, *Nápor* [Attack], demanded "separation from the Soviet Union and other socialist countries, achievement of sovereignty and independence in relation to the Soviet Union."[166] Although such requests were obviously Platonic and their intention was just to express collective anger and to support the government's resistance to Soviet demands, workers tried to hurt the Soviet Union when it was in their power; that is, in production of goods for delivery to the "first socialist country." This weapon was efficient. The "normalized" Scientific College of Economics at the Czechoslovak Academy of Sciences confirmed the success of this protracted action when it declared in its lengthy analysis of economic development: "Towards the end of 1968 the rate of growth of the industrial production slackened visibly [and] exports fell substantially. . . . This evolution reached its 'climax' during the first half of 1969. . . . The economy was approaching collapse."[167]

For quite some time, workers in many enterprises were able to stick together and prevent normalizers' attempts to break down their united front. In what seemed to be a pattern, employees in a shoe factory in Bardejov threatened to go on strike if the top Slovak collaborator, Vasil Bil'ak, visited their factory. He was not allowed to enter the enterprise. In Humenné, also in Eastern Slovakia, where a few loyalists invited Bil'ak to a meeting, the chairman of CPC enterprise council and of the trade union in *Chemostav*, together with workers, both members and non-members of the Party, protested against his presence and he had to leave the hall "unceremoniously through a back door."[168]

Tribuna, the first native weekly of collaborators, had to face several hurdles before it could appear and replace the occupation armies' *Zprávy*. First, its publication was postponed for three months from 1 October 1968 by a decision of the CPC CC Presidium. Then "a great majority" of editors of its board refused to work if another, Czech, collaborator, O. Švestka, became editor-in-chief. And finally, for one week, the typesetters refused to print the first issue until articles they objected to were withdrawn. The same procedure was repeated with the second number. After that several editors stopped cooperating with the paper. Even then for months the printed issues were being thrown into rivers and out of trains.[169]

Jan Štern became very active during the first months of the occupation. His weekly "Glosses" in the trade unionist paper kept attacking the new slogans

---

[166] *Rudé právo*, 30 July 1970.

[167] *Politická ekonomie*, no. 9 (Sept. 1972), p. 806. One year later, Don North, correspondent for ABC News, based in New York, reported from Prague that "factory production has dropped to about two-thirds of capacity, by the standards of the period before August 1968. In a clear expression of discontent with the occupation, workers are carrying out a prolonged nation-wide slowdown. . . . There is a feeling of fraternity between Czech intellectuals and the workers. . . . An estimated 5 per cent of factory workers have abandoned the common cause to gain privileges and higher positions." See his article "Prague: 'Nothing Is Forever'," *Nation*, 17 Aug. 1970, pp. 103–4.

[168] *Reportér*, 6 Mar. 1969, p. 2.

[169] O. Švestka, *Tribuna*, no. 33, 27 Aug. 1969, p. 2. Also a "Collective of workers of the national enterprise *Svoboda* Prague 5" refused to print in *Svět socialismu* material not in agreement with the Action Program of April 1968 and communicated its decision in a letter published in *Práce*, 14 Mar. 1969, p. 5.

which he found fraudulent. After the November 1968 Central Committee meeting, which marked an important step away from the Dubček Spring course, he defended the April Action Program as a viable one.[170] The next week he disproved the claim of Party conservatives that they represented the Left of the CPC, fighting against the supposed Rightists, led by Dubček and his allies.[171] Then he called as a witness the Italian communist leader Enrico Berlinquer for his thesis that the proper norm for "normalization" (as distinguished from "formalization") was still the Action Program. Against "realism," understood as acquiescence to the Soviet occupation, he repeated that realism should mean "accuracy, honesty to facts, respect for the meaning of conceptions:

> We hear obscure talking about "differentiation of opinions." I don't know — for the present we see that a small dogmatic minority more and more differentiates itself from the overwhelming majority. And on the contrary, exactly during the last weeks was accomplished an unusual coming together of universities and factories, creative unions with labor unions, and a situation developed when students request legalization of workers' councils and workers defend academic freedom. . . . Although the January in factories started to move slowly (it could be almost said, clumsily) then right now the factories became the steadiest and most unflinching bastions of our civic liberties.[172]

When an important state-wide meeting of representatives of workers' councils was taking place in *Škoda-Works* in Plzeň, Štern marked the occasion by an article in which he stressed their role: "The workers' class took the fate of socialism with a human face in its own hands and became the main guarantor of post-January policy. . . . The councils are not merely an economic factor. They are an extension and deepening of a really popular, workers' power."[173]

He was expelled from the Czech Journalist Union on 7 October 1969, along with eight other prominent reformist journalists, among them Jiří Pelikán (whose story will be told later). In a long condemnation of the trade union movement between 1968 and 1969, in a chapter devoted to major "Rightists" active in the labor press, Štern was named as a villain second only to his boss, editor-in-chief of *Práce*, L. Velenský.[174]

And so, in a system created out of his dreams and Soviet realities, Štern was able to work much longer as a Stalinist propagandist, helping to enslave and exploit the workers, than as a reforming socialist, defending their professional and human rights.

To liquidate the power of the workers took a little longer. In 1969 over twelve hundred trade union delegates, who represented about four million Czech workers, met from January 21 to 23 in Prague and endorsed a program of democratic socialism. One week later, Slovak unionists at their Bratislava meeting did not press for independence as strongly as their Czech colleagues. Nevertheless, they expected the Action Program to continue. The Seventh Czechoslovak All Trade Union Congress in Prague, 4–7 March, with 1,668 representatives present, again refused any subordination to the Communist Party. Consultations among

---

[170] *Práce*, 30 Nov. 1968.
[171] *Práce*, 7 Dec. 1968.
[172] *Práce*, 14 Dec. 1968.
[173] *Práce*, 9 Jan. 1969.
[174] *Práce*, 12 May 1972, supplement of 24 pages, p. 12.

individual enterprises and their resolutions about common attitudes in defense of workers' rights were frequent. On 6 June trade unionists from the Kladno Steelworks, ČKD Foundry in Prague, the Klement Gottwald Foundry in Ostrava, and five other plants met in Kladno and through the Metal Workers Union, largest in the country, presented the government with a list of strong political demands. They protested against sharp increases in prices, against dissolution of the Czechoslovak Society for Human Rights, and against "flagrant violation of our rights." They requested "undistorted application of the new economic system," implementation of workers' councils, an end to censorship, and "democratic elections to all representative organs."[175]

Although on 24 October 1968 the Černík government decided not to enlarge experimentation with *workers' councils*, their formation continued and picked up especially around the turn of years 1968/9. The first national conference of enterprise councils (or of their preparatory committees) was convened (not by the government or by the Party) in Plzeň on 9–10 January 1969, and was attended by over four hundred delegates representing almost a million workers from two hundred factories.[176] They elected a permanent "group of consultants" in order to coordinate their future activities.[177] A series of coordinating meetings also took place in plants and regions. Quite a few of the factories followed the model statutes of *Škoda* Plzeň, *Slovnafta* Bratislava, and *Synthesia* Pardubice. These statutes went beyond governmental proposals and in enterprises entrusted the workers' councils with decisive power.

At the Plzeň conference, one of the most active participants was engineer *Rudolf Slánský*, the son of the executed Party Secretary of the same name. As a representative of the Diesel Engines Division of the Prague *ČKD*, he stressed the need to "create political conditions for the economic reform." In the workers' councils he saw "self-managing organs, a certain embryo of a system of self-government": "We fight for the workers' councils as self-governing organs and not only as an expression of workers' participation in management. Thus, in fact, we fight for the same [goal] as we have started to fight for since January."[178]

A week later Slánský published an article in the Prague trade union daily in which he attacked the old command system as well as the State exclusive property rights to the means of production. In fact he requested the expropriation of the Party as the monopoly owner:

> The only possible method by which the bureaucratic-administrative model can be transformed into a democratic model is the *abolition of the monopoly of exercise of the proprietary rights on the part of the State and* a decentralization of this monopoly by *transferring it* to those in

[175] See *Rudé právo*, 12 June 1969, and especially an attack by V. Landa, in *Tribuna*, no. 24, 25 June 1969, since the author quotes large portions verbatim. In *Práce*, 4 Nov. 1969, eleven comrades from various workshops complained about the complete victory of democratic workers everywhere in Bohemia.

[176] *Radio Prague*, 9 and 10 Jan. 1969.

[177] *Zemědělské noviny*, 21 Feb. 1969.

[178] Page 20a of the minutes of the Plzeň conference, as quoted by Michael Lang, general director of the Lignite Mines and Briquette Works in Sokolovo, *Hospodářské noviny*, 10 July 1970, supplement of 8 pages, p. 6.

whose interest the socialist enterprises operate — i.e. *to the collectives of workers* of these enterprises.[179]

Two days later a popular cultural weekly came out with a demonstrative title over the front page: "All Power to the Workers' Councils!", echoing Lenin's slogan of 1917, "All Power to the Soviets!" The author of the article wrote:

> If the workers are deciding to take into their own hands the production, they do it because they do not want to be merely a part of the production process, but its creators. . . . It is a concrete form of a revolution opening a way to pluralism of a completely different kind than we can, for the present, imagine. . . . As the Soviets in February 1917, the workers' councils again arise spontaneously. . . . It is as if once more we could open the first pages of a revolutionary reader and after all the disappointments and despairs once more could endeavor after freedom in this world.[180]

In spite of the overwhelming presence of foreign armies in Czechoslovakia, the situation in factories approached revolutionary proportions. And it was supposed to be a movement returning to the democratic revolution of the Russian February 1917 and not to its perverted counter-revolutionary abolition by Lenin and Trotsky in October. As one of the leading normalizers, Peter Colotka, at the time CC Presidium member, said: "The Rightist forces had attempted, through the workers' councils, to establish a new power structure which was to weaken the Party's leading role."[181] The Party leaders need to have a great self-confidence in order to see themselves as Leftists and to denounce as Rightist the freely elected workers' councils.

According to incomplete data, at the end of June 1969, there existed in Czechoslovakia around three hundred workers' councils and the same number of preparatory committees that were not yet allowed to function legally. The workers were led, willingly, by intellectuals. The majority of members of the workers' councils were engineers and technicians.[182] "Employees felt that their interests as *co-owners* and as *entrepreneurs* would best be served by electing highly qualified people: white-collar workers. . . . In electing ROH [union] officers, workers voted for their own 'kind'."[183]

In the spring and especially during the summer of 1969, the Husák leadership began to crack down on trade unions and workers' councils. As a result, the unrest among workers in Ostrava, Brno, Prague, and other cities became very serious, as was admitted by the Party.[184] During mass demonstrations on the first anniversary of the invasion, 1,502 persons were arrested in Prague alone. A breakdown by occupation revealed that workers predominated.[185]

---

[179] *Práce*, 18 Feb. 1969. Emphasis added. Such a demand was then very popular. It appeared in a number of workers' resolutions.

[180] J. Chaloupecký in *Listy*, 20 Feb. 1969.

[181] *Pravda*, 6 Feb. 1970.

[182] In sixteen selected enterprises the elected councils were formed by 20.8% workers, 74.5% engineers and technicians, and 4.7% others. See Lang, *op. cit.*, p. 4.

[183] Karel Kovanda, "Czechoslovak Workers' Councils (1968-1969)," *Telos*, no. 28, summer 1976, p. 51. Emphasis is in the original. In 1969 the Institute of Technology in Prague studied ninety-five workers' councils and reported that 70% of elected members belonged to the technical intelligentsia and 25% were skilled workers. See Miloš Bárta, *Reportér*, 3 Apr. 1969, pp. 7-8.

[184] *International Herald Tribune*, 26-27 July 1969.

[185] *Mladá fronta*, 26 Aug. 1969.

In October, Ján Duži, deputy chairman of the Czechoslovak Trade Union Council, revealed that it was not easy to overcome workers' resistance and added: "We shall take the offensive and bring to an end the political struggle with Rightist opportunist forces."[186] And so in the name of a fictitious workers' class a merciless fight was going on against all democratically elected members of trade unions, workers' councils, and Communist Party organizations, since they backed about 95 per cent of the real workers and other employees in their attempt at self-government.

Practically it meant that whole organizations were liquidated and new ones, composed of loyal but hated comrades and often police agents, were imposed on unwilling masses. The enterprise CC committee of the *Iron- and Wire-Works* in Bohumín repeatedly refused demands coming from above to return to pre-January type of dictatorial policies, and was therefore declared dissolved by the new district Party leadership, which was itself installed by Husák and his group from Prague. After that the plant director was dismissed and a new one brought in. All was done in order to "strengthen discipline and order," although it was admitted that these "measures" were "unpopular."[187]

In the *First Machine Factory* in Brno, in order to "achieve a firm political and economic consolidation," after the local Party organization refused to budge from democratic principles, it was forbidden to function in December 1969. A newly established enterprise CP committee had to "execute changes in basic organizations and in-plant trade unions." General and branch directorships were replaced. "The workers' council was annulled, the enterprise trade union board was disbanded." Personal examinations of Party members and large-scale purges were initiated. Many employees lost their jobs.[188]

In the steelworks of the *Klement Gottwald New Foundry* in Kunčice, only in January 1970 a new enterprise CP organization could be installed, after the CP committee elected and recognized by workers was forced to resign. Comrades in protest stopped paying membership fees. Resistance in 1969 resulted in non-fulfillment of the local plan by 30,000 tons of steel. The "Dubčekist" trade union contained only sixteen communists out of forty-six elected committee members and was therefore abolished.[189]

The trade union at the *Institute for Nuclear Research* in Řež, under constant pressure from above from October 1969 till January 1970 to reverse its previous decisions and resolutions, refused to recant and was therefore "as a whole . . . relieved of its functions and its activity was terminated." All the trade union committee members of the workshops then resigned (with the exception of one) in a show of solidarity.[190]

In the *ČKD Locomotive Factory* in Prague support for the reforming majority of the CPC continued throughout 1969. Of their many activities at least one should be mentioned. On 16 April their trade unionists took part in a meeting of

---

[186] *Práce*, 7 Oct. 1969.

[187] Drahomír Blažej, "With New, Fresh Forces," *Rudé právo*, 29 Dec. 1969.

[188] *Rudé právo*, 30 July 1970.

[189] *Rude právo*, 15 Jan. 1970. In the Number Three plant — Maintenance — only thirty-three out of three hundred Party officials were allowed to keep their positions. See *Nová svoboda*, 12 Feb. 1971.

[190] Zázvorka, *Svět práce*, 24 June 1970, p. 5.

representatives of forty-five Prague enterprises with the Union of University Students, in order to send delegations with appropriate reformist resolutions to the CPC CC session. The attempts to destroy participatory democracy in the enterprise were being frustrated as late as March 1970 when its director Kalík, together with trade union and Party representatives, refused to recall and punish its personnel chief D. Dorn (discussed here previously) since he was "industrious, full of initiative, and constructive." The interference in the enterprise cost the Party and unions dearly: they lost 50 and almost 30 per cent, respectively, of their paying members.[191]

As late as May 1970, in Trenčín the CP organization at the district national committee defended its members and especially engineer Mišových (who considered talking to Soviet generals to be under his dignity). Then the whole Party organization was dissolved and fifty-two comrades were purged from the Party by commissars sent from above.[192]

The purges of directors and Party as well as trade union leaders in *Dioptra*, Turnov (also previously discussed), took effect in April 1970.[193] In the plant *Praga* proceedings similar to those in Turnov took place. Small groups of workers and members of their families, altogether ninety-nine in number, figured prominently in the Soviet claim that their troops were invited, since they sent a loyal letter to Moscow in 1968. The representatives elected by an overwhelming majority of non-loyal workers (who had ostracized the ninety-nine) were dismissed and their place was taken over by *apparatchiks* nominated from outside of the factory.[194]

In the important *V.I. Lenin (Škoda) Works* in Plzeň by 6 May 1970, twenty-nine Party organizations had been denied the right to conduct interviews with Party members during the purge. Appointees from above had to come (as elsewhere) and enforce the screening of comrades.[195] Jan Šimek, imposed upon the regional committee of the CPC in Plzeň as its leading secretary, boasted: "We have smashed Rightist centres in *Škodovka*" but the loss of Party members in *Škoda Works* was, according to him, "striking."[196] Voluntarily quitting the Party was one of the few weapons workers could use when they wanted to express their opinion about the post-Dubčekian course of the Party. The propagandists first described them (for instance, in this case, one-third of all CP cells of steel-workers in *Škoda*) as "honest and honorable people"[197] and attempted to picture them (elsewhere) as "disoriented" only:

> In one district, 300 persons, 75% of them workers, resigned from the Party within two weeks after the April Plenum [when Husák replaced Dubček]. They were good workers, honest

[191] *Rudé právo*, 23 and 24 July 1970.

[192] *Pravda*, 29 July 1970. The purge of the national committee members, supposedly elected by the people, was drastic. Before May 1970 "more than 12,700" deputies had been removed from their posts in the Czech lands and in Slovakia before April 5,689 deputies of district, local, and municipal national committees had been dismissed. The official agency *ČTK* quoting the Czech Premier Josef Korčák, 16 May 1970, and *Pravda*, 11 April 1970.

[193] Jarušek, *Tribuna*, 3 June 1970, p. 20.

[194] Jiří Hrubý, "All Power to Purification, Unification, and Activization," *Život strany*, no. 8, 13 Apr. 1970, pp. 41-4.

[195] *Rudé právo*, 6 May 1970.

[196] *Rudé právo*, 24 Nov. 1970, p. 3.

[197] *Večerní Praha*, 12 May 1969, p. 2.

and upright, but still disoriented. In their view, there was "nothing else left for them to do, unless they wanted to lose their honor and twist their character."[198]

The voluntary resignations from the Party took on massive proportions when the CP membership of Alexander Dubček was suspended and this suspension was announced by *Rudé právo* on 21 March 1970. In many ČKD workshops not a single worker remained in the Party and similar protest resignations took place in other factories.[199]

Although it is difficult to find documentary proof, since the regime did not announce fires and other accidents, sabotage was another weapon quite often used by workers who hated the return to "socialism with an inhuman face." One of the rare insights into problems the Husák normalizers had to cope with was offered by a CPC internal bi-weekly. The author of a substantial survey of growing criminality, himself a high police chief, complained that the usual pilfering of socialist property became much worse, was "the most widespread," had "mass character," and "affected every sector of the economy. . . . the actual damage is not known and cannot be objectively calculated." The major problem was "not only in the mass incidence of this sort of criminal activity, but also in the increased difficulty of uncovering it." Damages worth millions often result from "calculated, prepared in advance, systematically repeated, and continuing illegal activity." Also "the stealing of funds from the payroll is extensive." Workers and management cooperated in the creation of a "widespread special labor market" and "private enterprise . . . has almost completely evaded control." Black market, systematic corruption, and bribery are not at all exceptional but created a "mutually conditioned system." But something new was added to this increased and systematic stealing and corruption — a direct sabotage:

> Fires, industrial breakdowns, and major accidents become a very serious problem, since they inflict heavy losses upon our economy. In 1969 there occurred an *unprecedented growth of damages caused by fires*, totaling almost 470 million crowns. This represents only direct damage, but the consequent damages through disruption of production are often manifoldly higher. This is true especially of the great fires in large factories causing many millions of damages. *There were three times as many such fires in 1969 than in the preceding year.*

The police official found it intolerable that the public kept refusing to help the police which was regularly met with "mistrust and lack of cooperation."[200]

Between 1969 and 1970 the regime managed to "normalize" the situation in factories but at an enormous cost to the economy and to the popularity of the political system. As Dr. Husák once said, "it felt like in a burned out house."[201] People reacted to the fact that the country was stolen from them by stealing and damaging what they could not take back.

Considering the fact that all the documentation presented here was taken from official sources, which did not have any interest in acknowledging the truth more

---

[198] Oldřich Švestka, "To Win the Favor of the Working Class," *Tribuna*, 28 May 1969.

[199] UPI, Prague, 1 Apr. 1970.

[200] Pplk. [Lieutenant Colonel] Rudolf Pathy, chief officer of the Federal Criminal Headquarters at the Czechoslovak Ministry of the Interior, "Current Problems of Criminality in the National Economy," *Život strany*, no. 14, 6 July 1970, pp. 21–4. Emphasis was added.

[201] *Práce*, 4 Nov. 1969, p. 4. Quoted by a participant in a round-table discussion, editor-in-chief, Bedřich Kačírek.

than absolutely necessary for their purposes, the situation must have been, and most probably was, even more damaging than admitted, to their and Soviet interests.

The sullen mood and determined resistance of the working class did not abate after 1970 but continued to mar efforts of those in power, ruling in the name of the workers but against them, in spite of the apparent success of the "normalization." At the end of 1972, one of the *apparatchiks* working in the economic section of the CPC CC expressed the Sisyphian task of the men in charge of the ČSSR, ruled as a Soviet *guberniya*, when he wrote: "Undoubtedly, one of the most complicated tasks is to win the working people over to socialist ideas."[202]

[202] E. Podzemný, "Economics and Ideological Work," *Tribuna*, 13 Dec. 1972; trans. RFE Research: *Czechoslovak Press Survey*, no. 2467, 11 Jan. 1973, p. 7 of 8 polycopied pages.

Chapter 3.

Patterns of stratification:
Workers and intellectuals

The Theme

With some justification, it could be claimed that the Czechoslovak revolution of 1968 — in one of its major aspects — was the result of two conflicting sociological concepts. On one side, coming from the East, stood the Marxist-Leninist-Stalinist dogma asserting that the ruling class of Czechoslovakia was, and should be, the workers' class, fulfilling its historical mission in an anti-capitalist world revolution, under the leadership of its vanguard, the Communist party of Czechoslovakia, and supported in its efforts by the class of collective farmers and the social stratum of the intelligentsia. In opposition to this thesis was growing a more modern, Western, concept of a complex social stratification which, after the elimination of antagonistic classes between 1948 and 1960, should allow, in a democratized system, a competition of interest and pressure groups, in order to develop from below a common, non-class, societal programme. The intellectuals were acting as catalysts, as spokesmen, and, we should not forget, as formulators of the conflict.

At the same time, this ideological or sociological debate — depending on the position of the protagonists — about the class or pluralist character of Czechoslovak society in the 1960s, showed, at least in some instances, strong symptoms of a class conflict between two opposing sets of élites, the in and out, between subjects and objects of power, the governing and governed, or the managers and producers.[1]

The polarization into a bureaucratic-oligarchic regime of power on one side and, on the other, the reforming aspirants to a different system of pluralistic social democratic structures culminated in the years of 1967/8 in a temporary victory of the reformers. In 1969/70 a restoration of the previous autocratic government took place, with revenge.

The ambition of the CPC leaders, including Novotný, to proceed with a scientific exploration of societal trends and consultation with teams of scientists appointed to study them and propose necessary changes, permitted the evolution of the 1960s to take place and finally to climax in a challenge to the leadership which only too late realized the dangers implied. When in a mounting crisis leading politicians like Novotný and Hendrych lost their jobs in 1968 and with them a galaxy of bureaucratic supporters either saw their positions and prestige

---

[1] The last division uses the terminology adopted by Jaroslav Krejčí in his book *Social Change and Stratification in Postwar Czechoslovakia* (London: Macmillan, 1972), p. 138.

withdrawn or threatened, they mounted a counter-offensive which was encouraged and used by the Soviet Union and its allies in order to preserve their imperial and domestic interests.

In this chapter I will concentrate on inter-related issues of the membership of the Communist Party as the leading force in Czechoslovakia and seat of power after 1948, on changes in the composition of the CPC, on the relative strength and importance of workers and the intelligentsia in the Party and in the State, as well as on various interpretations of the roles of different groups in a socialist society.[2]

1. First stage: Imported Stalinism

Around the year 1948, the communist intelligentsia accepted the role assigned to it by the leaders of the CPC. Before the *coup d'état*, they were willing to support the efforts of the Party by their writings, speeches, and signing of manifestoes that helped to present the Party as a revolutionary but democratic force which has inherited all the best traditions of Czechoslovak history and would complement its progress towards an egalitarian, socially just, and humanistic Republic. Many leading intellectuals joined the Party and engaged themselves publicly towards its victory. Between the years of 1945 and 1949 the CPC was happy to accept almost anybody who expressed the wish. Individual Party organizations and districts competed as in a contest who would register more *new members*.

Although the CPC at its foundation in 1921 had some 350,000 members, in 1929 the number dropped drastically to just over 20,000. This seeming paradox — at the beginning of the great economic crisis — can be explained by the fact that the original enthusiasm did not survive the stabilization of the democratic system of the ČSR and especially the bolshevization of the Party under Klement Gottwald in 1929, after a direct intervention from Moscow. Till 1936 the membership grew again to 70,000 and after World War II the CPC started with some 30,000 members only. At a time when the prestige of the Soviet Union and of Czechoslovak communists as anti-fascist fighters was high, a great recruiting campaign brought the membership, before the end of 1945, to 800,000. The first million was passed in the middle of March 1946. The social composition of the Party then, at the time of the Eighth Party Congress, was: 57.7% workers, 12.8% farmers, 4.1% tradesmen, 9.2% intelligentsia, 16.2% others.[3]

Another large campaign to enlist new members, which started in September 1947, was almost as successful as the first and before February 1948 the number of communists reached 1,400,000.[4] The *coup* changed the situation. Since then, at least for some time, membership in the CPC was the only guarantee of job security, of access to responsible and well-paid positions, and of higher education for

---

[2] In communist usage the term "intelligentsia" refers to a social stratum whose work is mainly based on mental ("brain") capacities and usually requires higher than average education. It is roughly divided into the creative intelligentsia (the intellectuals), professional (lawyers, educators, physicians, etc.), and technical intelligentsia, e.g. engineers. Most writers accept this terminology since they depend on communist statistics.

[3] Jaroslav Fulka, *Nová mysl*, no. 3, 16 Mar. 1970, pp. 347-9.

[4] *Ibid.*, p. 351.

children. People in offices often found on their desks a Party membership form. Those who did not fill it out lost their jobs.[5]

The Social Democratic Party was forcibly incorporated into the CPC and in the process out of 363,735 members (in November 1947) 113,535 accepted Communist Party membership cards. Also in 1948, the Slovak Communist Party was incorporated into the C.P. of Czechoslovakia. Until then the Slovak Party was kept separate for tactical reasons — it appealed to Slovak nationalism. From pre-war 12,000 members it grew, before February 1948, to 210,000 and in the Fall of 1948 to 407,000. In comparison with pre-war figures the Slovak C.P. grew thirtyfold, the Czech C.P. seventy times greater. Before the end of 1948, the Communist Party of Czechoslovakia had 2,535,248 members, over one-third of the voting population.[6]

The *social composition of the CPC* changed radically. In 1948 the proportion of workers in the Party went down to 39.8 per cent[7]. But this trend was already started before the mass influx of officials and office employees; the workers began to leave the Party before the February *coup*: their relative representation in the CPC at the end of 1947 was down to 49 per cent from almost 58 per cent in March 1946.[8] One of the perennial problems of the Party claiming to be the vanguard of the working class thus manifested itself even before the seizure of total power in its name.

The relationship between the numbers of manual workers and the intelligentsia in the Party becomes even more revealing when we realize that by 1948 almost 50 per cent of the Czechoslovak intelligentsia joined the CPC,[9] but although workers in the material sphere of production in 1950 amounted to only 40 per cent of members of the CPC, they formed 78 per cent of all wage-earners and salaried employees.[10] Thus the self-appointed vanguard of the workers' class registered a perceptibly lower percentage of joiners from the workers than among the intelligentsia. The explanation is simple. There was no danger of losing a job for manual workers who did not join the Party. And a white-collar career was possible only with the Party card in the pocket.

After February 1948, the most politically active workers with the Communist Party card were *elevated to positions of leadership* in both economic and political systems. The statistics are not exact and often vary, according to source, between 200,000 and 300,000. At the same time, a few hundred thousand former specialists, managers, professors, scientists, etc., had to make place for the Party activists and enter the ranks of the working class.[11] From these times comes the joke that the workers' language changed for the better under the Party influence; you can

[5] *Ibid.*, p. 353.

[6] Bohumil Němec, *Život strany*, no. 15, 14 July 1972, p. 7. Fulka, *op. cit.*, p. 353, agrees. But according to *Dějiny Československa v datech* [*History of Czechoslovakia in Dates*] (Prague, 1968), p. 379, from the end of February to the end of August 1948, the CPC membership increased from 1,409,661 to 2,674,838.

[7] Karel Havlíček, *Život strany*, no. 13, 22 June 1970, p. 15.

[8] Fulka., *op. cit.*, p. 355.

[9] Antonín Vaněk, *Tribuna*, no. 24, 17 June 1970, p. 1.

[10] Radovan Richta *et. al.*, *Civilization at the Crossroads* (International Arts and Sciences Press, 1969), p. 328.

[11] J. Krejčí estimates that about 400,000 former professionals, self-employed, and non-manual employees had to become manual workers; *op. cit.*, pp. 44–5.

overhear workers telling each other; "Professor Doctor, could you kindly hand me the spade?" — "Sure, Your Excellency".

As a result of these radical changes, *the importance of education, qualification, and specialized knowledge diminished* and the economic as well as political consequences often were disastrous.

> In 1953, 60 per cent of directors and 85 per cent of foremen did not have any expert education. . . . In 1955 there were 85,000 unqualified persons in positions demanding university education and in places requiring secondary technical education even 248,000 unskilled personnel. The workers and the intelligentsia had to pay dearly for this notion of the "dictatorship of the proletariat." Still in 1961 out of 657,000 people with university or other higher education (between the ages of 25 to 59, more than half school finishers after 1950) only 11.3 per cent held management positions.[12]

Police did not ignore the workers. In 1951 among prisoners condemned for "political crimes" the working class was represented by 41 per cent, other employees by 21 per cent, former capitalists (mostly small tradespeople) by 15 per cent, and farmers by 23 per cent.[13]

For approximately six years (1948–54), the Communist Party of Czechoslovakia led the *process of a radical overhaul* of the State and of the whole society. The promises of a special and democratic road to socialism were forgotten and the country was fast bolshevized and turned into a Soviet satellite, more often than not with an eager assistance by the Czech and Slovak communists. Twenty years later would one of them, *Zdeněk Hejzlar* — born in 1921 and between 1945 and 1951 a leading functionary of the Czechoslovak Youth Organization (ČSM) — see it in a less positive way:

> In an atmosphere of ecstasy after an easy victory and out of subjectivist ideas about unlimited possibilities of the rate of societal transformation, and in an atmosphere of a game on a civil war, the Communist Party of Czechoslovakia in the years of 1949 till 1953 created a new economic and political system. What was realized was an *etatistic and bureaucratic model of the "proletarian dictatorship,"* as it was built up by Stalin in the Soviet Union . . . . Naturally, the result was not a dictatorship of a class but a dictatorship by the party, or rather by its *apparat*, and the formation of a peculiar bureaucratic system of managerial administration with a high concentration of power in the hands of a narrow group of party leadership.[14]

While between 1948 and 1958 the number of industrial workers grew exactly by the same amount as the number of farmers diminished (half a million), the growth of the white-collar employees was phenomenal — from 1,700,000 in 1948 to 2,300,000 ten years later, that is 100,000 larger than the industrial workers. Since in the same period the number of shops and similar services was drastically reduced, the political, economic as well as police and armed forces personnel clearly mushroomed.[15]

---

[12] Zdeněk Hejzlar, "On Politics and Internal Evolution of the CPC after 1948", in *Systémové změny* [Systemic Changes], ed. by Adolf Müller (Cologne: Index, 1972), p. 73. My translation.

[13] *Ibid.*, p. 75.

[14] Hejzlar, *op. cit.*, p. 72. Emphasis in the Czech original.

[15] Compounded from a table in *Zemědělské noviny*, 24 June 1971, p. 3. The growth of "other workers" continued and by 1968 reached the number of 3,000,000 as compared with 2,600,000 industrial workers and 1,200,000 collective farmers. *Ibid.*

The period 1948–53 was marked by nationalization of all industries, banking, and trade, by an extensive industrialization and production of armaments, and by collectivization of agriculture. The egalitarian Czechoslovak society was even more homogenized through general levelling of wages.

> In contrast to the Stalinist revolution in the U.S.S.R. during the 1930s, where one of the costs of rigid industrialization was gross inequality of income distribution and social prestige, Czechoslovakia's revolution had the opposite effect. . . . The effect of nationalization and collectivization was to "proletarianize" all individuals. All became employees, directly or indirectly, of the state. . . . In Czechoslovakia, as in all totally nationalized and collectivized East European countries, proletarian mass society came to be exploited in a very real way, by the party and managerial élites.[16]

It took years before this conclusion would be reached by the communist intelligentsia. When in the spring of 1953, after a monetary reform, which wiped out almost all savings, a rebellion took place in some of the most industrialized Czech and Moravian or Silesian cities, it was led by workers and not by intellectuals. It took another three years and Khrushchev's attack on Stalinism before at least a few of the writers would speak up at the Congress of their Union. In 1956 some literary and scientific journals started to publish critical articles on themes which would become popular in the 1960s, so that one on the "normalizing" studies could later contain this complaint:

> The theoretical thesis of the militant counter-revolutionary grouping of the intelligentsia that "in 1956 ends the dominion of ideology and the era of pure science begins" marked a public declaration of a political program, namely that this group of intelligentsia refused the hegemony of the ruling working class and its dominion — the State of proletarian dictatorship.[17]

A systematic campaign was mounted against all expressions of *"revisionism,"* which practically signified a political challenge by the intelligentsia to the claim of the bureaucratic bosses of the CPC that only they had the right to lead the society, as a sample will show:

> The best known and the most widely spread among our intelligentsia was the thesis about the leading role of the intelligentsia; this thesis was greatly stimulated by the known editorial article published by *Kultúrny život* in 1956 under the title "On the Duties and Problems of Our Intelligentsia." Revisionism of this thesis consists in the fact that it denies, in contradiction to the theory of Marxism-Leninism as well as to revolutionary practice, the leading part of the workers' class and the controlling and organizational role of the Communist Party in the socialist revolution. . . .
>
> The above-mentioned thesis about the "leading role of the intelligentsia in the nation" is still alive among one part of our intelligentsia. . . . Revisionist tendencies were apparent in various "resolutions" voted by some cultural institutions, etc. . . . Authors of satirical programs and stories concentrated on "criticism" of our officials and in particular of our cadre officials. . . . It has gone so far that some of our scientific and literary people explained their looking into the past saying that there is now not as much enthusiasm among our people as there was in 1948.[18]

Large-scale *purges* took place. Thus, in 1958, the *apparat* of the CPC created a

---

[16] David W. Paul, "The Repluralization of Czechoslovak Politics in the 1960's", *Slavic Review*, vol. 23, no. 4 (Dec. 1974), pp. 731 and 734.

[17] J. Obzina, *Nová mysl*, no. 3, Mar. 1973, p. 353.

[18] Michal Pecho (Secretary of the Slovak CP in Bratislava), "In the Interest of a Reform", *Predvoj*, 18 Dec. 1958.

special screening commission which purged 995 out of 4,560 Czech members of the Czechoslovak Academy of Sciences, which was founded in 1952 under the sponsorship of a governmental commission led by Ladislav Štoll. Roughly 21 per cent of academicians, who had passed strict political entrance requirements, lost their positions. Only one year before, the Academy was elevated to the role of adviser to the government on all fundamental questions of science. In 1969 the Academy made it clear that the purge was a case of gross manipulation of its organs and mistreatment of its, mainly communist, members by Party interference, contrary to law and common sense, and that it terribly harmed the interests of science and society.[19]

The search for an alternate program continued under the surface. The old system survived but was condemned and generally on the defensive. Probably to most of the people, including the communists, it became clear, as a popular joke expressed it, that if by definition "capitalism was exploitation of man by a fellowman, communism was just the opposite."

2.   Second stage: Reforms

On 11 July 1960 the Czechoslovak Communist Party had officially declared in a *New Constitution* that the country had reached the stage of socialism, the only state other than the Soviet Union to make this claim. The nationalization of mines, industries, trade, banking, etc., has been accomplished for some time and the collectivization of agriculture was completed in the same year. In November of 1960, the conference of eighty-one communist parties in Moscow proclaimed the independence of individual parties and their right to march towards the same goal of communism with due respect to local conditions, without fear of interference by other parties. A new era seemed to have started.

The Czechoslovak Republic officially became the Czechoslovak Socialist Republic. At first, the change in the name of the State by adding the adjective socialist and the promulgation in the new Constitution of a "class-less society" in an "all-people's State" were believed to be just another instance in a long series of empty propagandistic slogans. But a growing number of the Party intelligentsia took it seriously and demanded appropriate and real changes in society and its administration.

At a conference of social scientists in Liblice in 1961, the *theory of two distinct phases* in the formation of a communist society — first, *socialism*, and second, *communism* — became the base for future attempts to change the system from a dictatorship into a democracy. Since, according to Marx, people in communism would be free and happy, during a period of transition from socialism to communism, which was officially inaugurated, these aims, it was claimed at the conference, must be gradually introduced through liberal and democratic processes. Czechoslovak social scientists agreed that even in a socialist society *the fight between the old and the new goes on* and that conservative forces, often surviving the period of "vulgarization of Marxist principles in theory and errors in practice", and of the "cult of the

---

[19]   *Věstník ČSAV* [*Gazette of the CSAS*], no. 5, Sept.–Oct. 1969, pp. 489–99.

personality" (Stalinism) must be overcome.[20] And so in the name of Marx and progress, communist social scientists attempted to storm the fortress of Party conservatives.

The Party leadership was willing to listen to specialists and encourage *research*, especially as it was becoming obvious that the economy was failing. The ambitious Third Five Year Plan, which started on 1 January 1961, had to be abandoned after eighteen months and the CPC embarked upon a program of a solid research in social sciences. The Party intelligentsia had its chance. Reality could be studied, Western sciences explored, and alternate plans prepared. The intellectuals, instead of being disciplined and obedient servants, could aspire at least to the role of advisors if not mentors.

Between 1961 and 1963 the depleted Czechoslovak Academy of Sciences was reorganized, strengthened, and became the centre of a planned development of sciences. During the 1960s the number of scientific workers reached almost 10,000.[21]

Although the Twelfth Party Congress, meeting in December 1962, had a centralizing influence, it allowed a relatively frank *discussion* and encouraged the intelligentsia to demand more freedom for their professional endeavors.

The Party leadership was inviting the intellectuals to come to its rescue and offer scientific help. The *admission of failure* opened the door. The intellectuals moved into the corridors of power, did their work but as the old viziers, felt contempt for their useless and bungling masters who were standing in their way and kept postponing, stifling, or compromising their reform plans. Access to secret Party archives opened their eyes to the criminal activities of the leadership in the 1950s, study of truthful statistics about the whole society showed them its deep malaise, contacts with foreign arts and sciences strengthened their determination to act and create as free citizens with renewed dignity, and a return to their own nations' democratic traditions helped them to overcome the import of Soviet political culture.

During the first half of the 1960s, most of the alternate *seats of knowledge, information, and intellectual power* would be formed. The historians, writers, theatre and film artists, sociologists, other social and natural scientists would form themselves into more or less cohesive opinion and pressure groups. They had close personal contacts, professional loyalty was extended to non-communists, and an *alternate program* could be discussed in literary weeklies, published in hundreds of thousands of copies. Important books by Kosík, Mlynář, Šik, Lakatoš, etc., prepared the community for changes. Pavel Machonin published his first book *Cesty k beztřídní společnosti* [*Roads to a Classless Society*] in 1961. The leadership of the Party did facilitate the formulation of a socialist — but also democratic and pluralist — program by its creation of large *interdisciplinary teams*, composed of hundreds of specialists from various fields and led by Pavel Machonin, Zdeněk Mlynář, Radovan Richta, and Ota Šik. There was no strict separation between them and the political leaders of the Party; on the contrary, quite a few

[20] See František Velek "Hybnésily vývoje sociální struktury" [Driving Forces in the Evolution of a Social Structure"], in *Sociální struktura Socialistické Společnost.* [*Social Structure of Socialist Society*], ed. by Pavel Machonin (Prague: Svoboda, 1967), pp. 157-8.

[21] *Věstník ČSAV*, no. 6, Dec. 1972, pp. 289-96.

apparatchiks[22] became progressive and the alternate program (at least in parts) was winning supporters among the top leaders themselves.

> Impetus for a change did not come from the outside, apart from the regime, from oppositional forces and . . . had a socialist, reforming, not at all anti-socialist, contra-revolutionary character. To these pressures, to a certain degree, hesitatingly and partly with aversion, adapts itself even the power élite; all levels, it is forced both to take over partial reform thoughts, and to admit into its ranks their inherent or potential followers (qualified people).[23] people).[23]

As the intellectuals rightly claimed, the dividing line was between the new and the old, the progressives and conservatives.

According to the official census of the *population* in 1961 (March), Czechoslovakia had 13,746,000 citizens. There were 7,738,000 workers, 3,834,000 other employees, 2,114,000 farmers, 9,000 independent professionals, 51,000 craftsmen and tradespeople.[24] At the end of 1967, the same table gives these numbers: 8,359,000 workers, 4,243,000 other employees, 1,675,000 farmers, 11,000 independent professionals, 45,000 craftsmen and tradespeople. The number of farmers went down considerably and the number of other employees grew faster than the number of workers. But according to the authors of a collective work devoted to the exploration of the scientific and technological revolution this relative growth was far from ideal. Following their computation, between 1960 and 1966, the percentage distribution of wage-earners and salaried employees by branches of the national economy showed that in Czechoslovakia the workers in the material sphere of production declined from 75.1 to 71 per cent and the workers in other branches of the national economy (including commerce, education, science and research, health and social security) increased from 24.9 to 29 per cent.[25] They admired the U.S.A. inversion of the ratio of "immediate production" to "services" from 59:41 in 1940 to 47:53 in 1946 and the Canadian change from 61:39 (1940) to 54:46 (1960). Since they expected that "in the course of the scientific and technological revolution the volume of 'services' will grow to the point of occupying 40–60 per cent of national labour in coming decades" they were worried about the scientific and technological lag of Czechoslovakia behind other industrialized countries.[26]

Pavel Machonin and his team shared the ideas about necessary *changes in social structure in post-industrial societies:*

> Creative cooperation of workers as the leading social force and of the intelligentsia as the initiative force, carrying the scientific-technical revolution and further cultural transformations, determines continued destiny of socialism in our and other socialist countries.[27]

---

[22] In the summer of 1968, the Party *apparat* had 4,733 political workers; 34% had university and 28% specialist qualifications. In the *apparat* of the CPC Central Committee in Prague 69% had university education and in Bratislava 77%. See Z. Hejzlar, "On Politics. . . .," *Systemic Changes*, p. 88.

[23] Pavel Machonin, *Politika*, no. 3, 13 Mar. 1969, p. 15.

[24] V. Srb, *Demografie*, no. 2, June 1968, p. 181.

[25] Radovan Richta, *Civilization at the Crossroads*, p. 328.

[26] *Ibid.*, p. 121.

[27] P. Machonin, in *Sociální struktura . . .*, p. 150.

Some authors went further than that and demanded the recognition of the intelligentsia as brain workers politically equal in socialism to manual workers since without them the manual workers' class could not at all accomplish the mission assigned to it by Marx and history.[28] The intelligentsia demanded (at least) conceptual *equality with the manual workers*. Pavel Machonin expressed it categorically:

> The intelligentsia as a stratum of the socialist society possesses equal rights and in its creative sections fulfills a task of great import — it carries the scientific technical revolution and in general the progressive development of culture. That means that without an active participation and help by the creative intelligentsia, the working class cannot realize the leading role in a progressive development of a society and that without it [the intelligentsia] it cannot come at all to such a progressive development.[29]

On the same page, Machonin stressed that in order to solve some serious problems in the situation of the intelligentsia that would correspond to its great, objectively given, task, the highly qualified intellectual work must be materially rewarding, the qualification of the economic-technical and other leading managers must be greatly enhanced, and the conditions for scientific research and university work must be substantially improved. In such demands for recognition, as seen in this summary, the challenge to the actual, uneducated, rulers in the name of the workers' class of the day was apparent. A competent and competitive élite was raising its head.

How large was the intelligentsia? The categories in communist sources lack consistency but their statistics generally recognized two, sometimes overlapping, groups: The *intelligentsia* proper (white-collar and professional workers — literally "brainworkers") and *educated specialists* with specialized secondary or higher education. But fully "25 per cent (398,794 persons) of all white-collar and professional workers in 1966 had only a primary education."[30]

At the same time, "of the total number of 657,000 with secondary and higher education in the twenty-five to fifty-nine age group, only 11.3 per cent actually held leading posts.[31] A member of the *apparat*, who remained faithful to the Soviet line after 1968 and cannot be suspected of being biased in favor of the intelligentsia, wrote in 1971:

> The intelligentsia is the social group which has recorded the greatest increase in our most recent history. . . . While the groups of the population classified as intelligentsia numbered 426,000 persons in 1930, and 591,000 members in 1947, more than a million persons belonged to this category by 1962.
>
> In 1958, persons engaged in intellectual work constituted 19.8 per cent of the

---

[28] Zdeněk Valenta in *Sociální struktura. . .* , p. 468. Even the non-intellectual President Novotný in his speech to the Thirteenth Party Congress in 1966 admitted that the intelligentsia was becoming part of the working class. See *Práce*, 12 Oct. 1966.

[29] See his *Sociální struktura . . .* , p. 149. In order to make it clear that he does not include the Party bosses in this creative stratum he adds in a footnote: "Under the term of creative intelligentsia we comprehend all bearers of highly qualified and complex intellectual work."

[30] Vladimir V. Kusin, *Political Grouping in the Czechoslovak Reform Movement* (London: Macmillan, 1972), p. 57. See the author's discussion of difficulties with, and variations of, Czechoslovak statistics.

[31] *Ibid.*, p. 63.

total number of workers. In 1966, this figure was 24.1 per cent, that is, almost a quarter of the labor force. . . .[32]

Another author claimed even a higher number:

> According to the latest statistics, we have around 1.5 million brainworkers, among them 600,000 technical-economic workers; the others belong to a humanistic intelligentsia, scientists, health specialists, state organs and social organizations' workers.[33]

The Czechoslovak Statistical Yearbook 1967 listed the number of white-collar workers with secondary and higher education at 1,145,216 persons and divided them into 524,894 technical, and 620,322 cultural and other workers. In addition, 2,700 professional workers such as writers, artists, scientists, etc., were self-employed. The number of the intelligentsia more than doubled between 1955 and 1966.[34] Pavel Machonin in 1966 estimated that almost 30 per cent of the Czechoslovak population was professionally engaged in mental work.[35]

Although these figures often diverge, obviously in the Czechoslovakia of the 1960s the intelligentsia formed a large part of the working population.

The *societal tensions* at least partly stemmed from the disproportion of people in leading positions who did not have appropriate education, and educated people, who could not achieve social status and responsibility adequate to their specialized training and capacities. To this feeling of incompetents ordering around the competent ones should be added the vexing problem of poor remuneration for intellectual work after years of higher studies. The ratio of *average incomes* among manual workers, technicians and white-collar workers was, until 1967, under pressure, gradually improving for the latter two categories but, as the following table shows, it was by far not as differentiated as in other industrialized countries, not excluding the Soviet Union.

Income relations in per cent (Blue-Collar workers = 100)[36]

	1955	1960	1965	1966	1967	1968	1969
Engineers-technicians	126.3	132.9	135.3	140.5	142.2	140.9	139.7
White-collar workers	85.0	87.1	86.3	88.6	90.2	89.3	88.0

The incomes of Party and state leaders were six to ten times higher than the average worker's wage. In addition to wages they were used to very large

---

[32] *Rudé právo*, 22 Sept. 1972.

[33] *Práce*, 22 June 1965.

[34] Based on Table 23 in Jaroslav Krejčí, *Social Change and Stratification in Postwar Czechoslovakia* (London: Macmillan, 1972), p. 61.

[35] See his article "Socialistická rovnost a nerovnost v naší společnosti" ["Socialist Equality and Inequality in our Society"], *Nová mysl*, no. 12 (1966).

[36] *Statistická ročenka ČSSR 1973* [*Statistical Yearbook ČSSR 1973*] as quoted by Tibor Krajkovič, *Práce a mzda* [*Work and Wages*], no. 7, July 1974, p. 387. Beginning in 1968, the trend was reversed again, with workers' wages improving at the relative expense of the other two categories.

monetary and other privileges.[37] In 1965, to give an example of actual wages, a laborer was making 1757 crowns, graduate grammar school teacher 1907, a graduate lawyer 1937, locksmith 2010, doctor-practitioner with wide experience 2243, locomotive driver 2363, lathe operator 2422, graduate scientific worker 3022, skilled coal-face miner 3521, and leading manager in engineering industry 4692 Czechoslovak crowns.[38]

It is not surprising that spokesmen for *the intelligentsia* were *pressing for higher wages*, combining this demand with a thesis that without larger differentiation of incomes and higher rewards for intellectual work, there was no stimulus for continuing education and for improving the national economy by better standards of achievement. In an official analysis of Party activities and societal developments between the Thirteenth and Fourteenth Congresses of the CPC we can read:

> Income equalization hurts qualified, competent, diligent, and hardworking people who are in charge of complicated and demanding mental and physical work. . . . These circumstances contributed in their effects to a technical-economic stagnation, to a stagnation of living standards, to the broken dynamics of the social development. . . . Unqualified and incapable members of the leadership enjoyed the same (indeed greater) economic and social advantages as qualified and capable persons.[39]

Strangely enough, in 1968–9 as the intellectuals' share of power was growing, it was not accompanied by corresponding wage increases since the blue-collar workers' wages relatively outpaced theirs. As an explanation it could be stated that both types of élites, the reformists and conservatives, were then courting the working man, and the intelligentsia seemed to be more interested in fundamental societal changes than in the advancement of their own incomes.

What was the *class background of the intelligentsia?* And was the communist leaders' mistrust of it based on class origin?

One of the heads of the CPC scientific teams estimated that in the 1960s 45 per cent of the intelligentsia was of workers or small farmers origin and 55 per cent of other, mainly intelligentsia's background. This is his conclusion:

> At this time [1968], the intelligentsia in Czechoslovakia basically represented the social stratum, which was by a great and decisive majority formed by people to whom the privilege of belonging to the intelligentsia was given by the new political power after 1948.[40]

A Party ideological worker reported that in the ČSSR out of working people with secondary or university education 38.3 per cent came from working-class families and 24.9 per cent from the families of working farmers and tradesmen.[41] In Slovakia, in 1967, according to the social origin, out of all persons with secondary or university education 45.5 per cent came from manually working families; it was 48.8 per cent out of all specialized employees. Judging by their first occupation,

[37] Zdeněk Mlynář, *Československý pokus o reformu 1968: analýza jeho teorie a praxe* [*Czechoslovak Attempt at a Reform 1968: An Analysis of its Theory and Praxis*] (Cologne: Index, 1975), p. 207. It was also published in Italian, *Praga - Questione Aperta* (Bari: De Donato Editore, 1976).

[38] Krejčí, *op. cit.*, p. 72.

[39] This document was reproduced in Jiří Pelikán, ed., *XIV. Mimořádný sjezd KSČ: Protokol a Dokumenty* [*Fourteenth Extraordinary Congress of the CPC: Minutes and Documents*] (Vienna: Europa Verlag, 1970), pp. 193–4.

[40] Zdeněk Mlynář, *Československý pokus . . .* , p. 189.

[41] *Rudé právo*, 22 Sept. 1972.

37.7 per cent of university educated people and 39.5 per cent specialists with secondary education could be classified as originally manual workers. That means that almost half of the Slovak intelligentsia were of workers' class origin and two-fifths actually started their occupational careers as blue-collar workers.[42]

Turning our attention to the *Communist Party membership*, we can observe several interesting phenomena. In 1961 the CPC had over 1,600,000 members and candidates and continued to be a mass party. It had the highest relative membership of the country's population in the world. Since the Party leadership was worried about the constant tendency to deterioration of the social composition of the membership from the class point of view, the CC of the CPC in May 1959 decided that the Party organizations had to carefully select new candidates and attract among them 60 per cent of workers and 20 per cent of collective farmers or 80 per cent of workers and farmers plus 20 per cent of "other working people."[43] The main Party organ then claimed that "workers represented half of the membership of the Party and out of the total number of workers engaged in production almost every fifth is a member of the Party."[44] But it was admitted that if only workers actually engaged in production were counted, the half would shrink to 36 per cent and in addition 9.6 per cent workers, members of the party, were pensioners. Till 1967 a further deterioration would take place: "If in 1947 workers formed 50 per cent of the Party membership, then in 1967 the number of active manual workers represented only 26.4 per cent."[45] And till 1969 the number of retired workers went up to 15.9 per cent.[46]

At the end of May 1968, the CPC had 1,687,565 members.[47] It represented 12 per cent of the Czechoslovak population and 17 per cent of persons older than eighteen years. *The intelligentsia* formed *the largest group* — 40 per cent *of economically active members*. Almost 34 per cent of the intelligentsia was organized in the CPC, and among them up to 40 per cent of teachers were represented. We can agree with the author's conclusion: "The gradually diminishing share of workers in the Party, continuing in spite of measures taken by the CC of the CPC for almost twenty years, suggests that it concerns a deeper societal and Party problem."[48]

The vanguard of the workers' class was not only *losing workers* engaged in production but also fast *aging*. Before the purges of 1970, almost one-third of all Party members were over fifty-five years of age, out of them almost two-thirds no longer engaged in any work, and only a small part participated in social acitivities.[49] That the aging of the Party had a great correlation with its

[42] Róbert Roško, "On the Class origin of Our Intelligentsia," *Sociológia*, vol. iv, no. 3, Apr. 1972, p. 196.

[43] *Život strany*, no. 8, Apr. 1961.

[44] Editorial: "The Growth of the Party Must Be Directed Resolutely," *Rudé právo* (Bratislava edition), 4 May 1961.

[45] Lubomír Bakeš, "Triumf bolševismu" ["Triumph of Bolshevism"], *Rudé právo*, 27 July 1973, p. 3. A real triumph!

[46] K. Havlíček, *Život strany*, no. 13, 22 June 1970, p. 15.

[47] *Život strany*, no. 16, Aug. 1968, p. 14.

[48] Leopold Rykl, *"Nová mysl*, 4, Apr. 1970, pp. 458–64.

[49] K. Havlíček, *Život strany*, 22 June 1970, p. 16.

conservatism and that a regenerative effort was badly needed was shown persuasively by a Party investigation in July and August of 1968:

> Younger members of the Party (often possessing higher education and performing lower functions) prefer "innovative" tendencies (i.e. liberalistic and revisionist concepts of the Party)...; the "innovative" tendencies are stronger in factory than in village or local organization. . . . Political maturity of a "certain degree" [accepting the pro-Soviet line after the invasion] was proved by a group of communists of older age. . . . , possessing only basic or lower secondary school education.[50]

The tragedy of a party that wanted to represent the workers and needed young and educated progressive people could hardly be more clearly demonstrated.

Was the Czechoslovak society in 1968 *classless* or was a *class conflict* going on? A careful sociological investigation, initiated by the Party leadership, took place in 1967 and its results were published two years later.[51]

Pavel Machonin and his research team went a step further when compared with previous investigations and writings. Although the mass membership of the CPC made it impossible for all communists to take part in the management of the nation, membership in the Party was a necessary condition for such share in power:

> The higher the levels of power, the larger share of communists are their holders, while the addressees of power are predominantly non-communists. . . .
>
> Non-Communists work in industry and especially in agriculture. Members of the Party are mainly officials or belong to independent professions, non-members are mainly farmers and construction workers.
>
> The index of "household equipment" including the ownership of a car, mixer, washing machine, refrigerator, and television set presents a strong correlation with Party membership.[52]

Of leading officials of central institutions of power 85–90 per cent were communists. Of leading economic officials, 70–80 per cent, and of cultural and public education officials, 70 per cent.[53]

Although Pavel Machonin's team was in 1964 (when the conference at Hrazany took place) willing to describe the Communist Party as "sociologically speaking — a special social group"[54] and called for "moving forces to overcome its brakes"; for example, its isolation from other people, only the research of 1967 was used to point out the *class character of a supposedly classless society*. Another leader of a Party research team, Zdeněk Mlynář, on the basis of this study was able to stress the paradox of the situation when he wrote:

> The members of the CPC were, naturally, the social group that in the eyes of others stood out as the bearer and representative of the political power system, as the group responsible for its shortcomings, especially in the past, in the 1950s, out of which as a living factor of personal lives of great many people survived the consequences of power interests into the life of whole numerous classes and layers as well as consequences of lawlessness and obvious wrongs

[50] Rykl, *op. cit.*, p. 461.
[51] Pavel Machonin *et al.*, *Československá společnost: sociologická analýza sociální stratifikace* [*Czechoslovak Society: A Sociological Analysis of its Social Stratification*] (Bratistava: Epocha, 1969).
[52] See Lubomír Brokl's study in *Československá společnost*, pp. 257–9.
[53] A Vaněk, *Učitelské noviny*, 25 June 1970, p. 12.
[54] See René Rohan, "The Party and Changes in the Social Structure", in *Sociální struktura . . .* , p. 668 and 673.

towards many people. . . . The whole mass membership of the Party factually never held any power-directive functions and in a centralistic-bureaucratic system of management did not even have a chance of decisively influencing the politics of its own Party leadership.[55]

The question about existence of social differences in Czechoslovakia was in 1967 answered affirmatively by 74.9 per cent and negatively only by 9.5 per cent of those questioned. A social scientist identified the social group holding the economic and political power in Czechoslovakia of 1967 as 205,000 people.[56] Only in 1968 did it become possible to speak openly and describe the system with appropriate sharpness. Seventy-five members, P. Machonin and R. Richta among them, of the interdisciplinary team for research on the social and human implications of the scientific and technological revolution signed and published an *indictment of the regime*. A few quotations will show its frankness:

> Aversion to distortions which people obtained instead of socialism is universal. How heavy is the guilt of those who constantly talked about the interests of the working class, of workers, and in reality kept inflicting on them by their bureaucratic stupidity the most terrible wounds. . . .
> Socialism cannot exist as a society where instead of the deposed bourgeoisie the bureaucrats perform their supremacy, where the State in place of the capitalists changes the country into a single and huge industrial factory centrally directed. . . . Such a concept in fact denigrates socialism in a different form of a bureaucratic industrial machinery. . . . Socialism without democracy and its development is no socialism. . . .
> The system which declared itself as an incarnation of "workers'", "people's" politics, demonstrated a rude cruelty to laborer and worker as producer as well as consumer. . . . It forced him into unceasing hunting for missing goods, subjected him to shameless exploitation and humiliation from the services, made out of him a perpetual petitioner for an apartment, etc. The system that justified its centralist structure by requirements of scientific management, was unable to offer space to enterprising and technical initiative; did not open the way to capable and qualified people; deadened the inclination and vigour of a numerous army of engineers, technicians, economists, foremen, qualified workers. Instead of a dynamic social security . . . . it imposed a certainty, that the intolerable situation would be preserved . . . and fears that there is no other way out.

And the manifesto ended with this paragraph:

> The communists must put free socialist development of the society and of man against dictatorship and despotism, self-governing democratism against power-thirsty dirigism, socialist enterprising spirit against mediocrity, scientific reason against bureaucratic stupidity, modern tempo against negligence, patriotic and international responsibility against destruction of national and human sources, communism as a humanistic movement against narrow-minded partisanship, socialist progress against conservativism and capitulation. They must do it firmly and in time.[57]

The Czechoslovak communist intelligentsia, which in 1948 helped to install a Party dictatorship, gradually came to the conclusion that slogans of a raging class war served only as a defensive mechanism for the permanence of a *bureaucratic dictatorship*, which represented a new ruling class dominating and exploiting all other social groups, including the working class and the intelligentsia. The thesis of

[55] See his *Československý pokus* . . . , p. 209.
[56] Krejčí, *op. cit.*, pp. 110–11.
[57] "O nový československý model socialismu" ["For a New Czechoslovak Model of Socialism"], *Rudé právo*, 10 July 1968, p. 3; 11 July 1968, p. 5; 12 July 1968, p. 7.

an avant-garde of the proletariat was misleading. Pavel Machonin after the invasion spoke up more openly than before:

> In 1967 the workmen — people with original working occupation or of workers' origin — did not actually have any great privileges. In the light of facts, the theory that interprets the leading role of the working class as a stratification scheme of a direct government by the workers, is completely mistaken. On the contrary, the undemocratic features of the political organization were hurting, along with the farmers, primarily the workmen as the most numerous group of the population, as a mass excluded from an effective participation in government.[58]

What kind of a class dictatorship was it then? Machonin in the quoted article suggested that "the bureaucratization of the society was carried out 'behind the back' of the revolution" and that the social structure showed "relative equality in all fields, with the exception of the political power" which he repeatedly called "bureaucratic".[59] A Slovak scientist, *Michal Lakatoš* (who at a younger age used to celebrate Lenin as a "genial continuator of the work of Marx and Engels, who elaborated the theory of the dictatorship of the proletariat . . . . and revealed the theories about the withering away of the State during the building of socialism as hostile and undermining the power of the proletariat"[60]), in 1968/9 talked about "the power élite, surrounded by a barrier of privileges,"[61] "bureaucratic power regime,"[62] "bureaucratic power *apparat*,"[63] and "bureaucratic power system,"[64] as opposed to a "citizens" or "civic society."[65]

From a theory of a classless society the Czechoslovak communist social scientists finally came to the conclusion that *two classes* existed — the small élite of power holders against the large majority without power, or the Party bureaucrats against the rest of the people who were all working producers. Quite a few of the critics of the Czechoslovak 1948–68 system used terms, originally proposed either by Trotsky (the bureaucratic rule), or by Burnham (the managerial revolution). *Zdeněk Hejzlar* speaking about the system employed these words:

> After 1948 the CPC carried out its dictatorship by increasing its internal oligarchy and bureaucracy. Gradually, the Party and state apparatus merged. This led to the merging of political and economic powers and of the legislative and executive powers, creating a bureaucratic-centralistic Stalinist setup.[66]

Another long-term member as well as victim of the system, *Eugen Loebl*, repeatedly declared in his books and articles that the proletariat, obviously, was not a leading force in Czechoslovakia and that "the abolition of the classical type of the so-called 'Marxist-Leninist' party became in Czechoslovakia a precondition for the realization of the reform, i.e. to progress towards a socialist society."

[58] *Politika*, no. 3, 13 Mar. 1969, p. 15.
[59] *Ibid.*, pp. 14–15.
[60] *Lidové noviny*, 20 Jan. 1952, p. 1.
[61] *Zítřek*, 13 Nov. 1968, p. 2.
[62] *Ibid.*, 27 Nov. 1968, p. 2.
[63] *Ibid.*, p. 3.
[64] *Studentské listy*, no. 7, 9 Apr. 1969, p. 4.
[65] *Zítřek*, 11 Dec. 1968, p. 2; or *Svobodné slovo*, 12 July 1968, pp. 1–2. In 1966 Lakatoš published in Prague a book entitled significantly *Občan právo, a demokracie* [*Citizen, Justice, and Democracy*], and in 1968, after the invasion, *Úvahy o hodnotách demokracie* [*Essays on the Values of Democracy*].
[66] V. V. Kusin, ed., *The Czechoslovak Reform Movement 1968*, p. 111.

The Party was "the barrier against socialism."[67] He revived the old Saint-Simonian thesis about the important role of the technicians and scientists as the vital force in modern industrial society and, extending his experiences with the Czechoslovak revolution of the intellectuals, became something of a prophet of the intelligentsia in the modern world. Since the 1950s, from Eastern Europe, and including the Soviet Union, a message has been coming concerning the responsibility of the intellectuals for their countries and, in the final analysis, for the whole world.

3. Restoration and revenge

In the 1970s the old Stalinist slogan of a sharpening class struggle, both on the international and especially on the Czechoslovak scale was revived. Officially it repudiated the sociological concept of co-operation between interest groups of the 1960s and justified the political as well as professional liquidation of the reforming intellectuals. The class revenge was thorough. But for this purpose it was necessary to denounce the previous, victorious Party slogan that beginning with the 1960s, Czechoslovakia became a classless socialist state. The adjective "socialist" was allowed to remain incongruously in the name of the State — implying at least class harmony if not non-existence of classes. It was incorporated in the Constitution of 1960 was originally encouraged and accepted by the Soviet Union as valid. Now it was declared to be revisionist and coming from the arsenal of capitalist imperialists. The Party began a merciless "class struggle" against the communist intelligentsia — half of them of workers' origin and almost all of them products or beneficiaries of the regime.

Twenty years before it was written: "That the men who actually control the coercive machinery and are in a position to use it for purposes other than to establish socialism, will voluntarily give up the power they possess, is the great miracle of the Marxian belief."[68]

One of the main conditions of a "normalization" of Czechoslovak affairs that the Moscow leadership insisted upon, was a thorough *purge of the Communist Party* of Czechoslovakia. Many communists left the Party without waiting for the mass purge which took place mostly during 1970. So in 1968 the CPC lost 19,340 comrades (53 per cent workers), more than 1 per cent of its members and more than in any year since 1955. Most of them, 82.2 per cent, left during the second half of the year, after the Soviet invasion. The Party *Bulletin* commented:

> There is a growing number of Party members who decided to leave the Party because they do not agree with the situation, with the arrival and stay of Soviet armed forces, and with the consequences of this fact. In some letters sent to the CC of the CPC it is expressed entirely in concrete terms.[69]

The first day of 1969, the CPC had 1,671,637 members and the last day of that year 1,535,537, that means an additional loss through expulsions from membership

---

[67] *Ibid.*, pp. 338–40.
[68] Hans Kelsen, *The Political Theory of Bolshevism* (Los Angeles, 1948), p. 24.
[69] See *Zpravodaj KSČ*, no. 16/1969, supplement of *Zvot strany*, no. 18, 29 Apr. 1969, pp. 11-12. Also *Život strany, no. 15, 10 Apr. 1969.*

amounted in 1968 to 22,046, in 1969 to 96,823, and in 1970 to 326,817 communists, altogether in three years 473,731 members when other losses are taken into account, that is 28 per cent of membership between 1968 and 1970. That should have left some 1,200,000 strong mass Party.[70] But according to an interview with the influential CPC Presidium member and CC Secretary, Vasil Bil'ak, during the purge 461,751 communists were either expelled or struck off the lists. He also announced that some 30 per cent of them together with the Party card also lost their jobs.[71] That means that, officially, some 165,000 persons were dismissed from work for their political convictions which in 1968 were in agreement with the CPC policy. With family members it represents between 600,000 and 700,000 people, a colossal human tragedy in a nation of some 14 million.

An Italian journalist with excellent contacts in Prague, Mino Monicelli, reported that 600,000 Party members were expelled, among them 30,000 intellectuals.[72] According to reports emanating from the plenary meeting of the Central Committee in December 1970, only 880,000 communists accepted their new cards and 220,000 remained unclaimed.[73]

The purge was not an easy task. Only a relatively small number of communists were willing to take an active part in the liquidation of their comrades. The chieftain of the inquisition, Miloš Jakeš, chairman of the Control and Audit Commission of the CPC CC, complained during the purge that it was carried out in too liberal a manner, that *less than 10 per cent of Party organizations had followed Party orders*, and that in consequence many CPC organizations had to be dissolved. "Many, in spite of all explanations, mistake the Party card for a work permit." He also did not like that the conciliatory attitude of purgers was often accompanied by militancy on the part of those being purged who demanded facts and proofs or engaged in polemics with members of the tribunals for whom they ostensibly felt contempt.[74] The CPC had to create special purging groups and they travelled from place to place.

The disastrous *results of the purge* for the Party had to be expected. Miloš Jakeš repeatedly enumerated some of them. According to his account, many members remain passive, many keep excusing themselves and try to justify shortcomings; Party meetings are often formal and have only an informative character, only a few functionaries are involved, and criticism is being ignored or suppressed.[75] In 1970, on average, less than half of remaining members participated in Party meetings. Although the situation improved in following years, the percentage of members refusing to take part in Party activities remained high, one-third in 1973 and 1974.[76]

Another big problem was that *the Party* was *losing workers and growing old*. In 1970 the Secretary-General of the CPC reported that after the exchange of Party

[70] *Rudé právo*, Jan. 1971, p. 11.

[71] *Rudé právo*, 13 Sept. 1975, under the title "Socialism in the ČSSR Is Unshakable."

[72] Kevin Devlin, "Plight of Czechoslovak Intellectuals: 'Espresso' Interviews Kohout and Others," RFER, 5 July 1973, p. 2.

[73] *International Herald Tribune*, 28 Dec. 1970, p. 7.

[74] Miloš Jakeš, "Musíme vytvořit ve straně zdravé klima" ["We Have to Create in the Party a Healthy Climate"], *Tribuna*, 3 June 1970. pp. 1–3.

[75] See an interview with Miloš Jakeš in *Pravda*, 19 Apr. 1974, p. 3.

[76] *Život strany*, no. 26, 18 Dec. 1975, p. 11.

cards, the ratio of economically active workers in the Party was 26.4 per cent, of collective farmers 5.3 per cent, and of the intelligentsia 30.9 per cent.[77] That leaves, unmentioned, 37.4 per cent of "others", state and Party officials. For comparison, in the same year, the workers' share of the population was 58 per cent.[78] Such considerations led to a few unusually frank comments: "The present class, social structure of the Party membership is not in conformity with the Party's role as the vanguard of the working class."[79] One of the most influential and most conservative officials of the CPC CC, Alois Indra, endulging in wishful thinking, said: "What matters is that we wouldn't have to emphasize that we are the workers' party, but that the workers should say, the CPC is our party."[80]

More exact figures concerning the composition of the CPC could be found in reports complaining about the actual situation in parts of the State. In the *Party organization of the capital*, at the end of 1971, only 6 per cent of workers were members of the Party, one out of seventeen! But every fifth engineer, technician, or economic manager (18.6 per cent) was so organized. Although 60 per cent of all CPC members in Prague were of workers' origin, actual workers represented only 14 per cent. Out of pensioners, 23 per cent were workers, "that means that in the past a much higher percentage of workers belonged to the Prague Party organization."[81] In spite of determined efforts to improve the social composition of the CPC, the resistance of the workers remained high. On the first day of 1973 the share of blue-collar workers in the Prague Party organization was at 13.4 per cent and thanks to hectic activity it was improved in two years to 15.9 per cent. The "workers' party" in Prague proudly announced its goal for the Fifteenth Party Congress — to achieve 16 per cent of workers among its members! *At the beginning of 1975, one-third of all CPC members in Prague were pensioners*, and only 12.2 per cent were persons younger than 35 years, which was a great improvement since 1971, almost double.[82] And so the Party performed the greatest purge and professional liquidation of its intellectuals in history — in the name of the workers but almost without them.

One of the members of the CPC Presidium and of the CC secretariat in 1968, *Zdeněk Mlynář*, concluded:

> Isn't it strange that after almost thirty years of building of socialism at once one-third of members of the Communist Party [. . . in the most politically active layer of the Party it is rather 50 per cent and in some sections — especially in theoretical work of the Party — maybe 70–80 per cent] are on "enemy positions"?[83]

The police revenge against the best minds of the CPC was, and still is, so inhuman and devastating to the intellectual life of the country that Western commentators talked about "Biafra of the spirit" (Louis Aragon) or "*intellectual genocide* (Dr. Adolf Hermann). Tens of thousands of writers, journalists, teachers, humanist and natural scientists as well as economic managers and technicians were

---

[77] "December Plenum of the CPC CC in 1970," p. 14.
[78] *Demografie*, no. 2, July 1973, p. 176.
[79] Leopold Rykl, *Tribuna*, no. 28, 15 July 1970.
[80] *Brněnský večerník*, 3 July 1970, pp. 1–2.
[81] Bohumil Němec, *Život strany*, 24 July 1972, p. 9.
[82] František Trojáček, *Život strany*, no. 26, 18 Dec. 1975, p. 12.
[83] *Československý pokus o reformu 1968*, p. 163.

expelled from the CPC and lost their professional positions. Most of them were forced to work as unskilled laborers and some of them were not allowed to take any job at all, threatened by starvation. Research institutes, university and CPC CC seats of higher learning (especially those devoted to the study and propagation of Marxism-Leninism, Party history, and sociology) were closed and their professors and fellows pushed into street cleaning, sewage disposal, window washing, etc.[84] Between 1970 and 1975 more than 5,000 people, who were expressing or defending their scientific or political opinions, were condemned to prison terms, on an average of three and a half years. At the same time, the campaign against democratic socialism, pluralism, and any ideas not in perfect agreement with the Soviet official line, has been continuing until our day. Many articles are being published on the importance of the scientific-technological revolution, on the crucial role of the intelligentsia in its development, and on the low qualifications of managers and loyal specialists, but the conditions attached to participation are such that the Party leadership remains isolated, the intelligentsia alienated, and the economy, in spite of a slow improvement in the material standard of living, suffers from all the problems associated with the crisis of the 1960s.

4. Conclusion: The advantages and limitations of sociology

Although the *group theory* proved to be a useful tool for understanding some of the dynamics at work in communist countries and although its use in the 1960s by Czechoslovak scientists helped to undermine the totalitarian dictatorship of professional revolutionaries and bureaucrats over all producers of material or spiritual goods, it can answer our questions only to a certain extent. It cannot satisfactorily explain why individual members of the organs of power, opted, often in their majority, for the "progressive" instead of the "conservative" point of view, which could have more safely prevented their loss of privileged positions in the power hierarchy. Clearly, sociological method has its merits but also limits.

The class and even the group theory are based on the assumption that people gather around and fight for their *interests*. But if the interests turned out to be value-judgments, altruistic motivation, or character preferences instead of the more material advantages connected with a position of power and prestige, it leaves us without a proper tool. Sociology by its purpose, expressed also in its name, can give us only the macro, but not the micro, perspective on society. It talks in numbers but not about individual motivation as such, or only when many of them are computed together; but especially in times of crisis, of excitement, it could be misleading since people often change, act "irrationally", or not according to usual parameters.

Then it is up to other fields of study, for alternative approaches to scientific inquiry into human behaviour to comprehend the *motives* of people joining one or the other front in a conflict which is dividing the whole society. Why in the deepening polarization of Czechoslovak communists around the year of 1968 did comrades who spent years working together find themselves finally on the opposite side, Dubček or Husák, Černík or Kolder, Císař or Indra, P. Machonin or

---

[84] For one of the best accounts, see Peter Payne, "Four Years of 'Normalization': The Academic Purge in Czechoslovakia," *Index on Censorship*, summer 1972, pp. 33-52.

R. Richta, Mlynář or his normalized critic Matějíček, rebels L. Vaculík and Mňačko or loyalists Novomeský and Mináč? They belonged to the same groups, had the same material interests but decided according to some other criteria.

At the end of his long study of interest groups in the Soviet Union an author came to the conclusion that "every occupational group is divided into opinion groups and that 'reformists' and 'conservatives' are to be found in all of them." At the same time, "there is a wide spectrum of opinion within each group. . . . so that a simple 'liberal-conservative' dichotomy is not adequate. . . . Their attitudes are not static."[85]

A specialist on the Soviet intelligentsia agreed: "Any attempt at classifying Soviet intellectuals into two groups, the conformists and dissenters, is an absurd over-simplification."[86] Another author suggested that informal subgroups or opinion groups may be more revealing than established groups: "sets of *individuals* who share common attitudes." He proposed "an orientation that emphasized issues rather than groups, the process of tendency conflict on these issues rather than the conflict of structure invested with purposes and power of their own." Among non-material wants he mentioned also "the needs of human dignity."[87] Such "interests" are, naturally, hard to measure and difficult to quantify.

It seems that for the moment sociology does not yet possess tools that would help to explain why members of the same class or group arranged themselves on the opposite side of a dividing line, according to a cluster of *psychological motivations*: to joyfully go with the majority of the people or bitterly against it; to trust democracy or dictatorship; to welcome spontaneity or to fear it; to prefer cooperation or enforced compliance with orders; to be tempted by the new or to be afraid of it; to be optimistic about human nature or to be a cynic and pessimist; to risk a challenge to an overwhelming imperialist power or to despair of any chance and rather serve it. The secret of their decision, or just of an inclination and slipping in a position, remains in the hearts of men and often the balance leading to one or the other outcome is very complex.

There is evidence that *education* or lack of it and *intelligence* or lack of it played a constant role — but so did the natural *character* of the master/slave typology or social/anti-social disposition. Some people are adventurous and open, some get closed and petrified. Some love, some hate, also different things — but that can change in time. And so although we can eventually count numbers of people facing each other in a conflict at a certain moment, we cannot be sure that we know their motivation and that group or similar theory would give us a complete answer. Helpful might be autobiographies of political activists describing the development of their motivation from illusion to reality.[88]

[85] H. Gordon Skilling, ed., *Interest Groups in Soviet Politics* (Princeton, N.J.: Princeton University Press, 1971), p. 395.

[86] L. G. Churchward, *The Soviet Intelligentsia: An Essay on the Social Structure and Roles of the Soviet Intellectuals during the 1960s* (London: Routledge & Kegan Paul, 1973), p. 135.

[87] Franklyn Griffiths, "A Tendency Analysis of Soviet Policy-Making", in *Interest Groups in Soviet Politics*, pp. 342, 372, and 373.

[88] For the best one so far, see Zdeněk Mlynář, *Myráz přichází z Kremly* ('Cologne: Index, 1978'). The author left Czechoslavakia in 1977. His new book was also published in Germany as *Nachtfrost*.

Part III
Searching for truth and reality

Chapter 1.

In history

BETWEEN 1945 and 1955, history, for Czechoslovak communists, as so much else, had only a utilitarian aspect: something to be used in order to gain and keep total power over the population. For that instrumental purpose, the Party politicians and ideologues intended to use only those historical events from the past that suited their goal and to present them in such a way that the CPC would appear as the natural fulfillment of all past and present national aspirations. However, that ambitious concept, although at first eagerly followed by young historians, had to come into conflict with Czechoslovak traditions and with demands of professional standards. Once the supposed messianic role of Stalin, of the CPC's political leadership, and of the U.S.S.R. became subject to questioning, ethical and scientific postulates had to turn the majority of Marxist historians against such a partisan interpretation and misrepresentation of history. Leninist and Stalinist political Machiavellism could not be permanently grafted on a different cultural stock and sooner or later had to be rejected as a foreign implant.

1. The re-educators

The chief organizers of a cultural revolution, that was intended as complete re-education of the Czech and Slovak nations and their re-orientation towards Soviet communism, were the Minister for Information, Václav Kopecký, and the Minister for Education, Zdeněk Nejedlý. Both had a large staff and vast funds at their disposal and also, at least till February 1948, voluntary cooperation of many communist men of culture. Although after the *coup* their participation gradually diminished as the propaganda tones became more false, young enthusiasts took over and eagerly supplied intellectual ammunition whose untruth and idiocy often reached incredible levels.

The basis of the program of re-education was hardly believable. It was compiled out of one-sided anti-German, pro-Russian, and pro-Slav tendencies of the past, bound together with an amalgam of proud "heroic nationalism" and humble submission to, and crazy adulation of, Stalin. It lacked any reasonable balance and humanitarian ethos of T. G. Masaryk — it was modelled on the vast and uneven (in youth capable but later purely propagandistic) work[1] and rather unpleasant personality of Zdeněk Nejedlý.[2] The whole model was a derivative and artificial political construction.[3] Often it was very personal and silly. For instance, of Czech composers. Nejedlý favored only Bedřich Smetana and therefore Antonín Dvořák's music was almost never played, since Nejedlý could not forget his unsuccessful courtship of his daughter.

Before World War II Nejedlý wrote almost too devotedly a biography of T. G. Masaryk's childhood and youth in four volumes (Prague, 1930-6), but now started to denigrate him and came to this admirable class conclusion by which a gentleman's coachman became himself a gentleman: "Masaryk by the status of his father belonged to the nobility. His father as a gentleman's servant was, altogether indisputably, a man of the master class and the whole Masaryk's family were masters. That showed in all their social and official behavior."[4]

During the 1950s, in addition to physical terror, Czechoslovakia was flooded by intellectual terror in the form of propaganda bombardments in all newspapers and journals, on the radio, at meetings, as well as by countless books and brochures that had to be studied by millions of people through all possible venues.[5]

---

[1] "I worked with Zdeněk Nejedlý from July 1945 until his death. Already before February, I prepared first volumes of Nejedlý's work. At that time Masarykism was predominant in our philosophy and I fancied to place the work of Zdeněk Nejedlý against Masarykism. On the occasion of his seventieth birthday, it was just during the February days, the first volumes of his writings appeared. Against Masaryk's *Russia and Europe* I arranged and edited Nejedlý's book *Struggles for New Russia*; against Masaryk's *Humanistic Ideals* — Nejedlý's book *Great Personalities*. During Nejedlý's life I published some fifty volumes of his work. It was a great contribution to party's political and ideological armaments." *Tvorba*, no. 6, 4 Feb., 1976, supplement. The author, Pekárek, was a minor literary reviewer about whom Václav Černý, the recognized authority on literary criticism and editor of *the* literary and critical journal, *Kritický měsíčník* [*Critical Monthly*], remarked in his memoirs: "[Václav Pekárek] throughout the whole existence of *Kritický měsíčník* regularly, though in vain, never ceased to give notice of himself by sending contributions." Černý published many contributions by communist writers of real talent.

[2] According to the *Master of Spies*, F. Moravec, he was a "sexually perverse old man." See his *Špión, jemuž nevěřili*, p. 354. Nejedlý's daughter, Dr. Zdeňka Nedvědová-Nejedlá, in an interview called her father "an absolutely well-disciplined party man," who "really believed that Gottwald was right hundred per cent and the Party hundred and ten." She described his life as a "tragedy that a man who his whole life fought against smallness, suddenly began to allow it devotedly towards the Soviet Union," *Práce*, 18 Aug. 1968, pp. 4-5.

[3] Cf. Zdeněk Nejedlý, *Komunisté dědici velkých tradic českého národa* [*The Communists, Heirs of the Great Traditions of the Czech Nation*] (Prague, 1950). At a meeting of historians in the Town Committee of the Socialist Academy in Prague, on 30 April 1969, Jiří Brabec, from the Institute of Czech Literature, characterized it as follows: "This absolutely absurd and historically absolutely untenable show which happened was something so monstrous that only the oddity and specificness of the era might excuse for it." Quoted, disapprovingly, by Václav Král, *Slovanský přehled*, no. 2, Apr. 1973, p. 107.

[4] Quoted by Ferdinand Peroutka, "Masaryk a 21. století" ["Masaryk and the 21st Century"], *Hlas domova*, xxvi, no. 18, 6 Sept. 1976, p. 6.

[5] Typically, a speech by the Minister Václav Kopecký to cultural workers was introduced under the title "Ještě více rozvinout boj o duši národa" ["To Expand the Battle for the Nation's Soul Even More"], *Lidové noviny*, 11 Jan. 1952.

2. Karel Bartošek: From Stalinism to the New Left

The shameless character of this propaganda campaign, whose aim was to destroy all pillars of democratic traditions and humanitarian hopes of Czechoslovak citizens — coming so soon after a very similar Nazi campaign between 1939 and 1945, which often had exactly the same targets — can be shown by one of the heroes of the "Prague Spring" and of the subsequent resistance to "normalization," *Karel Bartošek*. It is hard to believe that his publications of the 1950s and of 1968/9 came from the same man. His later essays belong to the most lucid analyses of the late 1960s, but his earlier writings could be, at best, studied as documentary proofs of pathological deformation by senseless beliefs in any Party propaganda and by aggressive impulses liberated in the service of a program which most of all stressed hate in a sadistic/masochistic degradation of human values.

At first, Bartošek specialized in the American liberation of Western Bohemia and attempted to erase Czech memories of widespread raping, stealing, and murdering by Soviet soldiers through his vivid descriptions of alleged American crimes against the Czech population. (I remember only one complaint people had about the generally exemplary behavior of the American soldiers: they sometimes burned their underwear instead of washing it; this seemed to be inexcusable waste to a population that lacked everything.) Today Bartošek's excuse might be that everybody knew that it was all nonsense but his pamphlet was destined for young people and his propaganda of blind hatred based on lies was in perfect Party order.

His first book on that theme was entitled *The Shameful Role of the American Occupants in Western Bohemia in 1945*.[6] Two years later, in its new version, he dropped the "shameful role" from the title but his inflammatory pamphlet, prepared with a co-author, is full of crude comic-type drawings; for instance, the contrast between the American "occupation" and Russian "liberation" is depicted as a nasty American soldier shoots a distressed country-maiden and a blissful Russian soldier is being welcomed by a happy child with a bouquet of flowers.[7]

Under a chapter's title "Protectors of the Nazis for a New World War" a claim was elaborated that the Americans in 1945 made "agreements with the remnants of Hitler's armies, with Schörner and other bloodthirsty dogs about further battles against the Soviet army:"

> Defeated were not only the German Fascists. Crushed also were the plans of Western imperialists to destroy and enslave the Soviet lands. . . . The American army's command in Europe was making fast arrangements for saving the Nazis. Well, they were old and tried allies in the effort to destroy the Soviet Union. . . . The American army stopped its advance on purpose and according to its agreement with the Hitlerians was giving to its Nazi friends time to settle accounts with the Czech people.[8]

[6] Karel Bartošek, *Hanebná role amerických okupantů v západních Čechách v roce 1945* (Prague, 1951).

[7] Karel Bartošek and Karel Pichlík, *Američané v Západních Čechách* [*The Americans in Western Bohemia*] (Prague: Mladá fronta, 1953), p. 2. The quality of the co-author (who later would write much more responsibly) can be ascertained from this sample: "Sworn enmity of the American monopolists to our people marked not only the origin but every day of the existence of the Czechoslovak Republic." *Ibid.*, p. 17. Dialectically, the American monopolists were sometimes also blamed for helping with the foundation of Czechoslovakia as an imperialist bourgeois state.

[8] *Ibid.*, pp. 85-7.

The idea of an American-Nazi pact was dear to the authors and they kept coming back to it again and again:

> The American imperialist mercenaries . . . till the last moment enabled the Hitlerian murderers to kill hundreds of Czech men according to an agreed contract. With the Nazis and SS-men they united in plans to achieve the greatest possible destruction of our country and extermination of the Czech people.[9]

Young people were taught by Bartošek that the Americans were brutal barbarians:

> In many instances a Czech was bloodily beaten up just because to a question, "You Czech?" he answered, "Yes, I am Czech." . . . For six months the American mercenary gangs played havoc in Western Bohemia. For six months they were beating, shooting, and persecuting Czech people. For six months they were sneering at the national pride and self-confidence of the Czechs. Every baby knew about the atrocities of the American occupants.[10]

Naturally, the American murderous plans did not end in 1945:

> At the head of the American — English agency in the CPC, composed out of the worst gang of double-crossers, Trotskyites, Zionists, bourgeois nationalists, and cosmopolitans, the American imperialists placed their old agent Slánský.[11]

In an analogous style full of spite Bartošek denounced in the main Party daily the "American Imperialists — Plotters of the February Counter-Revolutionary Putsch:"

> In February 1948 the American billionaires, plotters of the reactionary counter-revolutionary *putsch*, were hard beaten by the Czechoslovak people. Since that time they had to sustain further defeats, the hardest one through the crushing of the Slánský gang, and therefore they are constantly getting more raging and beast-like.[12]

When after the monetary reform of 1953 Plzeň workers rioted against the regime, Bartošek with his pen-comrade Pichlík contributed to the campaign aimed at social-democracy by a new book in which they revived several Stalinist slogans of the 1930s:

> Social-Fascist policy of the rightist social democrats manifested itself fully in the years of economic crisis in the Plzeň region, too . . . Intentionally, they attacked the struggling people from the rear, by all means supported the extortionist system that was tossing about in the crisis convulsions.[13]

In their book the authors blamed the pre-war anti-Nazi armaments production in the Škoda Works as intended to be used against the Soviet Union [!], accused the social democrats of selling out the Republic to Hitler, named Beneš as the "head of the American Fifth Column in Czechoslovakia," and revealed that the "Rightist

---

[9] *Ibid.*, pp. 200–1; see also pp. 106 and 188–9.
[10] *Ibid.*, pp. 131 and 133.
[11] *Ibid.*, p. 207.
[12] *Rudé právo*, 25 Feb. 1953.
[13] Karel Bartošek and Karel Pichlík, *Z dějin dělnického hnutí na Plzeňsku: O úloze pravicových sociálních demokratů* [*From the History of the Workers' Movement in the Plzeň Region: The Role of the Rightist Social Democrats*] (Prague: Státní nakladatelství politické literatury [State Publishing House of Political Literature], 1954), pp. 113 and 115.

socialists" did it all since "they obstinately hate the working man."[14] Then, rather dialectically, they claimed that (1) in February 1948 social democracy was "crushed for good" and also that (2) "in the sharpening class conflict during the dictatorship of the proletariat" the events after the monetary reform showed "the necessity to purge the Party from obdurate social democrats who penetrated the CPC in 1948. . . . The strength of social democratic traditions was displayed."[15]

For the tenth anniversary of the February *coup* Bartošek wrote an article praising the successful communist tactics of coming to unshared power and singled out Gottwald as a master tactician who already in November 1947 prepared the Party for the *putsch.*[16]

Bartošek's next book, *Prague Insurrection 1945,*[17] although still written from a strictly partisan point of view, achieved higher historical standards and, to a certain degree, was aimed against the prevalent Party line. He admitted that non-communists sometimes had a larger share in anti-Nazi activities than the communists and that Prague was liberated before the arrival of Soviet troops. A careful reading of his study (very much as in the case of Trotsky's *History of the Russian Revolution*) reveals that communist leaders mostly fought for the Party *image* of the uprising and not so much against the German occupants to whom they kept propagandistically promising death. The book was, to a large degree, devoted to a defense of Josef Smrkovský, who was still on the list of proscribed personalities because the Russians had objections to his handling of the Prague uprising of 1945. It also belongs to the category of historical studies that tried to restore merits of the domestic efforts which have been completely suppressed in order to enhance the exclusive glory of the Soviet liberators. Bartošek praised "democratism, the beautiful trait of the Czech national character" which supposedly "received a deeper, revolutionary content"[18] and clearly was very much interested in the technique of revolts. At least partly he admitted that in his earlier publication on "the activities of the American army in Western Bohemia in 1945 . . . there were some errors and inaccuracies, but these errors do not relate to the assertion that the American army interfered in the internal affairs of the ČSR."[19] For his new book he obtained the prize of the Central Committee of the Union of Anti-Fascist Fighters.[20] For years Bartošek then kept writing commemorative articles on the Prague uprising but, from time to time, he also praised the Slovak National Uprising of 1944 and stressed "common Czech and Slovak revolutionary

[14] *Ibid.*, pp. 118, 142, 173, 185.
[15] *Ibid.*, pp. 189–92. At least since 1963 Pichlík started to write more objectively and during the period of "normalization" was therefore blamed for his "glorification of the role of Masaryk, Beneš, and Štefánik." See page 58 of the "strictly secret" document, written by the two normalizers in charge of the "historical front," Čestmír Amort and Václav Král, on Czechoslovak historiography, as partially published in *Listy*, nos. 4–5, July 1971, pp. 56–60. For comparison see his "Die Entstehung der Tschechoslowakei" ["The Origin of Czechoslovakia"], *Vierteljahreshefte für Zeitgeschichte*, xvii, 2 (Apr. 1969), pp. 160–80.
[16] "Proč muselo dojít ke střetnutí s reakcí" ["Why the Encounter with the Reaction Had to Come"], *Rudé právo*, 4 Feb. 1958.
[17] *Pražské povstání 1945* (Prague: Naše vojsko [Our Army], 1960).
[18] *Ibid.*, p. 246.
[19] *Ibid.*, p. 233.
[20] *Mladá fronta*, 2 Mar. 1961.

traditions.''[21] Typical for this stage of searching and hesitations was his statement in the May 1964 issue of *Plamen*: "We know where the untruth is, but not where the truth is."

In 1965 at the Scientific Conference on the Czechoslovak Road to Socialism at Liblice, his main report on the Czech society and revolution created quite some stir since he, a scientific fellow of the Historical Institute of the Academy of Sciences, proclaimed that "the specific mark of the Czechoslovak road to socialism is the gradual maturing of the notions of the workers' class about the close connection between democracy and socialism — about a peaceful democratic access to socialism."[22]

In quite a vivid style he wrote in 1963 a historical textbook for the ninth grade of the basic school, it was then praised,[23] but in the more relaxed and critical atmosphere four years later it was criticized by the majority of parents and pedagogues as "very bad."[24]

In 1966 he wrote a good survey of reforming historians' attempts to drop the lies and search for truth but in spite of his mild condemnation of the past Stalinist practices was quite apologetic about his own and his colleagues' propagandistic and bombastic lying of the 1950s; the *coup d'état* of 1948 was still described by him as "the victory of the people's democratic revolution" and the shameless distortions that followed were seen as something quite normal and natural:

> Every revolution must justify itself by history, and perhaps even more so after it has triumphed. It introduces a new point of view, a new outlook on the past, and it discovers new aspects of that past. It endeavours to instil its own concept of history into the social consciousness, and for this purpose makes use of all the means at its disposal. It is often onesided and demands an *apologia* for its present acts and measures. This is not the first time there has been this "revolutionary violation" of history.[25]

Bartošek had a few harsher words to say about his generation of communist falsifiers of history but even these fell short of a full admission of guilt, although he probably went as far as he safely could at the time:

> The basic core of research workers are people between the ages of 30 and 40, who are, for the most part, untainted by careers. In their callow youth they wholeheartedly believed everything that revolutionary practice and theory presented to them; then they suffered a painful shock. But the shock had a salutary effect . . . there is a genuine desire to seek and to comprehend the truth. The source of this new revolt against myth and illusions is probably to be sought in the affinities felt by this generation with the democratic spirit of the pre-war Czechoslovak intelligentsia and its fine tradition of avant-garde intellectual life.[26]

The pro-Soviet hurrah-communism was over and the prodigal sons were

[21] *Pravda*, 4 May 1960.
[22] *Svobodné slovo*, 17 Mar. 1965. The same year his book *The Prague Uprising* was published again and contained documents of adoration of the Soviet might. (The publisher: Artia in Prague.)
[23] *Dějepis pro devátý ročník základní devítileté školy*; see *Rudé právo*, 28 Jan. 1964, and *Kulturní tvorba*, no. 42, 17 Oct. 1963.
[24] *Mladá fronta*, 30 June 1967.
[25] "Czechoslovakia: The State of Historiography," *Journal of Contemporary History*, no. 2, Jan. 1967, pp. 143-55. The quote is on page 144.
[26] *Ibid.*, pp. 147-8.

returning home to traditions and ideals they now could appreciate. The closest Bartošek went to an acknowledgement that the past "histories" were artificially manufactured lies is this sentence: "During the 1950s historians defended and 'documented' theses invented by the political leadership of the day."[27] That is quite different from the earlier claim that all revolutions see things in a new way. It was admitted as well that the Party did not give up its manipulative use of historiography: "There still persists, however, the old idea of historiography which restricts this social science to its use as an 'instrument of education' and of vulgar apologetics."[28]

In the reforming year of 1968 Bartošek quite early in a new situation showed his revolutionary zeal when he advocated, as his title suggested, to progress "From Reforms to a Revolution:"

> Structural changes are necessary also in a socialist regime and system, especially in that which accepted as a model the bureaucratic-etatistic socialism, elaborated and enforced in Stalin's era. To achieve destruction of the system in which a group of self-appointed and democratically unelected bureaucrats decides about all basic questions, in which the citizen of a socialist state does not control the *apparat* but the *apparat* commands the citizen, is a revolutionary task corresponding to the principles of Marxism and Communism.[29]

A complete volte-face occurred in April 1968 when Karel Bartošek, who previously in many a text condemned Rudolf Slánský as the head of the American agency in Czechoslovakia, together with his son denounced the show trials of the 1950s and their presiding officer, Dr. Urválek.[30] In May, Bartošek appealed to Czechoslovak workers to establish workers' councils at once and participate in decision-making.[31]

One reason for Bartošek's spiritual growth might be the fact that for at least ten previous years he has been visiting France every year, keeping contact with French Leftist intellectuals. He was there also from September 1967 until April 1968 when he wrote for a Leftist weekly a historical review of Czechoslovak developments between 1948 and 1968. It was later published in the main Party daily in Prague as one of the first and best histories of the change.[32] He rejected the "Stalinist-bureaucratic concept of socialism and its construction" of 1949–52, the "concept of the Communist Party as a military organism," "uncontrolled power of the police and armed forces," and "unlawful trials" of 1949–54, followed by a "psychosis of fear."[33] Bartošek stressed the importance of the economic crisis but also paid due attention to cultural factors. Of special interest in our context is his paragraph devoted to historians:

> The work of historians of recent past of Czechoslovakia was of great significance. Deformation of this history served as justification of the existing system. . . . The historians of politics and culture gradually succeeded in bringing into public knowledge an array of

[27] *Ibid.*, p. 151, fn.
[28] *Ibid.*, p. 146.
[29] "Od reforem k revoluci," *Plamen*, no. 2, 1968, p. 65.
[30] Karel Bartošek and Rudolf Slánský, Jr., *Rudé právo*, 17 Apr. 1968.
[31] Cf. *Reportér*, vol. iii, no. 19, 8–15 May 1968, pp. 4–5. It was called "Open Letter to the Workers."
[32] "Revoluce proti byrokratismu?" ["Revolution Against Bureaucratism?"], *Rudé právo*, i, 18 July 1968, p. 3; ii, 24 July, p. 5; iii, 26 July, p. 3; iv, 30 July, p. 3; v, 31 July 1968, p. 3.
[33] See the first instalment, as above.

important problems: the importance of domestic anti-Fascist forces in the revolutionary changes of 1944-5 (almost without exception their leading personalities have suffered from reprisals at the beginning of the 1950s . . .); the importance of searching for a "Czechoslovak road to socialism" during 1945-8; the importance of the adjustment of Czecho-Slovak relations on the basis of equality . . .; the importance of cultural-political conceptions of the Marxist pre-war avant-garde.[34]

The systematic method of this "socialist opposition," as Bartošek called it, is obvious from the quote. As he explained, after 1963 the roots of it were in meetings with "rehabilitated" victims of the purges of the 1950s. The historians then discussed the possibility of a future Czech revolution.[35]

Soon after the Soviet invasion he took his distances from people, who in exchange for some hope of continuing post-January reforms were willing to make compromises, in an article in which he warned against the famous "Czech realism" of adapting to the unpleasant situation. Marx remained for Bartošek a man to quote and he reminded his readers that the world should be changed: "What to do then? Think and act as revolutionaries who belong to a small country where they were born and where they want to end their days.... What to do? Think and act in order to revolutionize our society."[36]

In March 1969 he condemned any collaboration with the occupiers as inevitably leading to treason. Even after Husák's replacement of Dubček, Bartošek continued his attacks on "Nejedlý's concept of the 'meaning of Czech history'" (in which he a decade before so eagerly participated):

> The "nation of Hus" was being educated to reverence and love towards the master at the stake and did not take much notice that in the present time the truth burned at new stakes-gallows, also ignited by foreign hands. We were a proud "nation of Comenius" — and in the contemporary education a disaster was realized in stages — shortening of school-attendance and general lowering of culture. The "meaning of history" had as its aim to cover up the absurdity of the present time.[37]

In the post-invasion period discussions of the meaning of Czech history became quite popular. Bartošek's cynical attitude toward the usual one-sidedness of such searching for regained self-confidence was part an attempt to get rid of illusions and to see the facts as coolly as possible in order to overcome them, instead of feeling sorry for them:

> We are heirs and children of both Hussitism and Baroque, Taborites and Jesuits, revolutionaries and reformists, revivalists and obscurantists, patriots and chauvinists, humanitarians and murderers, Catholics and Czech Brethren, internationalists and anti-Semites, radical democrats and Munich appeasers, anti-Fascists and Fascists.[38]

On 4 June 1969 Bartošek spoke to the students at the Charles University in Prague and proposed the formation of a New Left in order to prepare a new revolution in Czechoslovakia:

[34]   *Ibid.*, ii.
[35]   *Ibid.*, iv.
[36]   "Let's Not Howl with the Wolves," *Politika*, 19 Sept. 1968. Quoted from the French translation in Jiří Pelikán, ed., *Ici Prague: L'opposition intérieure parle* (Paris: Seuil, 1973), pp. 90-3.
[37]   "Nomocní dějinami" ["Sick by History"], *Doba*, no. 24, 19 June 1969, pp. 9-13.
[38]   *Ibid.* Bartošek followed here arguments of František Graus from his book, published in 1968, *Naše živá i mrtvá minulost* [*Our Living and Also Dead Past*].

An anti-bureaucratic revolution is a continuation (part of) the anti-capitalist revolution. . . . A real historical possibility is a *joint* struggle of small nations of Central, Eastern, and South-Eastern Europe for equality . . . . The revolutionary strategy of "Central-European revolution" by the New Left should then be based on a detailed study of the "eternal" dialectic of this revolution since 1848. The experience of 1968 is also an experience of our isolation.[39]

In January 1970 the Czech Ministry of the Interior announced the discovery of an anti-state organization, operating throughout the whole Republic. In March 1971 nineteen young people were condemned for "Trotskyism;" Bartošek was not among them. He was arrested in January 1972, accused of subversion and anti-socialist activities, and on 1 August 1972 condemned in Prague to a year in prison. He was released from court on probation. For seven months of detention he was charged 3,600 crowns.

According to reports from Prague in 1977, he looked sturdy and healthy, as a worker, after years of hard manual work. It is a strange and sad paradox that, like Bartošek, some young enthusiasts who used to dream about a workers' state after a victorious proletarian revolution, which they attempted to help, found themselves "elevated" from their intellectual preoccupation to the workers' class. The system they assisted forced them to really become workers. And those who pushed them to it — bureaucrats, policemen, manipulators — were often workers who thanks to the "revolution" managed to get away from hard manual work and moved into offices and positions of power. And so Bartošek joined the New Left dreaming about the next and, finally, as they all hope, victorious revolution without masters and slaves. The distance between dreams and reality was shortened at least in one instance, and maybe in one distance only: he is now an intellectual who really became a worker. Would he be trusted by them more than before? Would he understand them better? Would he be able to prepare a real "proletarian" revolution or would he start doubting Marxist parameters?

3. Josef Macek: Communist "Hussitism," a career, and cautious compromising

Dr. Josek Macek, who was born in 1922 and joined the CPC in 1945, during his Stalinist past specialized in non-religious but class explanation of the Hussite Reformation. He directed the streamlined Czech historiography and prominently participated in the communist front organization of the World Peace Council.

His fast career was assured since he closely followed Nejedlý's prescriptions of a strictly pro-communist history of the basically religious Czech Reformation whose obvious social aspects he one-sidedly exaggerated in his 1952 book *On the Hussite Revolutionary Movement*[40] for which he received the State Prize. In the same

---

[39] "Naše nynější krize a revoluce" ["Our Present Crisis and Revolution"], *Svědectví*, x, 38 (1970), pp. 231–40; quotes are from pages 237–8. His speech was published by the Italian journal *Il Manifesto* in November 1969 and in *Samizdat 1* (Paris: Seuil, collection "Combats,"), January 1970. For excerpts in French, see Pelikán, *Ici Prague*, pp. 120–3.

[40] *O husitském revolučním hnutí* (Prague, 1952). Another Hussite propaganda work of his was called *Ktož sú Boží bojovníci* [*Who Are the God's Warriors*]. A pamphlet reproduced his public speech of 29 May 1952 and was entitled *Proti kosmopolitismu ve výkladu našich národních dějin* [*Against Cosmopolitism in Interpretations of Our National History*].

crucial year of enhanced terror, Macek became the Dean of the Faculty of Social Sciences at the University of Political and Economic Sciences in Prague. He taught history and joined the editorial board of the Party theoretical monthly, *Nová mysl*. He also became director of the Historical Institute of the Academy of Sciences. He often lectured abroad; for instance, in June 1955 in Hamburg, usually trying to combine Hussitism, Communism, and world peace. In the Czech capital he was a regular speaker on the radio, praising the work of Zdeněk Nejedlý (2 February 1953), merits of deceased Klement Gottwald (18 March 1953), or extolling the doubtful blessings of communism for the country (e.g. 23 January 1955, 29 May 1955, and 18 March 1956).

Macek's contributions to the Party press showed much more propagandistic gibberish than scientific restraint; under the title "Stalinist Way of Our Science" he wrote:

> Progressive science of the whole world suffered an immortal [*sic!*] loss. The death of J. V. Stalin . . . is also for the Czechoslovak scientific community an immensely heavy and painful blow. Bowing in memory of the genial teacher of all progressive scientists, we realize again and again that the whole scientific work of Stalin is an eternally living source of knowledge and instruction for all scientific disciplines. Comrade Stalin prudently watched over permanent tempestuous prosperity of science . . . . At a time when in capitalist countries science turned away from life . . . , when it is directly in service of imperialist exploitation . . . , *Stalin with us and in us* — that's the slogan of Czechoslovak scientific workers, faithfully held together around the great pupil of Stalin, the President of the Republic, comrade Klement Gottwald.[41]

Unfortunately, the individual around whom all Czechoslovak scientists were supposed to gather, did not last long and so Macek fast had to find a substitute:

> Our native party, at head with comrade Gottwald, brought our nations over rivers of blood, prison, and battle-field [*sic!*] at the threshold of a society about which dreamed the Hussite fighters . . . . The Hussites after Žižka's death deeply regretted the departure of the great fighter for people's rights. Yet, the firmer they united together . . . . We all today, in these hard days, will unite even closer around the glorious heir of the Hussite tradition, our native Communist Party of Czechoslovakia, around its Central Committee and our Government.[42]

According to the Party line, Macek liked to contrast Russian love of peace with German militarism, although at the moment the country was clearly suffering not by German but by Russian militarism. He always managed to add to it Hussite traditions, as in his radio talk on 12 August 1956 or in his opening address to a scientific conference devoted to German militarism.[43]

His political career was much more successful than his partisan writings on history — as a member of many editorial boards, publication commissions, etc., he received a fabulous income. Foreign trips formed part of his privileged position: as chairman of the central committee of the Czechoslovak Society for Dissemination of Political and Scientific Knowledge he led a delegation to the Soviet Union in September 1957; in July 1961 he led a governmental delegation to Cuba; in

---

[41] *Rudé právo*, 11 Mar. 1953. My emphasis. Didn't he know at least the title of the book *Hitler in Us?*
[42] "Buďme husitsky a gottwaldovsky pevní a stateční" ["Let Us Be Firm and Brave the Hussite and Gottwaldian Way"], *Rudé právo*, 23 Mar. 1953.
[43] Reprinted the next day in *Rudé právo*, 18 July 1957. Another typical article of his was entitled "O ideologii soudobého německého imperialismu" ["On the Ideology of the Contemporary German Imperialism"], *Rudé právo*, 9 June 1959, p. 5.

July 1962 he headed a Czechoslovak delegation to the World Congress for a General Disarmament and Peace in Moscow; in September he participated in the Tenth Pugwash Conference in London; as presidium member of the World Council of Peace he was in October 1962 in Stockholm, in March 1963 in Malmö, in November 1963 in Warsaw, and in December 1964 in Berlin, etc. His domestic advancement was progressing apace — at the Twelfth Party Congress in December 1962 he became candidate member of the CPC CC and on 14 June 1964 he was "elected" deputy of the National Assembly for the South Moravian region.

Although at the Third Congress of Historians in September 1959 Macek in the main address still admonished everybody to follow Marxism-Leninism as the only acceptable historical doctrine and attacked "bourgeois influences;" and although in 1961 he published a new book on Jan Hus,[44] times were getting more complicated and difficult for a proper orientation. Encouraged from Moscow, at least partial truth was getting out. So in 1962 Macek became a member of the unfortunate "political-expert commission charged with preparation of a proposal for utilization of the space so far occupied by the Stalin monument." At meetings of members of the Academy of Sciences Macek's historical works were criticized and denounced as Stalinist. His own self-criticism was still cautious and very mild. Backed up by a motto from Marx and Engels, "The whole history has to be studied afresh," Macek wrote:

> Historical science in Czechoslovakia has been, for quite some time, successfully fighting with the remnants of the cult of the individual and in previous years substantially contributed to the development of scientific recognition of our past . . . . To the wrong, excessively simplified task of historiography was added dogmatism, the inseparable companion and jailer of thought from the era of the cult of the individual . . . . The job was to confirm the theses of the classics of Marxism-Leninism . . . . How many bravura somersaults it was necessary to make over the interpretation of Klement Gottwald's statements concerning an independent road of Czechoslovakia to socialism and again on general laws of building socialism in our country.

Macek then, moderately, denounced "campaigns against Masarykism" since even Masaryk's beginning scientific and political writings were "judged as entirely reactionary;" complained about "following in Stalin's footsteps with his completely erroneous theses on social-fascism," and mentioned that no one continued Nejedlý's work *Communists, Heirs of Glorious National Traditions*. Although Macek admitted: "We ourselves have produced a lot of worthless and unsocialist stuff by rude mistakes in building and education," he blamed for it the "birthmarks of the old world that sunk into irretrievability" and the necessary "fight against the political, spiritual, and especially moral and mental trash of capitalism." Viciously he attacked the "inflated and, besides, pitiful Czech provincialism" and nationalism but towards himself manifested much more benevolent criteria:

> If, as an example, I take my own studies of Hussitism, in spite of all efforts to comprehend the international significance of Hussitism, so far I did not succeed in expressing the universality of Hussitism because, among other things, I was not scientifically solving the relations of Hussitism to the Renaissance on one side and to the Reformation on the other.[45]

[44] For the congress record, see *Československý časopis historický*, no. 8 (1960), pp. 1–18 and 54–61. Macek's book was published in Prague by Svobodné slovo; see *Rudé právo*, 2 Dec. 1961, p. 1.
[45] "Naléhavé problémy historické vědy" ["Urgent Problems of Historiography"], *Nová mysl*, no. 9, Sept. 1963, pp. 1043–51. Quotes are on pages 1043, 1045–9.

After such a dubious, face-saving *mea culpa* Macek continued to serve as Party propagandist both at home and especially abroad (in January 1964 Moscow *Pravda* published his composition "Munich Tragedy — A Lesson,"[46] in July 1965 he was in Helsinki elected as member of the World Council of Peace,[47] and in June 1966 he was elected as member of the new board of directors of this communist front organization[48]). However, in his position of Party supervisor of historians he allowed the development of a new atmosphere of relative freedom of research and expression, backed up by loyal solidarity of a large professional group of historians. (We have encountered such split personalities, such a dichotomy of public professions of faith and private pursuit of reforming practices elsewhere; for instance, in the case of the writer Pavel Kohout or another historian, Karel Kaplan.)

The ideological bosses of the CPC did not like this situation and repeatedly attempted to break the growing loyalty and professionalism of historians. But when on 27 February 1964 Josef Macek, as a full member of the CPC CC (since 1966), reported on Party decisions concerning ideological questions (as usual he was supposed to enforce them), the scientific collegium of history, the highest organ of the historians in the Academy of Sciences, accepted a resolution which refused "administrative interference" and "any tutoring and bringing in *a priori* points of view" by the Party since "it makes impossible a really scientific approach to the solution of problems. Towards this end we have to create an atmosphere of perfect confidence and mutual cooperation."[49] It amounted to a local anti-totalitarian revolution since the historians as a collective professional body refused to follow the previously established authoritarian patterns and insisted, in a direct challenge to Party bureaucrats, on their independence and self-management.

The Ideological Commission of the CPC CC then prepared a review of the historians' views and activities. Administrative measures followed. Several historians were dismissed from their positions, others were publicly branded as renegades, and in March 1965 the editor-in-chief of the historical monthly, *Dějiny a současnost*, was replaced "for gross political mistakes." The majority of the members of the editorial board left in protest, to come back only three years later.[50] After prolonged skirmishes with the Ideological Commission, whose member Macek was and which several times tried to reimpose on the rebelling historians its supervision and strict cadre policies, the situation improved when the Academy of Sciences was taken out of the sphere of the Ideological Commission and entrusted to the CPC CC Commission for Education and Science.[51] The historians achieved a substantial victory.

Although the part of Macek in the whole affair was not prominent for his lack of fighting spirit (it is a different thing to admire the bravery of the Hussites and to be brave), it was important. His role remains unclear and hidden from a researcher's eyes. He was "very cautious and accessible to compromises" as was later reported

[46] Radio Prague, 12 January 1964.
[47] *Ibid.*, 14 July 1965.
[48] *Ibid.*, 16 June 1966.
[49] *Dějiny a současnost*, no. 7, July 1968, p. 26.
[50] Zdeněk Šikl, "Reminiscences and Perspectives," *Ibid.*, no. 5, May 1968, pp. 1–3.
[51] See Šikl's interview, as above, in footnote 49, p. 27.

from Czechoslovakia.[52] But somehow he made the whole evolution possible or at least did not succeed in arresting it. During the "Prague Spring" Macek claimed that in protest against the method of criticism of the journal *Dějiny a současnost* he resigned from his political function as chairman of the journal's publisher, the Society for the Dissemination of Political and Scientific Knowledge.[53] But he continued in many other functions (some were mentioned previously) and as a schoolmaster kept writing on the "tasks of historiography."[54] As chairman of the Czechoslovak Committee of Defenders of Peace (another communist front organization) he participated in the Stockholm conference on Vietnam and led a delegation to Belgium in order to support a Soviet initiative to convoke a large-scale conference on European security.[55] Less than a month later, on 5 June 1968, he took part in the session of the Presidium of the World Council for Peace in Nicosia, Cyprus.

During the first week of the Soviet invasion, Macek took part in the prolonged and beleaguered meetings of the Czechoslovak Parliament, which protested against the occupation. His participation provoked at least one admiring comment: "Such a scientist — yet he is remaining with other deputies in the parliamentary building, sleeps with them on the floor, notwithstanding that he lives in Prague."[56]

Although Macek allowed the publication of the *Black Book*, a historical documentation of the fateful week, and later would be blamed for it, one year after the invasion, on 28 August 1969, he still could open an international symposium on the theme "Fascism and Europe," but was not allowed to participate at the World Council for Peace celebration of its twentieth anniversary in East Berlin,[57] since the Russians might have objected. In November 1969 Macek was dismissed as director of the Historical Institute. The following month he had to resign as parliamentary deputy, and in January 1970 lost his place in the CPC CC, whose secretariat later confirmed his expulsion from the Party.[58] And so a long, devoted, and often disgraceful, service ended in an honorable disgrace.

In Macek the regime rejected a man who among historians more than anybody else was willing to engage himself fully in its service and faithfully follow the zigzagging Party lines. Truth and honesty were being discovered by him rather slowly but gradually, nevertheless, obviously with some help from the more determined and resolute colleagues. Finally, stimulated by humiliated nationalism, the most dogmatic manipulator of other historians and of historical truth had to give up trying and look for other, non-Party certainties or even a lack of them.

[52] Vratislav Prošek and Jiří Žemla, "Společenské vědy v údobí 1948–68" ["Social Sciences in the Period 1948–68"], *Svědectví*, viii, 52 (1976), p. 657. This interesting survey first appeared in the Czech *samizdat*.
[53] Radio Prague, 7 Mar. 1968.
[54] For instance, *Rudé právo*, 22 Mar. 1966, p. 3; or "Stav a úkoly historické vědy" ["State and Tasks of Historiography"], *Československý časopis historický*, no. 1, 1967, pp. 1–34.
[55] Radio Prague, 10 May 1968.
[56] *Ibid.*, 25 Aug. 1968.
[57] Richard Gott in *The Guardian*, 20 June 1969.
[58] *Život strany*, no. 6, 1970, p. 61.

His conversion was supposedly genuine as one of his former colleagues, himself a non-communist historian, testified: "[Macek] during the last years went through a tormenting but purifying and sincere (as I can personally bear witness to) internal regeneration."[59]

4. Milan Hübl, Gustáv Husák, and some other retrievers of the past

One of the most interesting cases of transformation is that of *Milan Hübl*, partly because of his close association with Gustáv Husák, whom he helped to get out of prison in order to be put there himself in due course by him.

Hübl was born in 1927 in Nitra, a Slovak town, and — as is very rare among Czechs who usually do not make the effort — speaks fluent Slovak, although at home Czech was spoken. Between 1942 and 1945, during the German occupation, he studied at the German textile school in Brno. In his first literary contribution I was able to find, the twenty-year-old Hübl, with help of a quote from Stalin attempted to prove that the Hitler–Stalin Pact was progressive and that "the Second World War against the Axis Powers had *right away from the beginning* (underlined by me, M. H.), unlike the First World War, the character of an anti-Fascist, liberation war:"

> In 1938–9 there was a danger of an English–French–German coalition, directed against the Soviet Union . . . Thanks to a skilful foreign policy of the Soviet Government and amateurish mistakes of Hitler, the Western Powers have got in this war in the camp of progress. . . . In case of victory by the Anglo-German coalition the life of our nation would have been finished! It is a so far underestimated merit of comrade Molotov that he prevented this coalition. He succeeded in taking advantage of conflicts between Anglo-American and German capitalists so that he managed to get those who ruled in their countries with the help of bourgeois democracy on his side and in this way they unwillingly became helpers of progress.[60]

Although in a rather contorted way — which still is typical for many young people of the New Left in the West — in this letter Hübl began to show his capacities for large-scale political schemes. At the time of its writing, Hübl was working in the Party *apparat* and its varied institutions. He had been a Party militant since 1945.[61]

All his public utterances before 1963 served established Party lines faithfully, although not as servilely as, for instance, those by Bartošek or Macek.

He celebrated the Eighth Congress of the Communist Party of China,[62] discussed exile literature 1945-8,[63] considered "lessons about advantages of the socialist regime,"[64] glorified "May 1945,"[65] and divulged the theme of his Ph.D. dissertation, defended in 1960, on "The Political Struggle in the ČSR During the

---

[59] Ivan Pfaff, "Mýtus a realita v proměnách Husova obrazu" ["Myth and Reality in Shifts of Hus' Image"], *Zpravodaj Čechov a Slovákov vo Švajcarsku*, iii, 8 (July 1970), pp. 9-11. The quoted part is on page 10.

[60] *Dnešek*, 31 Dec. 1947, p. 619.

[61] As claimed by Jiří Pelikán, *Ici Prague*, p. 178, and confirmed by Hübl, p. 193.

[62] *Nová mysl*, no. 1, Jan. 1957.

[63] *Ibid.*, no. 9, 1958, pp. 867-76.

[64] *Mladý svět*, 9 Jan. 1961.

[65] *Nová mysl*, no. 5, 1962.

Process of Transformation of a National and Democratic Revolution into a Socialist One."[66]

In 1963 Hübl published two articles that established him as one of the most daring and principled historians of the revisionist school which wanted to get rid of the Stalinist falsification of the past for temporary and doubtful partisan needs. First he criticized a recent book, devoted to Slovak history of 1945–8. He defended the record of Gustáv Husák and Laco Novomeský, both condemned as "bourgeois nationalists" in April 1954, and chastised the author for slanting historical facts: "Collaboration with a part of the bourgeoisie was a historical necessity at the time of the Resistance and just after the liberation." It was wrong to describe in the reviewed book Husák and Novomeský "only in negative context" and others, like Bacílek [a Slovak communist dictator, after January 1952 in charge of the police and trial investigations], "only in positive context and that often in a highly exaggerated manner." Hübl admitted that it was easy to be wise after the decisions of the CPC CC in April 1963 (when Bacílek was demoted from his post as First Secretary of the Communist Party of Slovakia) but as a final conclusion claimed: "The experiences of the past few years are a serious memento for us, admonishing us to put an end to every kind of subjectivism, inasmuch as only a truly scientific work is a partisan work in the proper meaning of the word."[67]

Although Hübl's resolute criticism was clearly part of a victorious Party faction's coming to at least a share in power and insisted only on replacing patent falsehoods by truth in the same and still necessary partisanship, it was an important step forward on the way away from lies to a closer adherence to some facts. This conflict about reality and false images of it was probably the major theme of the intellectual tug of war between 1963 and 1968 (and after the invasion the other way again, from facts to myths).

His second article was much more controversial. Hübl revealed (to the Czechs) that the Bulgarian communist leader Traicho Kostov was "after some hesitation" rehabilitated in the Fall of 1962 and that at his trial in December 1949, together with ten others, as "an enemy of the people," before his execution he twice refused to admit his treason as a supposed British spy. Hübl wrote about "monstrous deformations, usually called cult of the individual" and reminded his readers of Karl Marx's warning against mistakes of the Jacobin dictatorship.[68] Since at that time the CPC was in the throes of a continuing crisis about an eventual admission of its guilt for the Czechoslovak trials, about the gradual and limited publication of this reluctant admission, and about its very restricted rehabilitation of the victims, Hübl was publicly pushing for a denouement.

If in the 1960s Bartošek spoke for those who wanted to continue a proletarian revolution and Macek for holders of power on a slow and cautious retreat, Hübl was — directly or indirectly — helping those coming to power, such as Husák, Dubček, etc.

[66] *Příspěvky k dějinám KSČ*, no. 2, 1962, p. 308.
[67] *Československý časopis historický*, no. 4, 1963, pp. 473–6.
[68] "Trajčo Kostov," *Dějiny a současnost*, no. 6, June 1963, pp. 1–3.

It is not always remembered how important the year 1963 was for the final victory of the reformists in 1968. The "Slovak" anti-Slovak holders of power, Bacílek and Široký (one of Czech, the other of Hungarian origin), lost their posts in April and in September, respectively. Although Novotný, under strong pressure, dropped them both and some other *apparatchiks* in order to save himself, an important breach in his fortified position was achieved, since he could never recover the full support of the Communist Party of Slovakia on which he could count until then. From then on he kept counter-attacking but was, so to speak, limping on one leg which would never heal. With Alexander Dubček in Bratislava a more moderate, intelligent, liberal, and enlightened regime came to power which allowed Novotný's determined opponents, such as Husák, Loebl, Selucký, Hübl, and others to publish and agitate for further and substantial reforms.

Two closely connected Slovak problems were involved: the condemnation of the so-called bourgeois nationalists of 1954 and the uprising of 1944. In both cases the Czech historian Hübl supported the cause of the violated Slovak communists headed by *Gustáv Husák*, who was dismissed from his post of chairman of the Slovak Board of Commissioners in 1950 as a "bourgois nationalist". Husák was arrested the following year to be condemned in 1954, after repeated torture periods during thirty-nine months of detention, to prison for perpetuity.[69] He was amnestied in May 1960 and employed as a packer in a tailor's shop.

In 1962–3 Milan Hübl as a member of a CPC CC commission, which was discussing the problem of rehabilitations, fought for Husák's reinstatement and his political rights against strong opposition from other members, such as Bil'ak, Lenárt, and Šalgovič.[70] Hübl was in charge of a large group of historians, economists, and political scientists who were allowed to study secret Party archives in order to prepare a report on the trials of the 1950s, with special reference to the charges against Slovak communist leaders. Since this group worked in strict isolation in the "Barnabite Monastery" it was often called by this name. Their discoveries were terrible and extremely shocking; one of the participants expressed

---

[69] Husák was born in Bratislava-Doubravka on 10 January 1913 in a poor peasant family. He completed the *real gymnasium* in 1933. As a sixteen-year-old student he joined the Komsomol and before his entry to the Comenius University mastered Marxist theory. He studied law and at the age of twenty joined the Communist Party. As a capable Marxist speaker he became chairman of the Association of Socialist Students at the Bratislava University. He became member of the editorial board of the influential Leftist literary journal DAV. Another member was Vlado Clementis (executed in 1952) and Husák, after his graduation, worked in his law office. In 1941 he and the pro-Fascist Minister of Slovak State, Šaňo Mach, took part in a propaganda tour of the Ukraine, then occupied by the Nazis. In 1943, together with Laco Novomeský, he joined the illegal CC of the CPSl and the following year participated in the Uprising as deputy-chairman of the Slovak National Council. Later in Moscow he participated in talks about the post-war government and its program. His limited but successful career followed, once the war was over and he could return to Bratislava. But it was cut short by his dismissal and arrest at the beginning of the 1950s. Husák's biography was compiled from *Rudé právo*, 19 Apr. 1969, p. 2; Michael Mudry-Šebik, "Czechoslovakia: Husák Takes the Helm," *East Europe*, vol. 18, no. 5 (May 1969), pp. 2–7; and "A Slovak in Prague Castle," *Frankfurter Allgemeine Zeitung*, 21 Aug. 1976, weekend supplement.

[70] Pelikán, *Ici Prague*, p. 192.

himself about the guilt of the whole Politburo of the CPC as follows: "In the light of these documents it is a gang of hardened criminals."[71]

The report, although written in a conciliatory tone, was denounced by the secretary of the CPC CC, Vladimír Koucký, as a "provocation" and reworked by the secretariat. In its milder form it was confidentially communicated to Party organizations, in large doses for higher organs and smaller doses for lower cadre. Husák and Novomeský were rehabilitated only partly since they were still "guilty of political mistakes."[72] Even Dubček was supposedly against Husák's full rehabilitation since he did not wish to see him entering into public life again and therefore kept promoting Bil'ak.[73]

Throughout the year of 1963, primarily Slovak writers and journalists kept pushing for proper consequences to be drawn from the whole dirty affair. The Party leading dogmatists, responsible for the trials of the 1950s, were being attacked repeatedly: at the Slovak Writers' Union in April, at the Czechoslovak Writers' Congress in May, and at the Congress of Slovak Journalists, also in May 1963. Novotný counter-attacked but in vain. Five years later, Husák commented in an interview:

> During the era of Novotný's personal power, these last years — especially since 1963 — he was able to hold in check progressive forces more in the Czech milieu. In Slovakia the renewal process, after the rehabilitation of "bourgeois nationalism," after 1963, enforced certain changes. People of Bacílek's, David's, and Strechaj's type practically left political life in 1963. The new political leadership, headed by comrade Dubček, attempted changes in some political domains, namely in the attitude towards the intelligentsia, youth, and progressive democratic heritage of our history.[74]

The 10th of June, 1963, the Slovak Historical Society held its general meeting. The whole atmosphere was rather unusual in a police state for its frankness as described by a *compte rendu* in the Slovak cultural weekly:

> Comrade Miloš Gosiorovský, one of our leading historical workers, also courageously dwelt on the past period . . . . [He] explained his errors, particularly in connection with his study "The Underground Fight of the Slovak CP and the Slovak National Uprising," written in 1949.

He attributed his errors to his youth and "the former secretary-general of the Slovak CP, Štefan Baštovanský, [who] almost foisted on him one-sidedly selected documentary material." He had therefore "withdrawn, as errors, certain parts of his works" and promised to contribute "to the clearing of the names of all the brave

---

[71] "Poznámky a doplnky ke sdělení ÚV KSČ" ["Comments on the Additions to the Communication of the CPC CC"], *Svědectví*, vi, no. 28 (spring 1966), p. 357. See also impressions of another communist historian, Karel Kaplan, quoted earlier, Part I, Chapter 5. For a much fuller treatment of repercussions of the Barnabite commission, see my unpublished M. A. thesis, "On the Road to a Revolution: Czechoslovakia, 1960-1968," Columbia University, 1969, pp. 48-59.

[72] Excerpts from Husák's "Petition for Review of Trial and for Rehabilitation," written in December 1962, were published by David Burg, "A Smuggled Document from Czechoslovakia: The Ten-Year Hell of Dr. Husák," *Sunday Times*, 10 Aug. 1969, pp. 5-9.

[73] Moravus (pseud) "Alexandre Dubček de deux points de vue," *Ici Prague*, ed. by Jiří Pelikán, pp. 356-73.

[74] *Kulturní tvorba*, 18 July 1968, p. 1.

fighters in the heroic struggle of the Slovak nation.''[75] The stage was set for Gustáv Husák, working then in the Juristic Cabinet of the Slovak Academy of Sciences:

> He proved clearly how incorrect the claims were that the revolutionary Slovak National Council had been a body that was abused by the so-called bourgeois nationalists, . . . how nonsensical it was to decry the historical merits of the army and also of the Partisans so that, in the end, all that was left of the Uprising was the Moscow leadership and the brave, helpless Slovak people.

In this connection Husák revealed the reason for his own humiliation, repeated torture, and long persecution: during the uprising, they did not disobey Moscow instructions, they "merely refused to regard them as the only way." The reporter at the conclusion of his article stressed that Husák's "arguments . . . were accepted unanimously by the Slovak historians. After a long time, this was an organic unanimity based on an analysis of historical facts."[76]

A day after this report was published, the Slovak trade union daily well expressed in its editorial reasons for the excitment which was caused by the joy of openly expressing the truth after years of its suppression:

> It is neither unnatural nor preposterous that the scientists and artists, the journalists and all the workers of the ideological front are particularly active in the struggle for the overcoming of dogmatic and non-scientific way of thinking. . . . The attitude of the creative intelligentsia stems from the very nature of their work. Dogmatism and sectarianism bore down hard on truth in the social and natural sciences, they distorted the look at reality and created false theories which led to harmful practices.[77]

It was clearly hoped that a better recognition of reality would avoid criminal acts being committed in the name of false theories.

A Czech historian, Oldřich Janeček, and a Slovak writer, Michal Chorváth, proposed to reinstate the 28 October 1918 as the official birthday of the Czechoslovak Republic.[78] Every rebirth of domestic traditions had its anti-Soviet connotations, since it had to go against their past (and future) Soviet suppression.

Husák's full rehabilitation and return to previous political career was, however, not achieved in 1963. On 7 November 1963, at a meeting of the Barnabite commission, its member, the historian Karel Kaplan, proposed a full rehabilitation of the "bourgeois nationalists" and their return to positions they had occupied before their arrest, or to corresponding ones. His proposal was supported by some other members but vigorously opposed by V. Koucký, B. Laštovička, and by leading Slovak functionaries V. Bil'ak, R. Cvik, M. Lúčan, and M. Sabolčík. Ominously. Antonín Novotný used words which would be later remembered with a conference (25-6 August) in Ťaly, Slovakia. More than one hundred Soviet-bloc know him!''[79]

In 1964 Milan Hübl continued his "revisionist" writing[80] but the moment he

---

[75] *Kultúrny život*, no. 24, 15 June 1963.

[76] *Ibid.*, pp. 6-7.

[77] *Práca*, 16 June 1963.

[78] *Kultúrny život*, 31 Aug. 1963.

[79] Karel Kaplan, "Otevřený dopis Vasilu Bilakovi" ["Open Letter to Vasil Bilak"], sent 27 Sept. 1975 and published in *Listy*, vi, 1 (Feb. 1976), p. 40.

[80] See *Československý časopis historický*, no. 2, 1964, pp. 200-2; and *Historický časopis*, no. 4, 1964.

touched upon the sensitive issue of Moscow trials of the 1930s[81] he went too far and in April started to be attacked in an exemplary way — by Jiří Hendrych at the CPC regional conference,[82] by Vladimír Koucký in his address to the Academy of Sciences,[83] and in May[84] by President Novotný himself. Hübl was then dismissed from his position of pro-rector of the High Party School, expelled from the Party, but allowed to publish biting comments on the fall of another dictatorship.[85]

The twentieth anniversary of the Slovak uprising was celebrated by a two-day conference (25-6 August) in Ťaly, Slovakia. More than one hundred Soviet-bloc writers participated in discussions of Anti-Fascist literature and heard Laco Novomeský talk about "distorted socialism."[86] Together with some fifty others who managed to survive both the uprising and later purges, Novomeský and Husák then received in Khrushchev's presence commemorative medals from Novotný in Bánska Bystrica.[87] In 1964 Husák was able to publish his own version of the Slovak uprising in a book.[88] For an author who in 1948, in the victorious year of the *coup*, published an optimistic book *Zápas o zajtrajšek* [*Fight for Tomorrow*], the struggle for the past proved to be at least as demanding, complicating the joke: "Question: What is the most difficult task for a Communist historian? Answer: To predict the future."[89] Milan Hübl's and other historians' attempts at recovering the truth about the past were, of course, successful not only concerning the Slovak uprising. Gradually and systematically, the whole recent past was being uncovered as if archaeologists were digging up long lost civilizations.[90]

Naturally, the history of the Soviet Union was out of reach for Czech and Slovak historians but they could study the development of their own Communist Party which reflected it. Asking themselves what went so fatally wrong, they found that, more often than not, the tragic perversion of the original Marxist ideals they believed in was the result of Soviet interventions. At least briefly, one instructive case should be mentioned.

[81] *Literární niviny*, 21 Mar. 1964.

[82] *Svoboda*, 7 Apr. 1964, p. 3.

[83] *Rudé právo*, 11 Apr. 1964.

[84] *Ibid.*, 29 May 1964.

[85] "Pád jakobínské diktatury" ["Fall of the Jacobin Dictatorship"], *Dějiny a současnost*, no. 8, 1964; "Rehabilitace v S.S.S.R. pokračuje" ["Rehabilitation in the U.S.S.R. Goes On"], *Ibid.*, no. 9, 1964: "Počátek cesty" ["The Beginning of the Road"], *Slovanský přehled*, no. 2, 1965, pp. 74-80; *Literární noviny*, 8 Oct. 1966; and his celebration of a Slovak economist, discussed here previously, "Moudrý člověk: Eugen Löbl — 60" ["A Wise Man: Eugen Löbl — 60"], *Ibid.*, 20 May 1967, p. 7. Since 1965 Hübl became a regular contributor to this cultural weekly.

[86] *Kultúrny život*, 29 Aug 1964; his speech was partly translated in *East Europe*, xiii, 10 (Oct. 1964), p. 41.

[87] *Rudé právo*, 30 Aug. 1964.

[88] *Svedectvo o Slovenskom národnom povstání* [*Testimony About the Slovak National Uprising*]. A second, modified, version appeared in 1969. A non-communist collection of memoirs was edited by M. Kvetko and J. M. Ličko, *Zborník slovenského národného povstání* [*Volume on the Slovak National Uprising*] (Toronto: Stála konferencia slovenských demokratických exulantov [Continual Conference of Slovak Democratic Exiles], 1976.)

[89] Anatole Shub, *International Herald Tribune*, 28 Mar. 1969.

[90] For a survey, see especially Karel Bartošek, "Czechoslovakia: the State of Historiography," *Journal of Contemporary History*, no. 2, Jan. 1967, pp. 143-55; and Stanley Z. Pech, "Ferment in Czechoslovak Marxist Historiography," *Canadian Slavonic Papers*, no. 10, winter 1968, pp. 502-22.

Pavel Reiman, born in 1902 in Brno, one of the founders of the CPC, in 1931 published, in Czech, *Dějiny KSČ* [*History of the CPC*].[91] He expressed the view of some radical members of the Party that Czechoslovakia after the World War II was ripe for a proletarian revolution and that the leaders of the Communist Party spoiled the chance by bungling it. Some German bitterness towards Czech comrades was probably involved since the common Party was created out of nationalist factions on strong Soviet prodding. Till 1933 Reiman worked as the chief of the CPC CC's important department for agitation and propaganda. He lost his influential position for interesting reasons: a member of the Politburo, Josef Guttman, spoke for a Party faction which, quite rightly, was alarmed by Hitler's seizure of total power in Germany. But since Stalin's foolish policy, claiming that not the Nazis but Social Democrats represented the main danger, was still being enforced, Guttman was excommunicated and, together with Reiman, thrown on the famous "heap of history."

Thirty years later, in 1963, Reiman (who in 1961 was again able to publish in Prague his *History of the CPC*) became director of the Institute of History of the CPC. For five years he was in charge of studying and rewriting the Party history, which had been full of wrong policies, tragic mistakes, Soviet interference, factional infighting, and horrendous crimes. Many Party members who became their victims at one time or another, or on several occasions, were still around, clamoring for justice. Under his leadership a new generation of communist historians revealed hidden Party secrets and tore down the veil of a supposedly immaculate organization which has been "always right." A gradually emerging picture showed much less Party idealism and much more stupidity and brutality than expected.[92] Especially the complete bolshevization of the CPC since 1929, under Gottwald's name, its practical take-over by Soviet agents, and submission to Russian interests, came under scrutiny. Even the celebrated *coup* of 1948 began to be seen in its proper light as Soviet intervention, mainly through domestic agents; as the beginning of totalitarian satellization for the exclusive profit of the Soviet Union; and as the start of a new Dark Age in Czechoslovak history.

But let us return to the complementary work of Hübl and Husák; not much remains to be said about their activities until the end of the Novotný era. Husák as "the most influential man in Bratislava intellectual circles"[93] did not limit his ambition to Czechoslovakia but was spreading his wings farther afield. At the beginning of 1964 he sent several manuscripts of his articles (later to be printed in *Dějiny a současnost*) to the Polish historian Joseph Lewandovsky, who following the author's wishes, used them in the Polish press, where "they were read with interest," and also forwarded them, as intended by Husák, to the West.

[91] Also in 1931 it was issued in Hamburg as *Geschichte der Komunistischen Partei der Tschechoslowakei*. The author's name had its German version, Paul Reiman.
[92] In 1956 Reiman published in Prague and in Berlin his book *Main Trends of German Literature, 1750–1848*, and in 1966 in Prague his memoirs of the 1920s, *Ve dvacátých letech*. His last work of literary criticism, *Versunkene Welt: Acht Kapitel zur Geschichte Prager deutschen Literatur* [*The Sunken World: Eight Chapters from the History of the Prague German Literature*], was refused by the Publishing House of the Academy of Sciences since the author was expelled from the CPC and belonged to proscribed writers. Pavel Reiman died in Prague on 1 November 1976; for his obituary see *Listy*, vii, 1 (Feb. 1977), pp. 42–3.
[93] See Part II, Chapter 2, footnote 38, p. 91.

Meeting this Polish historian, Husák could hardly find anything positive about the existing regime. For the secretly circulating pamphlets and materials he coined the term "illegal communist press," and characterized it as "the biggest progress in Czechoslovakia during the last years." The Polish historian remarked: "At that time we were equal, both revisionist historians."[94]

Much was going on hidden from public eyes. An Italian communist intellectual who repeatedly visited Czechoslovakia and studied the situation both on the spot and from books, Luciano Antonetti, revealed that in 1964 he was present at a discussion of Togliatti's "Yalta memorandum" at the Prague school of economics where the teachers of Marxism-Leninism expressed views "quite different from the theses still held officially." At a conference on 8 February at the Historical Institute of the CPC, speakers criticized as nihilism the regime's lack of pursuit of national interests, sacrificing them for other doubtful goals, and its blocking of "the search for a democratic solution to the problem of the Czechoslovak state structure." He was especially pleased by the "flowering" of historical revisionism at the congress of historians held in Brno in September 1966.[95]

The previous year Milan Hübl praised a writer's report on Poland since thanks to him "for the first time the reader in Czechoslovakia could discover what really happened in Poznan on 28 June 1956."[96] He was later blamed for successfully having taken over at this 1966 congress the Czechoslovak Historical Society which until then was moribund. Although not a member of the Party, he and another historian, Jan Křen, had supposedly managed, "covered by the authority of the CPC," to take over the whole Czechoslovak historiography, "impose upon the whole historical community a new scale of values," and "gradually create an atmosphere of absolute hegemony, long before January 1968 . . . . At last in 1968 a complete identification of Macek's group took place with the militant and aggressive group around Hübl and Křen."[97] The authors of this secret report addressed to Party leadership, could see nothing but an enforced conspiracy in the organic unity of historians, who decided to serve the truth.

In this "atmosphere of absolute hegemony" Gustáv Husák, who worked in the Institute of State and Law in Bratislava, in 1966 successfully defended his new title of candidate of historical sciences.[98]

As became prevalent, in his articles Husák interpreted history in order to modify the present. At the beginning of 1967 he wrote a series of articles on Vlado Clementis and used them as a vehicle for attacks on Novotný's dictatorship, under the transparent pretense that his target was Premier Široký (deposed in 1963),

---

[94] Cf. Lewandovsky's open letter to Husák in the Polish monthly *Kultura* (Paris), no. 9, 1972, excerpted in *Listy*, iii, 1 (Feb. 1973), p. 51. In his letter the Polish historian reproached his Slovak erstwhile colleague for his persecution in the 1970s of other historians who helped him in his illegal activities of the 1960s.

[95] "Lenin e il Leninismo a Praga negli ultimi anni," *Critica Marxista*, vol. 8, no. 3 (May–June 1970), pp. 194-204; as quoted *in extenso* by Kevin Devlin, "Leninism and the Czechoslovak Spring: The PCI Stands Firm," *RFE Research*, 5 June 1970, 7 polycopied pages, pp. 3-4.

[96] "Oneskorená reportáž Ivana Klímu" ["Delayed Report of Ivan Klíma"], *Kultúrny život*, 5 Nov. 1965, p. 5.

[97] Čestmír Amort and Václav Král, "Tajně o historii" ["Secretly on History"], a document reprinted in *Listy*, i, 4-5 (July 1971), pp. 57-9.

[98] *Rudé právo*, 19 Apr. 1969, p. 2.

his "autocracy," his "undemocratic methods," and "insufficient knowledge of Slovakia's problems" as well as his "heartlessness."[99]

On 10 March 1967 the Institute of History of the Slovak CP in Bratislava organized an exchange of opinions about Czech-Slovak relations among nine historians from the Czech lands and twelve from Slovakia. A report was then published in the quarterly review of the Slovak Academy of Sciences. Husák declared that the topic was "one of the fundamental problems of our state." He deplored the fact that "after almost fifty years of the existence of Czechoslovakia, we must clarify the most elementary concepts;" namely, "the right of every nation to self-determination and of the democratic right of every nation to occupy a position of equality with all the other nations." He blamed the CPC for not having any actual program for the solution. In opposition, he sounded like a determined democrat (it is always easier to have high ethical standards in the opposition): "The guaranteeing of the democratic rights of the citizen and of the nation — numerically smaller — is a firm part of the struggle for the democratization of modern society, for the establishment and consolidation of democratic relations within the State and among states.[100]

At this meeting Miloš Gosiorovský described at length the formative influences American Slovaks and the U.S. democratic milieu had on the formulation of Slovak images of their future life in a common state with the Czechs. Clearly, the Slovak question was being used as a powerful tool against Novotný's dictatorship and his constant humiliations of the Slovaks. It also became clear that there existed a potentially dangerous difference between Czech intentions of a profound democratization of the whole State and the Slovak interest mainly in equality of two parts of a federalized State.

In the historical journal *Příspěvky k dějinám KSČ* a discussion resurrected the positive value of nationalism which until then was being constantly denigrated as something detestable and opposed to internationalism which term — and duty — practically meant serving exclusively Soviet interests. The historian Jan Tesař defended nationalism very much as T. G. Masaryk used to understand it; that is, as "responsibility for its own nation towards universal culture."[101] The national spirit was gradually being awakened in preparation for the coming challenge to Soviet imperialism.

Probably the first two personalities who publicly interpreted the change in Party leadership as an opening to profound changes in the country were Milan Hübl and Gustáv Husák. Hübl must have written his article for the Slovak writers' weekly during the protracted crisis at the top, when Czechoslovakia had a period of *interregnum*; it appeared on the day of Novotný's replacement by Dubček — what timing! The lecturer at the High Party School (proudly called University) anticipated the separation of powers, but stressed the necessity for "legal and institutional guarantees." He was able to foresee two main issues which would dominate the whole year of reforms:

---

[99] *Kultúrny život*, 16 Feb. 1968.
[100] Unsigned, "A Discussion About Czech-Slovak Relations," *Historický časopis*, no. 4, 1967.
[101] No. 3, 1967.

The experience of many socialist countries, especially after 1956, shows that it is not sufficient to count an outstanding, or only seemingly outstanding, qualities of those who would relieve the leadership . . . . The present situation is such that more than one of the socialist countries is endeavoring to find a solution that would make it possible to create a model of socialism which would not only be capable of life, but which also would stand up in comparison with the highly developed countries of the capitalist West.[102]

One week later Husák seconded his friend's demands for constitutional guarantees. The Czechoslovak society, he wrote, is composed of "mature, ripe, and cultured people" and should be treated as such, no longer like children in a kindergarten:

This is a problem of the progressing democratization of our social order, a problem of setting free and developing all creative forces of the population, its physical and intellectual potential, its commitment to activity, and a problem of the cooperation of millions of hands and brains institutionally expressed and guaranteed . . . .

The modern European wants to know what are the issues of state. He wants to understand, to have a say, to help decide his fate and living conditions, to elect his leaders, and then — according to their deeds — to praise them or even criticize them. In short, he wants to see the constitutional principle that "the people are the source of all power" implemented in everyday practice. The citizen wants to realize his civic and national self through his national and state representatives. He wants guarantees that he is free to apply his right of election, of control, and of civic responsibility.[103]

It sounded great but between 1967/8 and 1969/70 Husák must have either changed his speech-writers, his mind, or both. Just for comparison, Josef Smrkovský's similar call for basic reforms came out only nine days later.[104] After another seven days Hübl addressed his appeal, this time in Prague, to "the little Czech man" who started to complain that the Czechs were being ruled by Slovaks since both of the main positions, that of the First Secretary of the CPC and of the Prime Minister, happened to be in the hands of Slovaks, who formed approximately between one-third and one-fourth of the population. Hübl explained the multiple humiliations the Slovaks had to go through, especially since 1960 when their Board of Commissioners had been abolished and they became "a nation of deputies." He suggested that it was high time to "get rid of provincialism" and "strengthen Czechoslovakia as a common state of equal nations."[105]

As Hübl continued in his usual role as an advocate of the Slovak nation and of Slovak politicians, Husák concentrated on the issue of equality of Slovaks with the Czechs and began to work for an eventual federalization of the State.[106]

In the meantime, the director of the Historical Institute of the CPC, Pavel Reiman, in the name of an "initiative committee for the support of Alexander Dubček's policy," convoked a meeting of some 170 pre-war Party members, in order to send to the First Secretary a manifest of trust. It seems that there were some behind-the-scene maneuvers to unseat him or to limit his powers. Many future leaders of the reform movement took part in this meeting: Eduard Goldstücker,

[102] "Socialism for Us," *Kultúrny život*, 5 Jan. 1968, p. 3.
[103] "Old Anniversaries and New Hopes," *Kultúrny život*, 12 Jan. 1968, p. 1; excerpts in *East Europe*, Mar. 1968, pp. 25–6.
[104] *Práce*, 21 Jan. 1968.
[105] *Ibid.*, 28 Jan. 1968. He returned to the same theme in this daily of trade unions again on 21 Feb. 1968.
[106] See his series of articles, "February Meditations," in *Kultúrny život*.

Dr. Jiří Hájek, Dr. František Kriegel, Josef Pavel, Václav Slavík, Josef Smrkovský, and František Vodsloň. The strategy and tactics of radical changes in the future were planned at the seat of Party historians! On this occasion, Eduard Goldstücker, declared: "All that was progressive in the modern history of Czechs and Slovaks was formulated by the intelligentsia and brought by it into national consciousness." Soon the director of Czechoslovak Radio, Zdeněk Hejzlar, and the director of the Czechoslovak Television, Jiří Pelikán, both members of a younger generation, were cooperating. Large public meetings started to take place and since their fascinating revelations and stimulating discussions were sometimes broadcast without interruptions, large sections of the population realized that "maybe, hopefully," something very close to a bloodless revolution was going on.

At one such immense gathering in the Fučík Park (which used to be reserved for boring official manifestations with every word and gesture carefully planned in advance), on 20 March 1968, young people applauded every speaker but one. Gustáv Husák won disapproval when he "demonstrated his taste for normalization."[107] He clearly was more liberal and democratic with a carefully prepared text, away from other people, than faced with crowds that to his autocratic disposition must have always appeared unruly and dangerous when not carefully manipulated by Party display specialists. On other occasions, however, Husák even favored non-communist opposition when other communist members of a Slovak panel did not at all think about it, considering themselves as part of the élite chosen by history.[108]

At the May plenum of the CPC CC Husák resolutely attacked Novotný for his culpability for the political trials of the 1950s, especially the one he was personally involved in, against the Slovak leaders. It was Husák's first speech at this forum after eighteen years and it was a speech full of his justly bitter feelings over all the injustices suffered in the intervening period.[109] Husák even joined in the campaign against the top official of the Slovak CP, Vasil Biľak, when he said: "It would be a tragedy if Slovakia were to become a conservative bastion in the country's national development."[110] In short, it could be summarized that most of the time Husák pushed towards radical reforms. It suited his personal ambitions; little is known about his sincere attachment to these professed ideals.

He wanted to keep matters strictly in the hands of the Party *apparat* and therefore from time to time allowed his well-known authoritarian and intolerant nature to show. (But even Dubček and Smrkovský did not avoid such lapses into *apparatchik* instincts of strict manipulation of both intellectuals and masses.)

In April Husák became Vice-Premier of the Czechoslovak government in Prague and Hübl was appointed rector of the High Party School. Together they participated in an important commission charged with preparations for the federalization of the country. Hübl also took part in many vital bodies working on

---

[107] Pierre Daix, *J'ai cru au matin* [*I Believed It Was Morning*] (Paris: Robert Laffont, 1976), p. 404. Enthused, this old Party militant and editor-in-chief of *Les Lettres Françaises*, sent from Prague a postcard to Pablo Picasso: "This is a revolution!" *Ibid.*, p. 405.

[108] *Kultúrny život*, 29 Mar. 1968.

[109] His speech was published only several weeks later, *Rudé právo*, 15 June 1968, p. 3.

[110] Radio Bratislava, 5 July 1968, quoted by Mudry-Sebik, *op. cit.*, p. 5.

short- and long-term Party programs. As before 1968, when he visited Bratislava, he usually stayed in Husák's apartment.

Throughout the year 1968 the Czechoslovak historians achieved a magnificent victory. Not much remained tabu. As a sarcastic postscript to the ostentatious celebrations of the fiftieth anniversary of the Bolshevik revolution, *Literární listy* published in a serial Isaac Deutscher's *Unfinished Revolution, 1917–1967. Dějiny a současnost* in a series of articles written by historian Václav Veber, introduced to its readers the un-person of L. D. Trotsky as "the outstanding revolutionary."[111] The historians could write on the past much freer than ever before since 1948 and they had great and beneficial influence on the present society. It was an incredible achievement in a previously totalitarian and satellite state. The power of their determination and scholarship helped to destroy the carefully tailored strait-jacket in which the whole Czechoslovak people had been kept, foreigners in their own land. They were able to renew, quickly and firmly, the democratic and humanitarian traditions and ideals of their forerunners.

5. Husák and Hübl: Moscow time again

In his last speech, delivered a few hours (!) before the invasion, Husák complained that democratization was proceeding too slowly. Although some people were worried about anti-socialist dangers, he said, "the uneasiness about them might have originated in fear of freedom, fear of democracy, fear of losing position, or, simply, in fear of the people." He attacked those who "beg to close the door to this healthy air in our political life" and declared: "I am firmly convinced that the new current, represented in our country by comrade Dubček, is in both the Czech and Slovak nations so strong that there does not exist anybody able to close the door. No one can get us back, halt further progress and further perspectives."[112] Some of the tanks must have been already rolling towards that door.

Although Husák was not kidnapped during the fateful night as Dubček, Černík, Smrkovský, and other Czechoslovak communist leaders, he flew to Moscow and took part in the meetings from 23 to 26 August. (Hübl was surprised by the news of the invasion while vacationing in the Crimea[113] and at the secret Party Congress in Prague was elected (together with Husák) not only to the new Central Committee but, in recognition of his obvious services to the reform movement, also to its Presidium.) On his return from Moscow talks, Husák went straight to the regular session of the Congress of the CP of Slovakia and persuaded its delegates that the Fourteenth Congress of the CPC should not be recognized as valid because not enough of Slovak delegates were present in Prague and because one of the clauses of the Moscow Protocols requested its non-recognition. Since on 30 August he was elected First Secretary of the Slovak CP instead of the conservative Vasil Bil'ak, the result in Bratislava was a mixed bag and seemed to be a compromise. As it became

---

[111] "Trockismus — přisluhovač světové reakce" ["Trotskyism — Servant of the World Reaction"], *Zprávy*, no. 11, 15 Mar. 1969, pp. 4–5.
[112] Husák spoke at a Party meeting in Žiar nad Hronom and his speech was reported by Radio Bratislava. Quotes in "60 let G. Husáka" ["G. Husák Sixty Years Old"], *Listy*, iii, 4 (Aug. 1973), p. 40.
[113] Michel Tatu, *Le Monde*, 3 Sept. 1968.

gradually clear, it was an arrangement typical for the situation. Dubček, Černík, Smrkovský, and all the others who returned from abduction could throw out some hated collaborators with the Russians, but according to the Kremlin's wishes had to impose strict restrictions.

On 31 August both Husák and Hübl (with some others) were coopted in the enlarged old Central Committee of the CPC, as a sign of a partial acceptance and partial rejection of the "underground" elections by the recent, now "illegal," Party Congress in Prague. One week later Husák was elevated to the CPC CC Presidium.

From then on, Husák carefully began to maneuver his program and personality to the top, in stages, pushing aside all the leaders the Soviet Politburo wanted to get rid of. The difference was that they — slipping step by step — still hoped that Moscow will allow them to stop the downfall at a certain reasonable and dignified point, but Husák from the beginning took a "realist" attitude: "The hard and inexorable reality of the presence of Warsaw Pact troops on our soil" had to be recognized. "You can't go through a wall head first."[114] Climbing the stairs to the top, one by one, he gradually introduced and imposed all the Soviet demands, always sounding more resolute and contemptuous of the "anti-socialist forces" than the day or week before.

On 9 September 1968 Husák suspended the weekly that helped him most, *Kultúrny život*; a month later, he denounced the "anti-Soviet hysteria in the country" and spoke of the need to stop "criminal elements" and "agents working against the state;"[115] at a Central Committee session in November he deplored the "disintegration" of the secret police — "things can get out of hand." Journalists were involved in "heroic gestures, meetings, protests, and resolutions. I do not know any other word better fitting than Party irresponsibility for this."[116] Then he attacked "the excesses of the mass communication media" and journalists "with their anarchist interpretation of freedom of the press;"[117] and finally, he blamed Dubček and his colleagues for all the "mistakes" and the resulting need for an invasion:

> It was the fault of our leadership that it did not solve problems consistently, that it admitted anti-Soviet and hostile forces to public political life, that various irresponsible elements had the opportunity through millions of copies of newspapers and among millions of listeners and TV viewers to spread anti-Party, literally anti-state views, to fool people and to deceive part of our youth.[118]

One week later he replaced Dubček as the Party leader.

Milan Hübl, in the meantime, was more optimistic and less of a "realist" than his friend Husák (who was fast changing from a historian into a politician and replacing his democratic vocabulary by a Stalinist one). From our discussion of the economist Ota Šik, we know that Hübl through open letters attempted to lure him to Prague and tried to persuade him that the Central Committee, as the highest

[114] Radio Czechoslovakia, 28 Aug. 1968.
[115] Radio Bratislava, 19 Oct. 1968.
[116] *International Herald Tribune*, 25 Nov. 1968.
[117] *Pravda*, 13 Mar. 1969, pp. 4–5.
[118] *Četeka*, 11 Apr. 1969.

Party organ between congresses, at its December plenum "acted precisely in the spirit of principles fought through in January [1968]." Hübl implored Šik to come back and check for himself the real situation: "We are all on the same boat. You are one of us — your place shouldn't stay empty."[119] As we know, Šik came, stayed awhile; and left definitely, saving himself a lot of trouble or dividing the roles with those who preferred to remain at home.

In an article written before the end of 1968 Hübl explained some reasons for his optimism and persistence. The November strike of the students was an impressive success; the trade unions embarked upon great activity in factories and Hübl hoped that at least some capable communists would be able to get a number of comrades into the elected workers' organs which threatened to be without communists; the problem of sovereignty and interest in the realization of the Action Program of democratization would not abate; the selected persecution of "disturbers of the peace" did not work before and would never work; and, especially: "However romantic this may sound, it is chiefly up to us to decide in this country and at this time whether we shall be able to continue in the post-January policies — primarily through deeds — and to accomplish a socialism which is human not only because of its face, but also because of its substance." Hübl wrote, literally, "it is in our hands" and therefore he insisted that as many people as possible should take a stand and refuse to budge. Unfortunately, Husák was more of a realist than Hübl, who believed in a democratic reality: "The political reality of the first order, as clearly demonstrated by the events of the past few months, is the attitude and the efforts of the people of this country; its prudence, will, tenacity, and stubborn desire to live a life of its own." Hübl also tried to prove that even "external reality" might change, due to the growing importance of China, possible changes in American policies under a new president (Nixon), and the planned international conference of communist parties. Soviet policies might return to the program "abandoned or braked after 1964." He was looking to the future "with confidence."[120] Unfortunately, the confidence proved to be based on illusions which could not cope with Soviet armed and police power determined to finish with "Dubčekism."

Reasonable or sentimental appeals to Husák, not to serve as a Soviet tool in a new and brutal satellization of Czechoslovakia, had no influence on the "iron man" from Bratislava. Such was the case when a philosopher from Prague asked Husák, who violently attacked philosophy students as "hooligans," to remember that the same students in 1966 demanded for him the right to address the Thirteenth Party Congress and were therefore called "an ideological agency of the enemy".[121] The term was used again after the invasion. Then a Slovak historian objected to stigmatizing the 1968 reformers as a "danger from the Right:"

What happened in our country from January 1968 till 21 August of the same year has a direct continuity with everything that happened in our party since its foundation . . . . As a historian after years of study I arrived to a single conclusion: the main and decisive danger for the CPC in its entire history has always been the danger of Leftist sectarian dogmatism, obedient more of the center outside the Republic than of the will, voice, and feelings

---

[119] *Práce*, 16 Dec. 1968, pp. 1–2.
[120] *Práce*, 29 Dec. 1968.
[121] *Mladá fronta*, 3 Jan. 1969.

of this country's people. That's what in 1929–30 decimated the Party into a sect; that's what introduced into the Party the method of a "blow in its own ranks;" . . . that's what replaced battle of ideas by jails and gallows. That's what defamed the Czechoslovak communist movement by the most extensive executions out of all countries in Europe which after 1945 began building socialism.[122]

Husák was probably not influenced by some excellent historical essays either. In spite of heavy censorship, they continued to be published, in veiled form, until April 1969, before the curtain would gradually but definitely come down. The public was enlightened about the situation and its connections with similar events in the past. The nature of the regime and of the Russian empire was analyzed. Here are three such studies; examples of the intelligent way the historians went on serving their professional (and national) cause.

First, *Jan Tesař* wrote a series of articles entitled "Patriots and Fighters." In one of them, based on a detailed study of past collaboration by "realist patriots" with Hitler in Rumania, Slovakia, France, Bulgaria, Hungary, and in the Czech lands, he showed that the Nazis cleverly preferred even anti-German patriots, who wanted to save as much as possible, to fanatics who, though Fascist, could not get out of the population of occupied territories goods and work the Germans were interested in. Most they valued the *"realists* collaborating on the basis of the principle of a *smaller evil."* Tesař reminded his readers that although Czech fascists mostly ended their lives in German concentration camps, "Czech fascism *still exists."* He certainly had in mind some of the nasty pro-Soviet communists whose methods and language both before and after the invasion were much the same. The Germans invested some small amounts of money in foreign Fascist groups, using them as a constant threat of a possibly much worse regime; however, they governed in occupied territories with the help of *"realist patriots."* The article was written throughout in a scholarly way but Tesař did not want his readers to miss the real target; namely, the widespread belief among the intellectuals that Husák was, no doubt, bad but still better than Indra, Bil'ak, and similar comrades, since he represented a "lesser evil."

> Patriotism which gave up its democratic and generally humanitarian content became part of the German game with ignorant slaves . . . . In their experimental workshop on our soil was born their historical *deposit in the treasury* of tyranny and that is what the Nazis bequeathed to all future oppressors: the game with *fanatics and realists.*[123]

Second, *František Graus* published a long review of a new book written by Robert Mandrou (editor of the French version of the *Black Book*, the record of the Soviet invasion of the ČSSR), devoted to a study of the persecution of witches in seventeenth-century France.[124] Again, in the atmosphere of worry about new show trials, his scholarly review was a study of barbarian forces that manipulate ideas in order to hunt down actual or invented opponents who represent the evil:

---

[122] Ján Mlynárik, *Reportér*, 27 Feb. 1969, pp. 12 and 13.
[123] "Železná garda a 'realisté'" ["The Iron Guard and the 'Realists'"], *Listy*, no. 15, 17 Apr. 1969, p. 16. His own emphasis.
[124] *Magistrats et sorciers en France au XVIIe siècle. Analyse de psychologie historique* [*Magistrates and Sorcerors in France in the 17th Century: An Analysis of Historical Psychology*] (Paris: Civilisations et mentalités, 1968).

The belief that it is possible to influence the world by magic is ancient; the effort to change the environment by waving a magic wand is time-honored and perhaps eternal. Only the forms might differ: once people believe that it is possible to change this world by magical formulas, appealing to, and conjuring up, powerful forces; at another time people believe that it is possible to alter man totally by changing the societal forces, by influencing or harnessing them .
. . . .

A basic contradiction, a dualist view of history and of the contemporary world, can be found in most varied forms, kinds, and shapes. Deity can transfer into Hegel's *Weltgeist*, mythical "progress," in "sense of history," and into all other forms of a secularized theological world-view . . . .

Alas, faith in a mythical great Rival survived as well as persecution of his servitors . . . . In the twentieth-century trials of the witches returned in a new form . . . . Trials are taking place in a fog of whipped-up mass hysteria, of a general belief in omnipresence of evil and its attendants.

At the end of his article the author mentioned that "it is surprising how fast people sober up from illusions and superstitions" but "they soon fall for a new 'faith' as monstrous as the preceding one and they are willing to believe firmly and to burn the heretics and witches again."[125]

Third, *Milan Švankmajer* explained some Russian traditions under the title "The Gendarme of Europe" and with a motto from Nicholas I, 1848: "Gentlemen, saddle the horses, in Paris is a revolution." It was all written in minute detail about the Russian Czar, with proper old illustrations of Russian imperialism. But some sentences marked the real target as when, for example, the author discussed the Czar's "reorganization of the secret police and the attempt to 'put the souls right' (with the help of censorship and state ideology):"

Every future government began in an almost stereotyped way by ostentatiously abolishing the dreaded "Secret Office" but in no time renewing it (under a different name and without publicity) . . . .

All important governmental and public institutions were provided with permanent agents who were placed in all great military units . . . . Since Nicholas I the police did not belong to domains retarded behind Europe. Rather the other way about.

Then the author tried to explain the nature of Russian imperialism:

The Russian empire has been constantly exposed to the danger of disintegration which can be prevented only by a big central power . . . . Civic freedoms do not threaten only partial interests on the periphery of multinational empires but *their own existence*.

And talking in 1969 about the Russian invasion of Hungary in 1849, of course:

It was a stroke, soberly and coldly calculated and motivated by self-preservation, a stroke against European revolution which by its civic freedoms and efforts to assert the right of nations to self-determination threatened the very foundations of the Russian autocracy . . . .

The Russian empire was not led to its role as "gendarme of Europe" by differences of its civilization, culture, or opinions but by the fact that since the end of the eighteenth century the European evolution had permanently threatened the rudiments of its existence. It applies, of course, the other way around, too.[126]

Since the communist intelligentsia, obviously, in 1968 did not yet know enough of Russian and Soviet history, an attempt was made to underline the basic

[125] "Glosy: Hon na čarodějnice" ["Glosses: Witchhunt"], *Československý časopis historický*, no. 2, Apr. 1969, pp. 190–5.
[126] "Četník Evropy," *Dějiny a současnost*, no. 4, Apr. 1969, pp. 6–11. His stress.

characteristics that were markedly different from Czechoslovak history. The twilight of freedom was very short but some good work was done and the image of the "big Russian brother" became much more realistic than before. Naturally, the communist historians were only supplying additional details to pictures of the true Russia offered by Havlíček 125 years ago or by T. G. Masaryk more than 50 or 60 years before. But by their analyses the Czech and Slovak historians managed to substantiate the meaning of the invasion shock, which helped to heal the nations from their peculiar and undeserved attachment to the most Eastern Slavs, and they did their part in returning the country to its basically Western heritage and orientation.

There is no place here for a detailed study of the Husák era. Only the continuation and the end of his friendship with Hübl should be recalled as a sample of the First Secretary's ruthless character, of the limits of his power, or, probably, of a combination of both.

Although Husák in his first public speech as the new First Secretary of the CPC promised that there would be no return to the 1950s,[127] it seems that some Soviet and Czechoslovak comrades were clamoring for an exemplary trial of Dubček, or Kriegel, or some lesser representatives of the Prague Spring. It took Husák some time to sort things out and to get rid of some extremists who supposedly were even planning a *coup*.[128] In order to achieve that Husák had to rehabilitate and bring back into important Party and State functions comrades like Bil'ak, Indra, Švestka, and Šalgovič. They were willing to create a pro-Soviet puppet government during the invasion and therefore became hated as traitors. Husák also had to (or wanted to?) instigate a series of trials against some of his former supporters and colleagues in the 1968 liberalization.[129] Dubček, however, was saved, in spite of his repeated refusal to commit self-criticism.

Milan Hübl was ousted as rector of the High Party School by the Party Presidium at the end of June 1969, a few days after he delivered graduation papers to students. Since the May session of the CPC CC his Party membership had been suspended. He was expelled from the CC and from the CPC in September 1969. In his last speech to the Central Committee Hübl reminded his colleagues that in April 1969 he recommended the replacement of Dubček by Husák and that in 1963 he was a member of the Barnabite commission. He wanted to warn them that accusations against the so-called "Rightists" could lead to events similar to those in the 1950s.

---

[127] *Rudé právo*, 18 Apr. 1969, p. 1. Husák's speech concluding the CPC CC meeting at which he was elected was published *ibid.*, 19 Apr. 1969, pp. 1 and 3. He refused to accept for his group the term "henchmen of freedom." But K. S. Karol commented: "Willingly or not, Gustav Husák is no more than a front man for the Soviet Union's direct administration of an occupied country." See his article "Can Russia Survive Until 1980?" in *New Statesman*, 25 Apr. 1969, p. 573.

[128] Cf., for instance, a report of consistent rumors on the averted plot by General Rytíř, Josef Grösser, Czech Minister of the Interior, Jaromír Lang, an ideologue, and others was published by a rare journalist who had lived in Prague for years after the invasion, Laurent Rainer, *L'après Printemps de Prague* (Paris: Stock, 1976), pp. 65–70. All the named ones were very active, in a radical and sectarian way, till 1970 and then, at once demoted, disappeared from the scene.

[129] Ota Šik a bit later commented: "The objectivity of the old system will force him to rule by the same means and methods as his — by him personally hated — predecessor . . . . Today the number of persecuted and prosecuted persons in the ČSSR is larger than in the 1950s." See his essay "Husák jako Novotný" ["Husák Like Novotný"], *Listy*, i, 6 (Nov. 1971), p. 12.

"Personal guarantees don't have any value." The mechanism should be stopped in time. In April Novomeský wrote that there would be no humiliation of Dubček — but after five months this hope was shown to be naïve. The Party might have its last historical chance not to become just a "simple façade for a caste institution." Hübl explained his refusal to vote for a cancellation of the July and August resolutions of the CC. [They both criticized Soviet aggressive behavior, showed first in words and then by tanks.] He ended by repeating his pledge after his expulsion from the Party in 1964: as a communist and Marxist historian he will wait for a change in Party policy.[130] Around that time Husák received from Moscow the Order of Lenin.

After a letter from Hübl to Husák, sent on 18 February 1970, remained without an answer, Hübl wrote again on 5 October 1970. He wanted to tell his old friend about facts he should know so that later he could not claim that he had no knowledge of them. Since 1 July 1970 Hübl was unemployed, without any income. His ten months search for a job brought only refusals since he was on a blacklist. He had two children and on 1 October 1970 his wife was thrown out of her job as lecturer in the Russian department of Prague University. He himself had worked for the Party in various occupations since 1947: "If a private employer dared to treat his employees after twenty years of service in the same way, he would be rightly stigmatized as anti-social." And Hübl asked Husák: "Should that be natural, just, and normal, even normalized, in a country calling itself socialist?" He wrote: "A whole category of citizens has been arbitrarily deprived of all rights, including the right to make a living and to defend their honor. We are the pariahs of this society against whom anything is allowed. I don't exaggerate: literally anything." Then Hübl complained about Soviet authors attacking him as a Zionist. What can be still considered valid of the resolution of the CPC CC of 1963 which rehabilitated Husák? How easy it would be to mount again a process against not only Zionists but also bourgeois nationalists! It would be so handy to prove that he used to stay in Husák's apartments in Bratislava, that they collaborated on the preparation of the new Constitution in Koloděje [previously an ominous seat of protracted tortures for many victims of the Slánský trial]. In 1964, under Novotný, twelve lecturers lost their positions in the High Party School. In 1970, under Husák, their number was seventy-five! Where are the people today who helped Husák to get out of prison? And where are those who kept him there? In high positions. Hübl wrote: "All that is perhaps in agreement with the spirit of *The Prince* of Machiavelli: 'Who helps others in their ascent to power digs his own grave.' ... You are locked up in a knot of vipers of your former jailers."[131]

According to a letter from a Slovak historian, *Ján Mlynárik*, in addition to historians expelled from the High Party School, forty-five lost their positions in the Institute of History and about one hundred from institutes of learning.[132] Historians were among the hardest hit by the Party purge and by Soviet liquidation of the Czechoslovak science. The system obviously cannot live with history. Historical materialism changed into hysterical materialism.

In the autumn of 1971 Milan Hübl, as was officially hinted, helped

[130] The document is in Pelikán, *Ici Prague*, pp. 178–83.
[131] Pelikán, *Ici Prague*, pp. 192–7.
[132] *The Times*, 22 Jan. 1971.

Josef Smrkovský in the preparation of his interview for an Italian journal.[133] In the summer of 1972, in a trial against authors of a manifest which reminded Czechoslovak citizens of their right not to vote in elections, Hübl was sentenced to six and a half years of imprisonment (another historian, Jan Tesař, was condemned to five years). In spite of many domestic letters of protest and innumerable appeals to authorities for clemency; in spite of multiple foreign interventions, among them some by Italian communists, the ordeal of the victims was very hard and long lasting:

> The prisoners work in their cells, sewing buttons on cards, sorting and threading pins, hairpins, snap fasteners, sorting glass beads, and making artificial flowers and wicker-work chairs. Between 10 and 12 hours a day are spent in this fashion and non-fulfillment of the norm is punishable in various ways, such as reduced food rations. . . . Children can see and hear their fathers — touching is usually forbidden — for only four hours a year. . . . A single newspaper and one book a week from the prison library, selected by the warder, is not unusual. The same book is sometimes delivered to a cell several times.[134]

According to this document, Milan Hübl in 1973 wrote from the prison:

> During the most futile activities the worst is the feeling of wasted time. There has been no progress in it since the times of Chernyshevsky. . . . Read Gramsci's *Letters from prison* but don't infer from it any false comparison, as well as from N. Krupskaya's recollections of Lenin, how in the Siberian exile he was writing *The Development of Capitalism in Russia* and the Moscow University library kept procuring and sending him foreign literature.

Communist intellectuals clearly had it much worse in Communist prisons than Gramsci in the Fascist or Lenin in the Czarist prison.

The letters of Hübl and those addressed to him by his wife or his children were repeatedly kept or destroyed since they contained "concealed facts." Hübl's blood pressure became dangerously high, his poor eyesight markedly worsened, and he suffered head congestions. He blamed it on the prison conditions, provoked by such "abstract manifestations as disloyalty . . . ." Another time he wrote: "To put on unrepaired clothes full of spoiled in washing dirt, sound impressions of human beings wailing not only under blows of destiny, surroundings with an odd stinking atmosphere, faces from criminals' albums, touchy sensations from moral and other filth — literal, typical for the world of recidivism."

The rare visits of his family (permitted four times a year for one hour each time) were important: "It is just one hour, but for me it is precious because I can see and hear you. After three months for a moment, a little, I am myself again, otherwise I renew my identity partly in letters and reading." In 1975 Hübl wrote: "The spring sun does not shine on me. Only at the end of the month it will get so high that during our Saturday walk we would be able to catch its rays." And in 1976: "I would like to study systematically and work in my field, completing my knowledge of sociology, psychology, philosophy; this type of literature is not available here and neither are textbooks and dictionaries of foreign languages.[135]

---

[133] Milan Matouš, "Emigranti ve službách antikomunismu" ["Emmigrants in the Services of Anti-Communism"], *Tvorba*, 13 and 20 June 1973, a supplement of 16 pages, p. 12.

[134] *The Times*, 9 Apr. 1976, p. 9. From an English summary of a document in Czech, quoted next.

[135] Quoted from the "Documentation" annexed to an appeal addressed by the prisoners' relatives to Gustáv Husák on 1 Mar. 1976 and published in *Listy*, vi, 3 (June 1976), pp. 3–13.

Finally, before Christmas 1976, after five years in prison, Milan Hübl and the other remaining prisoners were released on probation for three years. It happened after a renewed campaign by Leftist and Communist parties, mainly in France and Italy.

In the meantime, while his former friend was counting colored beads and the days separating him from the next visit of an hour by his wife and children, *Gustáv Husák* continued his successful career. In 1973 the Presidium of the Supreme Soviet of the U.S.S.R. bestowed upon him a new Order of Lenin and L. I. Brezhnev himself brought it to Prague pinning it on his chest on the occasion of Husák's sixtieth birthday, in recognition of his "outstanding role in the development of friendship and cooperation among the peoples of the Soviet Union and Czechoslovakia."[136] In the first week of May 1975, after Husák withstood some difficulties with Dubček's letters and Smrkovský's memoirs, Andrei Kirilenko, one of the most important politicians in Moscow, came to Prague leading a Soviet delegation in order to condemn the reformers and praise Husák as "a loyal son of the working people, a patriot and internationalist, and an important figure in the world communist movement."[137] At the end of the same month, Husák added to his highest position in the Party also the honorific title of the President of the Republic.

On the first day of January 1977 the Charter 77 was signed reminding the Czechoslovak government of human rights which it should respect according to its own domestic laws and international agreements. Among the signatories were Milan Hübl, Karel Bartošek, Jan Tesař, Ján Mlynárik, and several other historians. A systematic harassment followed. Several of the best-known chartists were encouraged by the police to leave the country. Milan Hübl reportedly told Western journalists after leaving the passport office where they were ordered to go: "We made clear that we will not be robbed of our home country in that fashion."[138]

[136] *Nová mysl*, no. 2, Feb. 1974, p. 318.
[137] Thomas E. Heneghan, "Husak in Hradcany Castle," *RFER*, 6 Aug. 1975, 26 polycopied pages, p. 9.
[138] *The Times*, 29 Jan. 1977, p. 4.

Chapter 2.

In philosophy

CZECH and Slovak communist historians, after a few years of service to false, mainly Soviet, gods, denounced much of their own earlier work as worthless propaganda and attempted to give a truthful picture of the descent of their party and of their nations into the Stalinist hell. They had found themselves in a house, built with their own eager assistance, where all the floors and ceilings were painfully phony and unreal, where doors served as trapdoors, and windows led into blind walls. In order to save themselves, they had to get out of the madhouse of lies and illusions where celebrated party leaders were hanging on ropes and their ashes were spread on slippery roads. They had to ask themselves what went so terribly wrong and came up with a lot of bitter truth. They also helped to create a concept of a healthier society where crimes such as those they had so abundantly witnessed should not be repeated. Since 1969 they have been paying dearly for their courage to tell some partial truth about the naked king.

Party philosophers could not avoid similar problems but had to solve them in their own way. In philosophy it is in fact harder than in history to find the truth. Reality is an extremely elusive concept. Nevertheless, Czechoslovak philosophers of Marxist persuasion were gradually able to dismiss obvious falsehoods and advance on the road to the discovery of philosophical pitfalls first of Stalinism, then of Leninism, and finally even of Marxism. They achieved a better understanding of social reality. They also began to stress ethical values necessary for the creation of at least a relatively just community where, first of all, individuals must be free to develop their own creative energies.

In a cluster of short-case studies we will meet Arnošt Kolman, Karel Kosík, Ivan Sviták, Milan Machovec, and Miroslav Kusý. Although all of them had to get away from the Soviet ideology as false conscience and try to practice philosophy as a search for truth, we will observe in every one of them only certain, and different, aspects of the whole confrontation between Western and Eastern (Soviet) concepts and realities.

1. On the warpath (1945-8): Arnošt Kolman

To a high degree, the situation of philosophy in Prague between 1945 and 1948 reflected the intellectual and power relationship in the whole country. Non-communist philosophers (or rather professors of philosophy), who were called "bourgeois" by the communists but did not consider themselves as such, mainly believed that they were following Western democratic and liberal thought, especially in the form given to it by T. G. Masaryk. Not a single one of them then any international status as an original philosopher and some of them were a little more capable as teachers than others. They all looked with contempt on Marxism-Leninism as strictly a non-philosophical but political doctrine and did not feel threatened by it. However, the Soviet power and its manifested self-confidence exercised some attractiveness which, together with fears about the decline of the West, would weaken their resistance to coming Stalinism. Much deeper insight, brilliant wit, and philosophical erudition was displayed by a literary historian, professor Václav Černý, who in his University lectures, articles, and books capably and in an inspired way defended democratic principles then under attack or in limbo.

The bourgeois would-like-to-be proletarian and Marxist philosophers or students of historical and dialectical materialism, who fancied themselves as fighters on the side of the proletariat, were aggressive and happily carried on the wave of the approaching victorious future. They were better organized and disciplined, marching to what they believed would be not only power but also realization of the historical and philosophical truth. Their master was an old Bolshevik, *Arnošt Kolman*.[1] Our philosophical enquiry will start and end with him.

After a six-year long hiatus, the Charles University of Prague was opened again in the summer of 1945 and Kolman started to teach courses and seminars on Marxism. At the same time he acted as head of the CPC propaganda department. Most of the future Party philosophers attended his courses, as I could observe when I signed up for his seminar devoted to the study and refutation of T. G. Masaryk's philosophy. In spite of Kolman's concern for the weaknesses of Masaryk and his bias against Christian ethics as well as his own emphasis on Bolshevism and class struggle, the general level of his teaching was still, to a degree, scholarly.[2]

In the excitement about the successful *putsch* of 1948, the philosopher-propagandist Kolman declared that "the twenty-fifth February is a proof of the unconquerable power of the working people." He professed that "science should be united with politics."[3] Unfortunately for him, the "working people's power," exercising the "unity of science and politics," arrested him the same year and shipped him to Moscow, where he "spent three and a half years without trial — three of them in solitary confinement — in the Lubianka jail."[4] As Solzhenitsyn could say in the sarcastic style of his *Gulag Archipelago*, there clearly was great progress in the Soviet Union, especially in solitary confinement (by 600 per cent)

---

[1] Kolman was born in Prague in 1892. During World War I he became a prisoner of war in Russia and under Kerensky's rule spent six months in solitary confinement for anti-war propaganda. He joined the Communist Party and fought in the ranks of the Red Army. Later he was sent to Germany to do illegal work and became a member of the Central Committee of the German Communist Party. He was sentenced to five years hard labor, spent another six months in solitary confinement, but was exchanged in a deal with the Soviet Union. He worked in important positions in the Comintern, in the Central Committee, in the Moscow Party committee, and in the Soviet Academy of Sciences. Among his personal acquaintances was Lenin and his wife Krupskaya. Before he was sent in 1945 to Czechoslovakia, Kolman worked in the Political Command of the Red Army, charged with fomenting dissatisfaction in the German armed forces. During that time his sister was burnt in one of Hitler's gas ovens and his brother "was murdered by Stalin." See his letter to Brezhnev published in *The Times*, 6 Oct. 1976, pp. 1 and 8.

[2] Between 1945 and 1948 Kolman published many works, but rather propaganda brochures than books.

[3] *Svobodné noviny*, 27 Feb. 1948.

[4] See Kolman's letter to Brezhnev in *The Times*, 6 Oct. 1976, p. 8.

when compared to Kolman's half a year in Kerensky's Russia and another half a year in post-war Germany. However, he was an enemy of those two governments and a militant for the Soviet cause. But in the terrible years of Stalin's pogroms he was lucky to have his life spared.

2. Stalinist philosophy (1949–54): Karel Kosík

The incisive and original Marxist philosopher was born in Prague on 6 June 1926 and joined the CPC in 1945. As he soon showed, he was an avid reader of Marxist-Leninist literature and a devoted Party propagandist. The 23-year-old Kosík wrote:

> Lenin substantiated his ingenious thought that the proletariat can and must be the leader of the bourgeois-democratic revolution in his book *Two Tactics of Social Democracy in a Democratic Revolution* . . . . The Leninist teaching about the leading role of the proletariat in a democratic revolution is inseparably linked with teaching about the transformation of a bourgeois democratic revolution into a socialist revolution.[5]

Less than a year later, in a review of a newly published translation of Engels' *German Peasant War*, Kosík commented on Engels, Stalin, and Hus:

> Peasant uprisings can lead to success only when — teaches comrade Stalin — they are united to workers' uprisings and if the workers direct the peasant uprisings . . . . Bourgeois thick-headed persons cannot explain medieval religious struggles otherwise than as nonsensical quarrels about interpretation of the Bible and wrangling of scholastic theologians. . . . The Hussite revolutionary tradition is today in the hands of the workers' class an effective tool in the mobilization of broad masses for the battle to realize socialism.[6]

After another year of revolutionary blessings passed, Kosík, abundantly quoting from Lenin and Stalin, wrote, again in the obligatory and delightfully stupid, heavy-handed Stalinist style:

> To J. V. Stalin fell the historical role of terminating and culminating the epochal work of socialist revolution started by Lenin. Under the ingenious leadership of Stalin the socialist industrialization of the Soviet Union was realized, the collectivization of the agriculture, which by its importance equals the October Revolution of 1917, was carried through, the socialist society was constructed. . . . The Soviet Union under the wise leadership of Stalin became a firm bastion of progress and peace. . . . For all countries of people's democracy, passing to socialism, the law of the sharpened class struggle is absolutely binding. . . . Stalin's works on questions of linguistics [serve] as a matchless example of creative development of Marxism.[7]

The last two sentences quoted here had a portentous, but surely not intended, meaning for those few communists who were initiated into the details of the suicide of one of the best and most (also linguistically) sensitive communist poets, Konstantin Biebl, about whose death Marie Pujmanová published an article right after Kosík's celebration of exactly the reasons for Biebl's desperate jump from the window.

---

[5] "Buržoazně demokratická revoluce" ["Bourgeois Democratic Revolution"], *Tvorba*, 9 Nov. 1949, fourth page of the cover.

[6] "Také německý lid má svou revoluční tradici" ["Also the German People Has Its Revolutionary Tradition"], *Tvorba*, 23 Aug. 1950, pp. 810–11.

[7] "Sovětský svaz — bašta marxismu-leninismu" ["The Soviet Union — Bastion of Marxism-Leninism"], *Tvorba*, 22 Nov. 1951, pp. 1116–18.

A month later, just in front of Karol Bacílek's hateful report on the expulsion of Slánský from the Party, Kosík, again "philosophically," followed in the footsteps of his great teacher and as usual repeated the magic formula, "Comrade Stalin teaches us that. . . :"

> Such is the logic of history! Who does not faithfully serve the people, becomes a lackey of slave-dealers. Such is the fate of bourgeois hirelings, such is the fate of the traitors to the workers' class — of Slánský, Šling, and Co. Also for these trecherous monsters Stalin's words hold good by which he characterized the Trotskyist-Bukharinist gang of spies. . . . Only cosmopolitan bandits and wreckers of the type of Slánský, Švermová, Šling and Co., whom the people threw out from its midst, could dare to touch upon our alliance with the Soviet Union.... We are led by the great pupil of Stalin and the greatest man of our nation, dear comrade Gottwald.[8]

Reading the end of the article as quoted above, normally we would close the book on the author and would never bother again about anything such an obvious idiot would utter. But, incredibly, in a few years Kosík would grow out of this age of stupid babbling and become a major Marxist philosopher. Still, before that would happen, he had to use similar prattle in order to get in 1952 his degree "doctor of philosophy." His thesis was entitled "People's Democracy as a Form of the Dictatorship of the Proletariat." Also in order to be properly acceptable to the peripatetic academy of Stalinist philosophers he had to abuse T. G. Masaryk. He attacked an opinion, expressed by another Marxist philosopher, about whom more will be said in a while, Milan Machovec, who suggested that Masaryk's work during the last two decades of the nineteenth century had "in a sense, a relatively progressive mission." Kosík strongly objected:

> The most confused and harmful out of all these theories is the theory of a relative progressivity of Masarykism in the 1880s and 1890s. . . . It is necessary to demonstrate how Masarykism, entirely through inner logic, out of an ideology shared by a middling bourgeois group became the official ideology of the Czech financial capital and how it is ending as an ideology of traitors and agents of the enemy. . . . In fact it is possible to elucidate Masaryk's participation in the fight against the genuineness of the Manuscripts, against the Hilsner affair, [and] his stand on universal voting rights only as a *parasitic-opportunist pose* of a bourgeois politician, who temporarily "flows" with healthy currents in science and society, in order to make capital for *his* aims, that is "for saving capitalism."

Masarykism, according to Kosík, "served not only for cheating the workmen but in the 1930s also masked the progress of fascization of the Czech bourgeoisie." After 1945 it became the arsenal of the counter-revolutionary ideology of "democratic socialism." He denounced the concept of Czechoslovakia as a "bridge between the West and the East" (which, by the way, fourteen years later he would himself advocate) as "counter-revolutionary and anti-Soviet intrigues of the Czechoslovak bourgeoisie."[9]

[8] "Stalin nás učí lásce k vlasti a nenávisti k jejím nepřátelům" ["Stalin Teaches Us Love to the Fatherland and Hate to Its Enemies"], *Tvorba*, 20 Dec. 1951, pp. 1211–12.
[9] "O sociálních kořenech a filosofické podstatě masarykismu" ["On Social Roots and Philosophical Basis of Masarykism"], *Filosofický časopis*, no. 3, 1954, pp. 199–214. His emphasis.

3. Kosík's post-Stalinist rebirth

Stalin's death was followed in three years by Khrushchev's announcement that the "greatest genius of humanity that had ever lived" was a madman and mass murderer. It had great liberating influence on some communist philosophers; even their writing style improved enormously. A substantially changed Karel Kosík infuriated an unchanged Ladislav Štoll and other *apparatchiks* "in charge of philosophy" by his biting comments:

> A dogmatic lives in an illusion that he defends Marxism by "shielding" it from "unpleasant" facts. Actually, he compromises it. . . . Bad propaganda and bad theory, which believes that it is the master of facts because it selects facts according to its freest will (read, arbitrary power), degenerates into servile dependence on these *extracted* facts. . . . If someone asks about the meaning of life, the dogmatics reply by talking about pickling of sauerkraut and are sure that the inquiring trusting soul wouldn't reflect any more upon unhappiness and sorrow, upon sadness and sociability, but will descend from its "abstractions" to the plain reality of pickled sauerkraut. A mole who is an absolute ruler of the molehill, considers even a haystack, which is only a few meters higher, as an "abstraction" since by his mole's brains he is unable to grasp it as something equally entitled to existence as his little heap of dirt.[10]

In 1958 Kosík published a book which was sometimes hailed as the first swallow of the Prague Spring.[11] And at the beginning of the 1960s, he followed it by a major work,[12] devoted to a systematic exploration of Marxism, confronted with modern science and philosophy as well as with the everyday reality of life in a communist dictatorship; he seemed to be asking — in a difficult heuretic language, interspersed with clear brilliant passages — what are the basic theoretical mistakes or frauds committed in the name of Marxism which led us into this incredible mess?

Kosík condemned vulgarized Marxism, which attempted to explain everything from, and to reduce everything to, production relations. Manipulators made out of man an object but he must be again recognized as a subject who creates himself, society, and history: "Man as *real historical subject* (= praxis) . . . realizes an unending process of 'humanization of man'." For this praxis he needs to be free. He cannot be forced to live for the future "which does not *yet* exist":

> The future in itself does not overcome romanticism and alienation. In a certain form it evenly becomes an alienated escape from alienation, i.e. illusory overcoming of alienation. To "live in the future" and to "anticipate events" in a certain sense means denial of life: the individual does not live in presence but in future and because he negates

---

[10] As quoted from *Literární listy* by Petr Hrubý, "Je toho tak málo?" ["Is It Only a Little?"], *Československý přehled*, iv, 9, p. 15. Kosík's emphasis.

[11] *Dějiny filosofie jako filosofie: Filosofie v dějinách českého národa* [*History of Philosophy as Philosophy: Philosophy in the History of the Czech Nation*] (Prague, 1958). Kosík also published as editor *Čeští radikální demokraté: Výbor politických statí* [*Czech Radical Democrats: Selection of Political Essays*] (Prague, 1953) and *Česká radikální demokracie* [*Czech Radical Democracy*] (Prague, 1958).

[12] *Dialektika konkrétního: Studie o problematice člověka* [*Dialectics of the Concrete: Study of Man's Problems*] (Prague, 1963). I have translated here parts from the second edition in 1965. It was published in German, *Dialektik des konkreten* (Frankfurt: Suhrkampf, 1966) and in English, with the subtitle *A Study on Problems of Man and World* (trans. Karel Kovanda and James Schmidt; Boston: D. Reidel, 1976). By Paul Piccone in *Telos* it was welcomed as "phenomenological Marxism of a quality unreached since Marx's and Lukacs' early works." See also N. Lobkowicz's review in *Studies of Soviet Thought*, iv (1964), pp. 248 ff.

what is and anticipates what is not, his life happens in futility, i.e. in non-authenticity.[13]

This existentialist text, naturally, had much more meaning for people living in a system where everything was being planned for the future and they were daily victims of expected fulfillment of economic and other targets, always in a sense running after departing buses. In a constantly miserable situation their satisfactions were constantly postponed. Their actual life was stolen from them in the name of a non-existing impossible future.

The individual's personal life was also being taken away from him in the name of collectivism and man was replaced, according to Kosík, by "mystified I or mystified we, for whom the real individual changes into a tool or a mask." Therefore, Kosík wrote: "It seems to us that one of the main principles of modern art, poetry, and drama, fine arts and film, is 'violence' on everydayness, destruction of the pseudo-concrete. (Footnote: Also the work of Franz Kafka can be understood as destruction of pseudo-concreteness.)"[14]

In the communist state man lost his central position and was reduced to a *thing* which can be used and misused in a system, called by Kosík "social physics": "Social physics lives in an anti-metaphysical *illusion*: a doctrine of man as an object and its malleability (capacity to be manipulated) it can neither replace metaphysics (philosophy) nor solve metaphysical problems."[15]

In a country where economy became the main focus of attention, almost an article of faith, and where it was officially believed that poetry, law, ethics, and much else was just a superstructure dependent on, and only reflecting, the ownership of means of production and the relationship of classes, Kosík defended if not the primacy then at least the equality of cultural achievements.

> Poetry is not of a lower order than economics: equally it is a human reality, although of a different kind and form, with a different mission and significance. Economics does not give birth to poetry, directly or indirectly, immediately or through intermediaries, but man creates economics and poetry as products of human practice (praxis). . . .
> An art work is an integral part of societal reality, an element in the construction of this reality and a manifestation of social-spiritual production of man.[16]

In his book Kosík also attacked prevalent beliefs that in the name of supposed historical necessity some people had the right to commit acts (murders) which would normally be considered crimes but if done without private motivation are easily put on the altar of higher duties, as if performed "by the order of the Nation, Church, Historical Necessity."

> Hegel criticizes the "beautiful soul" of the romantics that knows that the world is dirty and does not want to pollute itself by touching it, i.e. by acting. This criticism, led from the point of view, of HISTORICAL ACTION cannot be identified with "criticism" of members of the "human bestiary" who condemn the "beautiful soul" only in order to mask by "historical" phrases their base and private costermonger's trade.[17]

---

[13] *Dialektika konkrétního*, pp. 41–2 and 52. Kosík's emphasis.
[14] *Ibid.*, pp. 58 and 60.
[15] *Ibid.*, p. 66.
[16] *Ibid.*, pp. 82 and 95.
[17] *Ibid.*, pp. 162–3.

In a society where many a cutthroat attempted to justify his crimes by "historical necessities" and proudly professed contempt for people who did not or did not want to "dirty their hands" and now dared to criticize those who "had to fight the enemy," such statements as Kosík's were bound to provoke anger. He was attacked but his often Aesopian language kept his text out of comprehension of Party "moles" who, however, recognized themselves and protested at being called Moles, Costermongers, etc.

Karel Kosík then headed the section of dialectical materialism at the Institute of Philosophy in the Czechoslovak Academy of Sciences. The director of the Institute had been, since his rehabilitation, Arnošt Kolman but he retired in 1963 and went to live in Moscow as a pensioner. (He was one of the first Soviet citizens to favor and work in cybernetics.)

For the Liblice Conference on Kafka in 1963, Kosík prepared an essay on two Prague writers who until then seemed to be at two completely different poles and therefore beyond comparison, although both were born in the same city in the same year, Josef Hašek and Franz Kafka. In his essay Kosík managed to say plainly what in his philosophical treatise was often hidden in a Hegelian and existentialist jargon:

> Hašek's analyses show man reduced to an object. Švejk, however, is irreducible. . . . people are constantly placed in a rationalized and calculable system where they are treated, disposed of, showed and moved, reduced to something inhuman and extra-human, i.e. to a calculable and disposable thing or variable. . . . Švejk cannot be calculated, because he is unpredictable. Man is irreducible to a thing, and is always more than a system of factual relations in which he moves and is moved. . . .
>
> What is the Kafkaesque world? It is the world of the absurdity of human thought and action, of human dreams, a world of a monstrous and unintelligible labyrinth, a world of human powerlessness in the network of the bureaucratic machines, mechanisms, reified creations. Švejkism is a way of reacting to this world of absurd omnipotence of the machine and of reified relations. . . .
>
> Kafka and Hašek described and exposed these phenomena, while subjecting them to criticism. . . .
>
> Man is irreducible to an object, he is more than a system. As yet we lack suitable description for the fact that man contains in himself the tremendous and indestructible force of humanity. The genius of both authors presented in the first quarter of this century two separate visions of the world. . . . One posited a negative, the other a positive scale of humanism.[18]

The philosophical and literary discussion at Liblice continued for some time in Czech journals. In a debate with Jean-Paul Sartre (who had earlier made Kafka *salonsfähig* in the communist society by his speech in Moscow)[19], Ernst Fischer, Eduard Goldstücker, and others in the monthly *Plamen*, Kosík returned to his basic

---

[18] "Hašek and Kafka," published in Karel Kovanda's translation in *Telos*, no. 23, spring 1975, pp. 84–8.

[19] Satre's help was really important. It was a good example of what fellow-travellers could do if they always tried to apply similar principles to both sides in the conflict. One of the observers who was able to realize it wrote: "Jean-Paul Sartre's real influence, and this more through his whole work and his indirect intellectual effect than through his political utterances proper, is felt in the communist world. Here it encourages — partly by antithesis — reflection, innovation, and a post-revolutionary liberalism." François Bondy, "Jean-Paul Sartre and Politics," *Journal of Contemporary History*, vol. 2, no. 2 (Apr. 1967), p. 48.

refutation of the Soviet political philosophy and of its model of government as applied in Czechoslovakia:

> The essence of technic are not machines and automatons but technical reason which plans reality as a system of disposability, perfectibility, and objectivation. . . . Man is not threatened by machines. . . . Man is threatened when technical reason identifies with reason itself, when technical reason takes over human reality to such a degree that all non-technical, non-disposable, incalculable, and unsuitable to manipulation will be set against it and against man as unreason.

Kosík then blamed the communist systems for such a reduction of man in the name of "metaphysics of modern times" which "lost respect for living and dead because it transformed all into objects of manipulation and thus opened up unlimited space to carelessness and bad taste." Socialist society in Eastern Europe represents a society that "only replaced a system of general marketability (supremacy of money and capital) by a system of general manipulation (supremacy of unlimited bureaucratic power)." Marxism-Leninism then buried the question "who is man and what is truth, what is existence and what is time, what is the substance of technic and science, what is the sense of revolution?"[20]

In 1965 Kosík was appointed by the presidium of the Academy of Sciences a member of the scientific collegium of philosophy of the academy. In June 1967 he participated in the celebrated Fourth Congress of Czechoslovak Writers but his contribution was rarely quoted in reports on its revolutionary importance, although it was remarkable. It did not attack the regime as directly as Vaculík, Liehm, Klíma, Kundera, or Kohout. It seemed to be strangely detached from the political and cultural conflict of the moment, but it acutely expressed one of the basic failures of the Czechoslovak experiment; namely, the missing unity of words and actions, of conscience and reason, and the need for such a unity in an integrated and courageous man. Kosík began by going back to the fifteenth century:

> On 18 June 1415, a great Czech intellectual [Jan Hus] wrote from prison: "A certain theologian said to me that for me everything is good and permitted, if only I submit to the Council, and he added, 'If the Council declared that you have only one eye, although in fact you have two, it would be your duty to agree with the Council that it was so.' I answered him, 'And if the whole world told me the same, I, possessing reason, would not be able to acknowledge it without my conscience being repelled.'"
> This text is unique in world literature and is among those immortal thoughts in which the fundamental truths about man and the world are expressed.

Kosík then proceeded to a careful analysis of the text and came up with the first conclusion:

> Man without this fundamental truth loses his base, he loses the ground under his feet and becomes a man uprooted, a man without a base. Who is a man uprooted and without a base? He who has lost his reason and conscience, answers the Czech intellectual of the fifteenth century. Let us take good note: reason and conscience exist together, they form a unity and only in this unity do they become the basis of human existence.

[20] As amply quoted by Ladislav Hrzal in his attack on Kosík, "Filozofie člověka" ["Philosophy of Man"], *Tribuna*, 30 Apr. 1975, pp. 8–9.

In modern times, according to Kosík, reason and conscience are usually separated and often viewed not only as independent of each other but rather indifferent, or even hostile qualities, as was already suggested by the tempter, the Council's spokesman:

> The man is offered the choice of gaining everything — everything will be permitted to him — if he renounces one thing. And who, in a dispute between everything and something, would not choose the everything and refuse the mere something? But above all who, in a dispute between "real" prospects and "illusory" prospects, would not prefer the first to the second and would not criticize from this realistic standpoint the intellectual who chose the second alternative for being a headstrong radical, an arrogant extremist, or an incorrigible eccentric?... In comparison with the authoritative and public reason, which asks me to admit that I have only one eye, although I know that I have two eyes, the voice of my conscience appears not only as a private affair, but above all as a small and futile nonentity. As this is a clash between an important and a futile authority, I can suppress the voice of conscience in good faith as something futile. In the realist reason always triumphs over conscience.

Kosík was here discussing one of the basic and for long an extremely efficient trick used to help the Soviet system to come to power in Czechoslovakia and to stay there with substantial help of the communist intellectuals. The capital difference between "objective laws," collective interest, history, workers' masses, and so on, on one side, and individual, purely subjective opinions on the other, was being constantly stressed and brandished in front of the intellectuals' eyes, especially when anybody wavered in his loyal obedience and dared to think for himself, or expressed anything else but Party dogmas and slogans. They were always asked, and even more often asked themselves, "I or the rest?", "What is my private opinion, just a possible subjective insight, not even a certainty, against this enormous truth of the whole Party, of history, of Marxism which is a science, of the mighty Soviet Union?" It was an uneven fight but in order not to lose, it was absolutely necessary to start by the first step of trusting his own individual idea and conscience. The whole monstrous system built on the fraudulent claim that it represented progress, the proletariat, humanity, history, everything, had to be challenged by the growing self-confidence of individuals trusting their own senses and reasoning, and sticking to them. Therefore I consider Kosík's speech remarkable since he expressed the conflict between the weak, isolated I (holding the truth) and the overwhelming organized power (using the lie). The balloon had to be pricked and the trick revealed. But let us return to Kosík's last conclusion:

> The realist has suppressed the "revulsion of conscience" in order to gain everything, but in this consideration of private interest he has in reality lost everything, he has lost both his conscience and his reason. . . . Unity is so important for the character of reason and the nature of conscience, that if this unity is lost, reason loses substantiality and conscience reality. Reason without conscience becomes the utilitarian and mechanical reason of computation and calculation, and a civilization founded on it is a civilization without reason, in which man is subordinate to things and their mechanical logic. Conscience divorced from reason sinks to an impotent inner voice, or the vanity of good intentions. . . .
> Only in this unity can conscience be what it is: the backbone and strength, the inviolable and inalienable property of man. . . . A man who agrees with the Council that he has only one eye although he knows full well that he has two gains nothing and loses everything, for to lose

reason and conscience means to lose the basis of his humanity. . . . A man without reason and conscience is a true nihilist.[21]

Kosík became persuaded that only "philosophy as wisdom" can avert the threat of "technical reason" and that it was necessary to start asking questions, so far untouched in communism, but all important if socialism should remain an alternative in the twentieth century.[22]

During the year of 1968 Kosík fully participated in the reform movement but did not forget that in that period more was needed than ideas:

> In view of the fact that politicians who have brought this country to the brink of economic, political, and moral disaster still hold strong positions and believe that there is a chance for them to survive the present period of rebirth, democracy must be on its guard and must not forget the basic historical experience, namely that, in politics, it is power and deeds, not words and promises, that decide.[23]

He signed the Two Thousand Words manifesto and at the Fourteenth Extraordinary CPC Congress was elected to the Central Committee. We will return to the year 1968 and to Kosík later but now let us look at another attempt to fill the gaping hole in the ruling ideology.

4. Milan Machovec: Could Jesus help the Marxists?

Now it seems quite logical that the lack of interest in non-economic human problems, displayed by Marxism-Leninism, and the series of inhuman crimes perpetrated in its name, had to lead its theoretitians and practitioners alike to renewed concern about ethics and other metaphysical questions. But when in the mid-1960s some communist circles began to propagate a *rapprochement* between Marxism and Christianity, it was easy to conclude that what was involved was only an attempt at converting Western Christians to communism, or that the secret police wanted to fish in troubled waters the usual way; namely, looking for fools who would be willing to do some voluntary work for the communist movement, or for victims who could be induced to it by newly provided compromising material of any kind. It seemed to be just another facet of Khrushchev's peaceful coexistence whose aim was to win without a nuclear war. No doubt, there were such interests involved, as they obviously are in the Italian slogan of a historical compromise between Marxism and Catholicism. But that was only part of the truth. Clearly, some Marxists were looking for a confrontation with Christians for similar

[21] "Rozum a svědomí" ["Reason and Conscience"], *Literární listy*, 1 Mar. 1968; trans. Andrew Oxley *et al.*, *Czechoslovakia: The Party and the People* (London: Allen Lane: The Penguin Press, 1973), pp. 26–9.
[22] "Naše nynější krise" ["Our Actual Crisis"], *Literární listy*, 11 Apr.—16 May 1968, as quoted by Hrzal, "Filozofie člověka," p. 9. This attack on Kosík is interesting since the author admits that Lenin talked about humanism and ethics very rarely and then only with contempt; also "Marx did never justify his communist demands by moral sentiments or by ethical valuations." According to Lenin, Marx deduced "the inevitability of the transformation of the capitalist society into a socialist one completely and exclusively from the economic law of motion of the contemporary society." *Ibid.* It makes Kosík's target — technical reason — clearer: "economic law of motion"!
[23] *Literární listy*, 7 Mar. 1968.

reasons that led others, like Kosík, who were encouraged by the recent publication of Marx's early work, the *Grundrisse*, to reverse the strictly economic interpretation of Marx and to return to his basic humanist inspiration. There was a pressing need in Czechoslovakia to humanize the system. At least a few Marxists were seriously looking at Christianity with hope that some help could be found there.

Naturally, they had books at their disposition. Access to them was in the 1960s much easier than in the 1950s; they made good use of them, in philosophy, as in other disciplines, and read eagerly and widely. At conferences they could sometimes surprise their Western colleagues by the scope of their knowledge of contemporary world literature on the subjects. The old Party hacks, whose horizons were limited rather than expanded by reading the *Communist Manifesto* and some Party pamphlets, had been, if not completely replaced, then at least complemented, by knowledgeable and sincere scholars who took their Marxism not as a club to beat others with it over the head but as a scientific method and challenge. However, they wanted more than just books. They wanted to meet living representatives of other beliefs and persuasions. They wanted to confront themselves with their views and to check their own opinions in an open clash of ideas. They needed a dialogue: "All monologues have been dull. . . . We must either de-dogmatize, de-fanaticize, de-bureaucratize our life or we shall go to the dogs together." That was Milan Machovec speaking at a Christian-Marxist dialogue held in Mariánské Lázně (Marienbad), between 27 and 30 April 1967.[24]

It was the third such conference. The first took place in Salzburg in 1965 and the second the following year on Herrenchiemsee. It should be noted that although the organizer was a West German, independent Catholic organization, the *Paulus Gesellschaft*, the initiative came from a meeting which took place in Munich in 1964 between members of this society and the Polish philosopher Adam Schaff, who was interested in the study of both Marxism and Christianity as much as his noted colleague and comrade Leszek Kolakowski.

The three-day dialogue in Mariánské Lázně was attended by 201 philosophers, theologians, natural scientists, and journalists. There were seventeen countries represented. The strongest delegation came from West Germany (85), the second in numbers was the Czechoslovak group (25). Not a single Russian arrived. Acting as co-chairmen at the symposium were Dr. Erich Kellner, a Catholic theologian from West Germany, and Dr. Erika Kadlecová, a Marxist sociologist and head of the Department of Theory and Sociology of Religion at the Czechoslovak Academy of Sciences.[25] There were some funny individuals present (supposedly agents) and some sharp exchanges of opinion took place, but the main surprise of the symposium were the open and undogmatic speeches of at least two Czech

[24] The quotation was taken from Charles Andras, "Christians and Marxists in Marianske Lazne," *RFER*, 10 July 1967, 30 polycopied pages, p. 25. For most of the following information on the conference and for the quotations I am indebted to this excellent paper which gives its rich Austrian, Czech, French, German, Hungarian, and other sources on pp. 1-3 and in some of the following footnotes.

[25] Sociology was officially abolished in Czechoslovakia in the academic year 1949/50 and allowed again in 1964 when a section of sociology was established in the Department of Philosophy at Charles University in Prague. For the local fate of sociology see Eduard Urbanek, "Sociology in Czechoslovakia," *Social Research*, xxxvii, 1 (spring 1970), pp. 129-46. Erika Kadlecová became in the Dubček era Minister responsible for Church affairs.

delegates, Milan Machovec and Milan Prŭcha. Both of them previously participated in a similar discussion at the West German *Evangelische Akademie* at Arnoldhain. In Mariánské Lázně twelve main lectures were delivered and followed by both prepared contributions and spontaneous discussions. The main theme of the conference was "Creativity and Freedom in Human Society."

At the opening meeting, Josef Macek did not talk about his usual topic, the fighting spirit and warlike prowess of the Hussites against the Germans, but on the ideal of tolerance which was a part of the Bohemian Constitution already in the fifteenth century. Among the "five most outstanding Marxist lectures delivered in Mariánské Lázně"[26] two came from Czech participants (the others were given by Roger Garaudy, Luciano Gruppi, and Manuel Azcarate).

Milan Prŭcha, a 31-year-old fellow of the Prague Institute of Philosophy, who had studied in Moscow and Paris, called for a Marxism which would be humanistically oriented and which would add to social and historical preoccupations also questions of life and death or of man's position in the cosmos. A confrontation with other schools of thought is necessary; they should not be treated only as adversaries:

> True philosophical activities can hardly protect themselves with class guarantees, hence they do not deserve *a priori* political and state guarantees. . . . To establish a monopoly [is] harmful not only to the interest of the philosophy but also to that of the State.[27]

Milan Machovec, since 1953 (terrible year!) professor of philosophy at the University of Prague who, beginning in the early 1960s has been organizing a seminar on Marxism and Christianity — often with participation of foreign Marxists and theologians — went much farther than that. Starting from similar premises as his colleague, he arrived at a sharper disagreement with the prevailing situation in his country:

> Marxism has, in my view, not yet answered the question about the meaning of human life.... In addition, the horizons of many Marxists have been reduced and limited to economic methods and political means. Hence, one can easily be inclined to think, and not without reason, that the Marxists are far more removed from the answer to this problem than members of other structures and schools. . . . For a humanist Marxist the dialogue is not only a matter of political pragmatism or of tactical consideration, but, above all, an existential necessity, because without a full openness, without a regular encounter with non-Marxists, he would necessarily remain, from the moral point of view, underdeveloped. I need then a dialogue to protect myself against de-humanization which is facing the *beati possidentes*.

Although the Czechoslovak government permitted the symposium only with the condition that no problems "directly related to existing social and economic systems would be discussed,"[28] he talked directly about some political matters:

> Each of us has to fight for an opening in his own country. It is said that as intellectuals we are powerless against the apparatus. But no person is powerless if only he holds out

---

[26] Andras, *op. cit.*, p. 18.

[27] *Ibid.*, pp. 22-3. His lecture was entitled in German, "Menschsein" ["Being a Man"]. Previously he published a study "Marxism and Existential problems of Man," in *Socialist Humanism*, ed. by Erich Fromm (New York: Doubleday, 1965). He wrote a report on the conference, *Kulturní tvorba*, 18 May 1967.

[28] *Ibid.*, pp. 24-5 and 1. His paper was entitled "Christians and Marxists in a Common Quest for the Meaning of Human Life." In 1965 Machovec published in Prague a book called *Smysl Lidského Života* [*The Meaning of Human Life*] in which he advocated a positivist humanism.

stubbornly. As professors of the Charles University, we must never tolerate that a young man may not study just because of his religion. We have to be firm on this.

In the discussion Machovec was again quite open:

> No historical school of thought should be forbidden for man. His searching for the sense (of life) being a difficult task, he must enjoy freedom of movement. . . . I feel a sense of connection with the searching Christian because I do not know whether I am 100 per cent right. This is not a fictitious problem. Antagonism is needed in thinking as well as in life. With the prophets of a single doctrine, we have gained enough of bad experience on both sides.[29]

As was shown previously in this work, there were other answers to the problem of alienation which, as was finally being admitted, existed even in communist states, and to the basic unhappiness of the "socialist" man, which the public opinion polls kept reporting. Just as a reminder of the humanitarian demands by the so-called scientific-technical revolution, a modern, Western, managerial concept should be mentioned as it was being introduced, for instance, by the writer of an article entitled "Institutional Alienation and Freedom of Man." *Jindřich Fibich*, substantiating himself with quotations from Marxist authors, especially Gramsci, who was very popular in communist intellectual circles, produced a series of Western "theorists of organization" in order to prove that there existed a requirement to base life and work on a "new conception of man," a "new conception of power, based on co-operation and justice, that replaces the model of power, based on compulsion and fear," and a "new conception of organizational values, founded on a humanist, existential orientation which would take the place of the dehumanized, mechanistic, marketable model." After this summary of W. G. Bennis, with recommendation he quoted P. Drucker: "The more an individual develops, so much the more can be accomplished by the organization."[30]

The communist philosophers were then approaching the problem of the inhuman nature of the regime from at least three different angles. For various reasons, however, they all came to the same conclusion: man should be returned his freedom and dignity. We have to note that all three approaches were inspired by Western developments in philosophy and sociology.

Milan Machovec continued his search for a basically ethical solution. In Czechoslovakia he quite logically had to meet T. G. Masaryk with his extraordinary unity of moral principles and activities. The result was a book simply called *Tomáš G. Masaryk*, published in Prague during the eventful year of 1968. It is a very decent Marxist confrontation with a great moralist and politician. One of the best evaluations of Masaryk ever written was followed by a good selection of the Czech philosopher's views, carefully chosen with an eye on moral and practical problems socialism had to face if it really wanted to acquire more human traits. Masaryk's arguments won even stronger persuasive power than they used to have in his own time, since in the meantime his countrymen had the unhappy chance of living under a system their old president had hoped to warn them emphatically against. How the perspective of Marxist philosophers changed in twenty years! Masaryk remained the same but Kolman, as we mentioned at the beginning of this chapter, kept looking for weak spots in his writings in order to

---

[29] *Ibid.*, pp. 24-5. In 1968 he published *Svatý Augustin* [St. Augustine].

[30] "Institucionální odcizení a svoboda člověka," *Filozófia*, no. 6, Nov.–Dec. 1967, pp. 607-17.

diminish, if not exclude, his influence, but Machovec was now showing Masaryk's strong points and setting him as an example to follow.

Machovec's next book, *A Marxist Looks at Jesus*,[31] manifests an even deeper study and a more thorough involvement with ethical matters than his book on Masaryk. At least to me, Machovec sounds completely sincere and believable. I read his book with joy. It is thoughtful and honest. He does not seem to be at all interested in converting Christians to Marxism (that would be under his level) but rather as someone who, as he says, feels the personal and societal need to check Christian values for the human ethos lacking in Marxism.

Machovec explains some of the motivations for the need to study Jesus (and other religious movements as well as he clearly did, as can be seen from numerous references to their texts and ideas). A few extracts are sufficient to show the fundamental disenchantment with the "distant cousin" of Marxism as has been applied in his country under the Soviet leadership:

> Early Marxists were often enchanted by the prospect of "a leap into the realm of freedom," and indeed bewitched by it; and this is a partial explanation for the tremendous dynamism and power of Marxism, as also for the possibility of its abuse. But it took twentieth-century Marxism a long time and involved much pain to learn how difficult it is in fact to make any real progress without secretly reviving the demons of the "past" in some new guise. . . .
>
> An ambitious and unscrupulously clever demagogue can toy with a somewhat limited but still sincere Marxist, or a cynical careerist and conformist can arraign and destroy as a traitor a colleague whose only crime is not being a yes-man: but there is nothing new in this, even if it comes in Marxist dress. . . . So there is no compassion, no responsibility for one's brother, when he is casualty of "historical forces". . . . That is not what the early socialists dreamed of and fought for. Age-old human egoism, cowardice and Phariaism reappear in new disguises. . . .
>
> When a Marxist who cares about honesty and truth wishes to serve his movement, he finds that he "must take up his cross"; . . . His own experience of life now teaches him that there are many situations in which he must suffer injustice rather than contribute to it. . . . Only truthfulness can provide a lasting principle for a humane society. And that also means that Marxists can never realize their aim of a classless humane society without promoting an unshakable love of truth.[32]

Machovec claims that he can bear witness that hundreds of thousands of Marxists are now on the threshold of this knowledge. The eschatological teaching of Jesus, according to the author's exploration of early Christianity, comes to a very meaningful precept that is valid for everybody, at all times:

> The future is not something that "arrives" . . . but something that *depends on us*, at every moment. . . . It would . . . be possible . . . to translate or rather interpret . . . Jesus's message in the following way: "Get a grip on life, the perfection of humanity is possible. Perfection is near, that is, you can grasp it, you can be morally better, purer, you can be more of a person — through your own action". In other words: no one ultimately forces you to be mean, vulgar, cowardly, egoistical — to live at a non-human or "reified" level, as we should say today. . . . Jesus shows not how to escape from the misery of real life but how to overcome one's own moral misery and lowliness.[33]

---

[31] It was published in Philadelphia by Fortress Press in 1976. It appeared earlier as *Jesus für Atheisten* (Stuttgart: Kreuz, 1972). The translation was made from the German edition but no translator was named. Some of the previous information in this part comes from the introduction to the U.S. edition by Peter Hebblethwaite, pp. 8–17.

[32] *A Marxist Looks at Jesus*, pp. 27, 29, 30, 34, and 35.

[33] *Ibid.*, pp. 88–9. His emphasis.

It is moral philosophy that Machovec is mostly interested in since he obviously came to the conclusion that his society desperately needed a revival of ethics. At the same time, very much as some of the Russian dissenters (including Solzhenitsyn) kept suggesting, while still in Russia, the ethical rebirth can and must start from the individual; the organized evil can be, as he clearly believes, opposed by every individual who makes his decision and perseveres in "bearing the cross." For that a whole mature man is needed and Machovec several times stressed the unity of word and action, as in this instance: "It worked only because Jesus was perfectly at one with his 'word', the human embodiment of his own teaching."[34]

At the end I would like to call attention to one of the few places in the whole scholarly work where Machovec directly reveals the political-philosophical meaning of his effort and of the conflict raging in Eastern Europe; he has as his target the "pseudo-revolutionary self-satisfaction" of Communist bureaucrats:

> It was the Sadducees who at the time of Jesus represented the type of the 'religious bureaucrats." Every age and every school has this type of person who busies himself (or herself) exclusively with the already established structure and, while preserving the original *form*, loses touch with the original *meaning*. Anyone, therefore, who has a real feel for older values must appear to them as a trouble-maker and a revolutionary.[35]

In the wholesale purge of "trouble-makers" when the "cynical careerists and conformists" decided to "destroy as traitors" all those who refused to be "yes-men" — or, remembering Kosík, all those who insisted during the "Party talks with comrades" that in August they did see with their two eyes an invasion, instead of closing one eye and welcoming the "fraternal help of allied armies" — Machovec was deprived of his professorship at the Faculty of Philosophy. When he appealed against the reason given for his dismissal; namely, that he was an anti-socialist, after six sessions at the court for labor law, he lost his case. Two professors affirmed that he has always been a persuaded socialist, but the new Dean of the faculty, Karel Galla, testified that Machovec was not a socialist. And so when his book was being published in Germany, he was making his living from translations and by giving private lessons in Latin.[36] With the invasion all attempts at a Christian-Marxist dialogue had ended, with the exception of Italy, where it remained an important part of the strategy of the Communist Party; and of Poland, where the discussion was switched to the highest level, between the Pope and comrade Gierek. But there, Italy is involved, too.[37] For the Czechs, at least for the moment, the dialogue was finished. It was just another example that the tide really had turned and that Soviet communism cannot afford ideological co-existence.

5. Ivan Sviták: The strategy of truth

Although during the fateful year of 1968 Czechoslovak philosophers (with the exception of Kolman who lived in Moscow) participated in the renewal process of re-Westernization of Marxism, Ivan Sviták was the most active. By the moderates

---

[34] *Ibid.*, p. 101.

[35] *Ibid.*, p. 101. The emphasis is his.

[36] *Listy*, ii, 3 (May 1972), p. 39.

[37] The election in October 1978 of a Polish Cardinal as Pope John Paul II brought this problem to a climax.

he was sometimes considered too impudent and provocative. But in his radical demands he was led by fear that without an active participation of workers and students the change would remain restricted to Party leadership and no real institutional reforms would take place. He did not trust the *apparat* and was worried that without· fast and basic democratic reforms only a new Gomulkian type of disappointment would follow as in Poland after 1956.

In 1968 Sviták repeatedly proved that he was a capable analyst of the situation, coining excellent slogans for action, and an effective stimulator of growing democratic movements on the part of the workers, students, and also in other new organizations, such as *Kan*, a club for non-Party people which provided a possible base for a future democratic party.

However, in his young years Sviták had sowed his wild oats. After the *putsch* he joined the Communist Party and actively participated in the brutal game at a supposedly progressive and proletarian revolution. Since 1952 he worked at the University of Political and Economic Sciences in Prague as a lecturer on history of philosophy. In 1957 he was criticized by the CPC CC for lack of discipline. He tried to prove himself by vigorous public agitation. His propaganda specialty was the fight for atheism and against religions. In this public campaign he delivered many speeches and wrote many an article.[38]

In 1964 Sviták became victim of one of the periodic attacks by the Party *apparat* on intellectuals who refused to follow the dogmatic Party line faithfully. He had sent to the weekly *Kulturní noviny* a study of forty-nine pages on the tasks of philosophy. The publication was refused and the highest Party organs studied his philosophical treatise. When the CPC CC made public its decision, it strongly objected to the following passage of the study: "A philosopher shouldn't be a household servant, a drudge of concocted laws, and a qualified clown who professes the spirit and depth of science where only yawns an abyss of spiritlessness."[39] Clearly, at the time he had to be all that.

Sviták was expelled from the Party in 1965 and after a protracted series of staff meetings at the University, where most of his colleagues refused to follow Party instructions and throw him out of the faculty, he was dismissed on higher orders. In unusually open letters (for the times) Sviták complained about his forced retirement to an Austrian monthly of the Congress for Cultural Freedom[40] and his case became known internationally. He contributed an essay called "Sources of Socialist Humanism" to Erich Fromm's book *Socialist Humanism* (published in 1965 in New York). His later contribution to a British quarterly "Kafka as Philosopher," probably suffered in the process of a double translation (through German),[41] since it does not possess the usual clarity of Sviták's thought and cannot compare with a previously mentioned essay on Kafka (and Švejk) by Kosík.

[38] For instance, "Stranická organizace a ateistická výchova" ["Party Organization and Atheist Education"], *Naše pravda* (Gottwaldov), 10 Feb. 1959, p. 2; "Překonat náboženské přežitky" ["To Overcome Religious Remnants"], *Naše pravda*, 19 Dec. 1959, pp. 2-3; "Ateistická výchova na vesnici" ["Atheist Education in the Village"], *Otázky marxistické filozofie*, no. 1 (1962), p. 49.

[39] *Rudé právo*, 3 Apr. 1964.

[40] "Brief aus Prag" ["Letter from Prague"], *Forum*, xiii (1966), no. 146; his first letter was published in no. 142.

[41] *Survey*, no. 59 (Apr. 1966), pp. 36-40.

Out of his many literary interventions in the 1968 developments Sviták himself selected the most interesting ones and published them, first in German[42] and then in English.[43] (Some of them were also translated for other collections of documents.)

The book starts with a great adoration of truth. Quotations from Hus and Marx (what a couple!) introduce the prologue whose title was used for the name of this part. Although Sviták sometimes seems to be keeping his basic belief in Marxist relativity of ideas (expressions of class interests) and consequently of their truth — "Political theories are a rationalization of social group interests" — at other times his concept of truth is almost absolute: "Truth is the best of tactics because it excludes tactics."[44] Since his articles combined philosophy and politics, he did not always try to avoid simplification and popular shortcuts: "The documents were formulated during that dynamic Prague Spring which made the city of Jan Hus the capital of truth and therefore a natural terrain for philosophy."[45]

He quotes his well-known answer to a public enquiry about national orientation: "If the question is, 'Where from, with whom, and whither?' we could briefly answer: 'From Asia to Europe, alone.'"[46] The bulk of Sviták's answer to this question should be cited at least partly, since it gives, in an abbreviated form, the main ideas of his numerous speeches and articles from this period. It involved him in one of the first and also most successful attempts at cooperation among workers and intellectuals.

> From totalitarian dictatorship to an open society, to the liquidation of the monopoly of power and an effective control of the power élite by the free press and public opinion. From a society and a culture bureaucratically directed by the "cut-throats of the official line" (Wright Mills) to the realization of basic civic rights at least as extensive as those of bourgeois-democratic Czechoslovakia. With the working-class movement, but without its *apparatchiks*; with the vast majority of the people, but without mindless collaborators, and with the intelligentsia as the leading force.[47]

The contribution of some sixty technicians of the Doubrava mine in Ostrava gave Sviták a chance of replying and explaining his points of view. His intention was to separate both the workers and the technical intelligentsia from the *apparatchiks* in order to create a common front "for the abolition of the decisive influence of the bureaucratic *apparat* on Party and national life:"

> The most pressing problem today is to replace totalitarian dictatorship with socialist democracy, which means changing the manner in which power is wielded without abandoning socialist achievements, in particular the social ownership of the means of production.[48]

Ivan Sviták was then invited to come to the mine for a meeting. It lasted

---

[42] *Verbotene Horizonte. Prag zwischen zwei Wintern* [*Forbidden Horizons: Prague Between Two Winters*] (Freiburg: Rombach, 1969).

[43] *The Czechoslovak Experiment 1968–1969* (New York: Columbia University Press, 1971).

[44] *Ibid.*, pp. 3 and 9.

[45] *Ibid.*, p. 8.

[46] *Ibid.*, p. 33.

[47] As quoted in "The Doubrava Technicians: Our Voice Joins the Discussion," *Literární listy*, 18 Apr. 1968; trans. Oxley *et al.*: *Czechoslovakia* . . . , p. 172.

[48] "Open Letter to the Workers and Technicians of the Doubrava Mine in Ostrava," *ibid.*, pp. 177–82.

eight hours and as a result one of the main Party bureaucrats, Drahomír Kolder, was not elected at Party meetings to the Fourteenth CPC Congress as their delegate, although Ostrava has been for a long time his power base. Another successful action of Sviták was his request to reopen the case of Jan Masaryk's death in 1948.

Sviták openly proclaimed the right of the intellectuals to lead the nation:

> The intellectual élite [is] the only true élite of modern times. . . . The intellectual's task it to destroy myth and illusions. . . . At all times an intellectual must defend suprapersonal, supraclass, and supranational values of truth, reason, and justice.[49]

In his article entitled "The Meaning of Our Regeneration Movement" he called for "the unity of working hands and working brains against the apparatuses of the power-élite:"

> Workers and the intelligentsia have a common enemy — the bureaucratic dictatorship of the apparatus, which equally despises manual labor and intellectual work, and for whom workers are only an obedient militia, just as the intelligentsia are only executors of power.[50]

After twenty years of sustained Party lies and dictatorship he kept coming back to the fundamental importance of truth and freedom, as in his "Ten Commandments for an Adult Intellectual: "1. Speak the truth regardless of tactical considerations. . . . 10. Commit yourselves to the cause of human freedom as the highest value of mankind."[51]

Several of Sviták's interventions had in effect but brought upon him the ire of the conservatives. Also some of the moderates sometimes thought that imprisonment of some of the leading reformists, foremost of Sviták, could have placated the Russians and averted the invasion. It would have been a solution à la Tito who for this tactic usually had sacrificed Djilas and/or Mihajlov. But that would have been the beginning of a self-imposed liquidation of the reform movement and might have led to student demonstrations and eventually even to a revolution.

6. Miroslav Kusý: The strategy of probing the limits

There is no doubt that the Slovak philosopher, Miroslav Kusý, in his mature years was as devoted as Sviták to telling and writing the truth as he saw it. The reason I am juxtaposing them is elsewhere. While after the invasion Sviták completely despaired of any chance that the Russians would allow Czechoslovak reforms to remain in force for any length of time — he was a skeptic even before[52] — Kusý hoped that sufficient space would be provided in which honest communists could continue their work. He was quickly disappointed.

In 1963, when he was a special assistant at the Faculty of Philosophy, Comenius University in Bratislava, he wrote for the main Party daily in Slovakia a piece with the provocative title, "The Social Function of Truth." He asserted that "people want to know the whole truth about our life, our problems and difficulties, our

---

[49] *The Czechoslovak Experiment*, p. 38.

[50] *Ibid.*, p. 75.

[51] *Ibid.*, pp. 112–13.

[52] Cf., Galia Golan, *Reform Rule in Czechoslovakia: The Dubček Era 1968–1969* (London Cambridge University Press, 1973), p. 125.

recent past and our perspectives in the near future." He disagreed with those who "raise the warning finger, cautioning that the truth may be used against us by the class enemy." (Here he spoke against Novotný, Hendrych, and Koucký who were doing exactly that.) Dogmatism and demagogy are the real dangers. "What the enemy . . . actually uses and misuses against us are our shortcomings and failures." The only proper way, according to Kusý, was to attend to them "uncompromisingly . . . through public acknowledgement."[53]

In 1968 Kusý published a well-timed book called *Czechoslovak Institutional Revolution: Questions of Politics and Democracy*. Since the "dictatorship of the proletariat changed into a dictatorship of leaders," he advocated, as the basic condition for a democratization of the public life, separation of the Communist Party from the State (an old idea of some Yugoslav communists). But the invasion spoiled such dreams; Kusý decided to combine forces with Husák and in November 1968 became head of the ideological department of the Slovak CPC CC, that means he joined the *apparat* in one of its highest functions. He was then thirty-eight years old. His scholarly career was quite remarkable: till then he was professor at the Comenius University, in the epistemological section of the Department of Philosophy, and chairman of the Scientific Council of the Slovak National Council Commissioner's Office of Culture and Information. His appointment as chief of Slovak ideology was regarded as a positive and progressive act by Husák, since Kusý's reformist credentials were excellent. But his political career would be very short — a mere four months. It was a very busy time during which the Professor, temporarily in the *apparat*, tried to accomplish a lot. We have to remember that Slovakia was substantially lagging behind the Czech lands in democratization of the State and of the Party, as well as in the liberalization of the press.

In Husák's political, cultural, and economic weekly Kusý had a regular column, "From an Open Notebook." He wrote on "The Duty of a Journalist:"

> We are making honest and sustained effort to fulfil the Moscow conditions. However, there is no clause in these conditions which would compel us to accept in silence every slander and malicious invective. . . . Therefore we can read daily information saying that this or that arms cache of counter-revolutionaries, which had been found, was actually nothing else than a strictly guarded and documented armory of our People's Militias.

Kusý then complained about editorial offices (in Moscow) that do not recall their correspondents "for grossly violating journalistic ethics and morality." The pathetic state of Czechoslovak "sovereignty" came to light in this passage:

> It is customary for a journalist to be expelled from a foreign country if the said journalist goes beyond the bounds of what hospitality permits and if he begins to insult the representatives and the people of this country. . . . Today, we have no possibility of proceeding in the same manner against certain journalists from allied countries who have grossly abused their positions. However, we would ask their editorial offices to do so in the interest of their good name and in the interest of truth and justice.[54]

---

[53] *Pravda*, 20 Aug. 1963, p. 2. The year before Kusý published a book *O vztahu teorie a praxe* [*On the Relation of Theory and Practice*] and another, *O vztahu tělesné a duševní práce* [*On the Relation of Physical and Mental Work*]. Other books followed: *Tvorba a poznání* [*Creation and Knowledge*] in 1964, *Filosofie politiky* [*The Philosophy of Politics*], in 1966, and *Marxistická filosofie* [*Marxist Philosophy*], in 1968. He also wrote *Úvod do filosofie* [*Introduction to Philosophy*].

[54] *Nové slovo*, 3 Oct. 1968.

That was written a few days before his new nomination and surely did not win him good points with the Soviet Embassy which was the headquarters of every gross abuse of hospitality. Kusý's study, "The Czechoslovak Political Crisis," which was written before the invasion, was published. It was an excellent analysis of the imported Soviet system and of the causes of the Prague Spring, as well as an exposition of the necessity to instigate profound institutional reforms:

> This is a revolution which aims at a qualitative change of the entire system of direction and of the entire institutional structure of our society in such a manner that this system and structure reflect to an optimal degree the new changed social structure of our society. Put in very simplified terms, what is involved is an institutional revolution, revolution in the sphere of the institutional superstructure above our social base.

Kusý deplored that the original "specific Czechoslovak road to socialism" was suppressed and "total nationalization," together with the "etatist model of the dictatorship of the proletariat" was enforced. It created an intolerant "bureaucratic *apparat*" whose "stabilized power élite set up a complicated system of corruption and favoritism:"

> Only the highest Party organs governed, only the Party *apparat* acted on behalf of the Party.... The fundamental quality, which was rigorously demanded of every rank and file Party member was an iron [literally, "military"] discipline, and unqualified adherence to the decisions made "above."

According to Kusý, the crisis could have been solved through reforms in 1953, 1956, and maybe even in 1960, but in 1968 only by an "all-embracing institutional revolution." He devoted a chapter to the Slovak specific need of federation but for him the major problem was the democratization of the whole Czechoslovak Republic.[55]

After his nomination as chief Slovak ideologue, Kusý talked about his attentive study of Italian Marxism, especially of Gramsci, who as a theorist "can be compared with Lenin." His main new task as he saw it was to create conditions for "as many educated people as possible."[56] That was exactly the opposite of Soviet plans for his country after 1968.

In a long interview for a Prague illustrated weekly, Kusý explained his hope for political activity in spite of the presence of Soviet occupation troops in the country:

> We can manage ourselves within the room left to us.... Certain rules of the game exist within the framework of the socialist camp. Therefore, let us accept these rules, and within their framework try to do everything that is in our power. But do not let us begin by wanting to change the rules, because in that case we would continually be rapped over the knuckles. And how large is this room? It is constantly changing. We must constantly scrutinize it and probe its limits. Of course, to a major degree how large a space we can win is up to us. We cannot just passively wait until we are given some room; we must always try to acquire this room by our own initiative. After all, we are not merely objects, but also subjects in this room.[57]

In this frank and remarkable (too frank, probably) interview Kusý also defended his Czech colleague Sviták; he might be radical but surely not counter-revolutionary.

[55] "Československá politická kríza," *Nová mysl*, no. 11, Nov. 1968, pp. 1315–28.
[56] *Večerník*, 16 Nov. 1968, pp. 1–2.
[57] "The Right, the Left, the Center, and the Others," *Světu obrazech*, 18 Feb. 1969.

Gradually, beginning in January 1969, Kusý started to sound less optimistic about the limits of the "constantly changing" room left and rules of the game, although he did not stop trying. On the contrary, judging by his public activity, he redoubled his effort. He kept defending what he called "the policy of the center" and there were days when two of his articles or interviews appeared in various newspapers.

Soviet field specialists obviously did not enjoy professor Kusý's probing of the limits left for self-rule and so Gustáv Husák made a quick end to the promising ideological career. As the first secretary of the Slovak CPC CC, he announced at a plenary meeting of this body that "the presidium of the Slovak CPC CC *was forced* on 17 February to release comrade Kusý from the function of the head of the ideological department." The headline of this part of Husák's speech read: "The Main Danger: Anti-Socialist and Rightist-Opportunist Forces." Husák introduced the news of the downfall of his close collaborator in his usual style: "I have to mention a case since there is developing a certain hum around it. Comrade M. Kusý performed a wicked service to the Party. . . . He kept flooding the Slovak and Czech press, radio, and television by his articles and utterances in which he discussed, in essence, Rightist-opportunist views."[58]

Kusý was allowed to have the last word — not in Bratislava but in Prague where other Slovak reformers as well could still publish. It was an interesting reversal from the years 1963–7 when Czech publicists were welcome in the Slovak press, but then Dubček was in power in Bratislava as he was now in Prague. But the privilege would not last long: Husák was already *ante portas*. Kusý wrote:

> I had a certain conception of modern ideological work: to assemble a team of Marxist theorists. [But] our partners passed from an exchange of opinions to diplomatic notes. . . . The political *apparat* has its own customary mechanism (the ideological department alone has some thirty people). One person can hardly change such a routine. . . . I am returning to the Faculty; I have considered the work in the *apparat* as only temporary. I do not regret, however, these four months; it was a great school.

Implicitly, he criticized Husák for misusing the Slovak question in order to exert pressure on Prague and thus for its lack of positive influence on the whole State. And he added: "For a modern nation the European context is of primary importance. We in Slovakia must open our windows wide to Europe, rather than to our own past."[59]

As often in the history of the Czechs and Slovaks, it was again proved that there was no effective way of coping with the overwhelming invading power — both the "strategy of truth" and the "strategy of probing limits" were bound to fail, but their protagonists at least had the courage and, in spite of their defeat, the satisfaction that they had really tried to do their best. What remained was to analyze the mistakes made. Ivan Sviták and Karel Kosík wrote a few good analyses.

Sviták, however, in spite of some infrequent doubts,[60] still professes belief in

[58] *Pravda*, 13 Mar. 1969, pp. 4–5. My emphasis.
[59] *Práce*, 20 Mar. 1969, p. 4.
[60] "Marx's categories survived the nineteenth century of class conflict and thus became an ideology — and not the true reflection of the social situation in the industrialized countries." "Illusions of Czech Socialist Democracy," *Telos.*, no. 22, winter 1974/5, p. 124.

Marxism and uses some of its language and images. Again, very much like Bartošek (and others as well), Sviták continues to believe in a special mission of the workers' class. Why should the workers be such a "chosen class?" Just because in the middle of the nineteenth century, when Marx was around, they were the obvious sufferers of the Industrial Revolution? Just because Marx assigned to them in his eschatological vision a mission which the workers never and nowhere seemed to be really interested in accomplishing? Why should any class be chosen for a messianic feat whose basic idea might be an interesting offshoot of the Judaic-Christian mythology but practically a dangerous illusion, in whose name countless murders could be and have been committed, both before and after Marx?

7. The question of internationalism

This chapter commenced with *Arnošt Kolman,* the patriarch of Czechoslovak Marxist philosophers and teacher of most of them. It can well end with him, too, since his paying of old scores with the Soviet system has great significance.

Arnošt Kolman in 1972 applied in Moscow for a passport to go to Stockholm and visit his daughter, married to a Czech nuclear physicist, František Janouch, and his grandchildren, all living in Sweden. When the fifteenth application of this Soviet and Czechoslovak academician, professor at both Prague and Moscow universities, was refused as all the previous ones, the 84-year-old Kolman complained about it in an interview granted to Swedish press and television: "How is it possible to believe declarations of the Soviet government on détente when the Soviet government does not fulfill the Helsinki agreement even in such a simple case, and does not want to allow parents to visit their only daughter?"[61]

After the publicity given to this interview in Sweden, Kolman's seventeenth application was granted by Soviet authorities and he was allowed to travel to Stockholm. From there he sent an open letter to Leonid I. Brezhnev. It is not only a moving human document but an important indictment of the Soviet system by one of the oldest Bolsheviks alive:

> I wish to inform you that I am leaving the Soviet Communist Party. I am 84 and have been a Party member for 58 years. I joined its ranks in order to fight for social justice, for a happy future for mankind. Now, after long and painful reflection, I have come to this difficult decision. . . .
>
> After Khrushchev's revelations about the bloody crimes of Stalin, euphemistically described as "the personality cult," I began to understand how deeply distorted the Soviet Communist Party and Soviet power had become, and that I, as a party member, must bear my share of responsibility for this.
>
> However, 1968 was the real turning-point for me, when I had occasion to observe the "Prague Spring" and see with my own eyes with what enthusiasm the united people of Czechoslovakia backed the strivings of the party to rekindle the socialist ideals and the fight for socialism with a human face.
>
> When your tanks and your armies occupied Czechoslovakia subjecting it to your political *Diktat* and merciless economic exploitation — in short turning it into your colony — I lost my illusions I may have had about the nature of your regime.

After this historical explanation of his loss of illusions and after a recapitulation of

---

[61] *Listy,* vi, 3 (June 1976), p. 48.

his work for the communist cause, Kolman devoted the second part of his letter to a Marxist description of the Soviet system:

> About what sort of socialism can one talk in the Soviet Union, when the place of the former capitalist and landowner exploitation classes has been taken by the privileged castes of the party and state bureaucracies? They are drowning in wealth, live isolated from the people, above them, and contemptuous of ordinary folk, not wishing to and incapable of understanding their needs and sufferings. . . .
>
> The Soviet Union lacks the most elementary democratic rights. . . . Basic human rights are crudely trampled on in the Soviet Union. . . . This makes the Soviet Union no less "a prison of the nations" than Tsarist Russia was. . . . It is preparing for the occupation of Romania and Yugoslavia. . . . It is also supplying arms and providing military support for most reactionary regimes and international terrorists. . . . The Soviet Union has one of the most conservative regimes in the world, with an aging leadership. . . . And is it not a tragedy that 60 years after the Revolution the agriculture of Europe's former granary is unable to produce enough bread, meat, fish and even potatoes to satisfy the needs of its own population?

Then Kolman complained about the inhuman treatment of families and the limitations or impossibility of contacts with their relatives abroad or in prisons:

> Can one live amid such conditions? And how long can one live like this? I can no longer go on living like this. . . . My staying in the ranks of the Soviet Communist Party would amount to a betrayal of the ideals of social justice, humanism and the building of a new and more human society. [62]

In a nutshell, Kolman's letter shows not only the reasons for pro-Soviet hopes of the Czechoslovak communist intellectuals but also their complete disappointment in the country and the system of their dreams. We cannot suspect Kolman of nationalism; his whole life of a man of three different national identities disproves that. When he talks about the joy of his stay in Prague of 1968, another, deeper sentiment than nationalism was involved; I recall it from the Hungarian revolution of 1956 when Tibor Déri and Gyula Hay felt and expressed it. It happened to many communists in Hungary of 1956 and in Czechoslovakia of 1968, when they really, for the first time in their lives of professional revolutionaries, could see and experience that the people were with them and responded to them enthusiastically because they were saying what people really believed; when they knew that they were not cheating them any more, lying to them as usual, or forcing them to anything but, on the contrary, felt like being carried with them on a wave of brotherly community of beliefs and interests. Then there was no pretense, no dead dogma, but living reality of mutual understanding and support. Then the revolution was a spontaneous and genuine people's revolution. Such an exalted moment of truth, naturally, makes it then possible to realize how the other "leading of the masses" had been always a fraud and a deadly game. That is what Kolman (Dubček, London, Daix, and so many others) recognized and loved in Prague of 1968 and what illuminated for them the enormous difference between a real, living, and genuine unity with the people, on one side, and on the other, the showy, unreal, and artificial pretense but total absence of it.

[62] Gabriel Ronay, "Lenin's old comrade hands in his party card," *The Times*, 6 Oct. 1976. pp. 1 and 8.

As we could see, Arnošt Kolman denied the substance of the "practical scientific communism" (as it is nowadays being called by its ideologues and politicians in Moscow and Prague), in whose name all the terror and sacrifices have been eventually excusable for the communists; namely, the supposed socialist character of the Soviet Union. Therefore, if there was no "Holy Grail," no higher sense, no excuse, no sanctification for the countless crimes — it was all just an enormous, destructive, and bloody lie.

There is another important observation which should be made and which in my mind ensues from the Kolman case, confirming many similar occurrences of recent years. It concerns one of the most potentially far-reaching developments of contemporary history. Admittedly, what follows could easily be criticized as a great generalization but I believe that there is in it more than a grain of truth.

It belongs to the common knowledge that the role of the Jews in the history of the preparation of the Russian revolution and in the creation of the Soviet Union was disproportionate to the small percentage of the Jewish population in the State. There is no place to repeat here the reasons for it (Jewish education, oppression, etc.). Russian (and Polish, Lithuanian, German) Jews helped to create the Bolshevik Party and the Soviet Union as an internationalist movement, as a hopeful fulfillment of a dream of a just, racially unbiased, supranationalist, socialist state. To the same degree, especially in Czechoslovakia, German-speaking Jews often participated in the creation of Central European Communist Parties (and later of communist states). Therefore, Hitler's claim that he had to save Western Christianity from a Jewish-Bolshevik-plutocratic conspiracy was often believable not only to simple anti-Semitic folks of Europe but also to sophisticated but prejudiced aristocrats in Great Britain, France, Poland, Hungary, and elsewhere. On the other side, we have to remember, this communist claim of internationalism and of cosmopolitan building of a new, alternate world order of people, liberated from oppression and narrow national boundaries and prejudices, had a great appeal to intellectuals who felt that it was the proper way for humanity to develop.

Arnošt Kolman, as we know, was a typical member of such an internationalist trend. He was a Czech, a Jew, but he also was a German and a Russian. What was he? A real internationalist. They were many like him. But then the tragedy started to evolve. With the death of Lenin, with the end of hopes that the Bolshevik Revolution or Soviet agents would trigger a world revolution, with the departure of Trotsky and with the advent of Stalin, orthodox Russia began to reassert itself. In a series of paroxysms, the fundamentally backward, anti-intellectual, anti-Semitic, barbarian, and anti-internationalist Russia, under Stalin's impetus, tried to get rid of the Jews in its leadership and its population, to shake them off as a foreign body (very much like barbarian instincts in Germany of Hitler), by killing them, organizing pogroms against them in show trials, or removing thousands of them to Asian parts of the Soviet Union. It is known how the semi-Fascist Soviet Government liquidated thousands of Jews by handing them over to the invading Nazis.

This anti-Jewish wave of pogroms came to Eastern Europe soon after the end of the World War II. The Slánský trial in Czechoslovakia was an anti-Semitic show *par excellence*. The Soviet Union was liquidating a large number of its internationalist agents who until then often were considered useful and were in charge of its takeovers of Eastern European countries and of Stalinist liquidations of the native, national, non-communist political leaders. One of the major themes of Stalinist propaganda campaigns in Czechoslovakia was a fight against "cosmopolitanism." Native, national heroes (Žižka, Jirásek, Smetana) were often artificially propagated beyond their comparative significance against foreign oriented, pro-Western, and internationalist personalities of the Czech history and culture. People who organized such campaigns, hidden in the Party secretariat, did not often even know Czech properly (Geminder, Frank, etc.). In the first stage they were used (it was easier for them to suppress the often hated natives), and in the second stage, they were liquidated. It was an extended arm of orthodox, conservative, anti-Western, anti-internationalist Russia.

The creation of the separate Jewish state of Israel was, to a large degree, due to efforts of Jews who originated in the Russian Pale and in Central Europe. After disastrous experiences not only with Hitler's *Reich* but also with Stalin's "Mother Russia" which thirty years after the Revolution was clearly unable and unwilling to fulfill the ideal of a supranational and non-racially biased world order, the interest and creative energy of Jewish leaders switched elsewhere, to the formation of their own national state. At the beginning, the Soviet Union and Czechoslovakia were helping with its evolution (against "British imperialism"); there were many Czechs (often Jewish) active as agents in the Palestine and large quantities of arms were sent there. Then, all at once, Stalin completely changed the policy and a huge anti-Jewish, anti-Zionist campaign was mounted. Its aim was to liquidate remaining power positions of Jews inside the Soviet empire (mainly among secret police agents) and to win Arab friends abroad: the Middle East could be used against the Western and "Jewish plutocrats" better from the Arab states than from Israel. This policy has been going on until our day, quite successfully, since, for example, it enabled the Soviet Union to turn in its favor the majorities in the United Nations and its agencies. Soviet leaders have been posing — unashamedly with the inherited Hitler's anti-Semitic mantle over their shoulders — as the center of mankind's alleged struggle against the Jewish, Zionist plot to take over the world in a conspiracy, led mainly by Israeli and American capitalist Jewry. It is not surprising that communist, internationalist Jews are watching this abortion of the original conception with horror.

Internally, as a consequence of the victory by the old orthodox, Muscovy, Asian, ultra-conservative tendencies of Russian Communism against the defeated internationalist trend, present in the Bolshevik Party around 1917, the Soviet Union is now in conflict — exactly as Czarist Russia was — with large numbers of its own Jewish population, which have been trying to get out of Russia in great numbers and which have been, to a large degree, allowed to follow its separatist inclination of an exodus, since it suits the long term "purity" of the Soviet population as the anti-Semitic Soviet leaders see it. In the global context, the Soviet Union had given rise to one of the first widely organized opposition to its cultural, social, and racial backwardness by Jews all over the world, even in Australia.

The case of Kolman, a genuine communist internationalist, helps to demonstrate the sad end of Soviet original internationalism. There is no place in the Soviet empire for people like him. For the Soviet Union, the word "internationalism" remained. But now its meaning is, without any doubt, equal to the exclusively national interests of Russian imperialism. At a time when Gustáv Husák can be honored as a "true internationalist," there is no place in Soviet communism for people like Kolman. It is only surprising how long it had taken them to realize it. But, at least, another illusion is dead.

Chapter 3.

In politics

WHAT is the character of communist parties and what is the reality of their power, as seen by an insider? One interesting source in looking for an answer to these questions is a recent book written by *Jiří Pelikán,* a Czech politician who spent more than twenty years in the service of the Communist Party of Czechoslovakia. After a few years as a national student leader, he represented it for ten years in leading functions of an international student body and five years as director of the Czechoslovak Television, both before and under Dubček. He can introduce us to the question of pro-Soviet collaboration of people like Husák or Richta long after the invasion and also to the problem of Euro-communism.

1. Student leader purging students

Jiří Pelikán, born in 1923 of a sculptor's family in the Moravian city of Olomouc, joined the Communist Party in 1939, was arrested by the Nazis in 1940 for distributing leaflets and jailed for six months. The rest of the war he spent "underground." According to his own memoirs he was first hiding in several localities under the name of Josef Plevák and then for three years, as Bohumil Paroulek, he was employed as municipal secretary in Korenec, a village of eight hundred peasants and workers, situated in the mountains. (Therefore, it seems, there is the slightly misleading mention in *The Times* biography, claiming that he "spent the rest of the war with the underground communist movement, partly in the mountains." That would turn a clerk, working in a mountain office, into partisan in a mountain cave, which is far above the much more modest claims of Pelikán in his own book.) Once he had to lead SS-men, searching for suspects, through all the village houses.[1]

After the liberation in 1945, Pelikán, as so many other bourgeois youngsters, sought salvation in a close attachment to the workers' class and made a good career of it, although he "never participated in the workers' movement."[2] He took an active part in the *coup d'état* of 1948 and even in 1975 still considered Gottwald's *putschist* tactics "valid and subtle: the resigning parties were being punished and divided." He also stressed that all parties naturally fight for power, to win it and keep it — without mentioning the subtle difference between democratic parties that continue to play according to democratic rules of the game and

[1] Jiří Pelikán, *S'ils me tuent* . . . (Paris: Bernard Grasset, 1975), pp. 40–5. *The Times,* 1 Oct. 1969.
[2] O. Ponomarjovova [clearly a Russian woman], "Runaway Herald of the 'Prague Spring'," *Týdenik aktualit* [one of several Soviet publications distributed in post-invasion Czechoslovakia in Czech for the enlightenment of the counter-revolutionaries], no. 26, 28 June 1971, p. 2.

totalitarian parties that destroy any limitations binding them to parliamentary habits.[3]

As chairman of the (closed shop) Association of University Students in Prague and in his new function as chairman of the revolutionary action committee of the National Front on universities, in 1948, Pelikán was responsible for large-scale purges of members of his association. Hundreds of students were not allowed to continue their studies and many of them were forced to work as miners, construction workers, or in other manual jobs. Quite a few disappeared in prisons and concentration camps or in the Jáchymov uranium mines as political slaves.

Almost thirty years later, a more experienced and wiser Pelikán, still considered his inhuman actions of 1948 as "politically justified and legitimate." Even the merciless purging of democratic professors and students from the universities the then secretary of communist students (who did the brutal job) considers "just in the whole." It "was all done for a democratization of the University" and in order to throw out "Fascist, reactionary elements, and their collaborators."[4] It is incredible and disgusting that Pelikán was not able to realize how unjust was the discrimination of students he presided over and what devastation of Czechoslovak education had followed as the result of these actions. Personally, I was not hurt since my personal Party supervisor had qualified me as "socially progressive" but I could observe that the best students and decent colleagues usually fell victim to these purges which were often led by stupid and reckless communists — of the type seen on American campuses in the 1960s bombing computers and searching Deans' offices for compromising documents. The talk about a democratization and about Fascist students was a lie in 1948 and remained a lie in 1975. Prime target of the purges were professors and students who dared to oppose communist nondemocratic methods.

According to Pelikán's memoirs, when Social Democratic student leader, Ivan Sviták (discussed in the chapter on philosophy), came to see him and warned him that injustice and mechanisms of revenge will turn against them, Pelikán persuaded him that it was all part of a great revolution and "When you cut down trees, chips fly."[5]

Finally, towards the end of this part of his memoirs, Pelikán added (thinking about future revolutionary communist actions in other countries) that now he realized that unjust acts, that at the beginning of a revolution do not seem to be important, tend to grow into larger injustice and finally crimes. But then he was "prisoner of a religions *optique.*"[6]

Let us return to 1948. In a leading article of a cultural periodical, entitled "The Road of the Young Intelligentsia," Pelikán expressed the hope, then often

[3] Pelikán *S'ils me tuent.* . . pp. 60-4.

[4] Ibid., pp. 65-6. In 1968, Professor Engst, The Deputy Dean of the Faculty of Philosophy, called it "acts of despotism." See *Literarní Listy,* no. 13, 23 May 1968, p. 5. Hugh Seton-Watson appropriately wrote: "The closest parallel to Hitler's revolution, both in the seizure of power and in the use of power, is the Communist revolution of 1948 in Czechoslovakia." See his *Nationalism and Communism. Essays 1946-63*(New York: Praeger, 1964), p. 78.

[5] *S'ils me tuent.* . ., p. 67.

[6] *Ibid.,* p. 68.

repeated, of representing the "good guys" in a propagandistic, though deeply felt, dichotomy of the world divided in two antagonistic classes:

> The whole generation of young intelligentsia will go with the new world that is growing out of ruins around us, with the young, energetic, and optimistic world of the working people, and not with the old, lewd world of greediness, falsehood, and martial destruction. . . . This is the only road to genuine freedom and real strength.[7]

A few weeks later, as a student candidate on the single list for the "elections" to the National Assembly, Pelikán called for "refusing the world of chaos, greediness, pecuniary stupidity, and hypocrisy" and for "choosing the world of truth and justice and socialism."[8] He became the youngest member of the streamlined parliament.

Soon, unfortunately, the class frontiers and the borders between the two worlds became blurred and many esteemed comrades had to be thrown on the growing historical heap of defeated enemies. One of the really great communist poets, František Halas, was denounced as a relic of the past by Ladislav Štoll, another believer in the slogan that chips must fly. Pelikán joined the attackers in order to "correctly apply in practice the instructions of comrade Zhdanov that are binding for us too". He condemned Halas for his "convulsiveness, apocalyptic fright, lack of faith, feeling of fate — all that is peculiar to the class which is perishing and is doomed to destruction."[9] With the stench of a dying class (his own) in his nostrils, Pelikán did not care that shortly before, the same cultural weekly of the Communist Party devoted a whole issue to the celebration of Halas, one of the most venerated writers and members of the Party, who after February 1948 was elevated to a high governmental position. Now he lost his honorary membership of the workers' class and became a target for vituperative attacks by those who wanted to merit their honorary memberships. Prague was importing Zhdanovism from the East and needed appropriate victims from its own ranks. Eager helpers did not realize that they were assisting the Soviet effort to cripple their nation's culture at a time when the armed services, police forces, the economy, and even the Party leadership were being purged and changed in order to better fit and serve the Soviet empire.

"The Party was doing exactly the opposite of what it had promised before." The agitators, and Pelikán was one of them, began to lose their persuasiveness: "The malaise was growing and we felt that people did not trust us anymore. . . . I lost the pleasure and audacity to speak at public meetings," remembers Pelikán.[10]

During the preparation of political show trials against Slánský and other prominent Party leaders, Pelikán spent nights without sleep, searching desperately for his own culpability. He gives almost no details about his work during these years — and he must have done a lot — but he mentions, casually, that he participated in the denunciation of Gustav Bareš, a Jew: "We, his close collaborators, met in order to discuss the best way of helping the Party to unmask him fast."[11]

[7] *Svobodné noviny,* 5 Mar. 1948.
[8] *Lidové noviny,* 27 May 1948.
[9] "An Example of a Principled Critique," *Tvorba,* 21 June 1950, pp. 603–5. Štoll's hatchet booklet was called *Třicet let bojů za socialistickou poesii* [*Thirty Years of Struggles for Socialist Poetry*].
[10] *S'ils me tuent. . .,* p. 80.
[11] *Ibid.,* p. 90.

2. Anti-colonial fight led from a colony

As a reward for his faithful following of the crooked Party line in the difficult and murderous period when "foreign spies" were being discovered in the leadership of the CPC, in 1953 Pelikán became, by the Party decision, general secretary of the International Union of Students. At the same time Enrico Berlinguer's brother, Giovanni, was named its president. Two years later, Pelikán became the president and in this important position travelled widely over all continents, and continued to steer the world student body in communist directions so that it served all its causes.

Who would like to learn about the work of this student union does not have to open Pelikán's book. It was all nice and platonic — meetings, speeches, resolutions, and "fighting against colonialism." But to someone who knows something about the way communists make politics, all this is just a surface behind which the real work is going on. On that, the real thing, there is not a single word on forty pages devoted to ten years of international activities.

Pelikán mentions some difficulties that were making his job hard. For instance, when the Soviet Union was massacring thousands of Hungarian students and deporting them to Siberia, some student unions would have liked to see an investigation of it. As Pelikán says, it had to be carefully handled in order not to offend the Russians by any criticism. They are so sensitive to it.[12]

During his numerous trips to the Soviet Union, Pelikán kept meeting the Russian rulers and could form an opinion of them: "The level of certain leaders was so mediocre, so low, that I have often asked myself how could they manage the Soviet Union."[13] In this connection Pelikán mentions an opinion, communicated to him by a member of the Politburo of the CPC, an old communist [Kriegel?], after his return from meetings at Čierná and Tisou: "Since Čierná, I cannot sleep. . . . I realized the incredibly low level of these people who had never read a single book by Marx or Lenin. . . . When I think that the fate of the world depends on such men, I can't sleep."[14]

There are also a few hints about the general degeneration of all communist systems everywhere, including Cuba. They all, despite their original swearing that they would not make the same mistakes, seem to be bound as if following some laws, to fall into the same traps and commit the same blunders. Pelikán also could not avoid seeing what he had already expressed in his Australian interview of 1971: "I realized there were many contradictions between the reality and the official propaganda which revolted me. . . . I felt that we were losing the moral right to condemn persecution elsewhere."[15]

Pelikán expected more from a younger generation of Soviet leaders, among whom he felt "a certain esteem" for Shelepin. As he says, he knew him well when he served as secretary of the Komsomol and even later when he was chief of the police and member of the Politburo. There are no details about their talks and collaboration, of course, but Pelikán indicates, without a word of doubts or disapproval, that when the Americans bombed Hanoi, Shelepin proposed that the

[12] *Ibid.*, p. 103.
[13] *Ibid.*, p. 118.
[14] *Ibid.*, p. 119.
[15] *Australian Left Review*, Mar. 1971, p. 45.

Soviet leadership respond with aerial attacks on the U.S. Eighth Fleet in the Vietnamese waters or by blocking West Berlin.[16]

After ten years of "the most beautiful period" of his life which "accelerated" his "political evolution,"[17] Pelikán in 1963 was named Director-General of the Czechoslovak Television where he, according to a later Soviet source, "little by little found himself under the influence of revisionist, antisocialist elements."[18]

3. A TV view of the Castle

The fourth part of Pelikán's autobiography, called "Behind the Scenes of the Bureaucracy," forms the center part of the book and is much more interesting than the rest, since it allows the readers some insight into the inner workings of a communist system. At any rate, in the second half of his memoirs, the author as reformer becomes more sympathetic and human than in the first, Stalinist, half.

He tells us that he had discovered the truth about the phony trials of the 1950s in 1956 when he happened to vacation in Bulgaria together with Arthur London, who was recuperating from his ordeal suffered at the hands of his comrades. From his friends Pelikán also heard about the other tortured victims, such as Husák, Loebl, and others. In addition, the anti-Yugoslav attacks were troubling him and his friends, too. That almost cost him his freedom, if not his life. For several years he has been followed by the police; his remarks about his observations abroad made in friends' houses had been taped, his telephone tapped, and especially his meetings with Yugoslav correspondents carefully shadowed.

In 1961 a group of high officials in the Party, completely hidden from the public eyes, but really operating the Party, including the grey eminence of the regime, Miroslav Mamula, decided to mount an anti-Yugoslav trial which would prove that Pelikán and other communist leaders had acted as Yugoslav spies, if not directly as agents of the C.I.A. Pelikán and some of his closest friends went through a long series of distressing interrogations when Pelikán realized that if he were treated as London he would finish by admitting everything they wanted him to, even complete fabrications. He and the other comrades were saved only by the Twenty-Second Congress of the Soviet C.P. since Khrushchev re-launched his anti-Stalinist campaign, thus spoiling plots that, for sure, could not have begun in Prague without the knowledge of at least some Soviet police officials. Czechoslovakia had to follow the new wave of de-Stalinization.[19]

The decision of the Party to put Pelikán in charge of the television network was communicated to him by one of the secretaries of the CPC CC,

---

[16] *S'ils me tuent. . .*, pp. 119–20.
[17] *Ibid.*, pp. 136–7.
[18] See Ponomarjovova, *op. cit.*, p. 2.
[19] *S'ils me tuent . . .* , pp. 15–20 and 142–50.

Čestmír Císař,[20] only one day before he was to start his new assignment! He was told by Císař: "We will develop a new line and you are the man we need because you are not from the *apparat* and not a sectarian functionary."[21]

Pelikán accepted and fixed himself three main tasks (it is possible to believe him since he clearly tried to follow all three of them):

> 1. Make out of the television an ideal instrument for a socialist, direct democracy, assuring a permanent dialogue between the country's leadership and the citizens.
> 2. Reflect the real state of society, function a little as its mirror and make its evolution sensible.
> 3. Contribute to the spread of culture to the masses of the population.[22]

To a large degree, he succeeded but had to lead a constant defensive fight against the conservative alliance of the *apparatchiks* and the police. Until then he did not know how organized and determined this reactionary force was:

> It is necessary to understand that the apparatus of the secret police in a country as, for example, Czechoslovakia, does not have only thousands of employees and officers, but also hundreds of thousands of informers, engaged by the police. Sometimes they are not paid but simply protected and "pushed" in their professional careers. They live obsessed by fear that a clean up would throw full light on their well-hidden responsibilities.[23]

According to Pelikán's account, even when the top leadership decides to begin a liberalization of the system, those in charge of it, members of the apparat, can brake it or kill it. The leaders are also completely dependent on the *apparat* and the secret police for information and therefore at their mercy: "I have often verified that the apparatus of the Party and of the secret police, that 'provides the picture' of the public opinion to the leadership, is perfectly conscious of the influence it can thus exert on the leadership's decisions."[24]

In addition, many factory managers are not up to their tasks and so are natural allies of conservative forces. They are afraid of any change. These cliques do not exist only on the national level, far from it:

---

[20] Císař in the 1960s became popular since he was responsible for some relaxation in culture, education, and information media. Naturally, he had his loyal Stalinist past. For example, on the liquidation of the Social Democratic Party he wrote: *"Our Party was born in a fight against the traitors of internationalism.* . . . Under the flag of internationalism we will win . . . against imperialist vampires." See his article, "Pod praporem internacionalismu" [Under the Banner of Internationalism"], *Tvorba*, xviii, 27 Apr. 1949, p. 383. His emphasis. Next year Císař wrote: "Churchill and other heralds of the American–English world domination are not hiding their inclination to destroy small nations and to subject them to the overlordship of the Anglo-Saxon race'. The supertraitors of our Republic and of its people, gentlemen Zenkl and Co., are ardently nodding to these cannibalistic plans and impudently lying. . . . The nations of the Soviet Union call Stalin their father. . . . The wise nationality policy of great Stalin will be victorious." *Tvorba*, 4 Oct. 1950, p. 960. Another year passed and Císař attacked the "criminal gang of spies and traitors" (Šling, Švermová, Clementis) and called the socialists Atlee, Morrison, Schumacher, Saragat, Vilím, and Laušman "the worst traitors and lackeys of imperialism as ferocious guarding dogs of capitalism." *Tvorba*, 22 Nov. 1951, pp. 1130–2.

[21] *S'ils me tuent . . .*, p. 151.

[22] *Ibid.*

[23] *Ibid.*, p. 152.

[24] *Ibid.*, p. 153.

It should be also understood (in the West it is not) that these conservative groups in Eastern states are bound together by invisible threads, are connected with ruling configurations in Moscow, and not only with the first secretary of the Presidium, but also with certain currents in the *apparat* of the Party and of the KGB, the Soviet secret police. If needed, they can mobilize a whole "international" of conservatives in order to exert pressures.

Such a conservative alliance was at work during the 1960s, retarding the liberalization, and "with tragic consequences" in 1968.[25]

Pelikán then described the complicated and vast system of censorship that operates everywhere. Not only all radio and television programs (including shows for children and sport reportages) as well as all press articles must be first read and passed by it, but even wedding and funeral announcements. A strict self-censorship develops but the problem is, there are no clear-cut guide-lines for the most loyal propagandist, since only the censors know the instructions, and these are constantly being changed. As a result, "more than one-third of Czechoslovakia, in fact, watched Austrian and German television, especially their political information."[26] Although the author does not mention it, the rest could not do it for technical reasons.

One of the best ways to discredit the regime was to organize question and answer programs of carefully selected journalists with Party and government leaders. Not only did the "avant-garde of the proletariat" replace the questions submitted in advance by their own, read their answers from prepared texts, but were also afraid of any meetings with other people. Quite rightly, they felt dead and ridiculous on a living screen. The program had to be stopped. It is a good example of how technological progress was undermining the carefully built up system of pretenses and appearances.

A fascinating insight into the communist bureaucratic *Castle* of Franz Kafka is provided by Pelikán's frank report on the "hierarchized information" according to which the Party *apparat* distributes news and advice of all sorts to Party leaders and propagandists on papers of different colors. Everybody knows his color scheme. When someone gets an information on a lower level of colored paper, he knows at once that for one reason or other he fell in disgrace. That means a smaller salary, a smaller apartment and country house, a less luxurious car and less expensive paid vacations in less advantageous countries (not in France but in Russia, in Bulgaria, or even in Bohemia), etc. He has to serve more devotedly in order to get back to his old layer or even to climb higher in the caste system of colored preferences. It all helps to create "a climate of political opportunism . . . where the essential preoccupations are not any more the truth about things and real problems but the reaction of your superiors to what you do or say." Everybody becomes "an opportunist and prisoner of the system."[27]

In 1964 the Party sent Pelikán to the Parliament again. The rest of the book is mostly an objective narrative of events known from many other books written by outsiders, but there are a few brief sketches of the idolatry and fear surrounding Novotný who was very sensitive about the image and who was furious when in one evening Dubček was shown on television twice talking to foreign representatives

[25] *Ibid.*, p. 154.
[26] *Ibid.*, p. 156.
[27] *Ibid.*, p. 161.

(Novotný did not allow TV crews to the Castle). It is interesting also to read that politicians' wifes watched television during their husbands' absence at political meetings and on their return told them all about it, so that the next day the General Director was called at seven in the morning to be reprimanded for what the politician (often the President of the Republic himself) did not see but only heard about. Pelikán also managed to describe the whole silly but deadly atmosphere of omnipresent police supervision, mutual suspicion, and a constant state of dread.[28]

4. Revolution by television

The resolute criticism and analysis of cultural, political economic, and social weaknesses of the regime of Novotný and the continuing pressure of communist intellectuals demanding improvements, finally forced the system to change its leadership. Pelikán's television and his skillful maneuvering of it had played its part. In 1968 he then surely, helped to make the "revolution by television." From January to August 1968 the communist intellectuals pushed the Party to further and further liberalization, winning for it large popular support but at the same time antagonizing vested interests at home and especially in the Soviet Union and in Ulbricht's and Gomulka's bureaucracies. Pelikán was one of the few pre-January media leaders who did not have to be changed.

The National Assembly elected him chairman of its Foreign Affairs Committee. It meant again meeting top foreign dignitaries.

During the invasion, Pelikán led the "underground" television broadcasting from improvized studios on more channels than had been in use until then, before Soviet soldiers occupied regular studios. A paper, published and distributed by the occupation forces in Czech, professed to know that Pelikán "gave an order to prepare all equipment already during the meetings in Čierná and Bratislava in order, in case of an eventual conflict, to start broadcasting without interruption from prearranged places."[29] In his book Pelikán does not boast about his exploits during the invasion week but praises his technicians. It would be only to his honor if he had acted as blamed.

Pelikán also helped to organize the clandestine Communist Party Fourteenth Congress in a Prague factory. Judging by some of his remarks about suggestions to Dubček to hide in a factory and lead at least a diplomatic fight, if not a military one, against the invaders, Pelikán belonged to the younger generation of communist leaders who could have led the Party in more decisive ways than was the case under Dubček's leadership or the lack of it.

5. Carnegijsky: How to turn friends into enemies

Because he was on the list of comrades the Soviet Party bosses insisted must be eliminated at once, he lost his directorship of the television networks but was sent to the Czechoslovak Embassy in Rome as councellor for press and culture. In 1969 he resigned, when he was being called back home, and as an exile published the

---

[28] *Ibid.*, pp. 158–67.
[29] *Zprávy*, no. 11, 15 Mar. 1969, p. 4.

proceedings and materials of the secret Party Congress in many languages,[30] as well as a top secret Party report, *The Czechoslovak Political Trials, 1950–1954.*[31]

Since 1969 Pelikán has been fighting for "socialism with a human face" from abroad, and in Rome publishing a journal, *Listy,* with occasional French and Italian editions. He seems to have established good contacts with some leading Italian and French communists as well as socialists. He often participated in public meetings, denouncing neo-Stalinist trends of international communism not only through speeches and interviews in France and Italy, but also elsewhere; for example, in Sweden.

On 30 October 1969 Pelikán was deprived of his Communist Party membership, exactly thirty years after his adherence. He did not feel any regrets but rather a relief: "Strangely, my refusal to obey orders of the Prague authorities and my decision to stay in exile, created in me a feeling of internal liberation."[32]

At a press conference in February 1974, when asked by editors of the Parisian weekly *Express* if he still considered himself to be a communist, Pelikán answered cryptically: "Who can say today about himself if he is a communist or not? It is sad that only experience teaches a man certain things."[33]

After a few suspicious events when he felt threatened by Soviet or Czech agents, on 4 February 1975 he received by mail a package with explosives. Unharmed — but for how long? — he decided to write his memoirs. He revealed quite a lot but, I suspect, by far not all that could be of interest to historians and political scientists. One reason for it might be that he still remained a fighter for socialism, if not for communism, and he still considers, as we could see, much of his political past just and right. Therefore, we should look up some of his own persistent illusions or misjudgements which, on one side, make it possible for him to range himself along with many West European Leftist militants but, on the other side, make it impossible for him to see the full truth about the communist movement and to completely break away from his past and from communist obsessions. But, naturally, he is a politician and as such, as other politicians, can hardly distinguish between his private, personal beliefs and his public postures. It is quite an organic political whole.

6. The beliefs of youth

For instance, judging from passages in his book, so often quoted in these pages, Pelikán still believes that the"October Revolution" was not a *coup d'état* executed by professional revolutionaries, organized in a para-military pro-totalitarian conspiracy, quite inappropriately called party (since it wanted to and did destroy all other parties), but a genuine, people's revolution which was good, progressive (and not retrogressive), as well as performed not only in the name of the proletariat, but actually by it and for it. He still believes that the originally quite democratic

---

[30] *Panzer überrollen den Parteitag: Protokoll und Dokumente des 14. Parteitages der KPC am 22. August 1968* (Vienna, Europa, 1969). In French, *Le Congrès clandestin* (Paris: Seuily, 1970). And *The Secret Vysočany Congress* (London, 1971).

[31] (London, Macdonald, 1971); *Das unterdrückte Dossier* (Vienna: Europa, 1970).

[32] *S'ils me tuent. . .*, pp. 239 and 242.

[33] According to Slovak *Pravda,* 19 Nov. 1974, p. 6.

soviets have lost their democratic character only under Stalin and not, as in fact, already under Lenin. I would say that, together with some ideological concepts, these are some of the bases of his rather authoritarian, non-democratic, and therefore dangerous message. He has never lost his admiration for Lenin and remains to this day a Leninist, with all the imminent threats to humanity implicit in this political attitude.

From Marxism Pelikán took over and keeps the supposed division of humanity into antagonistic classes. The world is for him still divided into the imperialist, capitalist world and the progressive, although deformed, socialist camp. He carefully remembers to attack American foreign policies every time he thinks it is appropriate, in order not to be accused of having sold out to the "Western imperialists."

Although Pelikán is probably the man who after the invasion did in politics in the West more than any of his comrades who stayed abroad, he seems to be proving again what during 1968 was quite obvious; namely, that writers, historians, philosophers, economists were better and faster willing to make admissions of past mistakes and to give up at least some of their Leninist or Marxist prejudices in order to start behaving in a liberal, democratic way than the politicians. It will be recalled that the intellectuals kept pushing the politicians into further reforms. As was recently said by an American practitioner of politics, power is the most potent aphrodisiac. It does not, however, only attract females to politicians, it has a great charm for its holders. They cannot give it up easily. Writers, philosophers, etc., are after other goals and virtues that can help in sustaining them but politicians usually do not have anything to fall back on in case of failure. Pelikán in 1975 clearly still believed that much of his own and of his Party's criminal activities between 1945 and 1968 are justified and proper. In 1979 he was elected in Italy to the European Parliament.

7. Why do they collaborate?

It is hard to give up the ideals and beliefs of youth. Pelikán, therefore, can introduce us to the problem of people who did not leave the country after the invasion as he did but who, on the contrary, decided to serve the occupying power. This question, how and why can they do it, was left without an answer in the sociological chapter of this work. Why collaborators such as Gustáv Husák or Radovan Richta, to name just two, can go on working for a system whose milder variation they themselves have decisively condemned previously?

First, it can be said that they, most probably, share the same beliefs just observed even in Pelikán who has exiled himself. It is hard and sometimes impossible to give up the ideals of youth. Gustáv Husák and Radovan Richta till August 1969 acted and spoke as if they could subscribe to Pelikán's nostalgic statement: "We were rehabilitating the ideal of our youth."[34] It is extremely hard to give up the whole life of devoted service to the Party and to admit that uncounted crimes were committed for false reasons. It is almost impossible to accept the fact that instead of

[34] *S'ils me tuent. . .*, p. 198.

serving progress and happiness, a whole life was spent serving a murderous tyrant and a criminal organization. An attempt, therefore, has to be made again and again to prove that it was not all wrong, that the principles were good, even most of the actions were beneficial and only some mistakes, some deformations have taken place against the will of the protagonists. There were quite a few suicides in Czechoslovakia during 1968 and later on of people who recognized the whole truth and could not go on living with this knowledge. Only very strong people can realize that throughout their life they had served a murderous cause. It was difficult for the Nazis; it is difficult for the communists.[35] Those who decide to continue their effort can still hope that they will help to make the system better and to sanctify by future progress the horrors of the past.

Second, in the twilight period of the closing half of the Dubček era, between August 1968 and April 1969, it was obvious that to cross the line definitely, to abandon the dream of cooperation with the Russians, and get to the other side of the border was very hard for people who grew up in the *apparat*. People like Černík, Císař, Mlynář, and others attempted to make some compromise that would allow them to stay in power, in spite of everything. There was even a popular slogan: do not give up your positions. Especially those *apparatchiks* who did not know anything about the other half of the world from their own personal experience, found it easy not to trust liberal and democratic trends since they did not believe in their practicality. Pelikán recalls how Husák sincerely did not believe when he mentioned that in France or in England a spokesman of the Opposition or even worse, a communist, would be allowed to criticize the government or to openly defend his views on the Radio or on state television. As Gomulka, he obstinately preferred to "remain prisoner of their own propaganda."[36]

People of a dogmatic, autocratic character found it impossible to really abandon the Party directives and its system of hierarchical power. All friends and enemies who know Husák agree on one point — and we have quoted some remarks to this effect previously — that his nature is very authoritarian. And the Communist party by its character kept attracting this type of person. A combination of all these features creates ideal bosses for the Party of police socialism. Without it, they would not know what to do in order to make a living and to feel supreme.

Third, in a tragic situation such as developed in Czechoslovakia in August 1968, it is understandable and natural that some leading communist personalities, with Husák at their head, decided to accept the situation as real and as "realists" to accommodate themselves to it, in spite of all the warnings expressed by historians, philosophers, and political scientists against it. The Soviets repeatedly threatened that in case of a lack of a viable solution à la Husák, they would create military havoc and drown the "counter-revolution" in a horrible blood-bath. People like Husák and Štrougal, I believe, preferred to "save as much as possible." Such a saving operation does not have to take place exclusively for nationalistic reasons. A mixture of nationalism and of an international feeling of responsibility for the

---

[35] A statement by Rudolf Margolius, previously quoted, could serve as a motto to this drama of conscience: "If it all really were a fraud, then all I have done would make me an accomplice in a monstrous crime." See Kovály-Kohák, *The Victors and the Vanquished*, p. 102.

[36] *S'ils me tuent. . .*, pp. 200–1.

whole movement could be involved. I can imagine that at least some of them might have been thinking along these or similar lines: "Here we are stuck with those stupid bullies, arrogant, determined idiots, with those Russians armed to the teeth. No one from the West will ever help us in the least, we must do as well as we can, save what can be saved and survive — till the moment when the Russian strength and imperialism weakens or disappears. Maybe a new relaxation and a new Thaw will come up in Moscow, it is bound to, they have such enormous economic and political problems on their hands. Then our time will come to improve the conditions again. Till then, we have to be tough, especially when talking, smile at the Russians, go on kissing these brutes, and to try to outsmart them."

Some of them might even have decided to stay inside the system, in spite of the nasty things they would have to do to keep their positions, in order to go on fighting on the enemy territory, in some kind of a personal partisan war, taking advantage of the program of integration of the whole satellite empire, in order to soften up the whole gigantic dictatorship from inside, with the help of similarly inclined Poles, Ukrainians, Russians, Hungarians, etc.; in a way they did this rather successfully in Novotný's Czechoslovakia. They know how rotten, senile, the empire is getting and they know also that individual satellite attempts at a revolution are clearly doomed in advance. Therefore, Moscow is the target. Is it too illusionistic to imagine anything like that? Knowing the character of some of the communists and realizing the enormity of the problem, I do not think that it is farfetched.

Fourth, some of those who stayed and joined the "normalizers," even some of the most important ones, could be American, British, French, or Yugoslav and Chinese agents. Western secret services, if they are not all run by Soviet agents, as sometimes happened and is probably still happening, should close shop if they do not have their people among the communist leaders in Eastern Europe. This and other things just said are naturally known to the Russians or at least suspected by them and therefore people like Husák are surrounded by concentrated circles of collaborators, agents, and supervisors, so that all possible danger could always be eliminated in time. But it would be really surprising if at least some of the communists who had spent decades in a conspiracy were not able to develop ways of using it for its own destruction or moderation.

Fifth, on the reverse side of this coin, are the "desperados" of the communist movement, people who have been Soviet agents for years, people who have committed innumerable crimes and who do not have any hope of saving their skin but by continuing collaboration. In Budapest these were the last fighters against the victorious revolution. In Prague those people kept sending anonymous letters, engaged in printing of anti-Semitic leaflets, cooperated with the Soviet invasion, and went on serving the secret police. They have nothing to lose any more except their lives in a change of the regime. They must defend it till the last breath. Here belongs also the category of sadists, mentally sick people, brutes who find their best time and employment only in this type of a system, where their criminal tendencies do not lead them into private crimes — as would be the case in a democratic, lawful society — but where they can use all their talents in the service of an organized criminal society. Every nation has a small percentage of potential criminals in its population. In totalitarian dictatorships these people, the real scum of the earth, get their best chance and can really enjoy themselves, at the same time feeling proud that they are serving the great cause of the pure race or of the pure class.

Sixth, there is the unfortunate group of people who at one time or another were caught in the net of the secret police whose files contained compromising materials about them. They colloborate because otherwise they would have their secrets exposed. Often, they become informers and join the category previously discusses. Sometimes they do it in order to save members of their families or relatives. Only a general burning of all police files and cadre records could save them from humiliation. That might be one of the reasons why burning of these files has been popping up in all attempts at a rebellion in Central and Eastern Europe.

After the invasion of August we can almost be absolutely sure of one thing: there are no more idealists helping the regime, but only cynics, opportunists, agents, hidden enemies, or very disreputable characters. That was one of the most interesting features of the new ruling and supporting group under the occupation — the very low professional level of people willing to work for the quisling government and also their moral and personal quality. The lack of available helpers was such that many police agents had to come out of hiding and take over editorial jobs in periodicals and other public places. The system had to reach the bottom. Desperately, it also tried to recruit willing youngsters but in contrast with the year 1948, when the same method was used (with the well-known incredibly low levels of literary production), this time there were no idealist enthusiasts among them.

Maybe it should be noted that any combination of the categories described above probably appears in practice more than any pure type.

According to some reports from Czechoslovakia, there are people who do not belong to the activists (as all the previous types do) but who are in charge of positions which are not too important. This category could be called "without any face" since the regime puts into some posts people who never, under any regime, stepped forward in any decisive way, who always remained neutral, colorless, and therefore cannot be blamed either for sectarianism, reformism, conservatism, or any other possible deviation from the changing but requested quality of X. They do not have and do not claim any merits, not even of workers' origin, they just are and always have been without any opinions of their own. They are now employed in positions they could never attain in any normal circumstance and therefore are willing to serve the regime as long as they are paid. They will never become fanatics, they will never win anybody for the system, and they are incapable of leading. But the system is happy that they exist and can be put behind the office desks.[37]

8. Towards Euro-communism?

Jiří Pelikán was disappointed when the Communist Party proved to be incapable of defending the country against a foreign invasion. Only the much more

---

[37] A good portrait of these servitors was drawn in an anonymous letter from Czechoslovakia, published in *Listy*, III, 2 (April 1973), pp. 8–10.

openly nationalistic communist parties of Yugoslavia, Albania, China, and Rumania managed to keep the brotherly Russian tanks away from their capitals. The Czechoslovak democratic version of communism — which appeared more *in spe* than *in facto* and did not have enough time to develop or stop the trend — by going beyond national communism made it possible for several West European communist parties to explore the possibilities of a larger conception, commonly now called Euro-communism.

Czech and Slovak communists stressed the importance of liberal and democratic principles for the implementation of a modern, European and not Asiatic, type of socialist society. In the meantime, the shock of the Soviet military suppression of this attempt and, thanks to Soviet dissidents, a better knowledge of the real conditions of life in the Soviet Union had become commonplace. It could no longer be denied by the communist parties of the West. In order to keep or augment their voting appeal, several of them began to disengage themselves publicly from the unattractive image of Soviet communism. The Czechoslovak program of 1968 came as a potent stimulation of a non-Russian variation of communism.

Because of the Machiavellian character of the whole communist movement since its re-formulation by Lenin, the problem is obvious: is it a sincere change of heart or is it just another in the long series of tactical maneuvers to fool the friends and enemies alike? Jiří Pelikán, who since 1969 has been working incessantly in order to spread in Western Europe the experience of his country with Bolshevism, at the end of his book stipulated three conditions for the creation of an "authentic socialism:" (1) transformation of communist parties; (2) existence of strong socialist parties that would not only co-operate but also compete with them; and (3) democratization of the Soviet Union and of the European East. According to Pelikán, without basic changes in East Europe, the West European communist parties would not be capable of successfully opposing the usual Soviet hegemony.[38] Especially the first and third conditions are so demanding and so far very poorly supported by factual evidence that it is not surprising to hear that their author, after he had met most of the protagonists involved, is very skeptical about their chance of really being fulfilled.

There is a vast and steadily growing literature on the subject. Most of the authors — with the exception of some hopeful Euro-communists — are not optimistic.

The worst enemy of Euro-communism is the history of Soviet and satellite communism. Every time the leopard tries to change its spots it can be pointed out that the same show has already been seen several times. In the Italian, and before that in the Portuguese, case, the successful strategy of a gradual but complete takeover by the Communist Party of Czechoslovakia has been serving as a warning to all who would like to trust their communist colleagues because they sound so trustworthy and seem to be so needed. A new book written on this instructive experience was published recently. Its last sentences read as follows:

> In fact, among models of the technique of seizure of power the one of Prague, perfecting the *salami tactics*, takes an honorable place on the side of the Leninist-Trotskyist technique of 1917 and of those used by Mao Tse-tung and marshal Tito. People always refer to it, feel inspired by

[38] *S'ils me tuent. . .*, pp. 283-6.

it, or dread it. However, as often happens in such a case, since the *Prince* of Machiavelli, a study of the Prague *coup* can serve not only those who dream about installing a Marxist totalitarian regime in their turn, but also those who in all lucidity wish to defend perspectives of social progress associated to democratic freedoms.[39]

Several years ago, the Italian writer and political theorist, Ignazio Silone, talked in an interview about the "ideological and institutional decadence" of the Russian State and answered his own question in a literary and persuasive style: "Can an institution change again into a free movement? . . . No, no one had ever seen a river remounting to its source.[40]

What is my opinion? I think that there are basically two different and largely contradictory trends involved.

First, the negative one. The character of any communist party is principally anti-democratic, and therefore reactionary and anti-humanistic. The Bolshevik party was created by Lenin according to militaristic rules as a disciplined, strictly hierarchical formation of professional political soldiers in order to seize power, destroy by any means the opposition and any nucleus from which resistance could develop to the absolute monopoly of the command system. From German military doctrine Lenin took over many tactics which would help his "party" (conspiracy) to storm any fortress and stay on the top. Throughout more than sixty years of its history, the Soviet Union, in the hands of the general staff of the Communist Party, enriched this Leninist patrimony of shrewd and ruthless techniques, so that the party militants could proudly see the modern Machiavellian system working successfully again and again. Naturally, with this mixture of political and military methods and structure, there is no chance at all of ever building any socialism or communism worth living under. But the real bosses of this police empire are cynical about such contemptible idealism. All they need Marxism-Leninism for is legitimacy of their dictatorial rule over the masses and of their imperialist domination of other countries. With such a movement in undiluted form there can be no lasting co-operation that would not lead to subjugation.

Second is the positive trend. There is a strong historical movement away from the Leninist misuse of Marxist and Leftist socialist ideals. It has been abundantly proved that the Soviet model is the wrong way: it leads to massacres of millions of people and it does not appreciably improve conditions which could be ameliorated easier and without so much destruction by other liberal and democratic means. Repeated failures of the Soviet Union and of its satellite empire in all fields of human endeavor have brought a substantial decline in the attractiveness of the Soviet Union and of its ideology. This trend cannot be reversed without a radical change in Soviet outlook and behavior. The last chance, offered by Czech and Slovak communists, the Russians badly missed. It could have meant a turning-point in history and could have offered the Soviet Union a dignified way out of the impasse of its Czarist and Stalinist past. Understandably, some Western

[39] Francois Fejtö: *Le coup de Prague* [*Prague Coup of 1948*] (Paris: Seuil, 1976), p. 233.

[40] In *L'Avanti*, quoted by J. N. in *Le Monde*, 4 Feb. 1970, p. 8. For a detailed review of major opinions on the subject, see my Ph. D. thesis, "Czechoslovakia between East and West: The Changing Role of Communist Intellectuals, 1948–1968," University of Geneva, 1978.

communists would like to save their movement from participation in this historical decline.[41]

The gradual moving away from the Leninist-Stalinist model could be observed everywhere — not onlu on the tragicomic heros presented here but in Western and other communist and Leftist circles, even in the Soviet Union itself. There is a historical chance of healing the split of the European socialist and liberal Left, which had originated with the demoniac Lenin, so full of determined hate. Lenin and Stalin knew how to concentrate and use all that is negative and destructive in human nature. It took humanity quite a long time to build enough antibodies against the new version of religious-political psychoses that have been plaguing it for thousands of years. Can there be a worse defeat for a movement, which began by a general attack on so-called bourgeois values of various freedoms, than when throughout its empire nations are demanding exactly those values as absolutely necessary for life? Lenin lost in a competition not only against Masaryk but also against Julius Martov and other democratic socialists. He showed that he and his party can grab power and hold it. But he also demonstrated that he or his followers cannot construct any decent system of socialism.

The problem of the unification of the Left, after so many decades of separation, is that it is taking place in a world basically divided into two antagonistic but also co-operating blocs, led by two superpowers whose leaders are in agreement that it is against their interest to face an eventually united socialist and democratic Left. So far not only the Russians but also the Americans repeatedly proved in Budapest, Santo Domingo, Prague, and Santiago that in their respective zones of influence they are not willing to allow any new combination of socialism and democracy. In such experiments both partners, rightly or wrongly, suspect the other side of a subterfuge that would upset the balance of power. The point of view, naturally, is different in the above named capitals and in Rome, Paris, Warsaw, or Geneva. For the moment, there does not seem to be any real possibility of an agreement on a progressive development towards both socialism and democracy in many parts of the world (with the notable exception of Great Britain and Scandinavia).

It is not sure if Soviet leaders (or how many of them) support the strategy of Euro-communism as a Trojan horse. But it seems that the U.S. Government still prefers the stalement as it is. Possibly it might also hope that the French pattern of evolution rather than the Italian one would continue its course, that the Communist Party would remain Stalinist and the Socialist Party would grow in strength, gradually out-distancing the communists.

Here we come to a crucial point. Euro-communism might be just another step on the sliding scale of an honorable retreat from Leninist-Stalinist positions. In a similar way Trotskyism used to serve as an intermediary station between the two opposite termini of Leninism and democracy. Disillusioned militants usually do not go all the way at once but proceed in stages, shedding one illusion after another, in

---

[41] "The Communist Parties of Western Europe do not want to be drawn along by the economic and ideological downfall of the U.S.S.R. . . . The West is henceforth an ideological threat to the Soviet system but the U.S.S.R. became a military threat to the West." Emmanuel Todd, *La chute finale: Essai sur la décomposition de la sphère soviétique* [*The Final Fall: Essay on the Decay of the Soviet Sphere*] (Paris Robert Laffont, 1976), pp. 302 and 163.

gradual steps. If this is true and if the democratic world could continue demonstrating its greater creativity, social justice, and endurance, then the waiting game might be just the right tactics for erosion of Soviet communism, without the risk that Latin countries of western and southern Europe would be swallowed up by the Soviet bloc or by a consolidation of a Western bloc of non-Soviet but communist states. That, of course, leaves Eastern Europe at the mercy of the Soviet Union which would probably be always willing to crush local rebellions by sending its armies on maneuvers into its "Allies'" territories. They would just help the Americans and other West European democrats in persuading new generations about the dangerous character of the Bolshevik monster. Although Czechoslovakia in 1968 might have been pointing in the right direction, in the stalemated situation it appears, at least for the moment, to be the biggest loser.

Conclusion

IN 1968 the communist intellectuals of Czechoslovakia lost everything materially but won much spiritually. In 1948 they could be used as fools by the Soviet Union for its takeover of Czechoslovakia but in 1968 not fanatical and naïve minds but well-oiled tanks were needed for the job. The difference between these two invasions — one shrewd, the other brutal — can be employed to measure the power of Soviet ideological influence: it was overwhelming in 1948, but almost nil in 1968. In twenty years, the charm had gone. What illusions did not disappear between February 1948 and August 1968, the tanks finished off. Some Czech caricatures expressed the conflict: pens against machine guns or Soviet armed forces progressing, in a military fashion, through art galleries. Soviet ideology and tactics were easily victorious in 1948 but almost useless in 1968. Ideological expansion had to be replaced by naked military occupation. After World War II, in West Germany and Japan, the Americans, incredibly, managed to make friends of defeated enemies. The Russians, surprisingly, achieved the opposite: they created enemies out of friends.

Aberration

On the basis of our case studies of some thirty communist intellectuals a list could be established of motivating attractions which, around the year 1948, led them to their pro-Soviet, anti-Western, and anti-democratic attitudes. After the experience with the economic crisis of the 1930s, after the Munich appeasement — considered in the ČSR as treason by the West — and after six years of German occupation during a destructive war, it was easier than ever before to believe in the complete breakdown of the West, with the coming end of capitalism, and in the definite rise of the East, with its socialism. The ideals of justice, equality, and progress could then be associated with the Soviet Union because of an almost absolute lack of knowledge of it or because of an obstinate refusal to see the nasty facts. For power-thirsty people its impressive power was hard to avoid. Its aggressive propaganda was skillfully disseminated by professional peddlers of millenial dreams. Important historical traditions, attaching the hope for survival of the Czechs and Slovaks to the big Slav brother in the East, helped to abandon the prevailing orientation to the West with its habits of rationalism, liberalism, and humanism. In the post-war situation, the native Masaryks and Benešes were no match for the foreign Leninists, Stalinists, and Zhdanovists.

The professed unity of the Left, cooperation with the Catholics, deceitful programs of pluralistic democracy and workers' self-management were seriously believed by many communist militants to be sincere programs. Fraudulent were the promises to preserve small shops and services as well as independent peasantry, and intellectual freedoms. All this was part of a supposedly special, national way to socialism. At the same time, communist intellectuals believed in the reality and historical necessity of a class struggle but thought that the means used will be mostly non-violent. Naturally, as communists, they shared the conviction that violence was necessary and beneficial every time that a "class enemy" refused to give up voluntarily. Anyway, all class enemies were condemned by science and history and had to be swept away. The image of the Devil was suitably modernized.

Among themselves, the communists enjoyed, at least for a short time, the feeling of a fighting fraternity, carried to victory by a well-thought-out and proved Marxist-Leninist-Stalinist conspiracy, which they considered to be a scientific theory.

The Soviet Union was, as they believed, a successful model to be copied in the main, voluntarily and with enthusiasm. The new world of truth, justice, and brotherly love was supposed to be winning over the old and doomed world of pecuniary interests, greed, destruction, exploitation, and alienation. A completely new man and a new society had to be built.[1]

Most of the communist intellectuals participated in the implementation of the Soviet example. Without much resistance, it quickly replaced the "Czechoslovak way to socialism" which was thoroughly condemned in the trials of the 1950s as treasonable. (A lot of material was then obtained, for future use, against Italian and French communist leaders, implicating them as American, British, French, etc., spies.) A Soviet *Gleichschaltung* was avoided only by Tito's Yugoslavia, in whose denouncement Czech and Slovak Party intellectuals participated as eagerly as in the political and often physical elimination of their own, as claimed, Zionist, bourgeois nationalist, and cosmopolitan Western agents.

The fanatical belief in Stalin and in the Party was not ostensibly shaken even by mass riots and strikes of the workers' class, culminating in 1953. Some propagandists were taken aback and from then on tried to avoid confrontation with the people. "Bourgeois remnants of capitalism" and "social-democratism and Masarykism" in workers' minds, however, could be blamed for their resistance.

Recovery

Only Khrushchev's attack on Stalin's anti-communist mass murders managed to undermine the foundations of the whole elaborate edifice. Those communists who were personally hurt during the purges and those who could hear from them about the horrors, perpetrated by the Soviet and Soviet-trained specialists in scientific torture, had to realize the criminal nature of the regime. For some Party educated professionals this discovery then waited in the CPC archives. It opened up a slow and incomplete rehabilitation of the victims.

In the 1960s, travelling finally permitted both in the Eastern and Western direction, helped people to see through the complex web of lies. It was possible

---

[1] "The dangers are obvious to the wise, while fools do not find anything difficult," Maimonides in his *Book on Asthma*, as quoted by Joshua O. Leibowitz, "Maimonides in the History of Medicine," *Ariel* (Jerusalem), no. 41, p. 38.

to learn the truth about the backwardness of Russia in almost everything. The freedom in the West seemed to be incredibly great and so was the consumer's paradise in Western countries when compared with their own scarcity of goods at home in all but military hardware. Access to Western literature, theatre, fine arts, and sciences stimulated their spirit, eager to live, create, and participate in an organic development of man and society. When the economic crisis in Czechoslovakia, together with the second wave of de-Stalinization, initiated by Khrushchev, liberalized the conditions first in Bratislava and then in Prague and Brno, the communist intellectuals, often prodded to it by their non-communist colleagues, began to create an alternate program of a less dictatorial and stupid socialism.

Gradually, they were able to take over many Party positions in the media, at universities, and scientific institutions, forcing the dogmatists into a helpless defense of lost causes. Using film, drama, literature, Marxism, sociology, journalism and television, they undermined the self-confidence of the masters by showing how ridiculous they were and how different a decent life should be. In spite of personal disagreements and jealousies, the communist intellectuals, encouraging and complementing each other, prepared the Party for a change in top positions and for a radical switch in policies. The anti-democratic Leninist party was used for a democratization by the cultural élite. They managed to win over the "superstructure" of the system but not its entrenched conservative power in the police and in the *apparat*. When they attempted, quite successfully, to base their continuing attack on these real seats of power by demanding and obtaining large public support, they also provoked the sensitive nerves of the bureaucratic, police, and armed forces of the Soviet Union, East Germany, and Poland who, in order to preserve their own monopoly of power and imperial hegemony, took over Czechoslovakia militarily. Then followed the gradual routing of the democratizing and liberalizing forces.

Lost and found

In the dark of the night light shines brighter than during a normal day. First, the communist intellectuals rediscovered ethical values and asserted their importance. Truth, justice, tolerance, decency — far from being bourgeois prejudices — proved to be extremely important principles for any society. Even materialist economists came to the conclusion that without them socialist economy cannot be healthy and prosperous. The government, courts, public and almost all in private life practiced the law of the jungle. No one could feel safe and in order to survive everybody had to lie, cheat, and steal, while, in addition, the big shots could, literally, get away with multiple murders.

In the 1950s, a Polish film, *Eve Wants to Sleep*, demonstrated the prevalent, selfish violence in the socialist paradise by a short sequence: In a street a man walks carrying a briefcase. From a door another man comes out, runs after him with a brick in his hand, hits him over the head with it, and takes the fallen man's briefcase. As he walks away, another man armed with a brick hits his target, grabs the briefcase, only to become himself a victim after a few steps, and so on and so on.

In the 1960s, Miloš Forman expressed the same situation in a people's democracy, just a little gentler, in his *Firemen's Ball*. Everybody steals; in the dark, everything disappears from the banquet table. Professional standards are at their lowest: when a house is on fire, the same stealing voluntary firemen (the Party workers' avant-garde is also voluntary) do not save the burning house, just pull the old man's bed out of the house into the snow. The old man is left to sleep out in the cold.

In the prevalent corruption and lawlessness the abandoned values had to be resurrected. We could observe how almost all of our selected characters dropped the ideas of a relative class truth or class justice and returned to plain, non-class ethics. A widow of one of the hanged Party leaders, Mariam Šlingová, entitled her book typically, with the Masarykian motto, *Truth Will Prevail*; not Party truth, that was a deadly lie, just truth.

Liberal and democratic rights, such as freedom of speech, of assembly, of opposition, and legal and constitutional safeguards became major catchwords because everybody had suffered from their absence. Their stress of them had the freshness of newly discovered basic values. In more sophisticated and spoiled societies that take them for granted or even see them sometimes misused by corrupted crooks or radical elements, their importance is often missed and is not so obvious as in criminal states. Workers deprived of their unions, voting power, strikes, and representatives realize how important they are for the level of real wages, standard of living, safety of work, and other basic benefits. Writers, depending on censors and policemen for permission to publish, understand the necessity of creative freedoms more than those who do not have to fight for them. All professional people soon discover that to have uneducated primitives, loyal to Party dogmas and proud of their stupidity, as bosses, can be very frustrating. The history of the 1960s was in Czechoslovakia mostly an uninterrupted attempt to get decision-making power out of the hands of Party hacks into the hands of specialists. All liberal and democratic values, about whose importance in a Western society it is so easy to doubt (and to dream about their replacement by some collectivist ideals or discipline), proved their validity and absolute necessity in a dictatorial regime, which had fulfilled the supposedly higher dream. To be submerged in a communist dictatorship seems to be the best way to open closed eyes to the significance of democracy and human rights. What else have the Chartists 77 been demanding?

Realism

Again and again, we could witness economists, writers, historians, philosophers, and others demanding *reality* and throwing away falsehoods and illusions. The tension between promise and reality became unbearable. Economists could not plan and manage factories on the bases of false and incomplete statistics. There were no "real" prices of anything. Writers were supposed to realistically describe non-existent socialism and celebrate an anti-social system. Historians felt lost in the labyrinth of constantly changing Party lines about the past and the present. Philosophers instead of dialectical materialism were obliged to handle subjective and idealistic Party dogmas and find properly sounding formulas for nonsense. All desperately tried but had to give up in complete disillusionment. Those who did not take refuge in cynicism and power, kept searching for truth and reality.

They had to find out that the Party did not represent the working class, that the bureaucrats were not an enlightened avant-garde of the proletariat but rather an organized self-appointed and self-perpetuating caste exploiting the masses who often felt class hate for them and blamed them for everything that was wrong. They had to discover that socialism without democracy meant a return to slavery, that barrack socialism could not make life pleasant and happy, and that the real masters of everybody were the secret police, the *apparat*, and Soviet agents. They also often came to the conclusion that the enormous difference between words and deeds, between the pretense and fact was particular to the Soviet version of communism and has been in the movement since Lenin's times. Ideals were confronted with reality and the gap between them had to be closed if all were not to be exposed as a complete fraud.

The school of realism continued after the Soviet invasion. Many Czechs and Slovaks became aware of the fact that statesmen crying, instead of fighting, in the moment of truth might be good enough for tragic stories but definitely not good at all for actual international conflicts. A lack of accurate knowledge of allies and enemies does not pay. A known lack of courage invites aggression. Czechoslovak leaders, beginning with Beneš and ending with Dubček, liked and idealized their French or Russian supports, asking for trouble and disappointment. A mature nation with an experienced leadership should be better able to get through crises and withstand adversity. Especially the young generation seemed to be making a decision that the next time the Czechs and Slovaks would not command just sorrowful pity for their pacific and decent loss but rather admiration for their courage and fighting qualities. Only time will tell if a nation's — or at least its leadership's — character can be so decisively modified. The determination to become realistic, however, was obvious.

Russian tyranny

In all fields of specialization, Czech and Slovak communist intellectuals little by little recognized that Soviet prescriptions were not suitable for a highly developed Central European country and that native traditions and trends should be substituted for the failing Soviet model of socialism. That also meant pluralism and democracy instead of a monopolistic dictatorship, trust of people instead of its systematic distrust, suggestions instead of commands, and allowance of freedom, spontaneity, organic evolution, and creative life instead of the Leninist-Stalinist system of marching orders and detailed directives from above. All changes in this direction were, naturally, revolting to Leninist dictators, used to administrative and militaristic methods of their command system. After all, the Russians did not have any experience with freedoms, except in the short period of a few months between the two autocrats, the last of the Romanovs and the first of the Bolshevik dynasty.

The longer they lived under the Soviet system the better the communist intellectuals of Czechoslovakia perceived the constants of Russian policies, apparent both in Czarist and Bolshevik times — a reactionary system of government, centralization, police methods, a certain perfidy towards friends and enemies alike, sentimental hypocrisy, cruelty, clumsiness, imperialism, narrowness of mind, intolerance, and possessiveness. At Čierná the members of the Czechoslovak Politburo were told: "You are ours, and we will not let you go!" All arguments about a human face of socialism, people's enthusiasm for the new course, attractiveness of reformed socialism to Western masses, about needs for democratization and liberalization, or for a real internationalist movement of equals were, of course, sounding like naïve dreams against such a brutal and simple attitude.

The recognition of the ugly truth about the Soviet Union and its export of a police and military socialism was, however, a relatively slow process, retarded by many layers of illusions. Even after the defeat in 1968 many Czech and Slovak communists would have liked to keep their hopes about the temporary character of Soviet imperialism and talked about "contemporary" Soviet leadership and its passing aggressivity, as if it were something exceptional in the history of the Soviet empire. They refused to realize, at least for some time, that these features had existed in Soviet domestic and external policies since Lenin's and Trotsky's times and that, equally, internal forms of Russian communism have never been "deformed" by Stalin or Brezhnev but formed by Lenin and kept ever since, even if on occasion, following Lenin's precepts, they were strengthened or temporarily relaxed by Stalin or other Soviet leaders.

The permanence of some basic constituent factors of Leninism-Stalinism has been and remains problem number one of the whole communist movement. They are hard to grasp and believe since to normal people, even to experienced politicians, they seem to be too inhuman to be possible. But the title of the Czechoslovak version of communism expressed more than is at first apparent about the difference between the Soviet and a European type of socialism. Therefore, there is hardly any realistic hope of democratic communism coming from communist parties without their express repudiation of all of these features. Enrico Berlinguer in 1976/7 sounded very much like Klement Gottwald in 1946/7. And then came the *coup* and all, including Gottwald, lived unhappily ever after.

Bibliography

A. Primary sources

1. Archives

Beseda Slovak, Geneva (especially letters to and from Eduard Beneš during World War II).
Dr. Johann Wolfgang Bruegel's private collection of main Czech dailies and weeklies from the 1940s
  and 1950s in the attic of his London house.
Johann Gottfried Herder Institut, Marburg an der Lahn.
Radio Free Europe, Munich and New York.

2. Unpublished documents

ČESKOSLOVENSKÁ AKADEMIE VĚD

Presidium. "Stanovisko." *Věstník ČSAV*, no. 5, Oct. 1968.
Komise k prošetření kádrových opatření a pro rehabilitaci v ČSAV. "Projev
  předsedy akademika Miroslava Katětova" and "Závěrečná zpráva komise." *Věstník
  ČSAV*, no. 5, Sept.-Oct. 1969, pp. 489-99.
Ústřední archiv. "Stručný přehled vývoje československé akademie věd v letech 1952-1972."
  Věstník ČSAV, no. 6, Dec. 1972, pp. 289-96.

3. Published documents

Czech Government. "Zpráva o vývoji národního hospodářství a plnění plánu v I. pololetí 1973:
  Naše hospodárství se rozvíjí dynamicky," *Rudé právo*, 23 July 1973.
CPC. *Akční program Komunistické strany Československa*. Prague, Svoboda, 1968; 64 pages.
"Why Was Alexander Dubček Expelled from Party Ranks."
  Rudé právo, 18 July 1970.
Presidium ÚV KSČ. "Dokumenty: Plán práce orgánu ÚV KSČ a II. pololetí 1969. Hlavní cíle a
  postup jejich zabezpečování," *Zpravodaj KSČ*, no. 22, 6 Aug. 1969.
ÚV KSČ. Plénum 14-17 November 1968. "Hlavní úkoly strany v nejbližším období. Rezoluce
  listopadového pléna," *Rudé právo*, 19 Nov. 1968, pp. 3-4.
Poučení z krizového vývoje ve straně a společnosti po 13. sjezdu KSČ, Prague, UV KSČ, 1971; 48 pages.
"Stanovisko ke kulturním časopisům," *Rudé právo*, 3 Apr. 1964.
"Výsledky prosincového pléna ÚV KSČ v roce 1970," *Rudé právo*, Jan. 1971, pp. 11-14.

SPEECHES OF CPC OFFICIALS

BĚLOVSKÝ, BOHUMIL. Secretary of the CPC regional committee in Ostrava. Public address. *Nová
  svoboda*, 7 Sept. 1957.
DOLANSKÝ, JAROMÍR. Politburo member in charge of the economy. Address to the CPC CC on
  27 February 1957. "Za vyšší efektivnost čs. národního hospodářství," *Rudé právo*, undated
  supplement of 16 pages.
GOTTWALD, KLEMENT. "Zpráva na zasedání ÚV KSČ dne 22. února 1951," *Tvorba*, 1 Mar. 1951,
  pp. 193-201.
HENDRYCH, JIŘÍ. "Některé současné ctázky ideologické práce strany," *Rudé právo*, 19 June 1957,
  supplement of 24 pages.
HUSÁK, GUSTÁV. "Cesta od mimoriadneho zjazdu Komunistickej strany Slovenska." Address
  delivered to ÚV KSS. *Pravda*, 13 Mar. 1969, pp. 4-5.

HUSÁK, GUSTÁV. From his concluding speech to the CPC CC on 17 April 1969. "Musíme hledat poctivé komunistické řešení," *Rudé právo*, 19 Apr. 1969, pp. 1 and 3.

HUSÁK, GUSTÁV. "O odpovědnosti A. Novotného." Speech to the May 1968 CPC CC meeting. *Rudé právo*, 15 June 1968, p. 3.

KÖHLER, BRUNO. CC secretary. Address to CPC members. *Život strany*, Mar. 1957.

KOLDER, DRAHOMÍR. Member of the Politburo. Report to the CPC CC meeting, 21-2 January 1964. *Rudé právo*, 26 Jan. 1964.

KOUCKÝ, VLADIMÍR. Chairman, ideological commission of the CPC CC. Speech at the CPC CC meeting in December 1963. *Rudé právo*, 21 Dec. 1963.

NOVOTNÝ, ANTONÍN. First Secretary of the CPC. Address to the Eleventh CPC Congress on 18 June 1958. "Zpráva o činnosti ústředního výboru KSČ XI. sjezdu a současné hlavní úkoly," *Rudé právo*, supplement of 23 pages, not dated.

NOVOTNÝ, ANTONÍN. Speech to the Thirteenth Party Congress in 1966. *Práce*, 12 Oct. 1966.

PAVLENDA, VIKTOR. Secretary of the CPSl CC. Address to the November 1968 meeting of the CPC CC. *Pravda*, 26 Nov. 1968, and *Rudé právo*, 4 Dec. 1968.

ŠIK, OTA. Speech to the CPC CC meeting in December 1963. *Rudé právo*, 22 Dec. 1963. Excerpts only.

OTHER CPC ORGANS

Kontrolní a revizní komise stranického výboru KSČ při ČSD — provozním oddíle v Přerově. "Zastavte vlak 5599!" *Tribuna*, 22 Apr. 1970, p. 20.

OTHER ORGANIZATIONS

ROH. "Závěry z krizového vývoje v ROH mezi VI. a VIII. všeodborovýn sjezdem," *Práce*, 12 May 1972, supplement of 24 pages.

Scientific Economic Collegium of the Czechoslovak Academy of Sciences. "K vývoji ekonomické theorie v šedesátých letech v Československu," *Politická ekonomie*, no. 9, Sept. 1972; 39 pages.

COLLECTIONS OF DOCUMENTS

The Birth of Czechoslovakia. Ed. Cestmir Jesina, Washington, D.C., *Czechoslovak National Council of America, 1968; ix, I-A*, 110 pages.

Československo 1968, Dokumenty a komentáre, ed. Pavel Tigrid, Paris, *Svědectví*, nos. 34-6, 1969; 113 pages.

Cesta ke Květnu. Ed. Miloš Klimeš, Prague, ČSAV, 1965; 2 vols.

Cesta k Únoru. Dokumenty, ed. Václav Král, Prague, 1963.

The Czech Black Book. Prepared by the Institute of History of the Czechoslovak Academy of Sciences, ed. Robert Littell, New York, Praeger, 1969; 303 pages.

Czechoslovakia's Blueprint for Freedom. Ed. P. Ello, Washington, Acropolis Books, 1968; 304 pages.

Defense of Socialism: Supreme International Duty. Moscow, Novosti Press, 1968; 35 pages.

Documents, annexed to an appeal addressed to President Gustáv Husák on 1 March 1976, *Listy*, vol. vi, no. 3, June 1976, pp. 3-13.

K událostem v Československu. Fakta, dokumenty, svědectví v tisku i očitých svědků, Moscow, Tisková skupina sovětských žurnalistů, 1968; 104 pages.

Les sept jours de Prague, 21-27 août 1968. Première documentation complète de l'entrée des troupes aux accords de Moscou, Paris, Anthropos, 1968; 417 pages, ed. Robert Mandrou.

"Moskevská jednání Beneše s představiteli KSČ v prosinci 1943." *Tvorba*, nos. 19 and 20, on 13 and 20 May 1970, supplement of 30 pages.

Sedm pražských dní. Sborník dokumentů, Prague. Historický ústav ČSAV, 1968; 494 pages.

Winter in Prague. Documents of Czechoslovak Communism in Crisis, Cambridge, Mass., The M.I.T. Press, 1969; 473 pages, ed. Robin A. Remington.

4.   Memoirs of non-Communists

ČERNÝ, VÁCLAV. *Pláč Koruny české*, Toronto, 68 Publications, 1977.

KVETKO, MARTIN, and J. M. LIČKO, eds. *Zborník slovenského národného povstání*, Toronto, Stála konferencia slovenských demokratických exulantov, 1976.

5. *Older Czech literature*

HAŠEK, JOSEF. *The Good Soldier Švejk*, trans. Cecil Parrott, London, Heinemann, 1973; 752 pages.
MASARYK on Marx. Ed. and trans. Erazim V. Kohák, Lewisburg, Bucknell University Press, 1972.
MORAVEC, FRANTIŠEK. *Špión, jemuž nevěřili*, Toronto. 68 Publishers, 1977.

6. *Books by Communist intellectuals – target of the study*

BARTOŠEK, KAREL. *Hanebná role amerických okupantů v západních Čechách v roce 1945*, Prague, 1951.
BARTOŠEK, KAREL. *Pražské povstání 1945*, Prague, Naše vojsko, 1960, 2nd edn. 1965.
BARTOŠEK, KAREL, and KAREL PICHLÍK. *Z dějin dělnického hnutí na Plzeňsku: O úloze pravicových sociálních demokratů*, Prague, Státní nakladatelství politické literatury, 1954.
BARTOŠEK, KAREL, and KAREL PICHLIK. *Američané v Západních Čechách*, Prague, Mladá fronta, 1953.
FILIPEC, J., and RADOSLAV RICHTA. *Vědecko-technická revoluce a socialismus*, Prague, Svoboda, 1972; 114 pages.
GOLDMANN, JOSEF, and KAREL KOUBA. *Economic Growth in Czechoslovakia: An Introduction to the Theory of Economic Growth Under Socialism*, White Plains, N.Y., I.A.S.P., 1969; 178 pages.
GOTTWALD, KLEMENT. *O kultuře a úkolech inteligence v budování socialismu*, Prague, 1954.
GRASS, GÜNTER, and PAVEL KOHOUT. *Briefe über die Grenze*, Versuch eines Ost-West Dialogs, Hamburg, Christian Wegner, 1968; 118 pages.
HÁJEK, JIŘÍ. *Dix ans après*, Prague, 1968–78; Paris, Seuil, 1978; 205 pages.
HAMŠÍK, DUŠAN. *Spisovatelé a moc*, Prague, Československý spisovatel, 1969; 193 pages.
HAMŠÍK, DUŠAN. *Writers against Rulers*, London, Hutchinson, 1971; 208 pages.
HAMŠÍK, DUŠAN, and JIŘÍ PRAŽÁK. *Bomba pro Heydricha*,. Prague, 1963.
HUSÁK, GUSTÁV. *Svedectvo o Slovenskom národnom povstanie*, Bratislava, 1964; 2nd edn., 1969.
KAPLAN, KAREL. *Znárodnění a socialismus*, Prague, Práce, 1968; 263 pages.
KOHOUT, PAVEL. *Aus dem Tagebuch eines Konter-Revolutionärs*, Luzern, Bucher, 1969; 295 pages.
KOHOUT, PAVEL. *From the Diary of a Counter-Revolutionary*. New York, McGraw-Hill, 1972; 307 pages.
KOSÍK, KAREL. *Česká radikální demokracie*, Prague, 1958.
KOSÍK, KAREL, ed. *Čeští radikální demokraté*, Výběr politických statí. Prague, 1953.
KOSÍK, KAREL. *Dějiny filosofie jako filosofie*. Filosofie v dějinách českého národa, Prague, 1958.
KOSÍK, KAREL. *Dialectics of the Concrete*. Study on Problems of Man and World, Boston, D. Reidel, 1976; viii, 158 p.
KOSÍK, KAREL., *Dialektika konrétního*, Prague, 1963; 2nd edn., 1965; 173 pages.
KOSÍK, KAREL. *Dialektik des Konkreten*, Frankfurt, Suhrkamp, 1966.
KOSÍK, KAREL. *La dialectique du concret*, Paris, Maspéro, 1970; 176 pages.
KOSÍK, KAREL. *Kritik der technischen Vernunft*, Frankfurt, Suhrkamp, 1973; 110 pages.
KOSÍK, KAREL. *La nostra crisi actual*, Roma, Editori riuniti, 1969; 106 pages.
KOVÁLY, HEDA, and ERAZIM KOHÁK. *The Victors and the Vanquished*, New York, Horizon Press, 1973; 274 pages.
KOVÁLYOVÁ, HEDA, and ERAZIM V. KOHÁK. *Na vlastní kůži*. Dialog přes barikádu, Toronto, 68 Publishers, 1973; 311 pages.
KUSÝ, MIROSLAV. *Marxistická filozófia*, Bratislava, Epocha, 1969; 431 pages.
LAKATOŠ, MICHAL. *Občan, právo a demokracie*, Prague, 1966.
LAKATOŠ, MICHAL. *Úvahy o hodnotách demokracie*. Prague, Melantrich, 1969; 187 pages.
LOEBL, EUGEN. *Conversation with the Bewildered*, London, Allen & Unwin, 1972; 192 pages.
LOEBL, EUGEN. *Geistige Arbeit – die wahre Quelle des Reichtums*. Entwurf eines neuen sozialistischen Ordnungs, Düsseldorf, Econ, 1968; 300 pages.
LOEBL, EUGEN. *Gespräche mit den Ratlosen. Ibid.*, 1970; 329 pages.
LOEBL, EUGEN. *Humanomics*.
LOEBL, EUGEN. *Marxismus – Wegweiser und Irrweg. Ibid.*, 1973; 232 pages.
LOEBL, EUGEN. *My Mind on Trial*, New York, Harcourt Brace Jovanovich, 1976.
LOEBL, EUGEN. *The New Source of Wealth: The Revolution of the Intellectuals*, New York, Grove Press, 1970.
LOEBL, EUGEN. *Sentenced and Tried*. The Stalinist Purges in Czechoslovakia, London. Elek, 1969; 272 pages.
LOEBL, EUGEN. *Stalinism in Prague*. The Loebl Story, New York, Grove, 1969; 327 pages.

LOEBL, EUGEN. *Svedectvo o procese s vedením protištátneho sprisahaneckého centra v čele s Rudolfom Slánskym*, Bratislava, VPL, 1968, 199 pages.

LOEBL, EUGEN. *Úvahy o duševnej práci a bohatstve národa*, Bratislava, VSAV, 1967.

LOEBL, EUGEN and LEOPOLD GRÜNWALD. Die Intellektuelle Revolution. Hintergründe und Auswirkungen des "Prager Fruühlings", Vienna, Europa, 1969; 308 pages.

LOEBL, EUGEN, and DUŠAN POKORNÝ. *Die Revolution rehabilitiert ihre Kinder.* Hinter den Kulissen des Slánský-Processes, Vienna, Europa, 1968; 228 pages.

LONDON, ARTUR. *L'aveu.* Dans l'engrenage du procès de Prague, Paris, Gallimard, 1968; 452 pages.

LONDON, ARTUR. *The Confession*, New York, Marrow, 1970; 442 pages.

LONDON, ARTUR. *Doznání*, Prague, Československý spisovatel, 1969; 412 pages.

LONDON, ARTUR. *Das Geständnis*, Munich, Kindel, 1968; 410 pages.

LONDON, ARTUR. *On Trial*, London, Macdonald, 1970; 453 pages.

MACHONIN, PAVEL *et al. Československá společnost.* Sociologická analýza sociální stratifikace, Bratislava, Epocha, 1969; 619 pages.

MACHONIN, PAVEL *et al. Sociální struktura socialistické společnosti*, Prague, Svoboda, 1967.

MACHOVEC, MILAN. *Jesus für Atheisten*, Stuttgart, Kreuz, 1972.

MACHOVEC, MILAN. *A Marxist Looks at Jesus*, Philadelphia, Fortress Press, 1976; 231 pages.

MACHOVEC, MILAN. *Tomáš G. Masaryk*, Prague, Melantrich, 1968; 282 pages.

MACHOVEC, MILAN. *Vom Sinn des menschlichen Lebens*, Freiburg, Rombach, 1971; 240 pages.

MARGOLIUS, HEDA. *I Do Not Want to Remember*, Auschwitz, 1941–Prague 1968, London, Weidenfeld and Nicolson, 1974; 176 pages.

MLYNÁŘ, ZDENĚK. *Československý pokus o reformu 1968.* Analýza jeho teorie a praxe, Cologne, Index, 1975.

MLYNÁŘ, ZDENĚK. *Mráz přichází z Kremlu*, Cologne, Index, 1978; 337 pages.

MŇAČKO, LADISLAV. *Dlhá biela prerušovaná čára*, Bratislava, Slovenský spisovatel, 1965.

MŇAČKO, LADISLAV. *Die Festrede*, Munich, Paul List, 1976.

MŇAČKO, LADISLAV. *Já. Adolf Eichman*, Bratislava, 1961.

MŇAČKO, LADISLAV. *Marxova ulica*, Bratislava, 1957.

MŇAČKO, LADISLAV. *Mosty na Východ*, Bratislava, 1952.

MŇAČKO, LADISLAV. *Oneskorené reportáže*, Bratislava, SVPL, 1964.

MŇAČKO, LADISLAV. *Partyzáni*, Bratislava, 1945.

MŇAČKO, LADISLAV. *La septième nuit*, Paris, Flammarion, 1968; 254 pages.

MŇAČKO, LADISLAV. *The Seventh Night*, New York, Dutton, 1969; 261 pages.

MŇAČKO, LADISLAV. *Die siebente Nacht.* Erkenntniss und Anklage eines Kommunisten, Vienna, Molden, 1969; 261 pages.

MŇAČKO, LADISLAV. *Smrt sa volá Engelchen*, Bratislava, 1959.

NEJEDLÝ, ZDENĚK. *Komunisté dědici velkých tradic českéno národa*, Prague, 1950.

PACHMAN, LUDĚK. *Boha nelze vyhnat.* Od marxismu zpět ke křesťanství, Rome, Křesťanská akademie, 1975; 110 pages.

PACHMAN, LUDĚK. *Checkmate in Prague.*

PACHMAN, LUDĚK. *Jak to bylo.* Zpráva o činnosti šachového velmistra za období 1924–72, Toronto, 68 Publishers, 1974; 391 pages.

PACHMAN, LUDĚK. *Jetzt kann ich sprechen*, Düsseldorf, Walter Rau, 1973; 450 pages.

PELIKÁN, JIŘÍ, ed. *Le congrès clandestin*, Paris, Seuil, 1970; 384 pages.

PELIKÁN, JIŘÍ. *Čtrnáctý mimořádný sjezd KSČ.* Protokol a dokumenty, Vienna, Europa, 1970; 294 pages.

PELIKÁN, JIŘÍ. *The Czechoslovak Political Trials, 1950–4.* The Suppressed Report of the Dubček's Government's Commission of Inquiry, 1968, London, Macdonald, 1971; 360 pages.

PELIKÁN, JIŘÍ. *Ici Prague.* L'opposition intérieure parle, Paris, Seuil, 1973; 427 pages.

PELIKÁN, JIŘÍ. *Panzer überrollen den Parteitag*, Vienna, Europa, 1969; 319 pages.

PELIKÁN, JIŘÍ. *Potlačená zpráva*, Vienna, Europa, 1970; 319 pages.

PELIKÁN, JIŘÍ. *The Secret Vysočany Congress*, London, Allen Lane, The Penguin Press, 1971; 304 pages.

PELIKÁN, JIŘÍ. *S'ils me tuent . . .* Récit recueilli par Frédéric de Towarnicki, Paris, Bernard Grasset, 1975; 293 pages.

PELIKÁN, JIŘÍ. *Socialist Opposition in Eastern Europe*. The Czechoslovak Example, London, Allison & Busby, 1976.
PELIKÁN, JIŘÍ. *Das unterdrückte Dossier*, Vienna, Europa, 1970; 442 pages.
PROCHÁZKA, JAN. *Politika pro každého*, Prague, Mladá fronta, 1968; 238 pages.
REINMAN, PAVEL. *Dějiny K.S.Č.*, Prague, 1931 and 1961.
REIMANN, PAUL. *Geschichte der Kommunistischen Partei der Tschechoslowakei*, Hamburg, 1931.
RICHTA, RADOVAN *et al*. *Civilizace na rozcestí*. Společenské a lidské souvislosti vědecko-technické revoluce, Prague, Svoboda, 1966; rev. edn. 1969; 417 pages.
RICHTA, RADOVAN. *La civilisation au carrefour*, Paris, Anthropus, 1969; 468 pages.
RICHTA, RADOVAN. *Civilization at the Crossroads*. Social and Human Implications of the Scientific and Technological Revolution, White Plains, I.A.S.P., 1969; 372 pages.
RICHTA, RADOVAN. *Technischer Fortschritt und die industrielle Gesellschaft*, Frankfurt, Makol, 1972; 228 pages.
SELUCKÝ, RADOSLAV. *Czechoslovakia: The Plan that Failed.*, London, Nelson, 1970; 150 pages.
SELUCKÝ, RADOSLAV. *Economic Reforms in Eastern Europe*. Political Background and Economic Significance, New York, Praeger, 1972; 181 pages.
SELUCKÝ, RADOSLAV. *Východ je Východ*. Cologne, Index, 1972; 242 pages.
ŠIK, OTA. *Argumente für den Dritten Weg*, Hamburg, Hoffmann und Campe, 1973; 213 pages.
ŠIK, OTA. *Czechoslovakia: The Bureaucratic Economy*, White Plains, I.A.S.P., 1972; 138 pages.
ŠIK, OTA. *Demokratische und sozialistische Plan- und Marktwirtschaft*, Zürich, Die Arche, 1971; 48 pages.
ŠIK, OTA. *Der dritte Weg*, Hamburg, Hoffmann und Campe, 1972; 460 pages.
ŠIK, OTA. *Ekonomika a zájmy*. Prague, Svoboda, 1968; 353 pages.
ŠIK, OTA. *Fakten der tachechoslowakischen Wirtschaft*. Vienna, Molden, 1969.
ŠIK, OTA. *Das Kommunistische Machtsystem*. Hamburg, Hoffmann und Campe, 1976.
ŠIK, OTA. *K problematice socialistických zbožních vztahů*, Prague, 1965.
ŠIK, OTA. *Plan and Market under Socialism*, White Plains, I.A.S.P., 1968; 382 pages.
ŠIK, OTA. *Plán a trh za socialismu*, Prague, Academia, 1968; 362 pages.
ŠIK, OTA. *The Third Way*. Marxist-Leninist Theory and Modern Industrial Society, London, Wildwood House, 1976; 431 pages.
ŠIK, OTA. *La vérité sur l'économie Tchécoslovaque*, Paris, Fayard, 1969.
SLÁNSKÁ, J. *Bericht über meinen Mann*, Vienna, Europa, 1969; 224 pages.
SLÁNSKÁ, J. *Rapport sur mon mari*, Paris, Mercure de France, 1969; 223 pages.
SLÁNSKÁ, J. *Report on My Husband*, London, Hutchinson, 1969, 208 pages.
ŠLINGOVÁ, MARIAM. *Truth Will Prevail*, London, Merlin, 1968; 126 pages.
SMRKOVSKÝ, JOSEF. *The Story of the Czechoslovak Invasion of 1968, As Told by an Insider*, Sydney, Red Pen, 1976.
SVITÁK, IVAN. *The Czechoslovak Experiment, 1968-1969*, New York, Colombia University, 1971; 243 pages.
SVITÁK, IVAN. *Lidský smysl kultury*, Prague, Československý spisovatel, 1968; 187 pages.
SVITÁK, IVAN. *Man and His World*, New York, Dell, 1970, 177 pages.
SVITÁK, IVAN. *Verbotene Horizonte*. Prag zwischen zwei Wintern, Freiburg, Rombach, 1969; 196 pages.
SYSTÉMOVÉ, ZMĚNY. *Příspěvky ke konferenci na universitě v Readingu v r. 1971*, Cologne, Index, 1972; 272 pages.
VACULÍK, LUDVÍK *et al*. *Čára na zdi*. Československé fejetóny 1975/1976, Cologne, Index, 1977; 187 pages.

7. Articles by Communist intellectuals – target of the study

BÁRTA, MILOŠ. "Rady pracujících a naše krize," *Reportér*, 3 Apr. 1969; pp. 7-8.
BARTOŠEK, KAREL. "Američtí imperialisté — osnovatelé únorového kontrarevolučního puče," *Rudé právo*, 25 Feb. 1953.
BARTOŠEK, KAREL. "Czechoslovakia: the State of Historiography," *Journal of Contemporary History*, no. 2, Jan. 1967, pp. 143-55.
BARTOŠEK, KAREL. "La nécessité d'une nouvelle gauche," *Samizdat*, collection "Combats", Seuil, Jan. 1970.

BARTOŠEK, KAREL. "Naše nynější krize a revoluce," *Svědectví*, vol. x, no. 38, 1970, pp. 231-40.

BARTOŠEK, KAREL. "Nemocní dějinami," *Doba*, no. 24, 19 June 1969, pp. 9-13.

BARTOŠEK, KAREL. "Nevyjme s vlky," *Politika*, 19 Sept. 1968.

BARTOŠEK, KAREL. "Od reforem k revoluci," *Plamen*, no. 2, 1968.

BARTOŠEK, KAREL. "Open Letter to the Workers of Czechoslovakia," *Reportér*, 8 May 1968.

BARTOŠEK,·KAREL. "Proč muselo dojít ke střetnutí s reakcí," *Rudé právo*, 4 Feb. 1958.

BARTOŠEK, KAREL. "Revoluce proti byrokratismu?" *Rudé právo*, 18, 24, 26, 30, 31 July 1968.

BARTOŠEK, KAREL. "Spoločné revolúčne tradície Čechov a Slovákov," *Pravda*, 4 May 1960.

BARTOŠEK, KAREL, and RUDOLF SLÁNSKÝ, Jr. "Zbabělost zůstává zbabělost," *Rudé právo*, 17 Apr. 1968.

BAUDISS, JIŘÍ. "Hovoří profesor Kusý: O současných myšlenkových proudech na Slovensku," *Práce*, 20 Mar. 1969, p. 4.

BELDA, J. *et al.* "K otázce účasti Československa na Marshallově plánu," *Revue dějin socialismu*, no. 1, Feb. 1968, pp. 81-100.

BROŽÍK, MARCEL. "Jak zrálo střetnutí" (interview with Ota Šik), *Kulturní noviny*, 29 Mar. 1968, pp. 1 and 3.

CHALOUPECKÝ, J. "All the Power to the Workers' Councils!" *Listy*, 20 Feb. 1969, p. 1.

CHUDÍKOVÁ, HELENA. "The Struggle for Progress Continues" (interview with Gustáv Husák), *Kulturní tvorba*, 18 July 1968, p. 1.

CÍSAŘ, ČESTMÍR. "Boj Lenina a Stalina za vytvoření bolševické strany," *Tvorba*, 22 Nov. 1951, pp. 1130-2.

CÍSAŘ, ČESTMÍR. "K otázce národního a 'všesvětového' jazyka," *Tvorba*, 4 Oct. 1950, p. 960.

CÍSAŘ, ČESTMÍR. "O některých současných otázkách ideologické práce plzeňské krajské organizace strany." A polycopied lecture from September 1953.

CÍSAŘ, ČESTMÍR. "Pro rozvoj socialistického budování," *Tvorba*, 13 Apr. 1949, pp. 336-7.

CÍSAŘ, ČESTMÍR. "Pod praporem internacionalismu," *Tvorba*, 27 Apr. 1949, pp. 383 ff.

čt. "Očista na vysokých školách: Pokrokovi vysokoškoláci se chápou iniciativy," *Svobodné noviny*, 27 Feb. 1948.

"Deset největších čs. podniků," *Svět hospodářství*, no. 10, 23 Jan. 1970, p. 1.

"A Discussion About Czech-Slovak Relations," *Historický časopis*, no. 4, 1967.

"Economic Conference in Prague." Speeches and Discussions, *Hospodářské noviny*, 8 and 15 Nov. 1963.

"The Economic Policy We Need." Statement by fifty Czech and Slovak economists, *Rudé právo*, 24 Sept. 1968.

"Ekonomové k nové soustavě." Statement of 13 Czech Economists. *Rudé právo*, 16 Sept. 1968, p. 2.

FERKO, VLADIMÍR. "Spring 1968 and Its Fashions," *Predvoj*, 28 Mar. 1968.

FIBICH, JINDŘICH. "Institucionální odcizení a svoboda člověka," *Filozófia*, no. 6, Nov.-Dec. 1967, pp. 607-17.

FRIŠ, EDO. "Eugen Löbl — šesťdesiatročný," *Práca*, 13 May 1967.

GOLDSTÜCKER, EDUARD. "Občané, pozor!" *Rudé právo*, 23 June 1968, p. 3.

GOLDSTÜCKER, EDUARD. "The Problem of Franz Kafka," *Literární noviny*, 16 Feb. 1963.

GRAUS, FRANTIŠEK. "Glosy: Hon na čarodějnice," *Československý časopis historický*, no. 2, Apr. 1969, pp. 190-5.

"S měnovou reformous se nepočítá," *Reportér*, 26 Sept. 1968, p. 9.

HAVLÍČEK, FRANTIŠEK. "Socialism Ensures the Free and Active Development of Everybody," *Rudé právo*, 7 Dec. 1963.

HENDRYCH, VÁCLAV. "Tasks in the Sector of Specialist Education in the Fight for Completing the Building of Socialism," *Pedagogika*, no. 4, Aug. 1959.

HIRŠ, PETER. "Svedectvo nielen o svedectve: S Eugenom Löblom o procesoch i problémoch súčasných," *Práca*, 15 May 1968, p. 4.

"Federation of Locomotive Crews: A Test of Democracy," *Lidová demokracie*, 18 Mar. 1969.

HLÁVEK, ANDREJ. "Seminár o socializme a demokracii," *Filozófia*, no. 1, Mar. 1969, pp. 91-5.

HOLINOVÁ, EVA. "Interview s prof. PhDr. Miroslavom Kusým, vedúcim ideologického oddelenia ÚV KSS: Slovenská politika," *Obrana lidu*, 1 Mar. 1969, p. 3.

HÜBL, MILAN. "Community of Czechs and Slovaks," *Práce*, 28 Jan. 1968.

HÜBL, MILAN. "Dopisy: Kdo se lépe osvědčil?" *Dnešek*, 31 Dec. 1947, p. 619.

HÜBL, MILAN. "Jak do roku 1969?" *Práce*, 29 Dec. 1968, pp. 1 and 4.

HÜBL, MILAN. "Moudrý člověk: Eugen Löbl — 60," *Literární noviny*, 20 May 1967, p. 7.

HÜBL, MILAN. "Oneskorená reportáž Ivana Klímu," *Kultúrny život*, 5 Nov. 1965, p. 5.

HÜBL, MILAN. "Pád jakobínské diktatury," *Dějiny a současnost*, no. 8, 1964.

HÜBL, MILAN. Review of Marta Vartíková's book *Roky rozhodnutia*. *Československý časopis historický*, no. 4, 1963, pp. 473-6.

HÜBL, MILAN. "Socialism for Us," *Kultúrny život*, 5 Jan. 1968, p. 3.

HÜBL, MILAN. "Trajčo Kostov," *Dějiny a současnost*, no. 6, June 1963, pp. 1-3.

HUSÁK, GUSTÁV. "February Meditations," *Kultúrny život*, Feb. 1968.

HUSÁK, GUSTÁV. "Old Anniversaries and New Hopes," *Kultúrny život*, 12 Jan. 1968, p. 1.

HUSÁK, GUSTÁV. "Revolúčne tradície slovenského národného povstánia," *Kultúrny život*, 31 Aug. 1963, pp. 1 and 10.

Interdisciplinary Team of Scientists for the Exploration of Societal and Human Implications of the Scientific-Technological Revolution. Statement. "O nový československý model socialismu," *Rudé právo*, 10, 11, 12 July 1968.

JELÍNEK, A., and M. SCHULZ. "On Pavel Kohout's Poetry," *Rudé právo*, 12 Dec. 1954.

JÍLKOVÁ, EVA. "Interview with Dr. Zdeňka Nedvědová-Nejedlá," *Práce*, 18 Aug. 1968, pp. 4-5.

JIRÁSEK, JAN. "Co s republikou — ekonomicky?" *Doba*, 17 Apr. 1969, p. 10.

—jk — "Criticism of Work Canteens Justified," *Pravda*, 9 Oct. 1957.

KANTŮREK, JIŘÍ. *Kulturní tvorba*, 5 Jan. 1967; trans. *East Europe*, vol. xvi, no. 2, Feb. 1967, pp. 29-31.

KAPLAN, KAREL. "The Class War After February 1948: A Contribution to the Process of forming the General Line of the Construction of Socialism," *Příspěvky k dějinám KSČ*, no. 3, 1963.

KAPLAN, KAREL. "Jak dál v demokratizaci?" *Reportér*, 3-10 Apr. 1968, pp. iii-v.

KAPLAN, KAREL. "Nebyla jiná cesta," *Svobodné slovo*, 23 Feb. 1966.

KAPLAN, KAREL. "The political Trials and the Present Day," *Doba*, 13 Feb. 1969.

KAPLAN, KAREL. "Včera a dnes," *Literární noviny*, 26 Feb. 1966.

KAPLAN, KAREL. "Zamyšlení nad politickými procesy," *Nová mysl*, no. 6, June 1968, pp. 765-94; no. 7, July 1968, pp. 906-40; no. 8, Aug. 1968, pp. 1054-78.

KAPLAN, KAREL. "Železná logika procesů: Zamyšlení nad padesátými léty," *Život strany*, no. 29, 27 Nov. 1968, p. 8.

KLEČKA, JAROSLAV. "One Cannot Be Silent," *Hospodářské noviny*, 27 Oct. 1957.

KLOFÁČ, J., and V. TLUSTÝ. "Socialism and Just Reward," *Reportér*, 6 Nov. 1968, pp. 5-13.

KOHOUT, LUBOŠ. "Kousek nedávné historie," *Mladá fronta*, 3 Jan. 1969, p. 2.

KOHOUT, PAVEL. "Co jsem byl . . .," *Literární noviny*, 21 Mar. 1964, p. 3.

KOHOUT, PAVEL. "Dopis," *Kultura*, 3 Aug. 1961.

KOHOUT, PAVEL. "Letter to the CPC CC," *Svědectví*, vol. ix, no. 33, winter 1967, p. 107.

KOHOUT, PAVEL. "Sebektritika," *Práce*, 4 Jan. 1969, p. 2.

KOHOUT, PAVEL. "Slovo k bratrům v těžkých dnech," *Rudé právo*, 10 Mar. 1953.

KOHOUT, PAVEL. Speech at the Third Czechoslovak Writers' Congress. *Kultúrny život*, 1 June 1963.

KOHOUT, PAVEL. "Stop, America," *Večerní Praha*, 6 Jan. 1962.

KOLDER, DRAHOMÍR. "Party management of National Economy," *Nová mysl*, no. 8, 1966.

KOSÍK, KAREL. "Buržoazně demokratická revoluce," *Tvorba*, 9 Nov. 1949, fourth page of the cover.

KOSÍK, KAREL. "Hasek and Kafka," *Telos*, no. 23, spring 1975, pp. 84-88.

KOSÍK, KAREL. "Illuze a realismus," *Listy*, no. 1, 7 Nov. 1968, p. 1.

KOSÍK, KAREL. "Naše nynější krise," *Literární listy*, 11 Apr.-16 May 1968.

KOSÍK, KAREL. "O sociálních kořenech a filosofické podstatě masarykismu," *Filosofický časopis*, no. 3, 1954, pp. 199-214.

KOSÍK, KAREL. "Rozum a svědomí," *Literární listy*, 1 Mar. 1968.

KOSÍK, KAREL. "Sovětský Svaz — bašta marxismu-leninismu," *Tvorba*, 22 Nov. 1951, pp. 1116-18.

KOSÍK, KAREL. "Stalin nás učí lásce k vlasti a nenávisti k jejím nepřátelům," *Tvorba*, 20 Dec. 1951, pp. 1211-12.

KOSÍK, KAREL. "Také německý lid má svou revoluční tradici," *Tvorba*, 23 Aug. 1950, pp. 810-11.

"The KOSIK — SARTRE Exchange of Letters." Trans. Andrew Feenberg, *Telos*, no. 25, Fall 1975, pp. 192-5.

KOSTKA, RUDOLF. "Úhelným bodem programu je hospodářská reforma." Interview with Prof. A. Červinka. *Rudé právo*, 25 Sept. 1968, p. 3.

KOUBA, KAREL. "Rady pracujících a ekonomická reforma," *Nová mysl*, no. 3, 10 Mar. 1969, pp. 327-32.

KOVALČIK, R. "Musel odísť," *Reportér*, 6 Mar. 1969, p. 2.

KOZÁK, JAN. "For the Clarification of Methods of the KSČ Central Committee in the Struggle for Gaining the Majority of the Nation in the Period before February 1948," *Příspěvky k dějinám KSČ*, no. 2, Mar. 1958.

KOZÁK, JAN. "Možnost revolučního využití parlamentu při přechodu k socialismu a úloha lidových mas," *Příspěvky k dějinám KSČ*, vol. 1, no. 1, autumn 1957.

KOZÁK, JAN. "The New Role of National Legislative Bodies in the Communist Conspiracy." U.S. House of Representatives, Committee on Un-American Activities, 30 Dec. 1961.

KRAUS, FRANTIŠEK. "Proti revizionismu," *Pochodeň*, 30 Jan. 1959.

-KT — "A Parting of the Ways," *Kulturní tvorba*, 24 Aug. 1967.

KUBÍČEK, IVAN. "Iniciativa zdola, nenaplánovaná shora," *Reportér*, 26 June-3 July 1968, pp. 9-11.

KUSÝ, MIROSLAV. "The Art of Leaving," *Nové slovo*, 20 Feb. 1969.

KUSÝ, MIROSLAV. "Československá politická kríza," *Nová mysl*, no. 11, Nov. 1968, pp. 1315-28.

KUSÝ, MIROSLAV. "From an Open Notebook," *Nové slovo*, 3 Oct. 1968.

KUSÝ, MIROSLAV. "The Right, the Left, the Center, and Others," *Svět v obrazech*. no. 7, 18 Feb. 1969.

KUSÝ, MIROSLAV. "Spoločenská funkcia pravdy," *Pravda*, 20 Aug. 1963, p. 2.

KUSÝ, MIROSLAV. "Z otvoreného zápisníka: O rozpoložení sil," *Nové slovo*, 27 Feb. 1969, p. 3.

LAKATOŠ, MICHAL. "Informace! Informace! Informace!" *Zítřek*. 11 Dec. 1968, p. 2.

LAKATOŠ, MICHAL. "Lenin o socialistickém státě," *Lidové noviny*, 20 Jan. 1952, p. 1.

LAKATOŠ, MICHAL. "Listopadové modality," *Zítřek*, 27 Nov. 1968, p. 3.

LAKATOŠ, MICHAL. "Morální autorita," *Zítřek*, 27 Nov. 1968, p. 2.

LAKATOŠ, MICHAL. "[O] kabinetní politice," *Studentské listy*, no. 7, 9 Apr. 1969, p. 4.

LAKATOŠ, MICHAL. "Prostor pro občanskou společnost," *Svobodné slovo*, 12 July 1968, pp. 1-2.

LAKATOŠ, MICHAL. "Ticho a mlčení," *Zítřek*, 13 Nov. 1968, p. 2.

LAŠTOVIČKA, BOHUSLAV. "Vznik a význam Košického vládního programu," *Československý časopis historický*, no. 4, Aug. 1960, pp. 449-71.

LAUŠMAN, BOHUMIL. "Let's Not Fear a Putsch!" *Právo lidu*, 22 Feb. 1948, p. 1.

LEDERER, JIŘÍ. "Wir stellen for: Pavel Kohout," *Volkszeitung*, 23 Sept. 1966.

LIČKA, PAVOL. "To Profess Historical Facts," *Kultúrny život*, no. 24, 15 June 1963.

LOEBL, EUGEN. "Book Review of Richta's *Civilization*," *Kultúrny život*, 16 Sept. 1966; and *Volkszeitung*, 7 and 14 Oct. 1966. p. 7.

LOEBL, EUGEN. "Dôsledně dokončiť rehabilitácie," *Smena*, 5 Mar. 1968, p. 4.

LOEBL, EUGEN. "Drobné podnikanie a socialistický trh," *Hospodářské noviny*, 6 July 1968, pp. 1, 6-7.

LOEBL, EUGEN. "Ekonomiku z hlavy na nohy," *Večerník*, 27 Mar. 1968.

LOEBL, EUGEN. "Nielen chlebom," *Kultúrny život*, 16 Jan. 1965.

LOEBL, EUGEN. "O čo išlo — o čo ide," *Kultúrny život*, 9 Aug. 1968, pp. 3 and 6.

LOEBL, EUGEN. "O dogmatizme v ekonomickom myslení," *Kultúrny život*, 28 Sept. 1963, p. 6.

LOEBL, EUGEN. "Pabĕrky z U.S.A.: O společnost s lidskou tváří," *Literární listy*, special issue in exile, Aug. 1970, p. 11.

LOEBL, EUGEN. "Právo na špecifickú cestu," *Pravda*, 12 Apr. 1968.

LOEBL, EUGEN. "Superstalinism: The New Soviet Foreign Policy," *Interplay*, June-July 1969, p. 22.

LOEBL, EUGEN. "Symmetrical Model, This Time in a Different Context," *Literární noviny*, 20 June 1968, p. 14.

LOEBL, EUGEN. "Večný smäd po poznaní," *Kultúrny život*, 19 Mar. 1965, pp. 3 and 8.

LOEBL, EUGEN. "Východiska z krízy (I. Dva pohledy na federáciu.)," *Kultúrny život*, 16 Aug 1968, pp. 1 and 10.

MACEK, JOSEF. "Buďme husitsky a gottwaldovsky stateční," *Rudé právo*, 23 Mar. 1953.

MACEK, JOSEF. "K některým otázkám historické vědy," *Rudé právo*, 22 Mar. 1966, p. 3.

MACEK, JOSEF. "Naléhavé problémy historické vědy," *Nová mysl*, no. 9, Sept. 1963, pp. 1043-51.

MACEK, JOSEF. "O husitském revolučním hnutí," Prague, 1952.

MACEK, JOSEF. "O ideologii soudobého německého imperialismu," *Rudé právo*, 2 Dec. 1961, p. 1.

MACEK, JOSEF. Opening address to a scientific conference on German militarism. *Rudé právo*, 18 July 1957.

MACEK, JOSEF. "Proti kosmopolitismu ve výkladu našich národních dějin." Public speech on 29 May 1952, pamphlet.

MACEK, JOSEF. "Stalinská cesta naší vědy," *Rudé právo*, 11 Mar. 1953.

MACEK, JOSEF. "Stav a úkoly historické vědy," *Československý časopis historický*, no. 1, 1967, pp. 1-34.

MACHONIN, PAVEL. "Socialistická rovnost a nerovnost v naší společnosti," *Nová mysl*, no. 12, 1966.

MACHONIN, PAVEL. "Sociální rozvrstvení v Československu 1969: geneze, stav, výhledy," *Politika*, no. 3, 13 Mar. 1969, p. 15.

"Máme nového ministra národní obrany?" *Práce*, 5 Nov. 1968.

MÁŠOVÁ, MILENA. "Hovoříme s Karlem Kosíkem: O literatuře a filosofii," *Divadelní noviny*, no. 14, 26 Mar. 1969, pp. 1 and 6.

MENCL, VOJTĚCH, and FRANTIŠEK OUŘEDNÍK. "Jak to bylo v lednu?" *Život strany*, nos. 14, 15, 16, June, July, August 1968.

MLYNÁRIK, JÁN. "O hlavním nebezpečí," *Reportér*, 27 Feb. 1969, pp. 12-13.

MŇAČKO, LADISLAV. "Dva průvody," *Rudé právo*, 1 May 1958.

MŇAČKO, LADISLAV. Interview: "Chatting about Night Talk," *Kultúrny život*, 22 June 1963, p. 6.

MŇAČKO, LADISLAV. "Nevymýcené býlí," *Rudé právo*, 10 Jan, 1960.

MŇAČKO, LADISLAV. "Nočný rozhovor," *Kultúrny život*, 8 June 1963, p. 7.

MŇAČKO, LADISLAV. "Pasca na myši," *Kultúrny život*, 1 June 1963, p. 1.

MŇAČKO, LADISLAV. "Pracovať a nebáťsa," *Kultúrny život*, 21 Dec. 1963, p. 1.

MŇAČKO, LADISLAV. Speech at the conference of Slovak writers in Bratislava on 22 Apr. 1963. *Kultúrny život*, 4 May 1963, pp. 3-6.

"MŇAČKO protestiert: Ich reise rach Israel," *Frankfurter Allgemeine Zeitung*, 11 Aug. 1967.

MUCHA, JAROSLAV. "The Right Tune," *Pochodeň*, 21 Mar. 1958.

NEPRAŠ, VLAD. "Hospodářská reforma nechce jen slova, ale činy," *Reportér*, 9 Oct. 1968, p. 6.

PACHMAN, LUDĚK. "Kdo je pro Leden a kdo je proti," *Obroda*, no. 6, 12 Mar. 1969, p. 5.

PACHMAN, LUDĚK. "Podivná normalizace," *Hlas domova*, 19 Feb. 1973, pp. 3 and 8.

PACHMAN, LUDĚK. "Šachistův šach," *Zítřek*, 5 Mar. 1969, p. 1.

PACHMAN, LUDĚK. "Výchovná práce v odborech," *Tvorba*, 30 Aug. 1950, pp. 838-40.

PAUC, LADISLAV (welder). Letter in *Pravda* (Plzeň), 27 Jan. 1959.

PAVLÍČEK, VÁCLAV. "Únor 1948," *Právník*, vol. cvii, no. 3, Mar. 1968, pp. 177-201.

PĚČEK, VLADISLAV. "Nepřipustíme sektářství v ČSM," *Mladá fronta*, 23 Aug. 1958.

PECHO, MICHAL. "In the Interest of a Reform," *Predvoj*, 18 Dec. 1958.

PELIKÁN, JIŘÍ. "Cesta mladé inteligence," *Svobodné noviny*, 5 Mar. 1948.

PELIKÁN, JIŘÍ. "Interview with . . .," *Australian Left Review*, no. 29, Mar. 1971, pp. 44-52.

PELIKÁN, JIŘÍ. "Příklad zásadní kritiky," *Tvorba*, 21 June 1950, pp. 603-5.

PELIKÁN, JIŘÍ. Speech as a student candidate to the National Assembly, *Lidové noviny*, 27 May 1948.

PELIKÁN, JIŘÍ. "Why I Have Disobeyed the Order to Return to Prague," *The Times*, 1 Oct. 1969.

PICHLÍK, KAREL. "Die Entstehung der Tschechoslowakei," *Vierteljahreshefte für Zeitgeschichte*, vol. xvii, no. 2, Apr. 1969, pp. 160-80.

PIOVARČIOVÁ, MARTA. "Rozhovor s profesorom Miroslavom Kusým: Pohľad na súčasnú polińckú klímu," *Práca*, 27 Feb. 1969, p. 5.

POLITICUS (pseud.). "Dopis," *Svědectví*, vol. ix, no. 33, winter 1967, pp. 75-82.

"Poznámky a doplňky ke sdělení ÚV KSČ," *Svědectví*, vol. vi, no. 28, spring 1966.

PRAVDA, VÁCLAV (pseud.). "Victim of Prague's Machinery of Revenge," *The Times*, 22 Feb. 1972, p. 12.

PRŮCHA, MILAN. "Dialog pokračuje," *Kulturní tvorba*, 18 May 1967.

RAŠLA, ANTON. "A Crisis of Discipline: the Eradication of the 'Cult' in the Economy," *Kultúrny život*, 14 Sept. 1963.

RAŠLA, ANTON. "For the Purity of the Workers' Class," *Kultúrny život*, leading article, 16 Nov. 1963. Excerpts in *East Europe*, vol. viii, no. 2, Feb. 1964, p. 24.

REIMAN, MICHAL. "Monopol leninismu a Československo," *Nová mysl*, no. 8, Aug. 1968, pp. 1027-33.

RICHTA, RADOVAN, and OTA ŠULC. "Forecasting and the Scientific and Technological Revolution," *International Social Sciences Journal*, vol. xxi, no. 4, 1969.

ROUBÍČEK, ZDENĚK. "Pavel Kohout and his dramatization of Švejk," *Mladá fronta*, 8 Dec. 1963.

RUPPELDTOVÁ. *Práca*, 6 May 1958.

ŠEDA, VÁCLAV. "The KSC Struggle for Revolutionary Changes in the Cultural Area in the Years 1945-8," *Příspěvky k dějinám KSČ*, no. 3, 1961.

SEKERA, JIŘÍ. "Po XII. sjezdu do nové etapy," *Nová mysl*, no. 11, Jan. 1963, pp. 1-11.

SELUCKÝ, RADOSLAV. *Kulturní tvorba*, 7 Feb. 1963. Parts trans. in *East Europe*, vol. xii, no. 5, May 1963, pp. 13-14.

SELUCKÝ, RADOSLAV. "Alternativy socialistického vývoje," *Nová mysl*, no. 8, Aug. 1968, pp. 1021-6.

SELUCKÝ, RADOSLAV. "The Cadres and the New System of Management," *Mladá fronta*, 21 Nov. 1964.

SELUCKÝ, RADOSLAV. "Ekonomika, politika, morálka," *Literární noviny*, 20 Oct. 1962, pp. 6-7.

SELUCKÝ, RADOSLAV. "Is There Danger of Unemployment in This Country?" *Příroda a společnost*, no. 11, 1967.

SELUCKÝ, RADOSLAV. "Myšlení, iniciativa, činy," *Kulturní tvorba*, 23 Jan. 1964, p. 1.

SELUCKÝ, RADOSLAV. "Otevřít dveře dokořán," *Svobodné slovo*, 31 Dec. 1967, p. 3.

SELUCKÝ, RADOSLAV. "Podnětné úvahy o duševnej práci a bohatstve národa," *Kultúrny život*, 2 June 1967, p. 3.

SELUCKÝ, RADOSLAV. "Review of E. Loebl's Book," *Kultúrny život*, 2 May 1967, p. 3.

SELUCKÝ, RADOSLAV. "The Socialist World As Seen by a Czech Economist" (ten parts), *Reportér*, nos. 6-16, 7 Feb.-17 Apr. 1968.

SELUCKÝ, RADOSLAV. "Tentokrát komentář pro ekonomy," *Práce*, 3 Dec. 1968, p. 3.

SELUCKÝ, RADOSLAV. "Východ je Východ," *Text 72*, vol. iv, no. 3 (32), 30 Mar. 1972, p. 8.

SELUCKÝ, RADOSLAV, and DUŠAN HAMŠÍK. "Mládež vede Brno," *Tvorba*, 18 May 1949, p. 470.

SELUCKÝ, RADOSLAV, and JAROSLAV VOJTĚCH, "Vodní schodiště: O stavbě pruplavu Volha-Don," *Tvorba*, 22 Nov. 1951, pp. 1122-3.

ŠIK, OTA. "Ako by nemal vyzerat 'antidogmatizmus,'" *Kultúrny život*, 2 Nov. 1963, p. 3.

ŠIK, OTA. "Husák jako Novotný," *Listy*, vol. i, no. 6, Nov. 1971, pp. 9-14.

ŠIK, OTA. "Jak dál v hospodářské politice," *Rudé právo*, 22 May 1968, p. 3, and *Bulletin československé společnosti ekonomické*, no. 3, 1968.

ŠIK, OTA. "Krize v ČSSR," *Literární listy*, special edition in exile, Aug. 1969, p. 1.

ŠIK, OTA. "Ma réforme était juste, la politique l'a fait échouer," *Preuves*, third quarter 1970, pp. 79-90.

ŠIK, OTA. "Na okraj těchto dnů," *Rudé právo*, 27 July 1968, pp. 1 and 3.

ŠIK, OTA. "Prohlášení," *Reportér*, 27 Mar. 1969, p. 12.

ŠIK, OTA. "Proti nemarxistickým teoriím 'decentralizace' řízení," *Tvorba*, 15 Jan. 1959, pp. 57-9.

ŠIK, Dr OTA on the Conflict between Capital and Wages: "The Maudling Memorandum: A Communist Critique," *The Times*, 4 Oct. 1972, p. 14.

ŠIK, OTA, and MILAN HÜBL. Exchange of Open Letters, *Práce*, 16 and 23 Dec. 1968. Editorial comments of *Práce* 22 Dec. 1968.

ŠIK, OTA Jr. Letter to *Práce*, 18 Dec. 1968.

"Sik versus Schweik in Czechoslovakia." *East Europe*, vol. xvi, no. 2, Feb. 1966, pp. 21-2.

ŠIKL, ZDENĚK. Interview with Pavel Oliva. "O řízení historiografie," *Dějiny a současnost*, no. 7, July 1968, p. 26.

ŠIKL, ZDENĚK. "Reminiscences and Perspectives," *Dějiny a současnost*, no. 5, May 1968, pp. 1-3.

SLÁNSKÝ, JOZEFA and MARTA. "Interview," *Borba*, 12 May 1968.

SLANSKÝ, RUDOLF Jr. "A Note by an Observer Lacking in Partiality: Councils of Workers or Councils of Directors?" *Práce*, 18 Feb. 1969.

SLEZÁK, DUŠAN. "Ešte raz s prof. M. Kusým: Filozofia k člověku," *Večerník*, 16 Nov. 1968, pp. 1-2.

SMRKOVSKÝ, JOSEF. Interview. *Giorni vie nuove*, 16 Sept. 1971.

SMRKOVSKÝ, JOSEF. Interview. *Student*, 20 June 1967.

SMRKOVSKÝ, JOSEF. "What Is Today's Issue?" *Práce*, 21 Jan. 1968.

SOSNAR, JURA. "Hovoří tajemník Pillerovy komise doc. Karel Kaplan: zodpovědnost očima historika," *Práce*, 23 July 1968, p. 3.

ŠPITZER, JURAJ. "Sila dějín," *Kultúrny život*, 31 Aug. 1963, p. 5.

SRB, V. "Třídní a sociální složení obyvatelstva v ČSSR v roce 1967," *Demografie*, no. 2, June 1968, p. 181.

ŠTERN, JAN. "Akord lásky: Čeští a slovenští básníci k 70. narozeninám J. V. Stalina," *Tvorba*, 11 Jan. 1950, p. 45.

ŠTERN, JAN. "Blíž k normě. Ani muže," *Práce*, 14 Dec. 1968.

ŠTERN, JAN. "Dopis straně." *Tvorba*, 25 May 1949, p. 492.

ŠTERN, JAN. "Epopej českého proletariátu," *Tvorba*, 27 Apr. 1949, p. 391.

ŠTERN, JAN. "Generace nebo 'generace'?" *Květen*, no. 9, May 1958.
ŠTERN, JAN. "Jeden za všechny, všichni za jednoho," *Práce*, 24 Aug. 1958.
ŠTERN, JAN. "Jsme s tebou, Koreo!" *Tvorba*, 2 July 1950, p. 643.
ŠTERN, JAN. "Kdo to tam kráčí pravou?" *Práce*, 7 Dec. 1968.
ŠTERN, JAN. "Měštácké svědomí," *Tvorba*, 30 Mar. 1949, p. 308.
ŠTERN, JAN. "Mládí mírového tábora," *Tvorba*, 21 Sept. 1949, p. 898.
ŠTERN, JAN. "Myslitel orlího zraku," *Tvorba*, 7 June 1950, p. 557.
ŠTERN, JAN. "Na stráži proti zradě," *Tvorba*, 12 Oct. 1949, p. 965.
ŠTERN, JAN. "Pište pro lidi," *Tvorba*, 23 Nov. 1949, p. 1114.
ŠTERN, JAN. "Plán jsou lidé: Ze staveniŠť Ostravska," *Tvorba*, 26 Oct. 1949, pp. 1019-20.
ŠTERN, JAN. "Poznámky z Budapešti," *Tvorba*, 17 Aug. 1949, p. 766.
ŠTERN, JAN. "Přehlídka mírové armády," *Tvorba*, 4 May 1949, p. 413.
ŠTERN, JAN. "Pruty Svatoplukovy," *Práce*, 4 Jan. 1969.
ŠTERN, JAN. "Rady se radí," *Práce*, 9 Jan. 1969, pp. 1 and 9.
ŠTERN, JAN. "Řecké děti," *Tvorba*, 6 July 1949, p. 634.
ŠTERN, JAN. "Staré dílny nových lidí," *Tvorba*, 19 Oct. 1949, p. 994.
ŠTERN, JAN. "Spojenectví angažovaných," *Práce*, 18 Aug. 1968, p. 1.
ŠTERN, JAN. "Velké spiknutí," *Tvorba*, 19 Oct. 1949, p. 1001.
ŠTERN, JAN. "Za socialistické vlastenectví," *Tvorba*, 17 Apr. 1949, p. 394.
ŠTERN, JAN. "Závěr k diskusi o míru," *Tvorba*, 6 Apr. 1949, p. 322.
ŠTERN, JAN. "Země se brání," *Tvorba*, 18 Oct. 1950, p. 1003.
ŠTERN, JAN. "Zpáteční cesta se trestá," *Práce*, 30 Nov. 1968.
ŠTEVČEK, PAVOL. "Reflections 1963," *Kultúrny život*, nos. 51-2, 21 Dec. 1963.
ŠTRAUB, A. "Od hospodářské reformy nelze ustoupit," *Reportér*, 6 Nov. 1968, pp. 14-15.
ŠULC, ZDISLAV. "The Significance of the Changes in the Control of Our Industry," *Rudé právo*, 26 Feb. 1959.
ŠULCOVÁ, OLGA. "Ani černá, ani bílá," *Kulturní tvorba*, 30 May 1963, p. 8.
ŠULCOVÁ, OLGA. "Umění neodejít," *Večerní Praha*, 12 May 1969, p. 2.
SUTOVEC, MILAN. "What We Need and What We Do Not Need," *Kultúrny život*, 29 Mar. 1968.
ŠVANKMAJER, MILAN. "Četník Evropy," *Dějiny a současnost*, no. 4, Apr. 1969, pp. 6-11.
SVITÁK, IVAN. "Ateistická výchova na vesnici," *Otázky marxistické filosofie*, no. 1, 1962, p. 49.
SVITÁK, IVAN. "Brief aus Prag." *Forum*, vol. xiii, no. 146, 1966. (First "Brief" by Sviták in no. 142.)
SVITÁK, IVAN. "Dívat se dopředu," *Listy*, vol. i, no. 6, Nov. 1971, pp. 23-4.
SVITÁK, IVAN. "Illusions of Czech Socialist Democracy," *Telos*, no. 22, winter 1974/5, pp. 118-30.
SVITÁK, IVAN. "Intellectuals and Workers in Czechoslovak Democratization," *New Politics*, vol. vii, Spring 1968, pp. 50-9.
SVITÁK, IVAN. "Kafka as Philosopher," *Survey*, no. 59, Apr. 1966, pp. 36-40.
SVITÁK, IVAN. "Překonat dědictví stalinismu," *Listy*, vol. iii, no. 2, Apr. 1973, pp. 18-20.
SVITÁK, IVAN. "Překonat náboženské přežcitky smysl vědecko-ateistické propagace," *Naše pravda*, 14 Dec. 1959, pp. 2-3.
SVITÁK, IVAN. "Slepá ulička české politiky," *Svědectví*, vol. ix, nos. 34-6, Winter 1969, pp. 127-30.
SVITÁK, IVAN. "Stranická organizace a ateistická výchova," *Naše pravda*, 10 Nov. 1959, p. 2.
TESAŘ, JAN. "Železná garda a 'realisté'," *Listy*, 17 Apr. 1969, p. 16.
URBANOVÁ, IRENA. Letter to the Editor. *Svět práce*, 30 Apr. 1969, p. 6.
VACULÍK, LUBOMÍR. "What Do You Want Us To Do?" *Rudé právo*, 12 Jan. 1964.
VACULÍK, LUDVÍK. "Pražský podzim," *Listy*, vol. vii, no. 1, Feb. 1977, p. 24.
VALENTA, V. "Interview: Teoreticky . . .," *Telegram*, vol. iii, no. 5, 15 Jan. 1973, p. 2 (Interview with Radoslav SELUCKÝ.)
V., E. "Čo vy na to, profesor Kusý?" *Smena*, 6 Mar. 1969, p. 5.
VOLNÝ, SLÁVA. "Rozhovor s Ladislavem Mňačkem. Zavinili jsme to sami," *Text 70*, no. 1, Jan. 1970, pp. 1-2.
VRABEC, VÁCLAV. "K míře odpovědnosti: Mlýn a mlynáři," *Reportér*, 24-31 July 1968, pp. I-VI.
VRABEC, VÁCLAV. "The Relationship of the CPC and the Public to the Political Trials of the Early Fifties," *Revue dějin socialismu*, no. 3, July 1969.
VRANOVSKÝ, PAVEL. "People Dissatisfied with Their Jobs?" *Práce*, 25 Aug. 1967.
"We Talk to Professor Kusý: What Menaces Democracy?" *Večerník*, 21 Feb. 1969.

"What Does February Mean for You Today?" A round-table discussion, *Reportér*, no. 7, 1968, pp. 1 ff.
ZAJAC, LADISLAV. "Worries of These Days," *Práca*, 16 June 1963.
zč. "Vědci o naší cestě k socialismu," *Svobodné slovo*, 17 Mar. 1965.
ZIMMER, DIETER E. "Was nicht passieren dürfte: Ein Interview mit Pavel Kohout," *Die Zeit*, 30 Aug. 1968, p. 10.
"Životopis soudruha JUDr. Gustáva Husáka, CSc.," *Rudé právo*, 19 Apr. 1969, p. 2.

8. Monitoring services and press surveys

Radio Free Europe, Munich: Press surveys in Czech, Slovak, and English; Czechoslovak Radio programs in Czech and Slovak; Czechoslovak Situation Reports; Analyses, and Studies.

9. Newspapers and periodicals in Czech and Slovak

Československý časopis historický, Dějiny a současnost, Dnešek, Doba, Echo, Filmové a televisní noviny, Filozófia, Hospodářské noviny, Kulturní noviny, Kulturní tvorba, Kultúrny život, Lidová demokracie, Lidové noviny, Listy, Literární listy, Literární noviny, L'ud, Mladá fronta, My 68, Nová mysl, Nové knihy, Nové slovo, Obrana lidu, Pedagogika, Plamen, Plánované hospodářství, Pochodeň, Politická ekonomie, Politika, Práca, Práce, Pravda, Právník, Právny obzor, Predvoj, Příspěvky k dějinám KSČ, Průboj, Reportér, Roľnícke noviny, Rudé právo, Sloboda, Slovenské pohľady, Smena, Student, Svědectví, Svět hospodářství, Svět práce, Svoboda, Svobodné noviny, Svobodne slovo, Text, Tvorba, Universita Karlova, Večerní Praha, Večerník, Zemědělské noviny, Zítřek, Život, Život strany, etc.

B. Sources from the normalization period

AMORT, Čestmír and Václav Král. "Tajně o historii." *Listy*, Nos. 4–5, July 1971, pp. 56–60.
BERNARD, Vladimír. "Na Leninských principech: Vymýtit kořeny pravicového oportunismu." *Tribuna*, 6 January 1971, p. 4.
DVORSKÝ, Petr. "Ota Šik odstraňuje třecí plochy." *Tribuna*, 30 September 1970, p. 7.
ek. "Spisovstel a strana: Beseda s literárním kritikem Václavem Pekárkem." *Tvorba*, 4 February 1976, supplement.
FIDRMUC, Jaroslav. "Ekonomická koncepcia trhového socializmu Otty Šika: Šik ako osoba a dielo, I." *Smena*, 25 July 1970, p. 6.
FULKA, Jaroslav. "Křst členské základny KSČ a únor 1948: Historická perspektiva I." *Nová mysl*, No. 3, 16 March 1970, pp. 347–49.
GERLOCH, Vladimír. "Muž s maskou: Paně Šikova 'třetí cesta'." *Tvorba*, 9 May 1973, p. 7.
GRYZLOV, Gavril. "Na dně." *Nové slovo*, 12 February 1970, p. 2.
HAVLÍČEK, Karel. "Sociální složení strany a její akceschopnost." *Život strany*, No. 13, 22 June 1970, pp. 15–16.
HOTHAR, Josef. "Poslední gesto Ladislava Mňačky." *Tvorba*, 28 January 1970, p. 2.
HRUBÝ, Jiří. "Všechny síly očistě, sjednocení a aktivizaci." *Život strany*, No. 8, 13 April 1970, pp. 41–44.
HRZAL, Ladislav. "Filozofie člověka." *Trubuna*, 30 April 1975, pp. 8–9.
HRZAL, Ladislav and J. Netopilík. "K analýze vývoje české filosofie: Poznánky k některým aspektům boje marxisticko-leninské a buržoanní ideologie v letech 1945–1949." *Filosofický časopis*, No. 2, April 1972, pp. 167–81.
JAKEŠ, Miloš. "Interview." *Pravda*, 19 April 1974, p. 3.
JAKEŠ, Miloš. "Lusíme vytvořit ve straně zdravé klima." *Tribuna*, 3 June 1970, pp. 1–3.

JARUŠEK, Oldřich. "Porážka ve druhém kole: 'Lidská tvář' pravice v Turnově — díl 2." *Tribuna*, 3 June 1970, p. 20.

KLIMPL, Vlastimil. "Urkulatého stolu: Cesty k ozdravění naší ekonomiky." *Nová mysl*, No. 7, July 1969, pp. 847-57.

KOTÚČ, Pavol and Josef Lúč. "Co sa skrývalo za žilinským štrajkom." *Pravda*, 22 June 1970, p. 4.

KRAJKOVIČ, Tibor. "Tendencia pohybu mzdových relácií medzi základnými kategóriami pracovníkov v ČSSR." *Práce a mzda*, No. 7, July 1974, p. 387.

KRÁL, Václay. "O marxistiokou koncepci národních dějin." *Slovanský přehled*, No. 2, April 1973, p. 107.

LANTAY, Andrej. "Nebudňe pesimisti." *Život*, 9 July 1969, p. 7.

LAUD, Michael. "Pravda o podnikových radách." *Hospodářské noviny*, 10 July 1970, supplement of 8 pages.

LAUDA, V. "Who Is Speaking in the Name of the Trade Unions?" *Tribuna*, No. 24, 25 June 1969.

LEŠA, Jiří. "Tečka za emigrantem Otou Šikem." *Tribuna*, 18 March 1970, p. 3.

MAREŠ, Jiří. "High Stakes." *Tribuna*, 18 February 1970, p. 20.

MAREŠ, Jiří. "'Lidská tvář' pravice v Turnově: Vysoká hra." *Tribuna*, 18 February 1970, p. 20.

MATOUŠ, Milan. "Emigranti ve službách antikomunismu." *Tvorba*, 13 and 20 June 1973, supplement of 16 p.

MOTTL, František. "Co byla Federace lokomotivních čet?" *Tribuna*, 28 January 1970, p. 7.

NĚMEC, Bohumil. "Růst členské základny — nedílná součást boje za upevnění její vedoucí úlohy." *Život strany*, No. 15, 14 July 1972, pp. 7-9.

NYUWIRTHOVÁ, Milena. "Podivná stávka v Libni." *Svět socialismu*, 11 June 1969, p. 6.

OBZINA, Jaromír. "Strana v výchova inteligence." *Nová mysl*, No. 3, March 1973, p. 351.

PATHY, Rudolf. "Současné problémy kriminality v národním hospodářství." *Život strany*, No. 14, 6 July 1970, pp. 21-24.

PETROVICKÝ, Milo and Luděk Dobeš. "Zahraniční politika ČSSR v roce 1973." *Nová mysl*, No. 2, February 1974, pp. 314-25.

PODZEMNÝ. E. "Economics and Ideological Work." *Tribuna*, 13 December 1972.

POMAIZL, K. "Jednostranný nacionalismus." *Tribuna*, 29 January 1975, p. 8.

PONOMARJOVOVA. "Runaway of the 'Prague Spring'." *Týdeník aktualit*, No. 26, 28 June 1971, p. 2.

PÓR, F. D. "Proč Ústav dějin socialismu, a ne Ústav dějin KSČ?" *Tribuna*, 30 December 1969, pp. 11 and 16.

ROŠKO, Róbert. "K otázke triednej genézy našej inteligencie." *Sociológia*, vol. IV, No. 3, April 1972, pp. 196-202.

ROUBAL. Květoslav. "Od dogmatismu k revizi marxisticke politické ekonomie: Vývoj ekonomických názorů Oty Šika." *Nová mysl*, No. 1, January 1971, pp. 63-84.

ROUBAL, Květoslav. "O umění metati kozelce anob Ota Šik — teoretik." *Tvorba*, 17, 24, and 31 March 197 , pp. 3, 15, and 14-15.

RYKL, Leopold. "Složení strany a dělníci." *Tribuna*, No. 28, 15 July 1970.

RYKL, Leopold. "Vývoj členské nákladny strany: Historická perspektiva, II." *Nová mysl*, No. 4, 15 April 1970, pp. 458-64.

"Šedesát let G. Husáka." *Listy*, vol. III, No. 4, August 1973, p. 40.

SOBOTECKÝ, Josef. "August August August." *Tvorba*, 27 May 1970, p. 16.

SOBOTECKÝ, Josef. "Opožděný reportér." *Tvorba*, 1 July 1970, p. 16.

ŠROUBHA, Jan. "Testimony of a Jest." *Tribuna*, 11 March 1970, p. 15.

ŠVESTKA, Oldřich. "Proč se to neřeklo dříve?" *Tribuna*, No. 33, 27 August 1969, p. 2.

ŠVESTKA, Oldřich. "To Win the Favor of the Working Class." *Tribuna*, 28 May 1969.

TAŠKÝ, František. "K problematike empirického výskuma robotníckej triedy." *Sociológia*, vol. IV, No. 2, March 1972, p. 113.

TAŠKÝ, František. "Robotnícka trieda na Slovensku po vítázstve socialistickej revolúcie." *Sociológia*, No. 1, February 1973, pp. 13-28.

TROJÁČEK, František. "Zkvalitňování členské základny strany vyžaduje důsledné řízení." *Život strany*, No. 26, 18 December 1975, p. 12.

VAJC, K. and M. Kolář. "O jounom výročí." *Tribuna*, 19 June 1970, p. 9.

ZÁZVORKA, J. "Co se všechno mělo 'obrozovat': Po očistě v ZO ROH v Ústavu jaderného výzkumu ČSAV v Řeži." *Svět práce*, 24 June 1970, p. 5.

C. Secondary sources

1. Bibliographies and references

DUBEN, J. *České a slovenské noviny a časopisy v zahraničí*, Září, 1970; New York, Společnost pro vědu a umění, 1970; 28 pages.

HEJZLAR, ZDENĚK, and VLADIMIR V. KUSIN. *Czechoslovakia 1968-1969*, Annotations, Bibliography, Chronology, New York, Garland, 1974; 316 pages.

KANET, ROGER. *Soviet and East European Foreign Policy*. A bibliography of English and Russian-Language Publications, 1967-71. Santa Barbara, Calif., and Oxford, ABC-Clio, 1975.

KUHN, HEINRICH. *Handbuch der Tschechoslowakei*, Munich, Lerche, 1966.

KUHN, HEINRICH. *Biographisches Handbuch der Tschechoslowakei*, I-II, Munich, Lerche, 1969.

KÜNZEL, FRANZ PETER. *Übersetzungen aus dem Tschechischen und dem Slowakischen ins Deutsche nach 1945*. Eine Bibliographie, Munich, Ackermann-Gemeinde, 1970.

PARRISH, MICHAEL. *The 1968 Czechoslovak Crisis*. A Bibliography, 1968-70. Santa Barbara, Calif., ABC-Clio, 1971; 41 pages.

ŠTURM, RUDOLF. *Bibliography on Czechoslovakia*, New York, Arno Press, 1968; 60 pages.

2. Unpublished materials

ANDRAS, CHARLES. "Christians and Marxists in Marianske Lazne," *RFER*, 10 July 1967; 30 pages.

ANDRAS, CHARLES. "Gustav Husak: A Political profile of the Slovak CP Leader," *RFER*, 6 Dec. 1968; 12 pages.

DEVLIN, KEVIN. "Leninism and the Czechoslovak Spring: The CPI Stands Firm," *RFER*, 5 June 1970; 7 pages.

DEVLIN, KEVIN. "Plight of Czechoslovak Intellectuals: 'Espresso' Interviews Kohout and Others," *RFER*, no. 1836, 5 July 1973.

HENEGHAN, THOMAS E. "Husak in Hradcany Castle," *RFER*, 6 Aug. 1975; 26 pages.

HRUBY, PETER. "On the Road to a Revolution: Czechoslovakia, 1960-1968." New York, Columbia University M.A. Thesis, 1969.

LYON, S. P. "The Communist Party of Czechoslovakia," *RFER*, 28 Mar. 1958; 49 pages.

"Situation Report, Czechoslovakia/76, 5 September 1969." *RFER*.

"Situation Report, Czechoslovakia," *RFER*, 4 June 1975; 15 pages.

S.L. "Husak and Strougal: Their Position and Prospects in Czechoslovakia Politics," *RFER*, 20 Aug. 1969; 16 pages.

STANKOVIC, SLOBODAN. "French Film on Stalinism in Czechoslovakia Enthusiastically Received in Yugoslavia," *Yugoslavia*, no. 0657, *RFER*, 16 July 1970; 7 pages.

STANKOVIC, SLOBODAN. "Russian Lieutenant Commanding Czechoslovak Academicians," *RFER*, 17 Jan. 1969.

TREND, HARRY. "Husak's 'Mini' Economic Reform," *RFER*, 2 Sept. 1969, 20 pages.

TREND, HARRY. "Pre-August Trends in Czechoslovak Economic Organization and Policy' III," *RFER*, 18 Nov. 1968; 30 pages.

TREND, HARRY. "The Return to Economic 'Normalcy' in Czechoslovakia," *RFER*, 9 Apr. 1970; 53 pages.

3. Books

ASHLEY, MAURICE. *England in the Seventeenth Century*, London, Penguin Books, 1968.

BECK, CARL *et al. Comparative Communist Political Leadership*, New York, David McKay Co., 1973.

BITTMAN, L. *The Deception Game*. Czechoslovak Intelligence in Soviet Political Warfare, Syracuse, Syracuse University Press, 1972; 246 pages.

BRODSKÝ, J. *Řešení Gama*, Toronto, Hlas nových, 1970; 200 pages.

ČERNÝ, VÁCLAV. *Boje a směry socialistické kultury*, Prague, Borový, 1946.

ČERNÝ, VÁCLAV. *První sešit o existencialismu*, Prague, 1948.

CHURCHWARD, L. G. *The Soviet Intelligentsia*. An Essay on the Social Structure and Roles of the Soviet Intellectuals during the 1960s, London, Routledge & Kegan Paul, 1973.

CZERWINSKI, E. J., and JAROSLAW PIEKALKIEWICZ, eds. *The Soviet Invasion of Czechoslovakia: Its Effects on Eastern Europe*, New York, Praeger, 1972; x, 214 pages.
DAIX, PIERRE. *J'ai cru au matin*, Paris, Robert Laffont, 1976; 444 pages.
DAVENPORT, MARCIA. *Too Strong for Fantasy*, London, Collins, 1968.
Dějiny Československa v datech, Prague, 1968.
DRACHKOVITCH, MILORAD M., ed. *Marxism in the Modern World*, Stanford, Stanford University Press, 1965; xvi, 293 pages.
DRACHKOVITCH, MILORAD M., ed. *Marxist Ideology in the Contemporary World, Its Appeals and Paradoxes*, New York, Praeger, 1966; xx, 192 pages.
ESSLIN, MARTIN. *Brecht*. The Man and His Work, Garden City, N.Y., Anchor Books, Doubleday & Co., 1961.
FEJTÖ, FRANÇOIS. *Le Coup de Prague 1948*, Paris, Seuil, 1977; 283 pages.
FONVIEILLE-ALQUIER, FRANÇOIS. *L'Eurocommunisme*. Essai. Paris, Fayard, 1977; 288 pages.
FREYMOND, JACQUES. *Lénine et l'impérialisme*, Lausanne, Payot, 1951; 134 pages.
FRIEDMAN, OTTO. *The Break-up of Czech Democracy*, London, Victor Gollancz, 1950.
FROLIK, JOSEF. *The Frolik Defection*, London, Leo Cooper, 1975.
FROMM, ERICH. *Socialist Humanism*, New York, Doubleday, 1965.
GATI, CHARLES, ed. *The International Politics of Eastern Europe*, New York, Praeger, 1976.
GOLAN, GALIA. *The Czechoslovak Reform Movement*. Communism in Crisis 1962–1968. Cambridge, Cambridge University Press, 1971; 368 pages.
GOLAN, GALIA. *Reform Rule in Czechoslovakia*. The Dubček Era 1968–1969, Cambridge, Cambridge University Press, 1973; vii, 327 pages.
GRIFFITH, WILLIAM E. *The Sino-Soviet Rift*, Cambridge, Mass., The M.I.T., 1964.
HALLE, LOUIS. *The Cold War As History*, New York, Harper & Row, 1967.
HARMON, ERNEST. *Combat Commander*. Autobiography of a Soldier, New York, Prentice Hall, 1971.
HERMANN, A. H. A. *History of the Czechs*, London, Allen Lane, 1975.
HODNETT, G., and P. J. POTICHNYJ. *The Ukraine and the Czechoslovak Crisis*, Canberra, Australian National University, 1970; 154 pages.
HORSKÝ, VLADIMÍR. *Prag 1968*. Systemverändergung und Systemverteidigung, Stuttgart, Ernst Klett, 1975; 534 pages.
IONESCU, GHITA. *The Break-up of the Soviet Empire in Eastern Europe*, Harmondsworth, Penguin Books, 1965; 169 pages.
ISENBERG, IRWIN. *Ferment in Eastern Europe*, New York, H. W. Wilson, 1965.
JANCAR, BARBARA W. *Czechoslovakia and the Absolute Monopoly of Power*. A Study of Political Power in a Communist System, New York, Praeger, 1971; 330 pages.
KAMENKA, EUGENE. *The Ethical Foundations of Marxism*, New York, St. Martin's Press, 1962 and 1969.
KELSEN, HANS. *The Political Theory of Bolshevism*. A Critical Analysis, Los Angeles, University of California Press, 1948; 60 pages.
KENNAN, GEORGE F. *Memoirs, 1925/1950*, Boston, Little, Brown & Co., 1967.
KING, F. P. *The New Internationalism*. Allied Policy and the European Peace 1939–1945, Newton Abbot, Devon, David & Charles, 1973.
KOLAKOWSKI, LESZEK. *Marxism and Beyond*, London, Paladin, 1971.
KORBEL, JOSEF. *The Communist Subversion of Czechoslovakia, 1938/1948*. The Failure of Coexistence, Princeton, N.J., Princeton University Press, 1959.
KORBEL, JOSEF. *Détente in Europe*. Real or Imaginary?, Princeton, N.J., Princeton University Press, 1972.
KORBEL, JOSEF. *Twentieth Century Czechoslovakia*. The Meaning of Its History, New York, Columbia University Press, 1977.
KREJČÍ, JAROSLAV. *Social Change and Stratification in Postwar Czechoslovakia*, London, Macmillan, 1972; 207 pages.
KUSIN, VLADIMIR V. *The Intellectual Origins of the Prague Spring*. The Development of Reformist Ideas in Czechoslovakia, 1956–1967, Cambridge, University Press, 1971; 168 pages.
KUSIN, VLADIMIR V. *Political Grouping in Czechoslovak Reform Movement*, London, Macmillan, 1972; 224 pages.
KUSIN, VLADIMIR V., ed. *The Czechoslovak Reform Movement 1968*. Proceedings of the Seminar Held

250   *Fools and Heroes*

at the University of Reading on 12–17 July 1971, London, International Research Documents, 1973; 358 pages.

LAZARCIK, GREGOR. *Comparison of Czechoslovak Agricultural and Nonagricultural Incomes in Current and Real Terms, 1937 and 1948–1965*, New York, Columbia University, 1968.

LETTRICH, JOZEF. *History of Modern Slovakia*, New York, 1955.

LEWY, A. *Rowboat to Prague*, New York, Orion, 1972; 531 pages.

LIEHM, A. J. *Closely Watched Films*. The Czechoslovak Experience, White Plains, I.A.S.P., 1974.

LIEHM, A. J. *Gespräche an der Moldau*, Vienna, Molden, 1968; 352 pages.

LIEHM, A. J. *The Politics of Culture*, New York, Grove Press, 1973; 412 pages.

LIEHM, A. J. *Trois générations*, Paris, Gallimard, 1970; 350 pages.

LOBKOWITZ, NIKOLAUS. *Marxismus-Leninismus in der CSR*. Die tschechoslowakische Philosophie seit 1945, Freiburg, Dordrecht, 1961.

LUTZ, WILLIAM, and HARRY BRENT, eds. *On Revolution*, Cambridge, Mass., Winthrop, 1971.

MAMATEY, VICTOR S., and RADOMÍR LUŽA, eds. *A History of the Czechoslovak Republic, 1918–1948*, Princeton, N.J., Princeton University Press, 1973; xi, 534 pages.

MARX, KARL. *Selected Works* in two volumes, vol. i, London, Lawrence & Wishart, 1947.

MAXA, J. *Die kontrollierte Revolution*. Anatomie des Prager Frühlings, Vienna, Zsolnay, 1969; 254 pages.

MASTNY, VOJTECH. *The Czechs under Nazi Rule*. The Failure of National Resistance, New York, Columbia University Press, 1971; xiii, 274 pages.

MAYER, M. S. *The Art of the Impossible*. A Study of the Czech Resistance. Santa Barbara, Calif., Center for the Study of Democratic Institutions, 1969; 47 pages.

MEDVEDEV, ROY A. *On Socialist Democracy*, London, Macmillan, 1975.

MILOSZ, CZESLAW. *The Captive Mind*, New York, Vintage Books, 1955.

OSTRÝ, A. (pseud.). *Československý pokus o reformu 1968*, Cologne, Index; 358 pages.

OXLEY, ANDREW, ALEX PRAVDA, ANDREW ROTCHIE, eds. *Czechoslovakia*. The Party and the People, London, Allen Land, The Penguin Books, 1973; vi, 303 pages.

PIELKALKIEWICZ, JAROSLAW A. *Public Opinion Polls in Czechoslovakia, 1968–1969*. Results and Analysis of Surveys Conducted During the Dubček Era, New York, Praeger, 1972; 357 pages.

RAINER, LAURENT. *L'après Printemps de Prague*, Paris, Stock, 1976.

RUSH, MYRON. *How Communist States Change Their Rulers*, Ithaca, Cornell University Press, 1974.

SALOMON, MICHEL. *Prague´ La révolution étranglée*, Janvier — Août 1968, Paris, Robert Laffont, 1968; 360 pages.

SCHWARZ, HARRY. *Prague's 200 Days*, New York, Praeger, 1969; 274 pages.

SCHWARZ, URI. *Confrontation and Intervention in the Modern World*, Dobbs Ferry, N.Y., Oceana Publications, 1970.

SETON-WATSON, HUGH. *Nationalism and Communism*. Essays, 1946–63. New York, Praeger, 1964.

SHAWCROSS, WILLIAM. *Dubček*, London, Weidenfeld & Nicolson, 1970; xvi, 317 pages.

SINANIAN, SYLVA, ISTVAN DEAK, PETER C. LUDZ, eds. *Eastern Europe in the 1970s*, New York, Praeger, 1972.

SIRC, LJUBO. *Economic Devolution in Eastern Europe*, London, Longmans, 1969; 165 pages.

SKILLING, H. GORDON. *Czechoslovakia's Interrupted Revolution*, Princeton, N.J., Princeton University Press, 1976; vi, 924 pages.

SKILLING, H. GORDON, and FRANKLYN GRIFFITHS, eds. *Interest Groups in Soviet politics*, Princeton University Press, 1971; vii, 433 pages.

ŠKVORECKÝ, JOSEF. *All the Bright Young Men and Women*. A Personal History of the Czech Cinema, Toronto, P. Martin Associates, 1971; 280 pages.

ŠKVORECKÝ, JOSEF. *Mirákl*. Toronto, 68 Publishers, 1972; 2 vols.

Slovník českých spisovatelů, Prague, 1964.

SOUČKOVÁ, MILADA. *A Literary Satellite*. Czechoslovak-Russian Literary Relations, Chicago, Chicago University Press, 1970; 179 pages.

STEINER, E. *The Slovak Dilemma*, Cambridge, Cambridge University Press, 1973; ix, 229 pages.

STERLING, C. *The Masaryk Case*, New York, Harper & Row, 1969; 366 pages.

SUDA, ZDENĚK. *The Czechoslovak Socialist Republic*, Baltimore, Md., John Hopkins Press, 1969; xii, 180 pages.

SVITÁK, IVAN. "Marxist Philosophy in Czechoslovakia: The Lesson from Prague," in R. T. De

George and J. P. Scanland, eds. *Marxism and Religion in Eastern Europe.* Papers presented at the Banff International Slavic Conference, 4-7 September, 1974. Dordrecht, Holland, D. Reidel, 1976.

SZULC, TAD. *Czechoslovakia since World War II,* New York, Viking, 1971; 503 pages.

TABORSKY, EDWARD. *Communism in Czechoslovakia, 1948-1960,* Princeton University Press, 1961; xii, 628 pages.

TATU, MICHEL. *L'hérésie impossible.* Chronique du drame tchécoslovaque, Paris, Bernard Grasset, 1968; 291 pages.

Tchécoslovaquie. Les ouvriers face à la dictature, 1938-1948-1968, Paris, Confédération Force Ouvrière, 1969; 208 pages.

TIGRID, PAVEL. *Amère révolution,* Paris, Albin Michel, 1977; 285 pages.

TIGRID, PAVEL. *La chute irrésistible d'Alexandre Dubček,* Paris, Calmann-Lévy, 1969; 319 pages.

TIGRID, PAVEL. *Kvadratura kruhu.* Dokumenty a poznámky k československé krizi 1968-1970, Paris, Svědectví, 1970; 200 pages.

TIGRID, PAVEL. *Politická emigrace v atomovém věku,* Paris, Svědectví, 1968; 100 pages.

TIGRID, PAVEL. *Le Printemps de Prague,* Paris, Seuil, 1968; 278 pages.

TIGRID, PAVEL. *Why Dubček Fell,* London, Macdonald, 1971; 229 pages.

TODD, EMMANUEL. *La chute finale.* Essai sur la décomposition de la sphère soviétique, Paris, Robert Laffont, 1976.

ULČ, OTO. *Politics in Czechoslovakia,* San Francisco, W. H. Freeman & Co., 1974.

URBAN, RUDOLF. *Tschechoslowakei zwischen Ost und West.* Entwicklung des Geisteslebens seit 1945, Hannover, 1962; 64 pages.

VICHNIAC, ISABELLE. *L'ordre règne à Prague,* Paris, Librairie Arthème Fayard, 1968; 193 pages.

WECHSBERG, J. *The Voices.* Garden City, Doubleday, 1969; 113 pages.

WEISSKOPF, KURT. *The Agony of Czechoslovakia,* 1938-1968, London, Elek, 1968; 234 pages.

WEISSKOPF, KURT. *Les Coups de Prague, 1938-1968,* Paris, Cite, 1968; 266 pages.

WESSON, ROBERT G. *Why Marxism?* The Continuing Success of a Failed Theory, New York, Basic Books, 1976.

WINDSOR, P., and A. ROBERTS. *Czechoslovakia 1968.* Reforms, Repression, and Resistance, London, Chatto & Windus, 1969; 200 pages.

WISKEMANN, ELISABETH. *Czechs and Germans.* A Study of the Struggle in the Historic Provinces of Bohemia and Moravia, London, Oxford University Press, 1938; viii, 299 pages.

WOLFE, T. W. *Soviet Power and Europe 1945-1970,* Sanata Monica, Rand Corporation, 1970; 512 pages.

ZARTMAN, I. W. *Czechoslovakia: Intervention and Impact,* New York, New York University Press, 1970; 127 pages.

ZEMAN, ZBYNĚK A. B. *Prague Spring.* A Report on Czechoslovakia 1968, Harmondsworth, Penguin Books, 1969; 169 pages.

ZINNER, PAUL E. *Communist Strategy and Tactics in Czechoslovakia, 1918-1948,* New York, Praeger, 1963; 264 pages.

4. *Articles*

ANDREUCCI, FRANCO, and MALCOLM SYLVERS. "The Italian Communists Write Their History," *Science and Society,* xl, no 1, spring 1976, pp. 28-56.

ANTONETTI, LUCIANO. "Lenin e il Leninismo a Praga negli ultimi anni," *Critica Marxista,* vol. 8, no. 3, May-June 1970, pp. 194-204.

BAILEY, GEORGE. "Kafka's Nightmare Comes True," *Reporter,* no. 30, 7 May 1964, pp. 15-20.

BARCATA, LOUIS. "Between Stalin's Winter and the Thaw," *Die Presse,* 5 Oct. 1966.

BASS, ROBERT. "The Post-Stalin Era in Eastern Europe," *Problems of Communism,* vol. xii, no. 2, Mar.-Apr. 1963.

BEER, MANFRED. Interview with Ota Šik. *Die Welt,* 20 Oct. 1969.

BOCHENSKI, JOSEPH M. "On Czechoslovakia," *Studies in Soviet Thought,* vol. x, no. 1, Mar. 1970, pp. 61-2.

BONDY, FRANÇOIS. "Jean-Paul Sartre and Politics," *Journal of Contemporary History,* vol. 2, no. 2, Apr. 1967, pp. 25-48.

BURG, DAVID. "A Smuggled Document from Czechoslovakia: The Ten-Year Hell of Dr. Husak," *The Sunday Times*, 10 Aug. 1969, pp. 5-9.

BYSTRICKY, RUDOLF. "La coopération économique industrielle entre l'Est et l'Ouest et les lois dites de l'édification socialiste," *Annales d'études internationales*, vol. 5, 1974; pp. 27-92.

CAMPBELL, F. GREGORY "Central Europe's Bastion of Democracy," *East European Quarterly*, vol. xi, no. 2 (summer 1977), pp. 155-76.

CARRÈRE D'ENCAUSSE, HELÈNE. "La fin du mythe unitaire. Vingt ans de conflits dans l'Europe socialiste," *Revue française de science politique*, vol. xviii, no. 6, Dec. 1968, pp. 1155-89.

CARUTHERS, OSGOOD. "Czech Economist Warns of 'Catastrophe'," *International Herald Tribune*, 4 Dec. 1968.

"A Congress of Organizers," *East Europe*, vol. xv, no. 7, July 1966.

Czechoslovak Society of Arts and Sciences in America: First European Conference, 26-8 June 1970 in Horgen by Zürich. A record.

DAVY, RICHARD. "The Intellectual Ferment in Czechoslovakia," *The Times*, 19 Sept. 1967.

DOBES, LEO. "Czechoslovak Industrial Relations, 1945-1970." University of Melbourne Research Paper, no. 27, Dec. 1974; 65 pages.

DOBES, LEO. "Towards a General Theory of Trade Union Development in Eastern Europe." University of Melbourne Research Paper, no. 29; 76 pages.

DUCHACEK, IVO. "Czechoslovakia," in Stephen D. Kertesz, ed., *East Central Europe and the World*. Developments in the Post-Stalin Era, University of Notre Dame Press, 1962, pp. 95-119.

DUCHACEK, IVO. "Czechoslovakia: New Course or No Course?" *Problems of Communism*. vol. iv, no. 1, Jan.-Feb. 1955, pp. 12-19.

DUCHACEK, IVO. "Deset let, která neotřásla světem: profil čs. komunismu 1948-1958," *Svědectví*, vol. ii, no. 3, 1958.

ELIÁŠ, ZDENĚK, and JAROMÍR NETÍK. "Czechoslovakia," In *Communism in Europe*, ed. William E. Griffith, vol. ii, Boston, M.I.T., 1966.

FARNSWORTH, CLYDE H. "Sik Says Prague Repression Is Worse than Under Novotny," *International Herald Tribune*, 16 Mar. 1970, p. 4.

FEUER, LEWIS S. "Marx and the Intellectuals," *Survey*, no. 49, Oct. 1963, pp. 102-12.

FREYMOND, JACQUES. "La crise du système international," *Annales d'études internationales*, Geneva, Association des anciens de l'IUHEI, 1970; pp. 191-202.

FREYMOND. "L'Europe à la recherche de la sécurité," *Annales d'études internationales*, vol. 5, 1974; pp. 11-23.

FROMM, ERICH. "Introduction" to John M. Steiner, *Power Politics and Social Change in National Socialist Germany*, The Hague, Mouton, 1975.

GATI, CHARLES. "The 'Europeanization' of Communism?" *Foreign Affairs*, Apr. 1977, vol. 55, no. 3, pp. 539-53.

GELLNER, ERNEST. "The Anti-Levellers of Prague," *New Society*, 5 Aug. 1971, pp. 232-4.

GRIFFITH, WILLIAM E. "Myth and Reality in Czechoslovak History," *East Europe*, vol. 11, no. 3, Mar. 1962, pp. 3-11, 34-36, 40-41.

HASSNER, PIERRE. "L'Europe de l'est entre l'est et l'Europe," *Revue française de science politique*, vol. xix, no. 1, Feb. 1969, pp. 101-43.

HEJL, LUBOŠ. Seminar on East-West trade at the Graduate Institute of International Studies in Geneva, 2 Dec. 1968.

HOFFMANN, PAUL. "Czech Communists Admit Labor Unrest Is Serious," *International Herald Tribune*, 26-7 July 1969.

HOFFMANN, PAUL. "Husak Ousts Sik, 5 Other Liberals from Party Power," *International Herald Tribune*, 2 June 1969, p. 1.

HOLESOVSKY, VACLAV. "Planning Reform in Czechoslovakia," *Soviet Studies*, vol. xix, no. 4, Apr. 1968, pp. 544-56.

HOLESOVSKY, VACLAV. "Problems and Prospects," *Problems of Communism*, vol. 14, no. 5, Sept.-Oct., 1965, pp. 41-5.

HOLZMAN, FRANKLYN D., and ROBERT LEGVOLD. "The Economics and Politics of East-West Relations," *International Organization*, vol. 29, no. 1, winter 1975, pp. 275-320.

HRUBÝ, PETR. "Je toho tak málo?" *Československý přehled*, vol. iv, no. 9.

IGNOTUS, PAUL. "Czechs, Magyars, Slovaks," *The Political Quarterly*, vol. xl, no. 2, Apr.-June 1969, pp. 187-204.

JANCAR, BARBARA. "The Great Purges and the 'Prague Spring'," *Orbis*, Summer 1971, pp. 609-24.

KAROL, K. S. "Can Russia Survive Until 1980?" *New Statesman*, 25 Apr. 1969, pp. 573-4.

KAVAN, JAN. "Arrests and Repression Are Not Stopping the Czech Chartists," *The Times*, 6 Jan. 1978, p. 12.

KOHAK, ERAZIM. "Italia Sinistra; A Report from Rome," *Dissent*, Fall 1976, pp. 328-32.

KOLAKOWSKI, LESZEK. "The Euro-Communist Schism," *Encounter*, vol. xlix, no. 2, Aug. 1977, pp. 14-19.

KORBONSKI, ANDRZEJ. "Bureaucracy and Interest Groups in Communist Societies: The Case of Czechoslovakia," *Studies in Comparative Communism*, vol. 4, no. 1, Jan. 1971.

KOTYK, VACLAV, PHILIP E. MOSELY, ARNOLD J. TOYNBEE *et al.* "East-West Détente: The European Debate," *Journal of International Affairs*, vol. xxii, no. 2, winter 1968.

KOVANDA, KAREL. "Czechoslovak Workers'·Councils (1968-69)," *Telos*, no. 28, summer 1976, pp. 36-54.

KOVANDA, KAREL. "Czechoslovakia in Transition," *Telos*, vol. 31, spring 1977, pp. 143-52.

KOVANDA, KAREL. "Works Councils in Czechoslovakia, 1945-47," *Soviet Studies*, vol. xxix, no. 2, Apr. 1977, pp. 255-69.

KUBAT, DANIEL. "Patterns of Leadership in a Communist State: Czechoslovakia 1946-58," *Journal of Central European Affairs*, vol. xxi, no. 3, Oct. 1961, p. 314.

KUBAT, DANIEL. "Writers in a Totalitarian State: Czechoslovakia, 1945-56," *The American Journal of Sociology*, vol. lxvii, no. 4, Jan. 1962, pp. 439-41.

LABEDZ, LEOPOLD *et al.* "The Future of East-West Relations," *Survey*, vol. xxii, no. 3/4 (100/101), summer-autumn 1976, pp. 1-16 ff.

LANGE, PETER. "What Is To Be Done About Italian Communism?" *Foreign Policy*, no. 21, winter 1975-6, pp. 224-40.

LEIBOWITZ, JOSHUA O. "Maimonides in the History of Medicine," *Ariel* (Jerusalem), no. 41, pp. 37-52.

LEWANDOVSKY, JOSEPH. Open letter to Gustav Husak. *Kultura* (Paris), no. 9, 1972; excerpts in *Listy*, vol. iii, no. 1, Feb. 1973, p. 51.

LICKLIDER, ROY E. "Soviet Control of Eastern Europe: Morality Versus American National Interest," *Political Science Quarterly*, vol. 91; no. 4, winter 1976-7, pp. 619-24.

LIEHM, A. J. "Franz Kafka in Eastern Europe," *Telos*, vol. 23, spring 1975, pp. 53-83.

LOBKOWICZ, N. "Partei-Philosophie," *Wort und Wahrheit*, no. 4, 1963, pp. 280-98.

LOBKOWICZ, N. "Philosophical Revisionism in Post-War Czechoslovakia," *Studies in Soviet Thought*, vol. 4, 1964, no. 2, pp. 89-101.

LOBKOWICZ, N. "Philosophy in Czechoslovakia since 1960," *Studies in Soviet Thought*, 1963, no. 1, pp. 11-32.

LOBKOWICZ, N. Review of Kosik's *Dialectics of the Concrete*, *Studies in Soviet Thought*, vol. iv, no. 3, Sept. 1964, pp. 248-51.

LOWENTHAL, RICHARD. "On 'Established' Communist Party Regimes," *Studies in Comparative Communism*, vol. vii, no. 4, winter 1974, pp. 335-58.

LUZA, RADOMIR. "The Communist Party of Czechoslovakia and the Czech Resistance, 1939-45." *Slavic Review*, vol. 28, no. 4, Dec. 1969, pp. 561-76.

MEDICI, MARINO DE. Letter to the Editor. *Foreign Policy*, no. 22, spring 1976, pp. 215-18.

MEISSNER, BORIS. "Die Auseinandersetzung zwischen dem Sowjet und dem Reform-kommunismus," in *Wirtschaftswissenschaftliche Südosteuropa-Forschung*, ed. Theodor Zotschen. Munich, Südosteuropa, 1963, pp. 75-100.

MONTIAS, JOHN M. "Economic Reform in Perspective," *Survey*, no. 59, Apr. 1966, pp. 48-60.

MORGAN, DAN. "Reform Economist Working in Prague," *International Herald Tribune*, 30 May 1969, p. 1.

MUDRY-SEBIK, MICHAEL. "Czechoslovakia: Husak Takes the Helm," *East Europe*, vol. 18, no. 5, May 1969, pp. 2-7.

MÜLLER, DIETRICH. "Die Ära Husak in der Tschechoslowakei," *Aussenpolitik*, vol. xxi, no. 6, June 1970, pp. 358-75.

NICHOLS, PETER. "On the Italian Crisis," *Foreign Affairs*, vol. 54, no. 3, Apr. 1976, pp. 511-26.

NORTH, DON. "Prague: Nothing Is Forever," *Nation*, 17 Aug. 1970, pp. 103-4.

NYERS, REZSO, interviewed by Bela Bagota and Jozef Garam. "The Hungarian Economic Reform," *Hospodářské noviny*, 25 July 1969.

OLIVER, ADAM. "What Went Wrong," interview with Ota Sik, *Manchester Guardian Weekly*, 22 Apr. 1972.

OSVALD, FRANK. "The Case of Ladislav Mňačko," *Survey*, no. 55, Apr. 1965, pp. 5-20.

PAUL, DAVID V. "The Repluralization of Czechoslovak Politics in the 1960's," *Slavic Review*, vol. 23, no. 4, Dec. 1974.

PAYNE, PETER. "Four Years of 'Normalization': The Academic Purge in Czechoslovakia," *Index on Censorship*, summer, 1972, pp. 33-52.

PECH, STANLEY Z. "Ferment in Czechoslovak Marxist Historiography." Canadian Slavonic Papers, vol. x, winter 1968, pp. 502-22.

PEROUTKA, FERDINAND. "Kritika kritiky čs. demokracie," *Hlas domova*, vol. xxiii, no. 10, 14 May 1973, p. 5.

PEROUTKA, FERDINAND. "Masaryk al. století," *Hlas domova*, vol. xxvi, no. 18, 6 Sept. 1976, p. 6.

PFAFF, IVAN. "Kontinuita revolučního komplexu," *Text 70*, vol. 2, nos. 8-9 (13-14), 25 Sept. 1970, p. 5.

PFAFF, IVAN. "Mýtus a realita v proměnách Husova obrazu," *Zpravodaj Čechov a Slovákov vo Švajcarsku*, vol. iii, no. 8, July 1970, pp. 9-11.

PFAFF, WILLIAM. "Reflections: Communism in Europe," *New Yorker*, 3 May 1976, pp. 118-29.

PIPES, RICHARD. "Liberal Communism in Western Europe?" *Orbis*, vol. 20, no. 3, Fall 1976, pp. 595-600.

POPOV, MILORAD. "'Eurocommunism' and the pan-European conference," *The World Today*, vol. 32, no. 10, Oct. 1976, pp. 387-92.

PRAVDA, ALEX. "Some Aspects of the Czechoslovak Economic Reform and the Working Class in 1968," *Soviet Studies*, vol. xxv, no. 1, July 1973, pp. 102-24.

"Před soudem — knihy!" *Listy*, vol. iii, no. 1, Feb. 1973, pp. 4-5.

"Příspěvek k česko-slovenské vzájemnosti," *Listy*, vol. vii, nos. 3-4, July 1977, p. 5.

PROŠEK, VRATISLAV, and JIŘÍ ŽEMLA. "Společenské vědy v údobí 1948-68," *Svědectví*, vol. iii, no. 52, 1976.

"Protest 149 evropských filosofů." *Listy*, vol. vii, nos. 3-4, July 1977, p. 5.

RONEY, GABRIEL. "Lenin's Old Comrade Hands in His Party Card," *The Times*, 6 Oct. 1976, pp. 1 and 8.

ROZEHNAL, ALOIS. "The Revival of the Czechoslovak Trade Union," *East Europe*, vol. 18, no. 4, Apr. 1969, pp. 2-7.

SCHUB, ANATOLE. "A Guide to Soviet Policy: 'Social Fascism' — 1928," *International Herald Tribune*, 28 Mar. 1969.

"Secrets from the 'Prague Spring'." *The Time*, 9 May 1977, p. 12.

SERKE, JÜRGEN. Interview with Pavel Kohout. *Die Welt*, 27 Mar. 1968.

SETON-WATSON, HUGH. "Eastern Europe," in *The Soviet Impact on World Politics*, New York, Hawthorn Books, 1974.

SETON-WATSON, HUGH. "George Kennan's Illusions: A Reply," *Encounter*, vol. xlvii, no. 5, Nov. 1976, pp. 24-35.

SHAFFER, HARRY. "Czechoslovakia's New Economic Model: Out of Stalinism," *Problems of Communism*, vol. 14, no. 5, Sept.-Oct. 1965, pp. 31-40.

SILONE, IGNAZIO. "Ce qui arrive à beaucoup de P.C. est bel et bien un schisme," interview with J.N., *Le Monde*, 4 Feb. 1970, p. 8.

SKILLING, H. GORDON. "Czechoslovakia," in Adam Bromke, ed., *The Communist States at the Crossroads*, New York, Praeger, 1965; pp. 87-105.

"A Slovak in Prague Castle," *Frankfurter Allgemeine Zeitung*, 21 August 1976.

TABORSKY, EDUARD. "Czechoslovakia: Out of Stalinism," *Problems of Communism*, vol. 13, May-June 1964, pp. 4-14.

TABORSKY, EDUARD. "Czechoslovakia under Husak," *Current History*, vol. 70, no. 114, Mar. 1976, pp. 114-18, 134-35.

TABORSKY, ÉDUARD. "Czechoslovakia's Abnormal 'Normalization'," *Current History*, vol. 64, no. 381, May 1973, pp. 207-11 and 229.

TABORSKY, EDUARD. "Czechoslovakia's March to Communism," *East Europe,*vol. x, no. 2, Mar.-Apr. 1961.

"Tchécoslovaquie: La 'lettre aux communistes' énumére les noms de cinquantesix 'opportunistes' et 'revionnistes'," *Le Monde*, 5 Feb. 1970.

TIGRID, PAVEL. "The Prague Coup of 1948: The Elegant Take-over," In *The Anatomy of Communist Take-overs*, ed. Thomas T. Hammond, New Haven, Yale University Press, 1975; pp. 399-432.

TRISKA, JAN F. "Messages from Czechoslovakia," *Problems of Communism*, vol. xxiv, no. 6, Nov.-Dec. 1975, pp. 26-42.

ULČ, OTTO. "Pilsen, the Unknown Revolt," *Problems of Communism*, vol. xiv, no. 3, May-June 1965.

URBAN, GEORGE. "Communism with an Italian Face? A Conversation with Lucio Lombardo Radice," *Encounter*, vol. xlviii, no. 5, May 1977, pp. 8-22.

URBAN, GEORGE. "A Conversation with Ota Sik," *Survey*, vol. 19, no. 2, spring 1973, pp. 256-7.

URBAN, GEORGE. "Eastern Europe after Czechoslovakia," *Studies in Comparative Communism*, vol. ii, Jan. 1969, pp. 50-68.

URBAN, GEORGE. "Have They Really Changed? A Conversation with Altiero Spinelli. Euro-Communism, Again," *Encounter*, vol. l, no. 1, Jan. 1978, pp. 7-27.

URBAN, GEORGE. "Removing the Hyphen," *Studies in Comparative Communism*, vol. i, no. 1-2, July-Oct. 1968, pp. 1-6.

URBANEK, EDUARD. "Sociology in Czechoslovakia." *Social Research*, vol. xxxvii, no. 1, spring 1970, pp. 129-46.

URBANEK, LIDA. "Some Difficulties in Implementing the Economic Reforms in Czechoslovakia," *Soviet Studies*, vol xix, no. 4, Apr. 1968, pp. 557-66.

SZULC, TAD. "Lisbon & Washington: Behind the Portuguese Revolution," *Foreign Policy*, no. 21, winter 1975/6, pp. 3-62.

WECHSBERG, JOSEPH. "Letter from Prague," *New Yorker*, vol. xi, vi, 27 Apr. 1968, pp. 97-140.

WISKEMANN, ELISABETH. "Masaryk and Czechoslovakia," *History Today*, vol. xviii, no. 12, Dec. 1968, pp. 844-51.

ZINNER, PAUL E. "A Nation Violated," *Saturday Review*, vol. lii, 29 Mar. 1969, pp. 21-3, 33-6.

5. *Films*

Eve Wants to Sleep.
FORMAN, MILOŠ. *Firemen's Ball.*
MAKAVEJEV, DUŠAN. *Innocence Protected*
MAKAVEJEV, DUŠAN. *W.R. or the Power of Organism.*

6. *Newspapers*

Frankfurter Allgemeine Zeitung.
International Herald Tribune.
Le Monde.
Die Neue Zürcher Zeitung.
The Times (London).

And occasionally other daily papers.

Name Index

(Bold-face numerals refer to pages devoted to the subjects of the study)

Subject Index